James Rowley

A smaller History of English Literature

For the Use of Schools

James Rowley

A smaller History of English Literature
For the Use of Schools

ISBN/EAN: 9783337205676

Printed in Europe, USA, Canada, Australia, Japan

Cover: Foto ©Paul-Georg Meister /pixelio.de

More available books at **www.hansebooks.com**

Sir Wm. Smith's Smaller Histories.

A SMALLER HISTORY

OF

ENGLISH LITERATURE,

FOR THE USE OF SCHOOLS.

By JAMES ROWLEY, M.A.,

PROFESSOR OF ENGLISH HISTORY AND LITERATURE IN UNIVERSITY
COLLEGE, BRISTOL.

FOURTEENTH IMPRESSION.

LONDON:

JOHN MURRAY, ALBEMARLE STREET.

1899.

LONDON: PRINTED BY WILLIAM CLOWES AND SONS, LIMITED,
STAMFORD STREET AND CHARING CROSS.

PREFACE.

THE important position which the study of English Literature is now taking in Education has led to the publication of this Work and of the accompanying volume of 'Specimens.' Both books have been undertaken at the request of many eminent teachers, and no pains have been spared to adapt them to the purpose for which they are designed, as elementary works to be used in schools. Neither will fully answer its object without the other; the two will be found to be of mutual assistance—the one as giving a rapid but trustworthy sketch of the lives of our chief writers, and of the successive influences which imparted to their writings their peculiar character; the other as supplying choice examples of the works themselves, accompanied by all the explanations required for their comprehension.

In both volumes a large proportion of the space has been given to the *great* Writers, so as to impress upon the minds of pupils the most important facts in English literature.

All living Writers are, for obvious reasons, excluded.

CONTENTS.

CHAPTER I.

PAGE.

Introductory 1

CHAPTER II.

English Literature to the Norman Conquest.. .. 7

CHAPTER III.

From The Conquest to Geoffrey Chaucer 14

CHAPTER IV.

Geoffrey Chaucer 21

CHAPTER V.

The Contemporaries of Chaucer 35

CHAPTER VI.

English Literature From Chaucer to Spenser .. 42

CHAPTER VII.

The Non-dramatic Elizabethan Poets 52

CHAPTER VIII.

The Dawn of the Drama 60

 CONTENTS.

CHAPTER IX.

PAGE.
SHAKESPEARE 73

CHAPTER X.

THE SHAKESPEARIAN DRAMATISTS 87

CHAPTER XI.

THE PROSE LITERATURE OF THE ELIZABETHAN PERIOD .. 95

CHAPTER XII.

THE SO-CALLED METAPHYSICAL POETS 104

CHAPTER XIII.

THEOLOGICAL WRITERS OF THE CIVIL WAR AND THE
COMMONWEALTH 110

CHAPTER XIV.

JOHN MILTON 114

CHAPTER XV.

THE AGE OF THE RESTORATION 123

CHAPTER XVI.

THE NEW DRAMA AND THE CORRECT POETS 137

CHAPTER XVII.

THE SECOND REVOLUTION 146

CHAPTER XVIII.

THE SO-CALLED AUGUSTAN POETS 154

CHAPTER XIX.

THE ESSAYISTS 168

CHAPTER XX.

PAGE.

The Great Novelists 176

CHAPTER XXI.

Historical, Moral, Political, and Theological Writers
of the Eighteenth Century 188

CHAPTER XXII.

The Dawn of Romantic Poetry 199

CHAPTER XXIII.

Walter Scott 212

CHAPTER XXIV.

Byron, Moore, Shelley, and other Poets 220

CHAPTER XXV.

The Lake School.—Wordsworth, Coleridge and Southey 235

CHAPTER XXVI.

The Modern Novelists 243

CHAPTER XXVII.

Prose Literature of the Nineteenth Century .. 263

Index 279

ENGLISH LITERATURE.

CHAPTER I.

INTRODUCTORY.

THE most ancient inhabitants of the British Islands, concerning whom history has handed down to us any certain information, were a branch of that Celtic race which appears to have once occupied a large portion of Western Europe. The Celts, when they first came under the notice of history, had not attained more than a low degree of civilization, a fact sufficiently indicated by their nomad and predatory mode of existence, by the comparative absence of agriculture, and above all by the universal practice of that infallible sign of a savage state, the habit of tattooing and staining the body.

Though the Phœnicians perhaps visited the southern coast of the island at an early period, yet the first *important* intercourse between the primitive Britons and any foreign nation was the invasion of the country by the Romans under Julius Cæsar in the year 55 B.C. The resistance of the Britons, though obstinate and ferocious, was gradually overpowered in the first century of the Christian era by the superior skill and military organization of the Roman armies: the country became a Roman province; and this domination subsisted about 400 years; during which time the invaders, as was their custom, endeavoured to introduce among their barbarous subjects their laws, their habits, and their civilization. Such of the Celts as submitted to the yoke of their invaders acquired a considerable degree of civilization; the inhabitants of the towns learnt the Latin language, and became a Latinized or provincial race, similar to the inhabitants on the other side of the Channel; but the rustic population probably continued to speak their own language. The other portion of the Celts, who inhabited mountainous regions inaccessible to the Roman arms, periodically descending from the rugged fastnesses in the country now called Scotland, carried devastation over the more civilized province, and taxed the skill and vigilance of the foreign soldiery. Upon the withdrawal of the Roman troops, at the beginning of the fifth century, the Romanized portion of the population, having in all probability lost, during their long subjection, their pristine valour, found themselves exposed to the furious incursions of hungry barbarians, eager to reconquer what they considered as their birthright. Swarms of Scottish and Pictish savages rushed down from their mountains; every trace of civilization was swept away; the furious devastation which they carried through the land is commemorated in the ancient songs and legends of the Cymry; and the objects of their vengeance, after vainly imploring the assistance of Rome in a most piteous appeal, had recourse to the only resource now left them, of hiring some warlike race of foreign adventurers to protect them. These adventurers were the Saxon pirates.

The traces left by the Celtic period in the language of the country are very few. It must be remembered that the Celtic dialect, whether in the form still spoken in Wales, or in that employed in the Highlands of Scotland and among the Celtic population of Ireland, has only a very remote affinity to modern English. In a vocabulary consisting of about 40,000 words, it would be difficult to point out a hundred derived *directly* from the Celtic. It is true that the English language contains a considerable number of words *ultimately* traceable to Celtic roots, but these have been introduced into it through the medium of the French, which, together with an enormous majority of Latin words, contains some of Gaulish origin. One class of words, however, is traceable to the Brito-Roman period of our history; and this is ineffaceably stamped upon the geography of the British Isles. Even in those parts of the country which have been successively occupied by very different races, many appellations of pure Celtic antiquity have survived the inundations of new peoples, and may still be marked, like some venerable Druidical *cromlech*, standing in hoar mysterious age in the midst of a more recent civilization. Thus the termination "*don*" is in some instances, as in "Lon*don*," the Celtic word "*dun*," a rock or natural fortress. Again, the termination "*caster*" or '*chester*" is unquestionably a monument of the Roman occupation of the island, indicating the spot of a Roman "*castrum*" or fortified post.*

The true foundations of the English laws, language, and national character were laid, between the middle of the fifth and the middle of the sixth centuries, deep in the solid granite of Teutonic antiquity. The piratical adventurers whom the old German passion

* In the same way some other Latin words appear in other names of places: as *strata*, "paved roads," in *Strat-ford*, *Stret-ton*; *colonia*, in *Lin-coln*; *port-us*, in *Portsmouth*, &c.

for plunder and glory, and also, perhaps, the entreaties of the
" miserable Britons," allured across the North Sea from the bleak
shores of their native Jutland, Schleswig, Holstein, and the coasts
of the Baltic, gradually established themselves in those parts of
Britain which the Romans had occupied before them. But the
same causes which prevented the Romans from penetrating into
the mountainous districts of Scotland, continued to exclude the
Anglo-Saxons also from those inaccessible fastnesses. The level,
and consequently more easily accessible, portion of Scotland was
gradually peopled by the Anglo-Saxon race; and their language
and institutions were established there as completely as in South
Britain itself. As to the half-Romanized Britons, one fact is
certain, that in general, whether friendly or hostile, as possessing
a less powerful organization and a less vigorous moral constitution
than the Teuton, they were in the course of time either quietly
absorbed into the more energetic race, or gradually disappeared.

The true parentage, therefore, of the English nation is to be
traced to the Teutonic race. The language spoken by the Northern
invaders was a Low-Germanic dialect, akin to the modern Dutch;
and, like the people who spoke it, was possessed of a character at
once practical and imaginative, at once real and ideal. In the
modern English, the emotions and the ideas that bring man into
relation with the great objects of nature still find expression to a
great extent in Teutonic words. The conversion of the Anglo-
Saxons to Christianity (597-681) exposed their language to the
modifying influences of the corrupt but more civilized Latin literature of the Lower Empire; and soon a very varied and extensive
literature arose, of which an account will presently be given.*

For a long period the English colonization of Britain was carried
on by detached Teutonic tribes, who formed several independent
kingdoms, generally denominated the *Heptarchy*, or Seven Kingdoms; which, after ages of mutual conflict, were at last absorbed
by Wessex, 827. But hardly was this accomplished when there
occurred the third great invasion and change of sovereignty to
which the country was destined, that of the barbarous and pagan
Danes, who endeavoured to treat the Anglo-Saxons as the latter
had treated the Celts. But, by the heroism and wisdom of the
illustrious Alfred, this catastrophe was averted; the two fierce races,
nearly allied in origin and blood, consented to an amalgamation
which did not produce any very material change in the language
or institutions of the country. In the North and East of England,
however, as in some of the maritime regions of Scotland, where

* See Chapter II.

colonies of Danes established themselves, there still survive, in the idiom of the peasantry and the names of families and places, evident marks of a Scandinavian instead of an Anglo-Saxon population. As examples of this we may cite the now immortal name of *Havelock*, derived from a famous sea-king, who is said to have founded the ancient town of Grimsby, so called after Grim in the story. But still the pure English element predominates, alike in the language and in the population.

Even before the Norman Conquest, many classical words had found their way into our language. The cultivation of the Latin literature in the monasteries, and the employment of the Latin language in the services of the Church, had incorporated with the Anglo-Saxon a considerable number of Latin words. Alfred, we know, translated into English the 'Consolations' of Boëthius: the Venerable Bede, and other English ecclesiastics, composed chronicles and legends in Latin, so that a considerable influx of Latin words may have become perceptible in it before the appearance of Normans on our shores. Besides, the family connexion between the last Anglo-Saxon dynasty and the neighbouring dukes of Normandy must have tended to increase materially the number of foreign words.

The most important change consequent upon the subjugation of the country by the Normans was obviously the establishment in England of the great feudal principle of the military tenure of land, of the chivalric spirit and habits which were the natural result of feudal institutions, and lastly, of the broad demarcation which separated society into the two great classes of the Nobles and the Serfs. But it is with the effects of the Norman Conquest upon the language of the country that we are at present concerned. On their arrival in France, the Northmen had exchanged for their native Scandinavian language a dialect of that great Romance* speech which extended during the Middle Ages from the northern shore of the Mediterranean to the British Channel, and which may be defined as the decomposition of the classical Latin. It was soon divided into two great sister-idioms, the Langue-d'Oc and the Langue-d'Oil (so called from the different words for *yes*), the general boundary or line of demarcation between them being roughly assignable as coinciding with the Loire. The Langue d'Oc, spoken to the south of this river, was subsequently called the Provençal; the Langue d'Oil was the parent of the French. In both, the language of ancient Rome, a highly

---

* *Romance* comes from the late Latin word *Romancius*, another form of Romanus. The old French language is constantly called *Lingua Romana*, "the Roman tongue."

inflected and complicated tongue, had lost all, or nearly all its
inflexions and grammatical complexity.   Thus the Latin sub-
stantive and adjective lost all those terminations which in the
original language expressed relation, as the various cases of the
different declensions; these relations being thenceforward indicated by the simpler expedient of prepositions.

But together with the institutions of feudalism the Normans
brought with them the poetry of feudalism, that is, the poetry of
chivalry.   The *lais* and *romances*, the *fabliaux*, and the legends
of mediæval chivalry soon began to modify the rude poetical sagas
and the tedious narratives of the lives of saints and hermits which
had formed the bulk of the literature of Saxon England.   The
Trouvère and *Troubadour*, which are obviously but two forms of
the same word as pronounced respectively by the population who
spoke the Langue-d'Oil and the Langue-d'Oc, displaced the old
English Gleeman, whose *joy* of the banquet was obliged to give
way to their *gay saber* and *guaye science*.   The imaginative or
poetical literature of the Trouvères, however, had taken a *narrative*, that of the Troubadours a *lyric*, form: for narrative is the necessary type in which the imagination, the sentiments, and the
memory, characteristics of a Northern race, are wont to clothe
themselves, while the ardent and transitory passion of the South
inevitably expresses itself in the lyric form.   Many of the inter-
minable romances of the Trouvères, as requiring literary culture
and leisure, may be traced to the ecclesiastical profession; while
the shorter and more lively lyric and satiric effusions which constitute the bulk of the Troubadour literature were frequently the
productions of princes, knights, and ladies, the power of writing
verse being considered as one of the necessary accomplishments of
a gentleman :

> "He coude songes make, and wel endite."

Though the native language was not altogether unaffected by
the Norman-French, which for three centuries was spoken by
the higher classes in England, yet it is an error to repr esent
English as springing from a mixture of Anglo-Saxon and
French; since a mixed language, in the strict sense of the
term, is an impossibility.   English still remained essen tially
a German tongue, though it received such large accessions of
French words as materially to change its character.   To fix with
precision the date when this change took place is manifestly an
impossible task.   It was a gradual process; and must have advanced with more or less rapidity in different parts of the country.
But this material change was brought about, according to Hallam :

" 1. by contracting or otherwise modifying the pronunciation and orthography of words; 2. by omitting many inflections, especially of the noun, and consequently making more use of articles and auxiliaries; and, 3. by the introduction of French derivatives."

The picturesque illustration, so happily employed by Scott in the opening chapter of *Ivanhoe*, has often been quoted as a good popular exemplification of the mode in which the Saxon and French elements were blended: the common animals serving for food to man, while under the charge of Saxon serfs and bondmen, retained their Teutonic appellation; but, when served up at the table of the Norman oppressor, they received a French designation. As examples of this, he cites the parallels *Ox* and *Beef*, *Swine* and *Pork*, *Sheep* and *Mutton*, *Calf* and *Veal*.* But the process of fusion continued through centuries; and it is the special glory of Chaucer that he harmonized the two elements, and put the last touch to the consolidation of the English language. Still traces of the peculiar alliterative system that prevailed before the Conquest, are perceptible for a period subsequent to the reign of Richard II., while the elaborate compositions addressed to the still purely Norman nobility retain much of the French spirit in their diction and imagery.

A consecutive account of the various English works produced before the Conquest will be given in the next chapter.

* This distinction, however, is of comparatively modern origin. As late as Shakespeare's time *Mutton* and *Beef* were used of the living animals. *Merchant of Venice*, Act I. sc. III.

CHAPTER II.

ENGLISH LITERATURE TO THE NORMAN CONQUEST.

No spoken language of modern Europe has so ancient a literature
as the English. For it is in the tongue which we now speak that
the thoughts, sentiments, and feelings of the English people have
found expression for more than fourteen centuries. Before a single
Englishman had set foot on British soil, while Roman and Celt
still grappled in desperate strife, or dwelt peacefully together as
conqueror and subject, our native tongue, rugged and meagre as
it must have been, was employed to express the simple wants and
simple conceptions of the English race. There was, strange as
it may appear, an English literature before there was an
England.

Differing in many particulars, the rude dialect that our forefathers
brought with them to Britain is the same in all *essential* respects as
our present language. It has undergone many changes and modifications, has been affected by external and internal influences, has
stripped itself of the great mass of its inflections, and, on the
other hand, acquired an immense amplitude of expression by the
unhesitating adoption of new words from all manner of sources—
in fact, has passed from early youth to mature manhood; but in all
the features that constitute identity it is the same.

Before proceeding any further, therefore, it were well for us
to get rid of the erroneous notion, that our present speech is not
the speech of our fathers, as well as of the unscientific classification of the various stages through which this speech has passed.
For the first is false in fact; and the second, by substituting the
terms *Anglo-Saxon* and *Semi-Saxon* for the plain word *English* that
Alfred used,* perpetuates the misconception. In the language of
Sir F. Palgrave,† the use of these expressions conveys "a most false
idea of our civil history. It disguises the continuity of affairs, and
substitutes the appearance of a new formation in the place of a
progressive evolution." And it is so with our native tongue as
well. It has *grown* to be what it is, obeying the spontaneous

---

* Ælfred Kyning wæs wealhstod ðisse bec, and hie of boclædene on *Englisc*
wende. "Ælfred King was commentator of this book, and it from book-language
into English turned"   † 'Normandy and England,' iii. 596.

impulse from within; not entirely uninfluenced by the Norman conquest and other events, but still steadily advancing in spite of them on its own predestined way, according to the law of its own nature.

Keeping these facts before us, then, and remembering that all classifications of the kind must be to a great extent arbitrary, we are justified in arranging these successive developments in the following way:—

1. *Old English*, from the earliest period to 1154. During this period English was highly inflected in its grammar, and mainly homogeneous in its vocabulary.

2. *Middle English*, from 1154 to about 1500. This is the transition period, during which the grammar was rapidly relieving itself of its complicated forms, and the vocabulary was freely taking in words from every quarter, principally from the French.

3. *Modern English*, from about 1500 to the present time. Grammar and vocabulary, though still undergoing slight modifications, are now practically fixed.

These periods will correspond respectively to the boyhood, youth, and manhood of the English language.

When then did our literature begin? Clearly with the first authentic utterance of the English race in the English tongue , and the first now extant is the poem of *Beowulf*.

1. Old English (commonly called Anglo-Saxon) Poetry.

The poem called BEOWULF seems to have originated in the primitive seat of the Angles, at Schleswig, and to have been brought over to England about the end of the fifth century. Its spirit is that of the old heathen Germans. Its subject is the expedition of Prince Beowulf, a lineal descendant of Woden, on the adventure of delivering a king from a destructive monster, called the Grendel, which enters the royal hall at midnight, and destroys many of the warriors who are sleeping there. The poem is supposed to be allegorical, this monster representing the poisonous exhalation from a neighbouring marsh; and it illustrates the early predilection of our ancestors for that kind of composition. The style is very similar to that of the old Scandinavian sagas; and the hero is connected with the races that appear in the *Lay of the Nibelung*.

The BATTLE OF FINNESBURH—"a small fragment, in which we meet Hengist, the mythical warrior "—and the TRAVELLER'S SONG are also assigned to the same period. The latter records the wanderings of a certain *gleeman*, the contemporary of Eormanric (Hermanaric), and Ætla (Attila).

But CÆDMON "was the first Englishman—it may be the first individual of Gothic race—who exchanged the gorgeous images of the old mythology for the chaste beauties of Christian poetry."* According to Bede, he was a monk of Whitby, and he died about the year 680. His *Metrical Paraphrase of the Scriptures* produced an extraordinary influence upon our national modes of thought and expression, and won for him the deep reverence of five centuries of Englishmen. The manuscript of his works first found its way into the hands of Junius in 1650, and by him was published in 1655. Indeed it has been maintained by some, that it was this work that first suggested to Milton the subject of his renowned Epic, whom they also assert to be under distinct literary obligations to the elder poet. Undoubtedly Milton commenced the composition of *Paradise Lost* not many years after the discovery of Cædmon; and in one passage at least—Satan's soliloquy in Hell—he bears a striking resemblance to the old Anglian. His subject also, to a great extent, carries him over the same ground. Cædmon, like Milton, describes the revolt of the wicked angels, their expulsion from heaven and descent into hell, together with the creation of the world, and other kindred events.

Next in order, both of time and merit, comes the BRUNANBURH WAR SONG, which in massive, ponderous verse, highly characteristic of the race, describes the great battle of that name (937), when "Æthelstan king, of earls the lord, and Eadmund ætheling" rolled back into utter rout the combined powers of Scot, Cymry, and Northman under their leader Anlaf, the Dane. This great national song of victory is preserved in almost every copy of the Saxon Chronicle, where only it is found; and it has kindled the enthusiasm of modern editors to an unwonted pitch. It is indeed a noble piece of verse, honourable to the race that produced it, giving utterance to the deep-toned exultation of the English people at their great deliverance, in the most powerful and glowing language.

It is to the same source—the Saxon Chronicle—that we owe many other magnificent outbursts of old English verse. The ANNEXATION OF MERCIA (942); the CORONATION OF EDGAR at Bath (973), as well as the *Brunanburh War Song*, are believed to have been popular songs which the compiler for the time being inserted in his copy of the Chronicle. There are other poems in the same work, however, which were evidently composed for the places in which they are found. On certain occasions, such as the death of Edgar, the murder of Edward the Martyr, the death of Edward

* Guest's 'English Rhythms,' ii. 23.

the Confessor, it would seem that the Chronicler found mere prose inadequate to the expression of his feelings, and was accordingly obliged to break out into verse.

But the BATTLE OF MALDON is a separate composition. It celebrates the valorous deeds and heroic death of the brave Ealdorman Brihtnoth, who with all his faithful *gesiths*, fell in desperate fight with the Pagan Northmen at Maldon in 991. This striking episode in the disastrous reign of the imbecile Ethelred appears to have deeply affected the national heart, and the result is one of the most spirit-stirring bursts of song ever written. The battle is described circumstantially; the warlike exploits of the several combatants, whose names are duly given, are minutely detailed in true Homeric fashion. No composition of the time possesses greater interest, not only for its rare poetic merits, but for the light it reflects upon the military principles, tactics, and usages of Englishmen before the conquest.

These works,—with the fragmentary JUDITH, King Alfred's *Paraphrase* of the Metres of Boëthius, and a few other scraps of verse which are found scattered through various prose compositions,—may be said to constitute almost all the poetical treasures of our nation before the Conquest. They are all written upon the same metrical principle, *alliteration*. Though appearing generally at long intervals, and rarely extending to any very great length, they are exceedingly valuable—revealing, as they do, the mental constitution of our ancestors, and showing that Englishmen were built pretty much on the same model then as now. They are the sincere utterances of a grave people, with an immense fund of radical fire deep-seated within them—not accustomed to give vent to their feelings save upon great occasions, and then expressing them with somewhat of solemnity, even in the midst of their excitement. The bright sparkle of lyric verse we cannot expect from them—neither the language nor the national character was adapted to its production—and, indeed, we can yet boast of but few brilliant pieces in that department of poetry.

2. OLD ENGLISH (commonly called ANGLO-SAXON) PROSE.

First in this province comes the honoured name of ALFRED (849-901). No sooner had the great King effected the deliverance of his people from their Danish enemies, than he eagerly set to work to lift them up from the ignorance and degradation into which they had sunk. Thinking that he would materially assist his purpose by translating into the vernacular such standard works upon religion, morals, geography, and history as were then current, he not only invited to his court men of learning and ability from whatever quarter he could find them, but proceeded by a careful course of training—irksome enough, we may be sure, at his time of life—to fit himself for the task. By these means he succeeded, to a great extent, in accomplishing the desire of his heart; and among Royal authors Alfred still stands pre-eminent. His most important translations were those of Bede's *Ecclesiastical History*, the *Ancient History of Orosius, Boëthius de Consolatione Philosophiæ;* to which last he added, by way of preface, the *Pastorale* of St. Gregory. To the second he prefixed an original geographical description of *Germania*, which he prepared himself with great care; and for which a considerable portion of the materials was supplied to the king by Ohthere and Wulfstan, both adventurous navigators, the first a native of Helgoland, in Norway.

Alfred was something more than a mere translator. Not only does he deal pretty freely with the text of his author—condensing some passages and expanding others—cutting away redundancies and making additions as he thinks fit; but the elaborate prefaces, and the new matter introduced by way of comment, illustration, or explanation, entitle him to be called an original author. He was mainly assisted in his preliminary course of training, and in the work itself, by ASSER, then a monk of St. David's, but afterwards Bishop of Sherborne, to whom we are greatly indebted for our knowledge of the life and character of the noble king. (See p. 13.)

Many works also were translated by the king's order, or after his example—as the *Dialogues of St. Gregory*, by WEREFRITH, Bishop of Worcester—a number of which have by the usual practice been fathered on the king himself, without having any claim whatever to such a distinction.

The principal representatives of the purely religious element in the literature of the time are ÆLFRIC, Archbishop of Canterbury, surnamed *Grammaticus* (d. 1006), WULFSTAN, Archbishop of York (d. 1023), and ÆLFRIC BATA, also Archbishop of York (d. 1051), who was a devoted disciple of his elder namesake. The first is distinguished as the author of eighty homilies—his chief work,—of the translation of the Books of Moses, and by his attempts to revive the study of Latin among his countrymen, with which view he wrote a *Latin Grammar* and *Colloquium*. The two others also enjoy some distinction, the first as a writer of homilies, the second as having republished the grammar and colloquium of his master, and written a life of Bishop Ethelwold (925-984).

One great monument of prose literature still remains, the SAXON CHRONICLE. This work exists in no less than seven separate forms, each named after the monastery in which it was compiled—of

which, however, the Winchester and Peterborough Chronicles are
the most valuable.   The ordinary account given of the origin
of this work is, that it was first composed, at the solicitation of
King Alfred, by Plegmund, Archbishop of Canterbury, who brought
it down to the year 891, whence it was continued as a contemporary
record, to the accession of Henry II. in 1154.   But there is absolutely no evidence of this.   Certain features of the earliest copy,
the Winchester, indicate a chronicle that was composed in Alfred's
reign, but there is nothing whatever to connect it with either
Alfred or Plegmund.   This chronicle—the earliest form of which
begins with the arrival of Julius Cæsar in Britain, and the latest
ends with the year 1154,—is remarkable as the first ever written in
Teutonic prose, and as furnishing us with almost our only trustworthy materials for the early history of the English people.   The
later entries are also the latest specimens of old English.

The contemptuous judgment that is sometimes pronounced on
this work is altogether unjust.   The earlier portions are certainly
meagre in their details, and altogether devoid of the qualities
we expect to find in an elaborate historical narrative; but in the
later the chroniclers, whoever they may be, occasionally rise into
sustained descriptions, characterised by vigour of style, and a
grave, sober eloquence.   One of the best passages is to be found
in the Peterborough copy under the year 1087, in which the
character of the great Conqueror is drawn with extraordinary
fidelity and force.   Mr. Earle is of opinion, that "putting aside
the Hebrew annals, there is not anywhere known a series of early
vernacular history comparable to the Saxon Chronicles."   Excepting
the Romance of Apollonius of Tyre, (which story is the same as
that of Shakespeare's Pericles), and a translation of the Gospels into
the vernacular, there is hardly anything of interest remaining
The various *laws* and *charters* emanating from our early kings and
princes, and written for the most part in the native language, do
not properly fall under the head of literature.

We shall now take a passing glance at our principal writers in
Latin.

3. LATIN WRITERS BEFORE THE CONQUEST.

Of these by far the greatest is BEDE, or Bæda, surnamed the
Venerable (672-735), who, born at Monk Wearmouth, spent the
greater part of his life at the monastery of Jarrow-upon-the-Tyne.
His *Ecclesiastical History* of the English was for many centuries the
only source of knowledge to the nation regarding its early history.
Written for the purpose of preserving among the Angles and
Saxons the memory of their conversion to the Christian faith, this

work embraces large sections of their political history as well,
more especially the rise and growth of the various petty Teutonic
states throughout the island.   In careful research, in arrangement of materials, in scrupulous fidelity and felicity of style he
rises far above all the Gothic historians of his time.   His other
compositions, theological, scientific, and grammatical, though
immensely voluminous, and not altogether without merit, do not
concern us here.

ASSER, Bishop of Sherborne (d. 910), the friend and associate of
Alfred, is the supposed author of an extant biography of his
master.   This is a work of great interest, but its authenticity
has been much disputed.   Though the question is surrounded
with difficulties, the balance of probability would seem to be in
favour of the substantial truth of what the book itself sets forth,
that it was written in 893.   At any rate, the majority of competent judges are fully satisfied that the bulk of it is the genuine
work of the learned bishop, though it is admitted that much has
been added to it in later times.   King Alfred was not the only
writer of the royal stock of Cerdic.   What Mr. Earle calls " the first
comprehensive Latin work founded upon the Saxon Chronicle,"
was written in the reign of Ethelred II. by ETHELWEARD, who
traced his descent from the brother of Alfred, the heroic Ethelred.
The work ends with the last year of Edgar (975); and though in
the main a mere translation from the vernacular chronicles, is not
without a kind of value, in spite of the author's ridiculous pedantry.
He occasionally throws a feeble glimmer of light upon the dark
passages of our early history.

There were many other distinguished Englishmen belonging
to this period who wrote in Latin,—WILFRED of York (d. 709),
afterwards canonised; EGBERT (678-766); ALCUIN of York (725-
804), who became the teacher and adviser of Charlemagne in the
education of his people; but their works possess but little interest
for modern readers, being composed for the most part of dry theological treatises, or wearisome verses.

CHAPTER III.

FROM THE CONQUEST TO GEOFFREY CHAUCER.

For more than a century after the Norman conquest English literature may be said to have ceased altogether.* This event, so fatal to the native aristocracy, seemed at first to have swept away in common ruin the laws, language, and arts of the English people, and to have blotted out England from the roll-call of the nations. A foreign King and aristocracy, an alien language and literature, ruled in the land; the old speech was no longer heard in the halls of the great, and lived only on the lips of the people; native genius no longer strove to utter itself in the native tongue, and the voice of the English nation seemed stilled for ever. But it was not the stillness of death; in a few generations signs of returning life began to show themselves; and the English nation emerged from the fiery trial, with its full equipment of language, laws, and literature—materially altered indeed, and perhaps improved—but still bearing the ineffaceable Teutonic stamp. The national life was not annihilated at Senlac; it was but suspended for a time.

The specific effect of the Conquest upon our native tongue has been referred to already, and need only be briefly spoken of here. Tendencies had set in—common to the English with other languages of the same stock—consisting mainly in an apparent desire on the part of our language to shake off the complicated net-work of inflections that seemed to fetter its free utterance. These tendencies existed before the Norman conquest; would have worked their way to the due result in spite of it; and the great political revolution did but give them an additional impulse. Nor was even this last a *direct* consequence. The vernacular speech was driven from literature altogether for a time, and obliged to take refuge in the cottages of the people; where, no longer fixed by the old steadying forces—for it is always the effect of a literature to give permanence to the forms of a language—and exposed to many varying influences, it fell into utter dislocation. The process of enfranchisement was thereby accelerated; and when, at the be-

* The Saxon Chronicle, confined to the Abbey of Peterborough, and accessible only to a few monks, can hardly be called literature.

ginning of the twelfth century, this speech rose to the surface once more, it had travelled much farther on its prescribed course, than it would have done had it been left to itself.	Still it was the old tongue.	In the words of Max Müller, "not a single drop of foreign blood has entered into the organic system of the English language. The Grammar, the blood and soul of the language, is as pure and unmixed in English as spoken in the British Isles, as it was when spoken on the shores of the German Ocean by the Angles, Saxons, and Juts of the continent."*

This—the Middle English Stage—may be called the revolutionary period of the language, during which it was in a state of apparently hopeless disorganisation.	There was a general break-up of the old grammatical system; and uncertainty, confusion, and fluctuation prevailed everywhere.	Three dialects—the Northern, the Midland, and the Southern, each with certain peculiar inflectional forms, and each represented by literary works of some note—now struggled for the mastery.	The influx of French words too, though trifling at first, had already begun; and for the next three centuries the process went on with increasing rapidity, until the vocabulary became to a great degree Romance.	Still there was a general movement towards simplification and new stability; each century brought with it a closer approximation to modern English; and the language was clearly gravitating towards a new fixed condition, in which "the fulness and purity of the ancient inflections" would no longer be found.

The interest of the writings which will form the subject of this chapter is almost exclusively philological and historical.	Their literary merits are but small; but they supply us with the means of tracing the course of the language through its many varying forms; and not a few of them occasionally throw a powerful light on the feelings and aspirations, the political and social condition of the people.

If we except a few fragments of verse—*the Hymn of St. Godric*, the Ely *Song of King Canute*, *The Here Prophecy*, none of them exceeding eight lines in length—the first to break the long silence was LAYAMON, author of the *Brut*, or Chronicle of Britain (A.D. 1200).	According to his own account he was a priest of Ernley-by-Severn (supposed to be Lower Areley); and his dialect will, therefore, represent that of North Worcestershire.	His work is mainly a translation from the *Brut d'Angleterre*, written in the French language by Robert Wace, a canon of Bayeux in the time of Henry II.; but Layamon has introduced into his work so much other matter that it extends to

* 'Lectures on the Science of Language,' 1st series, p. 40.

32,250 lines, or more than double the length of the original Brut.
Allusions to events that occurred late in the twelfth century enable
us to fix the date approximately. The style of the work—which
has come down to us in two texts, an earlier and a later—bears
witness to Norman influence, both in the structure of the verse
and the manner of the narrative, but not nearly to so great an
extent as might have been expected from the translator of a French
original. The earlier text has not fifty words taken from the
French; and both texts only about ninety. Though it still retains
a large proportion of the old inflectional forms, a broad chasm
separates it from the language of Alfred; and though composed
on the old metrical system, alliteration, it contains a considerable
number of rhyming couplets as well. "To the historical student,"
says Sir F. Madden, "the work is important, as the last and
fullest form of the old Celtic traditions concerning early British
history."

The ANCREN RIWLE, or Rule of Female Anchorites—a code of
monastic precepts, written for the guidance of a small nunnery—
is the work of an unknown author, who must have lived in the
early part of the thirteenth century. It possesses no literary value
whatsoever, but is of great importance philologically. Though
the quantity of matter is but half that of Layamon, it contains
twice as many French words; which circumstance is perhaps owing
to the fact that it treats of religious subjects, and was thereby
obliged to take in many words of Latin derivation.

ORMIN, or ORM, author of the *Ormulum*, so called "because that
Orm it wrought," was a monk of the order of St. Augustine, and
is supposed to have lived in the east of England some time in the
thirteenth century. His work is described by its editor, Dr.
White, "as a series of Homilies in an imperfect state, composed
in metre without alliteration, and, except in a very few cases, without rhyme; the subject of the Homilies being supplied by those
portions of the New Testament which were read in the daily
services of the Church." There is a great diversity of opinion
among critics as to the exact time of its composition, some making
it contemporary with Layamon, others finding in its forms and
grammatical structure evidence of a later date. And they are
equally at variance with one another as to the place. By some
scholars it is looked upon as a specimen of a North-eastern patois;
but Dr. Guest considers it "the oldest, the purest, and by far the
most valuable specimen of our old English dialect that time has
left us." If written, as generally supposed, in the north-east, it
tends to prove that the Anglian dialect was the first to throw off
the old inflections. Its peculiar spelling, which consists in the

doubling of the terminal consonant of a syllable when it has the *short* sound, to which device the author attached great importance, throws some interesting light on the history of the language. But few Latin words, and scarcely a trace of French, are to be found in the Ormulum.

ROBERT OF GLOUCESTER, who flourished about the year 1300, wrote a metrical *Chronicle of England*, of some importance to the history of both our language and nation. This work extends from the time of Brutus, the mythical founder of Britain, to the end of the reign of Henry III.; and from events it refers to must have been composed about 1297. In the earlier part it closely follows Geoffrey of Monmouth; but in the latter it contributes, from more trustworthy sources, some valuable information upon the physical and social condition of England in the thirteenth century. It is written in rhyming lines of fourteen syllables. To the same author a collection of the Lives of the English Saints is with confidence attributed; and short works on the *Martyrdom of Thomas à Becket*, and the *Life of St. Brandan* are undoubtedly his.

The last conspicuous production in English before Chaucer was a similar composition from the pen of ROBERT MANNYNG, or Robert of BRUNNE, who was born at Brunne (Bourne), in Lincolnshire, in the latter half of the same century. His work consists of two parts, which are both taken from the French; the first, coming down to the death of Cadwalader, from Wace's Brut; the second, ending with the death of Edward I., from the French of Peter of Langtoft. The second, which has been considerably enlarged and improved, is, like its original, in the Alexandrine twelve-syllable verse; whereas the first retains the octo-syllabic metre of Wace. The language is in a much more advanced state than that of Robert of Gloucester; the grammar having drawn a step nearer to modern English, and the vocabulary having received a considerable accession of Romance words.

A very curious composition of the first half of the fourteenth century is the *Ayenbite of Inwit*, or Again-biting—i. e., Remorse— of Conscience. It is a consistent attempt, made by DAN MICHEL OF NORTHGATE, in Kent, to write a work wholly in native Teutonic words. The title itself illustrates his ingenuity in word-building; but a more amusing specimen is the word " ontodelinde"—" that which cannot be divided into parts "—for individual.

But the immediate predecessor of Chaucer is LAWRENCE MINOT, whose ten poems on the battles and victories of Edward III. were most likely written at various times between the years 1333 and 1352. The series begins with Halidon Hill (1333), (Bannockburn being introduced for the purpose of showing how it had been avenged), and ends with the taking of Guisnes (1352). These poems were the first successful attempt to combine alliteration not only with rhyme but with Romance measures, both of verse and stanza. They are not without precision and force of expression; and breathe a strong martial and patriotic spirit, characteristic of the reign of Edward III.

This is the age of the METRICAL ROMANCE. For a long time after the conquest French was the only language of popular literature, and was used even by English writers in this kind of composition. It is probable that all our early English metrical romances were translations from the French; and their favourite metre is the octo-syllabic, found in the *Roman de la Rose* and Brut of Wace. The most considerable of them are the *Romance of Alexander; Tristrem; Richard Cœur-de-Lion; Ipomydon; William and the Werewolf;* the *Geste of King Horn;* and *Havelok* the Dane. The last of these, which relates the story of the foundation of Grimsby by Havelok's preserver, Grim, is especially noteworthy.

The free patriotic spirit of the people found an utterance for itself during the thirteenth and fourteenth centuries in POLITICAL SONGS, many of which are written in English. By far the most spirited is that which is oldest in subject if not in date, the *Song against the King of Almaigne,* the composition of some fervent admirer of Sir Simon the Righteous, who therein expresses his hearty satisfaction at the great victory of Lewes, and his deep contempt for the poor figure cut in it by Richard, Earl of Cornwall and King of the Romans.

Of the BALLADS and poems of genuine native origin—many of them satirical—the most remarkable are the *Owl and the Nightingale;* the *Land of Cockayne;* the *Body and the Soul;* all of which were produced in the fourteenth century, or not long after.

These works, however, were not all composed in the same dialect. Ralph Higden, writing about the year 1350, tells us that in his time the native speech was split up into three forms, the Northern, the Midland, and the Southern, distinguished from one another by well-marked peculiarities; and an examination of the writings described above fully bears out his statement. The Northern, spoken as far south as the Humber, with the Pennine chain as its western limit, formed all the persons of the present indicative, singular and plural alike, in *es*, and is represented by Minot's poems: the Midland, extending from the Humber to the Thames, and taking in the counties west of the Pennine chain, but excluding Somersetshire, Gloucestershire, and parts of Herefordshire and Worcestershire, formed its present indicative plural in *en*, and is represented by the Ormulum: and the southern, comprehending all the rest of

England, with the same parts of the verb in *eth*, is represented by Layamon, Robert of Gloucester, and Dan Michel of Northgate. Traces of the differences, at least between the second and third, can be discovered even in Chaucer; but it was the Midland that in the main became ultimately the language of England.

Writings in English are far from representing the entire intellectual wealth of the nation during this time; indeed they form but an insignificant portion of it. For almost three centuries after the conquest French continued to be the language of polite literature, and Latin of theology, philosophy, science, and history; and this country produced many men of great eminence in all these provinces. Strictly speaking, these have no claim to a place among the great names of English literature; but their works exercised so important and so lasting an influence on its form, tone, and subject-matter that they cannot be altogether passed over.

French *Romances*, composed principally in verse, either by professional minstrels, or by knights and even kings, were then the favourite reading of the cultivated classes; but the great mass of them can hardly be called ours at all, having been imported into this country from the Continent. They had a tendency to gather in clusters round some great name; and of these groups the most famous were those that had Charlemagne and Alexander as central figures. Still one cycle, the Arthurian, is of genuine native growth; and this one happens to possess the highest interest of them all— at least to the present generation of readers. Its origin, about which so much has been written, and so little is known, cannot be discussed here; but the names of three Englishmen, LUKE GALT, WALTER MAPES, the jovial Archdeacon of Oxford, and ROBERT BORRON, are the earliest mentioned in connection with it. The first is said to have translated the *Tristrem* from Latin into Romance; to the second is attributed the composition, in Latin, of the *Birth and Life of Arthur*, the *Lancelot*, the *Saint Graal*, and the *Death of Arthur*; and to the last a translation of the second and third of Mapes's productions is assigned. These all seem to have been in prose. Henry II. is believed to have suggested to Mapes the last part of his work; and to have imposed by express command his task upon Borron. Copies of some of these tales are found in Welsh; but to which of the two nations, Welsh or English, the original property belonged, still remains an unsolved question. Besides these romances the Anglo-Norman possessed great store of *Metrical Chronicles*, *Satires*, *Fabliaux*, many of which Chaucer afterwards used as materials.

The principal writers in Latin were LANFRANC (d. 1089), and ST. ANSELM (1033-1109), in theology; John of Salisbury (d. 1180),

ALEXANDER HALES, "the Irrefragable Doctor" (d. 1245), DUNS SCOTUS, "the Subtle Doctor" (d. 1308), and WILLIAM OF OCCAM, "the Invincible Doctor" (d. 1347), in philosophy; and ROGER BACON, author of the *Opus Majus* (d. 1292), in science. The chief historical writers were Churchmen, and, with a few exceptions, they confined themselves to the history of England. For the time before the Conquest FLORENCE OF WORCESTER (d. 1118), WILLIAM OF MALMESBURY (1140), HENRY OF HUNTINGDON (d. after 1154), are our principal authorities; WILLIAM OF POITIERS, and ORDERICUS VITALIS, for the events of the Conquest itself; and MATTHEW PARIS and ROGER OF WENDOVER, for subsequent times.

English literature has now reached the eve of its first great expansion. It has been in existence for a thousand years, but has as yet produced no work of pre-eminent merit, no name that is entitled to rank among intellects of the highest order. Force, energy of thought and expression, natural sweetness and simple pathos, are not wanting; but there is still a complete absence of artistic form, literary skill, and the higher qualities of true workmanship. Nothing would appear to portend the magnificent outburst that is at hand; but the student of history can discern forces, political, social, and spiritual, at work beneath the smooth surface, destined within a few years to produce momentous results in all three departments. The national life and thought of England is now passing through a mighty quickening process; a brilliant page in her history is about to open, in which will appear many bright names, but none brighter than that of the first man who, under these new conditions, spoke to the hearts of *all* classes of the English people—GEOFFREY CHAUCER.

CHAPTER IV.

GEOFFREY CHAUCER.

THE fourteenth century is the most important epoch in the intellectual history of Europe. It is the point of contact between two widely-differing eras in the social, religious, and political annals of our race; the slack water between the ebb of Feudalism and Chivalry, and the "young flood" of the Revival of Letters and the great Protestant Reformation. Of this great transformation from the old order to the new, the personal career, no less than the works, of the first great English poet, CHAUCER, will furnish us with the most exact type and expression; for, like all men of the highest order of genius, he at once followed and directed the intellectual tendencies of his age, and is himself the "abstract and brief chronicle" of the spirit of his time. And in the age in which he lived he was eminently happy; the magnificent court of Edward III. had carried the splendour of chivalry to the height of its development; the victories of Sluys, of Crécy, and Poitiers, by exciting the national pride, tended to consummate the fusion into one vigorous nationality of the two elements which formed the English people and the English language. The literature, too, abundant in quantity, if not remarkable for much originality of form, was rapidly taking a purely English tone; the rhyming chronicles and legendary romances were either translated into, or originally composed in, the vernacular language.

In endeavouring to form an idea of the intellectual situation of England in the fourteenth century, we must by no means leave out of account the vast influence exerted by the preaching of Wiclif, and the mortal blow struck by him against the foundations of Catholic supremacy in England. This, together with the general hostility excited by the intolerable corruptions of the monastic orders, which had gradually invaded the rights, the functions, and the possessions of the far more practically-useful working or parochial clergy, still farther intensified that inquiring spirit which prompted the people to refuse obedience to the temporal as well as spiritual authority of the Roman See, and paved the way for an ultimate rejection of the Papal yoke.

The date of Chaucer's birth is uncertain. By some it is fixed at

1328, by others at 1340, which latter date would harmonise better with certain known facts in his life. If, however, the first be correct, the poet's career almost coincides, in its commencement, with the splendid administration of Edward III., and comprehends also the short and disastrous reign of Richard II., which he survived for about a year. He seems to have sprung of wealthy, though not illustrious parentage, recent research having discovered his father and mother in a certain John Chaucer, a London vintner, and Agnes his wife. But London vintners were men of some consideration, and still more influence, in those days; we need not therefore be surprised to find young Geoffrey, during the years 1356-9, in the service of Elizabeth de Burgh, wife of Lionel Duke of Clarence, probably as page. And this connection with the royal family in all likelihood led to the first striking adventure of his life: he was taken prisoner in 1359 by the French, at the siege of Rhétiers, and being ransomed, according to the custom of those times, was enabled to return to England in 1360. We have, moreover, distinct proof, not only in the fact of his having been "armed a knight," but also in the honourable posts which he held, that he must have belonged to the higher sphere of society. He seems to have married about 1360; and if his wife—as is not unlikely, though satisfactory evidence is still wanting—were Philippa Röet, one of the maids of honour in attendance upon Queen Philippa, and the younger daughter of Sir Payne Röet, a knight who came from Hainault in the queen's train, it would still further tend to confirm this supposition. That he was educated at Cambridge rests only on an identification of him with Philogenet in the *Court of Love*, a work of questionable authenticity.

He next appears, in 1367, as one of the "valets of the king's chamber," and writs are addressed to him under the then honourable designation, "dilectus valettus noster." His official career appears to have been active and even distinguished: he enjoyed during a long period various profitable offices, having been for twelve years comptroller of the customs and subsidy of wools, skins, and tanned hides in the port of London; and he seems also to have been occasionally employed in diplomatic negociations. Thus, he was joined with two citizens of Genoa in a commission to Italy in 1373, on which occasion he is supposed to have made the acquaintance of Petrarch, then the most illustrious man of letters in Europe. Possibly because of his marriage with Philippa de Röet, whose sister, Catherine Swynford, was first the mistress and afterwards the wife of John of Gaunt, and partly perhaps from sharing in some of the political and religious opinions of that powerful prince, Chaucer was identified to a considerable degree both with the household and party of the Duke of Lancaster; and his *Complaynte of the Blacke Knyght*, his *Dream*, if indeed he wrote these poems, and his *Boke of the Duchesse* were suggested to him, the first by the courtship of the duke and the duchess Blanche, and the third by her death in 1369. One of the most interesting particulars of his life was his election as representative for Kent in the Parliament of 1386, which was dissolved in December of the same year. During the next four years he sustained a few disheartening reverses; for he was dismissed from all his offices in 1386, and he lost his wife in the following year. In 1389, however, he was appointed to the office of clerk of the king's works, which he held for only about two years: and there is reason to believe that, though his pecuniary circumstances must have been, during a great part of his life, in proportion to the position he occupied in the state and in society, his last days were more or less clouded by embarrassment. His death took place at Westminster on the 25th of October, 1400; and the house in which he died was afterwards removed to make room for the chapel of Henry VII.

If we may judge from an ancient and probably authentic portrait of Chaucer, attributed to his contemporary and fellow-poet Occleve, as well as from a curious and beautiful miniature introduced, according to the fashion of those times, into one of the most valuable manuscript copies of his works, our great poet appears to have been a man of pleasing and acute, though somewhat meditative and abstracted countenance, and to have grown rather corpulent towards the end of his life, at which time the *Canterbury Tales* were written. When, in the Prologue to *The Rime of Sir Thopas*, Chaucer is in his turn called upon by the host of the Tabard, himself represented as a "large man," and a "faire burgess," to contribute his story to the amusement of the pilgrims, he is rallied by honest Harry Bailey on his corpulency, as well as on his studious and abstracted air:

> "What man art thou?" quod he,
> "Thou lokest as thou woldest fynde an hare;
> For ever on the ground I se the stare.
> Approche ner, and loke merrily.
> Now ware you, sires, and let this man have space.
> He in the wast is schape as well as I:
> This were a popet in an arm to embrace,
> For any womman, smal and fair of face.
> He semeth elvisch by his countenance,
> For unto no wight doth he dalliaunce."

The literary and intellectual career of Chaucer divides itself naturally into two periods closely corresponding with the two great social and political tendencies which meet in the fourteenth century. His earlier productions bear the stamp and character of the Chivalric, his later and more original creations of the Italian literature. It is more than probable that the poet's visits to Italy, then the fountain and centre of the great literary revolution, brought him into contact with the works and the men by whose example the change in the taste of Europe was brought about. The religious element, too, enters largely into the character of his writings. It is probable, that though he sympathised—as is shown by numerous satirical passages in his poems—with Wiclif's hostility to the monastic orders and the corruptions of the clergy, the poet did not share in the theological opinions of the reformer.

On a rough general inspection of the longer poetical works, which until recently were all confidently ascribed to Chaucer, it will be found that about eight of them are to be ascribed to a direct or indirect imitation of purely Romance models, while four fall naturally under the category of the Italian type. Of the former class the principal are the *Romaunt of the Rose*, the *Court of Love*, the *Assembly of Fowls*, the *Cuckow and the Nightingale*, the *Flower and the Leaf*, *Chaucer's Dream*, the *Boke of the Duchesse*, and the *House of Fame*. Under the latter we must range the *Legend of Good Women*, *Troilus and Creseide*, *Anelyda and Arcyte*, and above all the *Canterbury Tales*.

But before giving an account of these works, we must observe that the authenticity of many of them has been denied by recent scholars upon two grounds—their absence in the most authoritative manuscripts, and their failing to conform to a rule of rhyming observed in all the unquestioned works of the poet (that of treating a final *ye* as a dissyllable. The doubtful works are the *Romaunt of the Rose* (of which, however, some translation was certainly made by Chaucer), the *Court of Love*, the *Cuckoo and the Nightingale*, *Chaucer's Dream*, the *Flower and the Leaf*, and the *Complaint of the Black Knight* (probably by Lydgate).

(1.) The *Romaunt of the Rose* is a translation of the famous French allegory *Le Roman de la Rose*, which forms the earliest monument of French literature in the 13th century. The original is of inordinate length, containing, even in the unfinished state in which it was left, 22,000 verses. It was begun by Guillaume de Lorris, who completed about 4070 lines; and was continued after his death by the witty and sarcastic Jean de Méun: the former of these authors died in 1260, and the latter probably about 1318. According to the general practice of the old Romance poets, the story is put into the form of a dream or vision. Lover, the hero, is alternately aided and obstructed in his undertakings: the principal of which is that of culling the enchanted rose which gives its name to the poem, by a multitude of beneficent or malignant personages, such as Bel-Accueil, Faux-Semblant, Danger, Male-Bouche, and Constrained-Abstinence. Chaucer's translation, which is in the octosyllabic Trouvère measure of the original, and consists of 7698 verses, comprehends the whole of the portion written by Lorris, together with about a sixth part of Méun's continuation; the portions omitted having either never been translated by the English poet in consequence of his dislike of the immoral and anti-religious tendency of which they were accused, or left out by the copyist from the early English manuscripts. The translation gives incessant proof of Chaucer's remarkable ear for metrical harmony, and also of his picturesque imagination; for though in many places he has followed his original with scrupulous fidelity, he not unfrequently adds vigorous touches of his own. The most remarkable illustration of this is the description of the character of a true gentleman, not a hint of which can be found in the original.*

(ii.) The *Court of Love* is written in the name of " Philogenet of Cambridge," clerk (or student), who is directed by Mercury to appear at the Court of Venus. The above designation has induced some critics to suppose that the poet meant under it to indicate himself, and they have drawn from it a most unfounded supposition that Chaucer had studied at Cambridge. The poet proceeds to give a description of the Castle of Love, where Admetus and Alcestis preside as king and queen. Philogenet is then conducted by Philobone to the Temple, where he sees Venus and Cupid; and where the oath of allegiance and obedience to the twenty commandments of Love is administered to the faithful. The hero is then presented to the Lady Rosial, with whom, in strict accordance with Provençal poetical custom, he has become enamoured in a dream. The most curious part of the poem is the celebration of the grand festival of Love on May-day, when an exact parody of the Catholic Matin service for Trinity Sunday is chanted by various birds in honour of the God of Love.

(iii.) In the *Assembly of Fowls* we have a poem not very dissimilar in form and versification to the preceding. The subject is a debate carried on before the Parliament of Birds to decide the claims of three eagles for the possession of a beautiful *formel* (female or hen), by which the Lady Blanche of Lancaster is probably intended.

(iv.) The *Cuckow and the Nightingale*, though of no great length, is one of the most charming among this class of Chaucer's productions: it describes a controversy between the two birds, the former

<hr>

* Lines 2187–2274.

of which was among the poets and allegorists of the Middle Ages the emblem of profligate celibacy, while the Nightingale was the type of constant and virtuous conjugal love. In this poem we meet with a striking example of that exquisite sensibility to the sweetness of external nature, and in particular to the song of birds, which was possessed by Chaucer in a higher degree, perhaps, than by any other poet in the world.*

(v.) The *Flower and the Leaf* is an allegory, probably written to celebrate the marriage of Philippa, John of Gaunt's daughter, with John, king of Portugal. A lady, unable to sleep, wanders out into a forest on a spring morning—an opening or *mise en scène* which often recurs in poems of this age—and seating herself in a delicious arbour, listens to the alternate song of the goldfinch and the nightingale. Her reverie is suddenly interrupted by the approach of a band of ladies clothed in white, and garlanded with laurel, agnus-castus, and woodbine. These accompany their queen in singing a roundel, and are in their turn interrupted by the sound of trumpets and by the appearance of nine armed knights, followed by a splendid train of cavaliers and ladies. These joust for an hour, and then advance to the first company, and each knight leads a lady to a laurel to which they make an obeisance. Another troop of ladies now approaches, habited in green and led by a queen, who do reverence to a tuft of flowers, while the leader sings a "bargaret," or pastoral song, in honour of the daisy, "si douce est la Marguérite." The sports are broken off, first by the heat of the sun which withers all the flowers, and afterwards by a violent storm of thunder and rain, in which the knights and ladies in green are pitifully drenched; while the white company shelter themselves under the laurel. Then follows the explanation of the allegory: the white queen and her party represent chastity; the knights the Nine Worthies; the cavaliers crowned with laurel the Knights of the Round Table, the Peers of Charlemagne, and the Knights of the Garter, to which illustrious order, then recently founded, the poet wished to pay a compliment. The Queen and ladies in green represent Flora and the followers of sloth and idleness. In general the flower typifies vain pleasure, the leaf, virtue and industry; the former being "a thing fading with every blast," while the latter "abides with the root, notwithstanding the frosts and winter storms." The poem is written in the seven-lined stanza, and contains many curious and beautiful passages.

(vi. vii.) The title of *Chaucer's Dream* was formerly given to the poem which is better named the *Boke of the Duchesse*. *Chaucer's*

See the inimitable passage from line 65 to 85.

Dream, proper, is one of the works of doubtful authorship, and refers under an allegorical form to certain real persons and events; but who and what these were it is now impossible to ascertain. The *Boke of the Duchesse*, as already mentioned, was suggested by the death of Blaunche of Lancaster.

(viii.) For its extraordinary union of brilliant description with learning and humour, the poem of the *House of Fame* is sufficient of itself to stamp Chaucer's reputation. Under the fashionable form of a dream or vision, it gives us a vivid and striking picture of the Temple of Glory, crowded with aspirants for immortal renown, and adorned with myriad statues of great poets and historians, and the House of Rumour, thronged with pilgrims, pardoners, sailors, and other retailers of wonderful reports. The Temple, though originally borrowed from the *Metamorphoses* of Ovid, exhibits in its architecture and adornment that strange mixture of pagan antiquity with the Gothic details of mediæval cathedrals, that strikes us in the poetry and in the illuminated MSS. of the fourteenth century. In richness of fancy it far surpasses Pope's imitation, *The Temple of Fame*.

(ix.) The *Legend of Good Women* is supposed, from many circumstances, to have been one of the latest of Chaucer's compositions; and to have been written as a kind of *amende honorable* or recantation for his unfavourable pictures of female character. Though the matter is closely translated, for the most part, from the *Heroïdes* of Ovid, the colouring given to the stories is entirely Catholic and mediæval; and Dido, Cleopatra, and Medea are regarded as the Martyrs of Saint Venus and Saint Cupid. The poet's original intention was to compose the legends of nineteen celebrated victims of the tender passion; but the work having been left incomplete, we possess only those of Cleopatra, Thisbe, Dido, Hypsipyle and Medea, Lucretia, Ariadne, Philomela, Phillis, and Hypermnestra. The poem is in ten-syllable heroic couplets, the rhymed heroic measure, and exhibits a consummate mastery over the resources of the English language and prosody; and many striking passages of description are interpolated by Chaucer. A few droll anachronisms also may be noted, as the introduction of cannon at the Battle of Actium.

(x.) The poem which the generations contemporary with, or succeeding to, the age of Chaucer placed nearest to the level of the *Canterbury Tales*, was unquestionably the *Troilus and Creseide*; for which work the poet indubitably drew his materials from Boccacio's poem entitled *Filostrato*. The story itself, which was extremely popular in the Middle Ages and later, Shakespeare himself having dramatized it, has been traced to Guido di Colonna, and to the mysterious book entitled *Trophe* of the equally mysterious author Lollius, so often quoted in Chaucer's age, and respecting whom all is obscure and enigmatical.* Some of the names and personages of the story, as Cryseida (Chrysois), Troilus, Pandarus, Diomede, and Priam, are obviously borrowed from the *Iliad*; but their relative positions and personality have been most strangely altered; and the principal action of the poem, being the passionate love of Troilus for Cryseida, her ultimate infidelity, and the immoral subserviency of Pandarus, bear the stamp of mediæval society, and have no resemblance whatever to the incidents and feelings of the heroic age. Chaucer has frequently adhered to the text of the *Filostrato*, and has adopted a modification of the Italian stanza of seven lines; but in the conduct of the story he has shown himself far superior to his original, the characters of Troilus, Pandarus, and Creseide in the *Filostrato*, contrasting very unfavourably with the pure, noble, and ideal personages of the English poet, whose morality is far higher and more refined than that of his great Florentine contemporary.

Chaucer's greatest and most original work is, beyond all comparison, the *Canterbury Tales*. It is in this that he has poured forth in inexhaustible abundance all his stores of wit, humour, pathos, splendour, and knowledge of humanity: it is this which will place him, till the remotest posterity, in the first rank among poets and character-painters.

The plan of this great work is singularly happy, enabling the poet to give us, first, a collection of admirable daguerreotypes of the various classes of English society, and then to place in the mouths of these persons a series of separate tales highly beautiful when regarded as compositions and judged on their own independent merits, but deriving an infinitely higher interest and appropriateness from the way in which they harmonise with their respective narrators. The poet informs us, after giving a brief but picturesque description of spring, that being about to make a pilgrimage from London to the shrine of St. Thomas à Becket in the cathedral of Canterbury, he passes the night previous to his departure at the hostelry of the Tabard in Southwark. While at the inn the hostelry is filled by a crowd of pilgrims bound to the same destination:—

> "In Southwerk at the Tabard as I lay,
> Redy to wenden on my pilgrimage
> To Canterbury with ful devout corage,
> At night was come into that hostelrie

---

* In the opinion of Mr. Henry Morley this mysterious personage is none other than Boccacio himself.

> Wel nyne and twenty in a companye *
> Of sondry folk, by aventure i-falle
> In felawschipe, and pilgryms were thei alle,
> That toward Canterbury wolden ryde."

This goodly company, assembled in a manner so natural in those times of pilgrimages and of difficult and dangerous roads, agree to travel in a body; and at supper the host of the Tabard, a jolly and sociable personage, proposes to accompany the party and serve as a guide; and at the same time suggests that they may much enliven the tedium of their journey by relating stories as they ride. He is to be accepted by the whole society as a kind of judge or moderator, by whose decisions every one is to abide. As the journey to Canterbury and the return journey then occupied several days, the plan of the whole work, had Chaucer completed it, would have comprised the adventures on the outward journey, the arrival at Canterbury, a description, in all probability, of the splendid religious ceremonies and the visits to the numerous shrines and relics in the Cathedral, the return to London, the farewell supper at the Tabard, and dissolution of the pleasant company, which would separate as naturally as they had assembled. Harry Bailey proposes that each pilgrim should relate two tales on the journey out, and two more on the way home; and that, on the return of the party to London, he who should be adjudged to have related the best and most amusing story should sup at the common cost. Such is the *setting* or framework in which the separate tales are inserted; and the tales themselves are admirably in accordance with the characters of the persons who relate them, and the remarks and criticisms to which they give rise are no less humorous and natural: some of the stories suggesting others, just as would happen in real life under the same circumstances. The pilgrims are persons of almost all ranks and classes of society; and in the inimitable description of their manners, persons, dress, horses, &c., with which the poet has introduced them, we behold a vast and minute portrait gallery of the social state of England in the fourteenth century. They are—(1.) A Knight; (2.) A Squire; (3.) A Yeoman, or military retainer of the class of the free peasants, who in the quality of an archer was bound to accompany his feudal lord to war; (4.) A Prioress, a lady of rank, superior of a nunnery; (5, 6, 7, 8.) A Nun and three Priests, in attendance upon this lady; (9.) A Monk, a person represented as handsomely dressed and equipped, and passionately fond of hunting and good cheer: (10.) A Friar; (11.) A Merchant; (12.) A Clerk, or Student of the University of Oxford; (13.) A Serjeant of the Law; (14.) A Franklin or rich country-gentleman; (15, 16, 17, 18, 19.) Five

---

* But in his subsequent enumeration (see next page), Chaucer counts 30 persons.

wealthy burgesses or tradesmen, a Haberdasher, or dealer in silk
and cloth, a Carpenter, a Weaver, a Dyer, and a Tapisser, or
maker of carpets and hangings; (20.) A Cook, or rather what in
old French is called a *rôtisseur*, i. e. the keeper of a cook's-shop;
(21.) A Shipman, the master of a trading vessel; (22.) A Doctor of
Physic; (23.) A Wife of Bath, a rich cloth-manufacturer; (24.) A
Parson, or secular parish priest; (25.) A Ploughman, the brother
of the preceding personage; (26.) A Miller; (27.) A Manciple, or
steward of a college or religious house; (28.) A Reeve, bailiff or
intendant of the estates of some wealthy landowner; (29.) A Sompnour, or Sumner, an officer in the then formidable ecclesiastical
courts, whose duty was to summon or cite before the spiritual jurisdiction those who had offended against the canon laws; (30.) A
Pardoner, or vendor of Indulgences from Rome. To these thirty
persons must be added Chaucer himself, and the Host of the Tabard,
making in all thirty-two.

Now, if each of these pilgrims had related four tales, viz., two on
the journey to Canterbury, and two on their return, the work would
have contained 124 stories, independently of the subordinate incidents and conversations. In reality, however, the pilgrims do not
arrive at their destination. and there are many evidences of confusion in the tales which Chaucer has given us, leading to the
conclusion that the materials were not only incomplete, but left in
an unarranged state by the poet. The stories that we possess are
twenty-five in number,—three of which, the Cook's, the Squire's,
and Chaucer's first, are " left half," or less than half, " told," and
one, *Gamelyn*,* is either entirely spurious or written by the poet for
a different purpose. Thus we have only twenty-one complete tales.
so that several of the personages are left silent. Besides, a Canon
and his Yeoman unexpectedly join the cavalcade during the journey,
but it is uncertain whether this episode, which was probably an
afterthought of the poet, takes place on the journey to or from
Canterbury. The Canon, who is represented as an Alchemist, half
swindler and half dupe, is driven away from the company by shame
at his attendant's indiscreet disclosures; and the latter, remaining
with the pilgrims, relates a most amusing story of the villanous
artifices of the charlatans who pretended to possess the Great Ar-
canum. The stories narrated by the pilgrims are admirably introduced by what the author calls "prologues," consisting either of
remarks and criticisms on the preceding tale, and which naturally
suggest what is to follow, and of the incidents of the journey itself.
The Tales are all in verse, with the exception of two, that of the

* The Cook's Tale of *Gamelyn*, if really written by Chaucer, was perhaps intended
to be related on the journey home.

Parson, and Chaucer's second narrative, the allegorical story of Melibeus and his wife Prudence. Those in verse exhibit a considerable variety of metrical forms, all of which Chaucer handles with consummate ease and dexterity; indeed, it may be boldly affirmed that no English poet whatever is more exquisitely melodious than he: and the nature of the versification will often assist us in tracing the sources from whence Chaucer derived or adapted his materials. Indeed he appears in no single demonstrable instance to have taken the trouble to invent the intrigue or subject-matter of any of his stories, but to have freely borrowed them either from the multitudinous fabliaux of the Provençal poets, the legends of the mediæval chroniclers, or the immense storehouse of the Gesta Romanorum, and the rich treasury of the early Italian writers, Dante, Petrarch, and Boccacio.

The Tales themselves may be roughly divided into the two great classes of serious, tragic, or pathetic, and comic or humorous; in both styles Chaucer has seldom been equalled, and assuredly never surpassed. The finest of the elevated and pathetic stories are the *Knight's Tale*—the longest of them all, in which is related the adventure of Palamon and Arcite;—the *Squire's Tale*, a wild half-oriental story of love, chivalry, and enchantment, the action of which goes on "at Sarray (Tzarev, near Sarepta) in the lond of Tartary;" the *Man of Law's Tale*, the beautiful and pathetic story of Custance; the *Prioress's Tale*, the charming legend of "litel Hew of Lincoln," the Christian child murdered by the Jews for so perseveringly singing his hymn to the Virgin;[*] and, above all, the *Clerk of Oxford's Tale*, perhaps the most beautiful pathetic narration in the whole range of literature. This, the story of Griselda, the model and heroine of wifely patience and obedience, is the crown and pearl of all the serious and pathetic narratives, as the *Knight's Tale* is the masterpiece among the descriptions of love and chivalric magnificence.

We will rapidly note the sources from which, as far as can be ascertained at present, Chaucer derived the subjects of the narratives above particularised. The *Knight's Tale* is freely borrowed from the *Teseide* of Boccacio, many of the incidents of the latter being themselves taken from the *Thebais* of Statius. Though the action and personages of this noble story are assigned to classical antiquity, it is needless to say that the sentiments, manners, and feelings of the persons introduced are those of chivalric Europe; the "Two Noble Kinsmen," Palamon and Arcite, being the purest ideal types of the knightly character, and the decision of their claims to the

<hr>

[*] Though the scene of this tale is laid in Asia, yet the principal incidents of the well-known English legend are retained.

hand of Emilie by a combat in *champ clos*, an incident completely alien from the habits of the heroic age. The *Squire's Tale* bears evident marks of Oriental origin ; but whether it be a legend directly derived from Eastern literature, or received by Chaucer after having filtered through a Romance version, is now uncertain. It is equal to the preceding story in splendour and variety of incident and word-painting, but far inferior in depth of pathos and ideal elevation of sentiment; yet it was by the *Squire's Tale* that Milton characterised Chaucer in that inimitable passage of the *Penseroso* where he evokes the recollections of the great poet :—

> " And call up him that left half-told
> The story of Cambuscan bold,
> Of Cambal, and of Algarsife,
> And who had Canace to wife
> That owned the virtuous ring and glass ;
> And of the wondrous horse of brass
> On which the Tartar king did ride."

The *Man of Law's Tale* is taken with little variation from Gower's ' *Confessio Amantis*,' unless indeed, which is more likely, both Chaucer and Gower drew from the same source.

The pedigree of the most pathetic of Chaucer's stories, that of Patient Griselda, narrated by the clerk of Oxford, is traceable to Petrarch's Latin translation of the last tale in Boccacio's *Decameron*, which Petrarch sent to Boccacio in 1373, the year before his own death.

The finest of Chaucer's comic and humorous stories are those of the Miller, the Reeve, the Sompnour, the Canon's Yeoman, and the Nun's Priest. Though all of these are excellent, the three best are the Miller's, the Reeve's, and the Sompnour's; and among these last it is difficult to give the palm of drollery, acute painting of human nature, and exquisite ingenuity of incident. It is much to be regretted that the comic stories turn upon events of a kind which the refinement of modern manners renders it impossible to analyse but it should be remembered that society in Chaucer's day, though perhaps not less moral in reality, was far more outspoken and simple, and permitted and enjoyed allusions which have been proscribed by the more precise delicacy of later ages. The first of these irresistible drolleries is probably the adaptation to English life—for the scene is laid at Oxford—of some old fabliau; the *Reeve's Tale* may be found in substance in the 6th novel of the Ninth Day of the *Decameron:* the *Sompnour's Tale*, though probably from a mediæval source, has not hitherto been traced. The admirable wit, humour, and learning, with which in the *Canon's Yeoman's Tale* Chaucer exposes the rascalities of the pretenders to alchemical knowledge, may have been derived from his own expe-

rience of the arts of these swindlers. The tale may be compared
with Ben Jonson's comedy of the *Alchemist*. The tale assigned to
the Nun's Priest is an exceedingly humorous apologue of the Cock
and the Fox, in which, though the *dramatis personæ* are animals,
they are endowed with such a droll similitude to the human character, that the reader enjoys at the same time the apparently
incompatible pleasures of sympathising with them as human
beings, and laughing at their fantastic assumption of reason as
lower creatures.

A remark has been made, some pages back, on the circumstance of
two of the stories being written in prose. It may be not uninteresting
to investigate this exception. When Chaucer is applied to by the
Host, he commences a rambling puerile romance of chivalry,
entitled the *Rime of Sir Thopas*, which promises to be an in-
terminable story of knight-errant adventures, combats with giants,
dragons, and enchanters, and is written in the exact style and metre
of the Trouvère narrative poems—the only instance of this versification being employed in the *Canterbury Tales*. He goes on gal-
lantly " in the style his books of chivalry had taught him," and,
like Don Quixote, " imitating, as near as he could, their very
phrase ;" but he is suddenly interrupted, with many expressions of
comic disgust, by the merry host :—

> " ' No mor of this, for Goddes dignite !'
> Quod our Hoste, ' for thou makest me
> So wery of thy verray lewednesse,
> That, al so wisly God my soule blesse,
> Myn ecres aken for thy drafty speche.
> Now such a rym the devel I byteche !
> This may wel be rym dogerel,' qued he."

Chaucer, then, with great goodnature and a readiness which
marks the man of the world, offers to tell " a litel thing in prose ;"
and commences the long allegorical tale of *Melibeus and his wife
Prudence*, in which, though the matter is often tiresome enough, he
shows himself as great a master of prose as of poetry.

The other prose tale is narrated by the Parson, who, being represented as a somewhat simple and narrow-minded though pious and
large-hearted pastor, characteristically refuses to indulge the company with what can only minister to vain pleasure, and proposes
something that may tend to edification, " moralité and vertuous
matiere ;" and commences a long and very curious sermon on the
Seven Deadly Sins, their causes and remedies—a most interesting
specimen of the theological literature of the day. It is divided and
subdivided with all the painful minuteness of scholastic divinity;
but it breathes throughout a noble spirit of evangelical piety, and
in many passages attains great dignity of expression.

Besides these two Canterbury Tales, Chaucer wrote in prose a translation of Böethius *De Consolatione*, and an incomplete astrological work, *On the Astrolabe*, addressed to his son Lewis in 1391.

The Testament of Love, long regarded as one of the poet's undoubted works, has been lately ruled by the best judges to be spurious, a decision in which Chaucer's admirers are only too glad to acquiesce.

The general plan of the *Canterbury Tales* is believed to have been suggested by the Decameron of Boccacio, though the English poet's conception must be allowed to be infinitely superior to that of the Italian, whose ten accomplished young gentlemen and ladies assemble in their luxurious villa to escape from the terrible plague which was then, in sad reality, devastating Florence.

The difficulty of reading and understanding Chaucer has been much exaggerated. The principal rule that the student should keep in mind is that the French words, so abundant in his writings, had not yet been so modified, by changes in their orthography and pronunciation, as to become anglicized, and are therefore to be read with their French accent; and secondly, that the final *e* which terminates so many English words had not yet become an *e mute*, and is to be pronounced as a separate syllable, as *love, hope, lové, hopé;* and finally, the past termination of the verb *ed* is almost invariably to be made a separate syllable. Some curious traces of the old Anglo-Saxon grammar, as the inflexions of the personal and possessive pronouns, are still retained; as well as of the Teutonic past participle, in the prefix *i* or *y* (*ifalle, yron,* German *gefallen, geronnen*), and a few other details of the Teutonic formation of the verb.

Many attempts have been made to reduce Chaucer's writings to the language and diction of modern times; and even some distinguished poets have tried their skill in this way, but with very indifferent success. Wordsworth has adhered with tolerable fidelity to the language, and consequently to the spirit, of the original. His *Cuckoo and Nightingale, Prioress's Tale,* and *Troilus and Cresida,* really do retain a good deal of Chaucer; but the less sympathetic minds of Dryden and Pope made even this moderate degree of success impossible. The *Palamon and Arcite, Wife of Bath's Tale, Cock and Fox,* and *Flower and Leaf* of Dryden, are perhaps very pleasant reading; but everything characteristic of the greater poet, that subtle essence which is everywhere present in his works, has evaporated utterly. Pope's failure in the *Prologue to the Wife of Bath,* and in the *Merchant's Tale,* is no less marked.

CHAPTER V.

THE CONTEMPORARIES OF CHAUCER

INTELLECTUAL power, it is said, has a tendency, in all countries where it has been developed, to gather in clusters. It seldom, if ever, occurs in literature that a single isolated figure is found standing alone—that a "bright particular star" shines forth unattended by the lesser lights, which shed a steady though less brilliant lustre over the literary firmament. Throughout the history of English, as well as of classical literature, we invariably find the great names grouped into distinct constellations round some one star of the first magnitude, whose surpassing radiance, by attracting the gaze exclusively to itself, often serves to make us insensible to the no less real splendour of its humbler companions. And so it is with the age of Chaucer. From one poet of transcendent merit it has gained a distinct character and a distinct interest; by him mainly it has been made fruitful throughout all time; but he, too, is but the central figure of a group—the most splendidly endowed genius in a band of rare intellects.

No writings—not even those of Chaucer himself—so faithfully reflect the popular feeling during the great social and religious movement that forms so striking a feature of the latter half of the fourteenth century, as that very remarkable series of poems which appeared under the name of PIERS PLOUGHMAN. In these works the deep-seated discontent of the Commons with the course of affairs in Church and State found a voice. The most important of them are three in number, the *Vision*, and the *Creed, of Piers Ploughman*, and the fragment of a Poem on the *Deposition of Richard II.* They bear the closest resemblance to one another in form and spirit, as well as in style of execution, and were all written, though at considerable intervals, within the same half-century. The first in merit as in date (1362?), which also formed the model for the others, and is much the longest, is the *Vision.* Allusions to the treaty of Bretigny, made in 1360, and to the great tempest of 1362, would seem to fix the latter year, or thereabouts, as the time of its composition in its earliest form—for it was subsequently twice enlarged—and tradition confidently assigns its authorship to one Robert Langlande, who is otherwise unknown. If, indeed, we believe the author to have so entirely identified himself with the seer of the *Vision* as to give him his own name, we must admit that he was called William; but in that case we must also assume that he wrote the later versions after his own death, the end of the first having left Will " enclosed under clay." Two things are tolerably clear from the work itself—that the writer was a Churchman, and that he sympathised heartily with the new spirit that was spreading through the labouring classes of the nation. In this work *Piers Ploughman* (or *Peter the Ploughman*) is a purely allegorical personage—a sort of personification of the peasantry—and is the subject, not the seer, of the *Vision*. The Latin title more exactly conveys its nature; it is *Visio Willelmi de Pietro Ploughman*—a vision seen by the author, who is here called William, concerning the working men of England. The dreamer, exhausted by his long wanderings—" wery for-wandred," he says himself—goes to sleep on the Malvern Hills, and soon becomes aware of a goodly company gathered before him in a field. In a word, representatives of every section of society are there assembled. He is somewhat puzzled at first to understand what all this may mean, when a " lovely lady," descending from a castle, announces herself as Holy Church, expounds to him the meaning of the scene that lies before him, and, after leaving with him the key of the mystery, departs. The poet then proceeds to describe the various incidents that took place in this typical assembly, each of which shadows forth in an easily-penetrated allegory some move in the great game played by king, ecclesiastic, and noble. The second version of the work, which is supposed to have been written about 1377, consists of nearly 8000 double verses (or couplets), arranged in twenty *passus,* or sections, so little connected with one another as to appear almost separate poems. A few years later the author still further enlarged it. Its prevalent spirit is that of satire, aimed against abuses and vices in general, but in particular against the corruptions of the Church, which are assailed with great force and spirit.

The second, or *Creed of Piers Ploughman* (1393?), is supposed to have been written some thirty years later than the *Vision*. Though an evident imitation of the earlier work, it differs from it in many important respects. In it Piers Ploughman is no longer an allegorical personage, but a real flesh and blood representative of the sons of the soil: the author is an ardent disciple of Wiclif, who attacks the doctrines as well as the discipline of the Church; and it contains no political satire whatever.

The third, or Poem on the *Deposition of Richard II.* (1399), is a mere fragment—for, in common with the *Creed,* it seems to have been rigidly proscribed by the ruling powers—and its tone is entirely political. It was composed during the few months that intervened between the capture of King Richard and the accession of Henry Bolingbroke in 1399.

All three are constructed on the same metrical principle, which is a mixture of alliteration and rhythmical accent, without rhyme; and they are the last and most perfect specimens of the kind in any form of the language. In this respect, as well as in the character of the allegory and their somewhat obsolete style, they would seem to indicate a distinct return to the ancient models; but the proportion of French words found in them is just as great as in Chaucer. But, though the earliest of them is later in date than the earliest of Chaucer's works, their diction is more archaic, and a more considerable number of their words has fallen out of use.

A notable fact in the history of these works is the great popularity they afterwards attained on their being first printed in the year 1530, when they not only materially promoted the growth of Reformation principles, but contributed to the mental development of more than one great intellect. The character of the poet Sponser was probably moulded by them and their great contemporary.

But the name that is most closely linked with Chaucer's is that of JOHN GOWER (1325 ?–1408). Born some time before Chaucer, this excellent poet and man lived in the most intimate, though it would seem not unbroken, friendship with him during a great part of their joint lives, and finally survived him for eight years. It is to " moral Gower" that the 'Troilus and Creseide' was dedicated: he, too, became the poet's representative when he was absent in Italy in 1373; and he pays a high compliment to his friend in the first edition of his English work, the *Confessio Amantis*. The omission of this passage in the later edition, and the emphatic language in which Chaucer, in the Man of Law's prologue, denounces the " corsed stories" introduced by the other into his work, are supposed to indicate a rupture of this famous friendship; but there is happily no necessity for so unwelcome an explanation.

The course of Gower's life was by no means so active or so full of vicissitudes as his friend's. A member of an affluent county family in Kent, he appears to have passed his life mainly in the management of his property and in the composition of his literary works. Yet he was not an unconcerned spectator of the stirring events of his time, as all his extant works evince. From a loyal subject of Richard of Bordeaux he changed into an avowed partisan of Henry of Lancaster, whose badge, the collar of the silver swan, still adorns the recumbent effigy that covers his bones in St. Saviour's, Southwark.

And the three books, on which the poet's head is there represented as reclining, are typical, not only of the work of his life, but of the three great literary principles that were at war in his time,

The French language still maintained its ground as the language of the educated classes; and accordingly even our countryman, when addressing himself "al universite de tout le monde," felt himself constrained to use the alien tongue; but the one great result of his labours therein, the *Speculum Meditantis*, is no longer extant, the poem once taken for it having turned out to be an entirely different work. This was the last considerable contribution to French literature in England.

Again, when Gower undertook to describe the diseased condition of English society in his time (1382?), not even then did he adopt the native tongue; but in the *Vox Clamantis* he strove to give utterance to his oppressed feelings in alternate Latin hexameters and pentameters. This, generally believed to be the best of his works, is a poem in seven books, written on the subject of the great insurrection of the Commons in 1381, of which he gives us a lively picture in the first Book. The following Books are taken up mainly with elaborate treatises on religion and society, and addresses to the different professions. To this work he afterwards appended the *Tripartite Chronicle*, written in leonine hexameters.

Finally, when Chaucer had shown the great capabilities of the native speech under a skilful hand, Gower in his old age produced the *Confessio Amantis* (1393) in that tongue. This work, which, though not the ablest, is by far the most interesting to us, was first undertaken at the request of King Richard, to whom, the poet says,

> " Belongeth my legeaunce,
> With all min hertes obeisaunce,"

and was finished in the " yere sixtenthe " of the same king's reign (1392-3). This edition contains the celebrated passage, in which Venus represents Chaucer as her disciple and poet, and expresses a wish, that in his " later age " he should " sette an end to all his werke" by writing the ' Testament of Love.' Subsequently, however, a second edition of the poem appeared, differing from the first merely in the omission of this compliment to his great contemporary, and in the introduction of a new prologue, which, without a single reference to King Richard, professes an entire affection for Henry of Lancaster, to whom the book is now dedicated.

The *Confessio Amantis* is a poem in the octo-syllabic metre, consisting of eight Books, in addition to the Prologue; one being given to each of the seven deadly sins, and another inserted in the body of the work on the subject of philosophy generally. It is in reality a collection of stories, strung together upon a very simple, but not over felicitous plan, which is much inferior to Chaucer's, and hardly equal even to Boccacio's. Instead of a number of characters,

we have but two, Lover and Genius; the former, by direction of
Venus, confessing his sins to the latter, who, as the goddess's own
clerk, listens to the penitent, and then, before shriving him, illustrates the enormity of his offences by an immense number of appo-
site stories.   These are taken from all manner of sources—the
Bible, Ovid, the ' Gesta Romanorum ' (the oldest collection of tales
extant), Godfrey of Viterbo, French lays and fabliaux, &c.—and
illustrate the varied and extensive reading of the author.   The
Confessio Amantis possesses real merit, and is not without a certain
charm for congenial minds; but its excellences, such as they are,
are balanced by many defects.   It is tedious, overlaid with learning
to a wearisome extent, and utterly without Chaucer's humour, passion, and love of nature.   The author, while sensible of and de-
ploring the disjointed state of society in his time, and the offences
of men in high place, is yet a stout supporter of the old order of
things.   His popularity with the cultivated classes continued for
many generations.   James of Scotland, in the fifteenth century,
describes him and Chaucer as

> "Superlative as poetis laureate,
>   In moralitee and eloquence ornate;"

and Shakespeare, in the sixteenth, not only borrows from him the
materials of ' Pericles,' but brings him upon the stage as chorus to
the same play.

A greater poet than Gower still remains to be noticed—JOHN
BARBOUR (1316-1395?), Archdeacon of Aberdeen, whose life was
almost strictly contemporaneous with Chaucer's.   Though a Scotchman, he fairly deserves a place among English poets, for the growth
of the literary dialect had not yet produced any material divergence
in the language of the two countries, nor had their union under the
same king yet converted the Northern speech into a patois.   There
were differences certainly between the two tongues, but hardly more
considerable than those existing between parts of England itself.
His great poem is the *Brus*, or *Bruce*, a chronicle in rhymed octo-
syllabics of the adventures of King Robert, extending to about
12,500 lines.   It is a work of great merit, both poetical and historical; for, while occasionally embellishing the great king's history
with romantic incidents and details, it apparently contains a good
deal of trustworthy information.   After Chaucer no writer of the
fourteenth century is so readable as Barbour.   He also paid several
visits to England and studied at Oxford in his old age, where two
curious memorials of him have been lately discovered—a versified
translation of the ' Troy Book,' and a collection of fifty lives of the
Saints

Prose Literature in the Time of Chaucer.

The most meritorious writer of English prose in Chaucer's time was undoubtedly Chaucer himself; but his rare power in this department has been eclipsed completely by his transcendent genius as a poet. Of those writers whose fame depends on prose works alone, the chief are MANDEVILLE, TREVISA, and WICLIF. The first, Sir John Mandeville (1300-1371), who is sometimes, but erroneously, called the father of English prose, published his well-known volume of travels in 1356. This, which Mr. Hallam calls our earliest English book, professes to be an authentic account of what the author saw on his travels through the most distant countries of the East, but is, in reality, a lying collection of marvels, worthy only of being classed with the adventures of Baron Munchausen. There is, doubtless, a real element of truth in the work, but it is blended with such a large proportion of falsehood as to make the whole narrative worthless. The style, however, is straightforward and unadorned, and the composition may still be read with but little difficulty.

JOHN OF TREVISA (fl. 1387), besides other works, translated into English the Latin *Polychronicon* of Ralph Higden, which he finished about the year 1387—a work which Caxton printed in 1482, with an additional chapter from his own pen, bringing the narrative down to the year 1460. From these two productions we learn historically, what is otherwise a matter of reasonable inference, that the three languages still existed side by side in England, but that English was gradually recovering the supremacy. Mandeville, in his Prologue, tells us that he had "put this boke out of Latyn into Frensche, and translated it agen out of Frensche into Englyssche, that every man of his nation may understand it;" and to Trevisa we are indebted for the fact that in 1385 "in al the gramere scholes of Engelonde childern leuth Freynsch and construeth and lurneth an Englysch."

No name of the time perhaps will be longer remembered than that of the man who first gave a complete copy of the Scriptures to the English people in the English tongue, JOHN WICLIF (1324-1384). This remarkable man, of almost as great importance in the literary as in the political history of our nation, was born, it is said, near Richmond, in Yorkshire, in 1324, studied at Oxford, and eventually rose to considerable academical and ecclesiastical preferments, though his life was marked by many vicissitudes. After having been alternately supported and abandoned by men of great influence, of whom John of Gaunt was the greatest, he closed his life peacefully at his Lutterworth parsonage in 1384. It was here, after his enemies had driven him from his Chair at Oxford, that he com-

menced his great translation, which, with the assistance of a priest,
named HEREFORD, he is said to have finished about the year 1380.
The latter is believed to have been the author of the work as far as
Baruch in the Apocrypha, and Wiclif himself of the remainder. A
revision of their version was made about ten years after by PURVEY,
who introduced many important alterations into the text of his predecessors.

But this is not our only obligation to Wiclif. He was perhaps
the first English scholar who made his native tongue the vehicle
for attacks on the ecclesiastical system: for his *Apology* for the
Lollards, and *Harmony of the Gospels* are written in English.

It is impossible to overrate the importance of Wiclif's great work
both to the language and the nation. Translated, as it was, from
the Latin Vulgate, it supplies the principal reason that the theological vocabulary of our language is taken mainly from the Latin;
and more than any other literary work, it contributed to keep alive
in the people that irrepressible spirit of free inquiry that led to the
great Reformation of the sixteenth century. Few English writers
are more deserving of the gratitude of the nation than John
Wiclif.

CHAPTER VI.

ENGLISH LITERATURE FROM CHAUCER TO SPENSER.

WITH the death of Chaucer in 1400 terminates our first great manifestation of intellectual power. To it succeeds a somewhat lengthened period of literary decay, as remarkable for the absence, as the preceding was for the presence, of original genius, when the mental energies of the nation seemed well nigh exhausted. For more than a hundred and fifty years we meet with no first-rate intellect, with hardly a single name worthy to stand even in the second rank. But though singularly deficient in great men, the time was by no means barren in results. It is distinguished by one event at least, the importance of which cannot possibly be over-estimated—the invention of printing; and it witnessed the revival of learning, and the emancipation of the human mind from ecclesiastical tyranny. It was also a period of unwearied accumulation of materials, when the spiritual activities of the nation were gathering themselves up for another marvellous outburst. Nor, indeed, was there any break in the chain of succession which links the nineteenth century to the fourteenth; the continuity of literature in both verse and prose was preserved uninterrupted by a line of men of real, though not brilliant, ability; foremost among whom, at least in order of time, come the immediate disciples of Chaucer, OCCLEVE, LYDGATE, and JAMES OF SCOTLAND.

Of the first, THOMAS OCCLEVE (1370-1454?), little need be said. Born about 1370, he was in early life the friend, and in later the poetical disciple, of Chaucer, whose death he bewails with simple earnestness, in his most meritorious work the *De Regimine Principum*. This lament is the most striking passage in the poem, which is partly autobiographical and partly reflective.

JOHN LYDGATE (1374-1460?), known sometimes as Dan John of Bury (Bury St. Edmund's), where he passed the greater part of his life as an inmate of its famous monastery, deserves a much higher place. His works were in great repute in his own century and long after, the fastidious Gray, no less than James of Scotland, finding in him many poetical excellences. He was a very prolific writer; but his longest and best known productions are the *Story of Thebes*, the *Troy Book*, and the *Fall of Princes*. The first, which is a translation of the Thebaid of Statius, is given as an additional Canterbury Tale, told on the return journey by the author, who represents himself in the prologue as having fallen in with Chaucer's pilgrims at the Canterbury inn, and been allowed to go home in their company. The *Fall of Princes* is a translation from the 'De Casibus Illustrium Virorum' of Boccacio, and is chiefly remarkable for the famous reference to his "maister Chaucer," "the lode-sterre of our language," whose Monk's Tale is constructed on the same plan. The Latin prose romance of Guido Colonné, a Sicilian poet, whom Edward I. brought to England, supplied him with the materials for the *Troy Book*,—a work of some interest to the antiquarian, as pre-serving many features of the social life of the fifteenth century. To these may be added, as worthy of special notice, the *London Lackpenny*, a short poem of much spirit in the tumbling metre. Its moral will commend it to the sympathies of all but a very few —the little that can be got in this world without money to pay for it.

But the most brilliant poetical name of the fifteenth century is James I. of Scotland (1394–1437). This, the only really eminent king of the Stuart line, was no doubt indebted for the develop-ment of his royal qualities to the same early adversities to which we owe his great poem, the *King's Quair*, written in the nineteenth and last year of his captivity in England. In 1405, when but eleven years old, he fell into the hands of Henry IV., by whom and whose successors he was detained a prisoner for almost a quarter of a century; which period, however, was not without results to himself and his nation. His *Quair* (Quire or Book) is a poetical record of the circumstances under which he first met, and won the heart of, his devoted Queen, Jane Beaufort, daughter of John Earl of Somerset, and consequently grand-daughter of John of Gaunt and of Chaucer's supposed sister-in-law, Catherine Swyneford, of whose bright figure,

> "The fairest or the freschest young flowre,"

he caught a glimpse from the window of his prison, as she walked with her attendants "under the Toure." In six cantos, or about 1400 lines, the royal captive describes his sad reflections in his prison-house, the sudden appearance of this beautiful vision, its peerless loveliness, his many fluctuating emotions, his hopes and despairs, and the happy ending of his courtship. No poem of equal merit was produced in the long interval between Chaucer and Spenser; it is distinguished by a genuine poetic sensibility, a manly delicacy of feeling, and tenderness of expression not often found. Many other effusions are ascribed to King James, some of which undoubtedly belong to his more licentious namesake of the following century. His English training, his devotion to English models, and the fact that he composed his great work in England, fully justify us in calling him an English poet.

Besides these three, this century produced not a single respectable versifier. They are connected with one another by a sort of affinity, in being all professed disciples of Chaucer, whose influence upon them is shown by the very metre in which they wrote—the rhyme royal. This stanza, first made popular by Chaucer, and a great favourite with the poets of the next two centuries, is said, indeed, to have gained its name from being that of the *King's Quair*, though other explanations are suggested. It consists of seven heroic lines, of which the first and third, the second, fourth, and fifth, and the sixth and seventh rhyme together, being in fact the well known *ottava rima* with the fifth line omitted.

Prose literature made much greater progress in this century than her elder sister, though half of it had already elapsed before any striking composition appeared even in this department. REGINALD PECOCK (1390–1460?), Bishop of Chichester, whose somewhat remarkable career extends over a large portion of this century, after combating the doctrines of the Lollards in several English pamphlets and sermons, finally published, unfortunately for himself, about 1450, the elaborate work entitled the *Repressor of Overmuch Blaming of the Clergy*. In his zeal for the Church he seems to have overstepped the prescribed limits of orthodoxy; and he paid the penalty of his rashness in the Abbey of Thorney, where he lay a prisoner from 1457 until his death. "In diction and arrangement of sentences," says Mr. Marsh, "the *Repressor* is much in advance of the chronicles of Pecock's age; the grammar, both in accidence and syntax, is in many points nearly where Wiclif had left it," his language being more obsolete even than Lydgate's. It is not improbable that, like Spenser after him, he affected a sort of archaism in his style.

The *Difference between Absolute and Limited Monarchy* was written by Sir John Fortescue (1395–1485), Chief Justice to Henry VI., about the year 1470. The *De Laudibus Legum Angliæ* in Latin was a contribution from the same pen to the education of the young Prince of Wales, whose mental training during his years of exile was under the direction of Sir John. Both these works, and especially the latter, are of great value to the historical student, to whom they furnish direct evidence of the constitutional and legal procedure of the time.

Few English names of this age will live as long as that of William Caxton (1412–1491), to whom England owes her participation in the benefits arising from the greatest invention of modern times—the art of printing. The original author of this invention, which was nothing more than the use of moveable types in place of the old engraved wooden blocks, is now generally believed to have been John Gutenberg of Mentz. He had already, it is said, thought out the plan about 1438, but through poverty was unable to put it into execution until twelve years afterwards, when he met with John Fust, a wealthy merchant, by whose assistance he brought out in 1455 the first printed book, the Latin Bible now known as the Mazarin. The art was introduced into England by Caxton, the first-fruits of whose printing-press, set up at Westminster under the patronage of Anthony Woodville, Earl Rivers, is supposed to have been the *Game of the Chesse*, in 1474. From that time until his death, in 1491, Caxton laboured assiduously at his vocation, giving to the world sixty-three books, of which the vast majority were in English, consisting partly of translations and partly of original works. Many of these translations are from the printer's own pen. To others of the books he added prefaces of his own composition, so that he is fairly entitled to a place, though not a very high one, among English authors.

To one of the original writings published by him, the *Mort D'Arthur* of Sir Thomas Malory, great interest is attached by the present generation. It is the quarry out of which the greatest of our living poets has hewn the materials for one of his finished works, as well as for his earlier essay in the same province. Notwithstanding its name, " it treateth," says Caxton, "of the byrth, lyf, and actes of the sayd Kynge Arthur, of his noble Knyghtes of the Rounde Table, their marvayllous enquestes and adventures;" who also states that it was taken by its author out of certain books in the French and reduced into English, and printed by himself in 1485. It is a romance of real chivalry, written in a plain, unadorned English style; free from most of the extravagances of the earlier romances and from many of the repulsive passages which deformed the more ancient Arthurian cycle. The *Paston Letters*, the earliest collection of the kind in the language, form a regular series extending from before 1422 until 1509, and are so numerous that they filled five volumes on their first publication. By far the greatest number are written either by or to members of the Paston family, then and afterwards well known in Norfolk and elsewhere, of which Sir William, the " Good Judge," was the first representative of distinction; but the collection contains not a few from the most prominent men of the time, the Duke of

York, the Earl of Warwick, the Duke of Norfolk (Shakespeare's "Jockey of Norfolk"), and many others. They were published at intervals, between the years 1787 and 1823; the first four volumes under the editorship of Sir John Fenn, a Norfolk antiquary, and the fifth under that of his nephew, Serjeant Frere. This collection is of the greatest historical importance, not only from the light it throws upon some of the dark passages of our history, but also from the valuable illustrations it supplies of the domestic manners, and modes of thought and action that prevailed in the fifteenth century. The inner life of the period is laid open before us; its character and spirit are revealed to us through the very thoughts and words of those that lived in it. No other literary monument could so effectually bring us into contact with the very "form and pressure" of the age.

The early part of the sixteenth century is in some respects an improvement upon its predecessor, though in England at least it failed to produce any poet of equal merit with King James. The *Pastime of Pleasure* of STEPHEN HAWES, a favourite of Henry VII., is a rather dull allegorical poem in rhyme royal; and ALEXANDER BARCLAY's *Ship of Fools* is merely a translation of the once celebrated satire of Sebastian Brandt. These works, though of little value in themselves, testify to the marked progress that our versification was making towards grace and harmony; and in this respect, if in no other, they indicate an approach to the manner of Spenser and Shakespeare.

The most prolific versifier of this period was JOHN SKELTON (1460-1529), who, with WILLIAM ROY, author of the *Satire upon the Clergy*, is generally taken to typify the then prevalent spirit of revolt against ecclesiastical arrogance and authority, especially as represented by our last great churchman, Cardinal Wolsey. Skelton was himself a much humbler member of the same profession, being rector of Diss, in Norfolk; and we have the testimony of Erasmus, then a resident in England, to his eminence as a scholar and man of letters. His bitter tongue, however, is said to have drawn down upon him the Cardinal's wrath, from which he was obliged to take refuge in the Sanctuary at Westminster, where he died in 1529. His Latin poems, in the headings of which he loved to style himself "Poeta Skelton Laureatus," (an allusion to the honour of the laurel, or degree in verse which he gained at Oxford), evince not a little classical elegance. His serious efforts in English are exceedingly heavy and tedious; but his satiric writings, coarse and vulgar as they too often are, show so much force and spirit that they still retain some degree of popularity There is, perhaps, too much reason for the opinion of Puttenham who calls him "a rude, rayling rimer;" but any manifestation of intellectual vigour, whatever form it may take, is sure to gain a certain amount of respect in England. The peculiar doggrel measure too, called by himself "breathlesse rhymes," in which his satiric works are composed, and his use of the familiar speech of the people, have attracted to him a degree of attention which his intrinsic merits by no means entitle him to. His principal attacks upon Wolsey are found in the *Booke of Colin Clout, Why come ye not to Court?*, and the *Bouge of Court* (*i.e.* Bouche à Court, diet allowed at Court), which last is written in the favourite stanza of the day—rhyme royal. The Scottish King and nation also fell under the lash of Skelton; and he exults in no very generous spirit over the terrible overthrow they sustained at Flodden. Notwithstanding the admiration that is often expressed for this writer, his so-called satirical compositions hardly rise above the dignity of lampoons; most of them are simply venomous pasquinades on one of the most magnanimous of our statesmen. His happier efforts, indeed, were of a much less ambitious kind. The bright sparkle and animation of his *Book of the Sparrow* go far to redeem his fame; and the somewhat boisterous liveliness of the *Tunning of Elinor Rummyng* well nigh compensates for its almost indecent coarseness. The first, one of the most famous of his productions, is a mock heroic dirge or lamentation on the death of a tame sparrow belonging to the "fair Jane Scrope," and consists of a description of a funeral service performed by all the birds for the repose of Philip Sparrow's soul, to which is prefixed a humorous excommunication of cats in general, and the cat that murdered poor Philip in particular. Some notice of Skelton's dramatic works will be given in a subsequent chapter. "His learning," in the opinion of Mr. Marsh, "certainly did little for the improvement of his English style; and it may be said of his diction in general, that all that is not vulgar is pedantic."

Inferior to Skelton's works in force and vivacity, but vastly superior in elegance and grace, the poems of WYATT and SURREY are the earliest indications of the dawn of the brightest day that our literature has ever seen. These two poets, though unequal in merit, possess so much in common; there is so marked an affinity in their manner and tone of mind that their names are now indissolubly associated together. The higher place is invariably assigned to the younger, HENRY HOWARD, EARL OF SURREY (1517–1547), whose early death on the scaffold in 1547 has deepened the romantic interest that surrounds his name. His contributions to poetry are not very extensive, but are of considerable importance, as well from their own peculiar excellence as from the new metrical

form and new style in which many of them are written. It is to
Surrey that we owe two of the greatest literary innovations—the
introduction of the Sonnet, and the use of Blank Verse; from him
we have received our first translation in verse from a classical
author made south of the Tweed, and he was the first to write in
that involved style which so strikingly distinguishes the language
of Shakespeare from that of Chaucer. A version of the second and
fourth Books of the Æneid, in what Milton called "English heroic
verse without rhyme;" numerous sonnets on many subjects, chiefly
amatory; a satire on the citizens of London, together with para-
phrases of Ecclesiastes and some of the Psalms, constitute the
main portion of his writings. The fanciful theories of some later
editors have attached a greater significance than it deserves to
his connection with the fair Geraldine, daughter of the Earl of
Kildare, in whose honour many of his best sonnets were written.

SIR THOMAS WYATT (1503-1542), though fourteen years older
than his friend, is generally regarded as his poetical disciple, but
is undoubtedly a poet of a much lower type. He, too, composed
many songs and sonnets on the one inexhaustible topic—love; and
there is some reason to suppose that the lady who forms the subject of these was the ill-starred Ann Boleyn. His satires and
metrical versions of the Penitential Psalms supply an additional
point of resemblance between him and Surrey. In both the
highly beneficent influences of an acquaintance with Italian literature are manifest; influences which affected the entire structure
and spirit of our poetry for the next century and longer, imparting
to it a smoothness and melody unknown before, without impairing
in the slightest degree its native strength and manliness of tone.
Their collected works were first published ten years after Surrey's
death, in Tottel's Miscellany; and with them some poems of
Nicholas Grimoald, who is chiefly remarkable as having been the
first to follow Surrey in the use of blank verse.

Though this century has left us but few monuments of good
prose, yet these are generally very excellent in their kind. The
first name of any distinction is that of SIR THOMAS MORE (1478-
1535), whose best known work, however, the *Utopia*, is written in
Latin, though familiarly known to most modern readers by
Burnet's translation. It is a philosophical romance belonging to
the same class as Bacon's 'New Atlantis,' and Harrington's
'Oceana;' its object being to give a picture of an ideal commonwealth, where the laws and social and political usages are in strict
accordance with philosophical perfection. As the author tells us,
it takes its name from King Utopus (οὐ τόπος, nowhere), though
Milton in his 'Areopagitica' calls it Eutopia (εὖ, well). Many of its

theories and suggestions are of a most enlightened character, and
some of them are far in advance, not only of the author's own
time, but even of the present. The contrast between his advocacy
of religious toleration in this work, and his own subsequent conduct, when he was brought face to face with the question, should
teach a powerful lesson to all statesmen. More's other writings are
not voluminous, and, with one notable exception, are of a controversial nature; and display an amount of bitterness and in-
tolerance strangely out of harmony with his traditional character.
This exception is a work called indifferently a Life of Edward V.,
or a Life of Richard III., which was first printed anonymously in
the edition of Hardynge's Chronicle, published in 1543, and has
been ever since confidently ascribed to More. Mr. Hallam pronounces it " the first example of good English language, pure and
perspicuous, well chosen, without vulgarisms or pedantry."

One of the best translations ever made is LORD BERNERS' *Chronicle
of Froissart*, so exactly does the archaism of its language reproduce the picturesque old French. Its author was Governor of
Calais under Henry VIII., at whose instigation he is supposed to
have undertaken the work. The first volume was published in
1523, the second in 1525.

This period also witnessed the earliest approximation to history
in the modern form of the English language; and in the pages
of FABYAN and HALL we possess the first attempts at a systematic
compilation of past events. The first, who was an alderman and
sheriff of London, reduces to a regular narrative, called *The Con-
cordance of Histories*, the mythical, semi-mythical, and authentic
events of our history from Brute the Trojan to his own time; and
Hall, a judge in the Sheriff's Court of the same city, under the
title of the *Union of the Two Noble and Illustrious Families of York
and Lancaster*, gives a history of England under those two houses,
and so on down to the year 1532, which Grafton afterwards continued until the death of Henry VIII. These writings, though
totally devoid of any pretensions to history in the genuine sense
of the word, are valuable not only as storehouses of facts for
modern narrators, but also as monuments of language and examples
of the popular feeling of the time. It is from Hall that Lord
Bacon derived the principal materials for his 'History of Henry VII.'

The *Toxophilus* of ROGER ASCHAM (1515–1568), published in
1545, was written to revive the then decaying interest in the use
of the bow, and is distinguished by quiet dignity of style and
manliness of spirit. It is composed in the form of a dialogue
between Philologus and Toxophilus. Eighteen years afterwards,
when tutor to Queen Elizabeth, this same author brought out his

more important work, *The Schoolmaster*, which is still valuable
for the principles and rules of teaching expounded therein. One
memorable passage, quoted repeatedly since, will long retain an
interest from its connection with Lady Jane Grey.

No literary monument of this age, and few of any age, wrought
such momentous results to the nation and language as the first
authorized version of the Scriptures, which was given to the
English people in 1536. It then appeared under the editorship
of MILES COVERDALE, subsequently Bishop of Exeter; but the
entire work bears the impress of the mind of WILLIAM TYNDAL,
who in 1526 published at Antwerp his translation of the New
Testament, afterwards added the Pentateuch, and finally, in the
year of his martyrdom (1536), the Psalms and the Prophets,
written either by himself or under his supervision. It is thought
that no writer, not even Shakespeare himself, so deeply affected
the character and form of the language as Tyndal. He contributed
more than any other to fix in their present shape its grammatical
structure, idiom, and diction.

During this period there took place in the northern kingdom
the earliest original development of the national genius, whose
productive energy contrasts honourably with the mental torpor
that prevailed in the south. The impulse communicated by Barbour had carried Scottish literature to still nobler triumphs; and
the writings of Henryson, Gawin Douglas, and Dunbar, first
stamped upon it that distinct national impress which is yet un-
effaced. Though Henryson's *Testament of the Faire Creseide* is a
continuation of a work of Chaucer's, yet his exquisite pastoral of
Robin and Makyne breathes the peculiar national spirit. The
exploits of *William Wallace* gave a congenial subject to the muse
of BLIND HARRY, otherwise HARRY THE MINSTREL, of whose life
we have a very imperfect knowledge. GAWIN DOUGLAS (1474–
1522), Bishop of Dunkeld, prided himself on his freedom from
southern influences, and wrote in the very broadest form of his
native dialect his translation of Virgil, as well as his *King Hart*,
and *Palace of Honour*, the diction of which is defaced by the
unnecessary introduction of a great mass of French and Latin
words, far beyond the proportion usual in contemporary English
writings.

But the special glory of Scotland in the beginning of the sixteenth century is WILLIAM DUNBAR, a truly powerful and original
genius, and the greatest Scotch poet before Burns. His *Thistle
and Rose*, which celebrates the marriage of James IV. of Scotland
with Margaret Tudor, daughter of Henry VII., is a poem of great
merit; and his *Dance of the Seven Deadly Sins* possesses an almost

fearful force and picturesqueness. To these might be added as
favourable specimens of his genius *The Design of the Golden Terge*,
and the *Lament for the Makars* (poets). His strength and liveliness of imagination are beyond all praise; but a degrading licentious-
ness both in thought and expression often pollutes his pages.

Sir David Lindesay (1490–1557), a name familiar to the readers
of 'Marmion,' is the last conspicuous member of this group. He,
too, is remarkable rather for vigour than grace; and his temperament naturally projected him into the department of satire, which
in his most elaborate effort, the *Satire of the Three Estates*, takes
a dramatic form. This is the earliest work of the kind in the
northern dialect. Other compositions of his are *The Monarchy*,
Squire Meldrum, and the *Complaint of the Papingo;* which last
is one of his most successful pieces. The effect of Sir David's
works on the progress of the Reformation in Scotland is generally
supposed to have been considerable, a circumstance which Scott
finely glances at when he ascribes to him—

> " that satiric rage,
> Which, bursting on the early stage.
> Branded the vices of the age,
> And broke the keys of Rome."

CHAPTER VII.

THE NON-DRAMATIC ELIZABETHAN POETS.

THE Age of Elizabeth is characterized by features which cause it to stand alone in the literary history of the world. It was a period of sudden emancipation of thought, of immense fertility and originality, and of high intellectual cultivation. The language had reached its highest perfection; the study and imitation of ancient or foreign models had furnished a vast store of materials, images, and literary forms, which had not yet had time to become commonplace and over-worn. The poets and prose writers of this age, therefore, united the freshness and vigour of youth with the regularity and majesty of manhood. It will be our task to give a rapid sketch of some of its great works.

The first distinguished name is that of THOMAS SACKVILLE, Lord Buckhurst (1536-1608), a kinsman of Queen Elizabeth, who late in life filled the office of Lord High Treasurer. It was for his children that Ascham wrote the *Schoolmaster*. He projected, and himself commenced, a work entitled *A Mirrour for Magistrates*, which was intended to contain a series of tragic examples of the vicissitudes of fortune, drawn from the annals of his own country, serving as lessons of virtue and warnings to future kings and statesmen. Sackville composed the *Induction* (introduction), and also the first legend or complaint, which relates the power and the fall of the Duke of Buckingham, victim of the tyrannical Richard III. The work passed through many forms, the earliest, of which the authors were Richard Baldwin and George Ferrers, having appeared in 1559, and the latest in 1610. It was to the second, or edition of 1563, that Sackville contributed. The conception was not original, but was simply an application to English history of that of Boccacio's 'De Casibus,' which both Chaucer and Lydgate had already followed. The *Mirrour for Magistrates* is written in rhyme royal, and exhibits great occasional power of expression, and a remarkable force and compression of language, though the general tone is gloomy and somewhat monotonous.

The illustrious EDMUND SPENSER (1552?-1599), unquestionably the greatest English poet intervening between Chaucer and Shakespeare, was born in London about 1552—a cadet of the illustrious family whose name he bore, though not endowed with fortune—and was educated at the University of Cambridge, where he undoubtedly acquired an amount of learning remarkable even in that age of solid and substantial studies. He is supposed to have gained his first fame by the publication, in 1579, of the *Shepherd's Calendar*, a series of pastorals divided into twelve parts or months, in which, as in Virgil's *Bucolics*, under the guise of idyllic dialogues, his imaginary interlocutors discuss high questions of morality and state, and pay refined compliments to illustrious personages. These eclogues, to which Spenser endeavoured to give a national air by painting English scenery and the English climate, and by selecting English names for his rustic persons, attracted to him the favour and patronage of the great. Through his friend, the learned Gabriel Harvey, whose mania for employing in English verse the ancient classical metres, founded on quantity, for some time infected the poet himself, he acquired the notice and favour of the accomplished Sidney; and it was at Penshurst, the fine mansion of the latter, that he is supposed to have revised the *Shepherd's Calendar*, which he dedicated to "Maister Philip Sidney, most worthy of all titles of both of learning and chivalry." Sidney made him known to his uncle, Lord Leicester, and also brought him under the personal notice of Elizabeth, to whom he naturally sought to recommend himself by all the refinements of literary homage; but the poet inevitably exposed himself to the hostility of those who were the enemies of his protectors; and he has left us a gloomy picture of the miseries of courtly dependence.

In 1580, on the nomination of Lord Grey de Wilton as Deputy of Ireland, Spenser accompanied him to that country as secretary; and six years afterwards he received a grant of land not far from Cork, which had formed part of the confiscated domains of the Earls of Desmond. At Kilcolman Castle, where he resided for several years, with occasional visits to England, he composed the most important of his works, among which the *Faëry Queen* holds the first place. In October, 1598, the great rebellion, called Tyrone's Insurrection, spread from the neighbouring province of Ulster to Spenser's retreat. Kilcolman Castle was attacked and burned by the insurgents. Completely ruined, and overwhelmed by the loss of a young child, which perished in the wreck of his house, the poet returned to London, where he died (in the greatest poverty it is said) in 1599, and was buried with great pomp in Westminster Abbey, near the tomb of Chaucer.

Spenser's greatest work, *The Faëry Queen*, the subject of which is chivalric, allegorical, narrative, and descriptive, was originally planned to consist of twelve books of moral adventures, each typify-

ing the triumph of a Virtue, and couched under the form of an
exploit of knight-errantry. The hero of the whole action was to be
the mythical Prince Arthur, the type of perfect virtue in Spenser ;
who is supposed to have become enamoured of the Faëry Queen in a
dream ; " with whose excellent beauty ravished, he awaking resolved to seek her out ; and so being by Merlin armed, and by
Timon thoroughly instructed, he went to seeke her forth in Faerye
land." While he is pursuing the quest, Gloriana is keeping her
annual feast of twelve days, on each of which an adventurous
knight is represented as riding forth to redress some specially
flagrant wrong, or to rid the world of some terrible monster. The
First Book relates the expedition of the Red-Cross Knight, who
is the allegorical representative of *Holiness*, while his mistress Una
represents true *Religion ;* and the action of the knight's exploit
shadows forth the triumph of Holiness over the enchantments
and deceptions of Heresy. The Second Book recounts the adventures of Sir Guyon, or *Temperance ;* the Third, those of Britomartis,
a female champion, or *Chastity.* Each of these books is subdivided
into twelve cantos. The three first books were published separately in 1590, and dedicated to Elizabeth, who rewarded the
delicate flattery which pervades innumerable allusions in the
work with a pension of 50l. a year. After returning to Ireland,
Spenser prosecuted his work ; and in 1596 he gave to the world
three more books, namely, the Fourth, containing the Legend of
Cambell and Triamond, allegorizing *Friendship ;* the Fifth, the
Legend of Artegall, or *Justice ;* and the Sixth, that of Sir Calidore,
or *Courtesy.* Thus half of the poet's original design was executed. Tradition asserts that the latter portion was completed, and
lost at sea ; but more probably the dreadful misfortunes of the poet's
later life prevented him from completing his design. This is perhaps no matter of regret, as the vigour, invention, and splendour of
expression, that glow so brightly in the first three books, manifestly
decline in the fourth, fifth, and sixth. In this poem are united and
harmonized three different elements which at first sight would appear
irreconcilable ; for the skeleton or framework of the action is derived
from the feudal or chivalric legends ; the ethical or moral sentiment
from the lofty philosophy of Plato, combined with the most elevated
Christian purity ; and the form and colouring of the language and
versification are saturated with the flowing grace and sensuous elegance of the great Italian poets of the Renaissance. The principal
defects of the *Faëry Queen,* viewed as a whole, are a want of unity,
involving a loss of interest in the story ; and a monotony of character inseparable from a series of adventures which, though varied
with inexhaustible fertility, are all, from their chivalric nature, fun-

damentally similar, being either combats between one knight and another, or between the hero of the moment and some supernatural being—a monster, a dragon, or a wicked enchanter. Besides, hardly can any degree of genius long sustain the interest of an allegory indeed those who read Spenser with the intensest delight are precisely those who entirely neglect the moral lessons typified in his allegory, and follow his recital of adventures as those of human beings, giving themselves up to the mighty magic of his unequalled imagination. But Spenser, though extremely monotonous and tiresome to an ordinary reader, is the most enchanting of poets to him, who, endowed with a lively fancy, confines his attention to one or two at a time of his delicious episodes, descriptions, or impersonations. Moreover, many of his allegorical persons and adventures were intended to contain allusions to facts and individuals of Spenser's own time. Gloriana, the Faëry Queen herself, and the beautiful huntress Belphœbe, shadow forth Elizabeth; Sir Artegall, the Knight of Justice, Lord Grey; and the adventures of the Red-Cross Knight typify the history of the Anglican Church.

None of our poets is more exquisitely and uniformly musical than Spenser. Indeed the sweetness and flowingness of his verse is sometimes carried so far as to become cloying and enervated. The metre he employed, called after him the *Spenserian*, consists of nine lines, and was formed by adding an Alexandrine to the eight-line stanza of Chaucer. As it is somewhat complicated, and necessitates a frequent recurrence in each stanza of the same rhymes—namely, four of one ending, three of another, and two of a third—he was obliged to take considerable liberties with the orthography and accentuation of the English language. In doing this, he shows himself as unscrupulous as masterly. By employing an immense mass of old Chaucerian words and provincialisms, nay even by occasionally inventing words himself, he furnishes his verse with an inexhaustible variety of language; but at the same time the reader must remember that much of the vocabulary of the great poet was a dialect that never really existed. Its peculiarities have been less permanent than those of almost any other of our great writers.

The power of Spenser's genius consists in an unequalled richness of description, in the art of representing events and objects with an intensity that makes them visible and tangible. He describes *to the eye*, and communicates to the airy conceptions of allegory, the splendour and the vivacity of visible objects. Among the most important of his other poetical writings are his *Mother Hubbard's Tale;* his *Daphnaida* and *Astrophel*, idyllic elegies on the death of Lady Howard and Sir Philip Sidney; all his *Amoretti*, or love-sonnets; and, above all, his beautiful *Epithalamium*, or Marriage-

Song on his own nuptials with the "fair Elizabeth," which is certainly one of the richest and chastest marriage-hymns to be found in the whole range of literature. His single prose work, the *View of the State of Ireland*, was not published until many years after his death. It is a faithful description of the manners and condition of the native Celtic race, which Spenser seems to have carefully studied, when a resident among them.

SIR PHILIP SIDNEY (1554-1586) exerted so powerful an influence on the intellectual spirit of the epoch, that our notice of the age would be incomplete without some allusion to his life, even did not the intrinsic merit of his writings give him a place among the best poets and prose-writers of the time. He was born in 1554, and died at the age of thirty-two (October 7, 1586), of a wound received in the battle of Zutphen, fought to aid the Protestants of the Netherlands in their heroic struggle against the Spaniards. His contributions to the literature of his country consist of a small collection of *Sonnets*, called *Astrophel and Stella*, (*his* Stella being Penelope Devereux, Lady Rich), remarkable for their somewhat languid and refined elegance ; and the prose romance, once regarded as a manual of courtesy and refined ingenuity, entitled *The Countess of Pembroke's Arcadia*, which was written at the request of his noble sister Mary, wife of Henry Herbert, Earl of Pembroke. A great portion of the work is chivalric, and the grace and animation with which the knightly pen of Sidney paints the shock of the tourney, and the noble warfare of the chase, is not surpassed by the luxurious elegance of his pastoral descriptions. In the style we see perpetual traces of that ingenious antithetical affectation called Euphuism, an account of which will be given afterwards ; but the story, though occasionally tiresome and involved, is related with considerable skill, and abounds in happy thoughts and graceful expressions. Sidney wrote also a small tract entitled *An Apologie for Poetrie*, in which he strives to show that the pleasures derivable from imaginative literature are powerful aids, not only to the acquisition of knowledge, but to the cultivation of virtue.

SAMUEL DANIEL (1562-1619), who is said to have succeeded Spenser as poet laureate, and who enjoyed among his contemporaries a respect merited not only by his talents but by his character, wrote, in the eight-line stanza, *The History of the Civil Wars*, a poem on the Civil Wars between the houses of York and Lancaster, in that peculiar style of poetical narrative and moral meditation which was at this time a favourite type among the literary men of England. The language is exceedingly pure, limpid, and intelligible. The poem entitled *Musophilus* is an elaborate defence of learning, cast into the form of a dialogue. Many of Daniel's minor poems, as his *Elegies*, *Epistles*, *Masques*, and *Songs*, together with his contributions to the dramatic literature of the day, justify the reputation which he possessed.   Good sense, dignity, and an equable flow of pure language and harmonious versification, are the qualities which posterity will acknowledge in his writings.

The longest and most celebrated productions of MICHAEL DRAYTON (1563-1631) were the topographical and descriptive poem entitled *Polyolbion*, in thirty cantos or songs, *The Barons' Wars*, *England's Heroical Epistles*, *The Battle of Agincourt*, *The Muses' Elysium*, and the delicious fancies of *The Court of Fairy*. The first is a minute poetical itinerary of England and Wales, composed in the long-rhymed verse of twelve syllables, known as the Alexandrine, and is, both in design and execution, absolutely unique in literature. Drayton has described his country with the painful accuracy of the topographer and the enthusiasm of a poet; and the *Polyolbion* will ever remain a most interesting monument of industry and taste. *The Barons' Wars*, a poem, describing the principal events of the unhappy reign of Edward II., is a recast in Spenserian stanza of the author's earlier *Mortimeriados*, which was in the *ottava rima*. The *Heroical Epistles* are imagined to be written by illustrious and unfortunate personages in English history to the objects of their love. They are therefore a kind of adaptation of the plan of Ovid to English annals. In the so-called Pastoral, too, Drayton attained great excellence; in the series entitled *The Muses' Elysium*, and above all in the exquisite little mock-heroic of *Nymphidia*, everything that is most graceful, delicate, quaint, and fantastic in that form of national superstition—almost peculiar to Great Britain—the fairy mythology, is accumulated and touched with a consummate felicity.

The vigorous versatility of the age is well exemplified in SIR JOHN DAVIES (1570-1626), Chief Justice of Ireland, who has left two works of unusual merit and originality, though on widely different subjects. The subject of one of them, *Nosce Teipsum*, is the proof of the immortality of the soul; that of the other, entitled *Orchestra*, the art of dancing. The first is written in four-lined stanzas of heroic lines, afterwards made famous by Dryden's *Annus Mirabilis*; and the second in a peculiarly-constructed seven-lined stanza. In both the language of Davies is pure and masculine, his versification smooth and melodious.

The manner, spirit, and in a sense even the metre of Spenser were copied with considerable success by the brothers GILES (1588-1623) and PHINEAS FLETCHER (1584-1650), cousins of Beaumont's colleague, who, along with WILLIAM BROWNE (1590-1645), author of *Britannia's Pastorals*, are usually classed as the immediate followers of the great Elizabethan poet. The first published in 1610 a poem entitled *Christ's Victory and Triumph*, written in an eight-line modifi cation of the Spenserian stanza; and the second gave to the world in 1633 his strange production, the *Purple Island*, written in a seven-line stanza of the same type. These works are chiefly remarkable for the extraordinary ingenuity with which the allegorical style of their model is pursued under the most unfavourable conditions; in the latter especially, whose subject is the mind and body of man, this misapplication of ability is almost ludicrously conspicuous. Allegorical anatomy, however skilfully managed, is not attractive to an ordinary reader; nor is the canto on the intellectual and moral powers much more successful. Both seem, however, to have been well known to Milton; and one scene of the 'Paradise Regained,' the first meeting of Christ with Satan, is said to have been taken from Giles's work.

To this time is generally assigned the origin of English satire as a specific branch of poetical literature, with distinctly marked features of its own. Many passages, indeed, of social and personal invective are found in earlier writers; Chaucer's pictures of the monastic orders and other classes of mankind abound in both open and implied censure; both the spirit and matter of Langlande's work are almost wholly satirical; but in neither of these authors is satire an essential characteristic,—a certain infusion of it was inevitable to the task they undertook, but it was far from being a primary condition with either. Skelton was too ribaldrous, too full of mere venom and spite against individuals, to be ranked as anything more than a mere lampooner; and Surrey and Wyatt rather pointed out the way to this kind of composition than followed it themselves. The first English writer who distinctly calls himself a satirist is Joseph Hall (1574-1656), and the general opinion of later critics has acquiesced in his assertion; but the distinction has also been claimed for George Gascoyne (1530-1577), whose *Steel Glass* appeared in 1576, as well as for the better known John Donne (1573-1631), whose satires were composed as early as 1594, though not published until long afterwards.

However this may be, in 1597, Joseph Hall, then fresh from Cambridge, published three books of *toothless satires*, which one year afterwards he followed up with three more of *biting satires:* and to the collective work he gave the name of *Virgidemarium*, or of rod-harvests. These poems seem to fulfil all the conditions of satire; they attack, with great energy and some humour, the prevailing follies and affectations both in literature and social life. Though the numbers are often harsh and the meaning obscure, they possess enough of the spirit of Juvenal to make them still readable.

In later life Hall won greater distinction still, more especially by his sermons; and as bishop of Norwich and champion of episcopacy, he ventured to grapple with Milton himself. John Donne will take his place more appropriately in a subsequent chapter (see p. 104). His satires, which were notorious for ruggedness and want of polish, were translated by Pope into the language of his own time, under the name of ' The Satires of Dr. John Donne, Dean of St. Paul's, versified.' Many other writers of the day followed in the footsteps of Hall, among whom the most noteworthy is JOHN MARSTON, author of the *Scourge of Villainy.*

No fact is more significant of the unparalleled literary activity of the Elizabethan Age than the almost incredible number of smaller poets that it gave birth to. As many as two hundred have been reckoned who gave evidence in that time of a certain amount of skill in constructing verses. From among these, the rank and file of the army of letters, we may select as worthy of some notice WILLIAM WARNER (1558-1609), whose *Albion's England*, an historical poem in ballad metre, published in 1586, supplanted in popular esteem the ' Mirror for Magistrates *;* " silver-tongued " JOSHUA SYLVESTER (1563-1618), whose translation of Du Bartas was an early favourite with Milton; and ROBERT SOUTHWELL (1560-1595), executed as a Jesuit priest in 1595, author of the *Burning Babe*, which Ben Jonson admired so much.

It is besides a special distinction of the same age that it produced, among many of a rather indifferent kind, one or two translations of unusual excellence. The *Iliad* and *Odyssey* of GEORGE CHAPMAN (1557-1634), which appeared at different times early in the seventeenth century, have won the enthusiastic admiration of several generations of poets from Waller to Keats. " The earnestness and passion," says Charles Lamb, " which he has put into every part of these poems would be incredible to a reader of more modern translations." High commendation, though of a different kind, must be awarded to EDWARD FAIRFAX's translation of Tasso's ' Jerusalem,' published in 1600, and SIR JOHN HARINGTON's version of the ' Orlando Furioso,' which appeared nine years earlier.

But the grandest phenomenon of the epoch of Elizabeth is the Drama, and to it we shall now address ourselves.

CHAPTER VIII.

THE DAWN OF THE DRAMA.

SPAIN and England alone, among all the modern civilised nations, possess a theatrical literature independent in its origin, characteristic in its form, and reflecting faithfully the features, moral, social, and intellectual, of the people among which it arose; the dramas of both countries being strongly romantic, though otherwise very dissimilar. It is possible to trace the first dawning of our national stage to a period not far removed from the Norman Conquest; for the custom of representing, in a rude dramatic form, legends of the Lives of the Saints and striking episodes of Bible History existed as early as the twelfth century. To these the name of *Mysteries* or *Miracle-plays* was given; of which the earliest on record is the *Play of St. Catherine*, written in French, and in all probability a rude dramatised picture of the miracles and martyrdom of that saint, which was represented at Dunstable in 1119. These performances were obviously an expedient employed by the clergy for communicating some elementary religious instruction to the people, and, by gratifying the curiosity of their rude hearers, extending and strengthening the influence of the Church. At first these plays were composed and acted by monks; the cathedral was transformed for the nonce into a theatre, the stage was a species of graduated platform in three divisions—representing Heaven, Earth, and Hell—rising one over the other, and the costumes were furnished from the vestry of the church. On many of the high religious festivals the personage or event then commemorated was represented in a visible form, with such details as Scripture, legend, or the imagination of the author, could supply; nor did the simple faith of the monkish dramatists and their audience see any impropriety in the introduction of the most supernatural beings, the persons of the Trinity, angels, devils, saints, and martyrs. It was absolutely necessary that some comic element should be introduced to enliven the graver scenes; and this was supplied by representing the wicked personages, whether human or spiritual, of the drama as placed in ludicrous situations; thus the Devil generally played the part of the clown or jester, and was exhibited in a light half terrific and half farcical; and the modern puppet-play of Punch, with his struggles with the Devil, is unquestionably a direct tradition handed down from these ancient miracles in which the Evil One was alternately the conqueror and the victim of the human Buffoon, Jester, or Vice, as he was called.

Some idea may be formed of these ancient religious dramas from the titles of some of them which have been preserved. The *Creation of the World*, the *Fall of Man*, the story of *Cain and Abel*, the *Crucifixion of Our Lord*, the *Massacre of the Innocents*, the *Deluge*, besides an infinite multitude of subjects taken from the lives and miracles of the saints; such were their materials. They are generally written in mixed prose and verse; and, though abounding in anachronisms and absurdities both of character and dialogue, they sometimes contain passages of simple and natural pathos, and sometimes scenes of genuine, if not very delicate, humour. Thus, in the *Deluge*, a comic scene is produced by the refusal of Noah's wife to enter the Ark, and by the beating which justly terminates her resistance and scolding; whilst, on the other hand, a mystery on the subject of the *Sacrifice of Isaac* contains a dialogue of much pathos and beauty between Abraham and his son. The oldest known manuscript of a miracle-play in English is that of *The Harrowing of Hell*, i. e. the Conquering of Hell by Christ, believed to have been written about 1350; but *The Play of the Blessed Sacrament*, which is as old at least as the year 1470, is more artistically constructed than any other of the kind.

These Mysteries, once the only form of dramatic representation, continued to be popular from the eleventh to the end of the fourteenth century, when their ascendency was disputed by another kind of representation, called a *Morality*. In a sense, indeed, the Miracle-play is not quite extinct even yet; in the retired valleys of Catholic Switzerland, in the Tyrol, and in some little-visited districts of Germany, the peasants still annually perform dramatic spectacles representing episodes in the life of Christ. The subjects of these new dramas, which became popular from about the beginning of the fifteenth century, instead of being purely religious, were moral, as their name implies; and the ethical lessons were conveyed by an action and *dramatis personæ* of an abstract or allegorical kind. Thus, instead of the Deity and his angels, the Saints, the Patriarchs, and the characters of the Old and New Testament, the persons who figure in the Moralities are Every-Man, a general type or expression of humanity—Lusty Juventus, who represents the follies and weaknesses of youth—Good Counsel, Repentance, Gluttony, Pride, Avarice, and the like. The action was in general exceedingly simple, and the tone grave and doctrinal, though of course the same necessity existed as before for the introduction of comic scenes,

The Devil was therefore retained; and his battles and scoldings with a new character, the Vice, furnished forth many "a fit of mirth." The oldest English Moral-play now extant is *The Castle of Perseverance*, which was written about 1450. It is a sort of dramatic allegory of human life, representing the many contending influences that surround man in his way through the world. Another, called *Lusty Juventus*, contains a vivid and even humorous picture of the extravagance and debauchery of a young heir, surrounded by companions, the Virtues and the Vices; ending with a demonstration of the inevitable misery and punishment which follow a departure from the path of virtue and religion. The Morality had a strong tendency to partake of the character of the court masque, in which the Elements, the Virtues, the Vices, or the various reigns of nature, were introduced either to convey some physical or philosophical instruction in the guise of allegory, or to compliment a king or great personage on a festival occasion; of which class Skelton's masque of *Magnificence* is an excellent specimen.

Springing from the Moralities, and bearing some general resemblance to them, though exhibiting a still nearer approach to the regular drama, are the *Interludes*, a class of compositions in dialogue, much shorter in extent and more merry and farcical in subject; which were exceedingly fashionable about the time when the great controversy was raging between the Catholic church and the Reformed religion in England. A prolific author of these grotesque and merry pieces was JOHN HEYWOOD, a man of learning and accomplishment, who seems to have performed the duties of a sort of jester at the court of Henry VIII. His *Four P's*, his *Johan, Tyb, and Sir Jhan*, are very creditable productions, and exhibit powers of humour far above the ordinary.

The national taste for dramatic entertainments was still further fostered by those *pageants* which were so often employed to gratify the vanity of citizens, or to compliment an illustrious visitor. These either simply consisted of the exhibition, on some lofty platform, in the porch or churchyard of a cathedral, in the Town Hall or over the city gate, of a number of figures suitably dressed, or which accompanied their action with poetical declamation and music; and necessarily partook in all the changes of taste which characterised the age: the Prophets and Saints who welcomed the royal stranger in the thirteenth century with barbarous Latin hymns were gradually supplanted by the Virtues and allegorical qualities; and these in their turn, when the Renaissance had disseminated a universal passion for classical imagery, made way for the Cupids, the Muses, and other classical personages, whose influence has continued almost to the literature of our own time. Such spectacles were of course frequently exhibited at the Universities, where, partly from the multitude of *nations* composing the body of the students, who required some common language which they could all understand, and partly for more obvious reasons, the Latin tongue was invariably employed. Soon afterwards the fashion became general of producing Latin plays at the Universities and Inns of Court; and a large number of pieces, generally written upon the models of Terence and Seneca, were produced and represented, especially in the great outbreak of revolt against the authority of scholasticism which preceded the Reformation. These dramas, however, do not appear to have exercised any appreciable influence on the growth of the English stage.

We have now traced the progress of the Dramatic art from its first rude infancy in England; and have seen how every step of that advance removed it farther and farther from a purely religious, and brought it closer and closer to a profane character. The last step of the progress was the creation of what we now understand under the term dramatic, viz., the scenic representation, by means of the action and dialogue of human personages, of some event of history or ocial life. As in the first appearance of this, the most perfect form which the art could attain, the influence of the great models of ancient literature must have been very powerful, dramatic compositions class themselves, by the very nature of the case, into the two great categories of Tragedy and Comedy; and even borrow from the classical models details of an unessential kind, as, for example, the use of the Chorus, which, originally consisting of a numerous body of performers, was gradually reduced, though its name and functions were retained to a certain degree by the old English playwrights, to a single individual, as in several of Shakespeare's dramas. It was about the middle of the sixteenth century that a considerable activity of creation was first perceptible in this department. JOHN BALE (1495–1563), the author of many semi-polemical plays, partaking in some measure of the character of the Mystery, the Morality, and the Interlude, set the example of extracting materials for rude historical dramas from the chronicles of his native country. His drama of *King John* occupies an intermediate place between the Moralities and historical plays. But the earliest composition in our language that possesses all the requisites of a regular tragedy is the play of *Gorboduc*, or *Ferrex and Porrex*, written by Thomas Sackville, Lord Buckhurst (the principal writer in the ‘Mirror for Magistrates’), and Thomas Norton (?), and acted in 1562 for the entertainment of Queen Elizabeth by the gentlemen of the Inner Temple. Its subject is borrowed from the old mythological Chronicles of Britain; but the principal event is similar to the story of Eteocles and

Polynices ; and the treatment exhibits strong marks of classic imitation. The dialogue of *Gorboduc* is in blank verse, which is regular and carefully constructed; but it is totally destitute of variety of pause, and consequently is a most insufficient vehicle for dramatic dialogue. The sentence almost invariably terminates with the line; and the effect of the whole is insupportably formal and heavy; the action also is oppressively tragic, being a monotonous, dismal succession of slaughters, ending with the desolation of an entire kingdom. Another work of a similar character is *Damon and Pythias*, acted before the Queen at Christ Church, Oxford, in 1566. This play, which is in rhyme, is a mixture of tragedy and comedy. Its author was RICHARD EDWARDS, the compiler of the miscellany called *The Paradise of Dainty Devices*. He also wrote *Palamon and Arcite*, the beautiful story so inimitably treated by Chaucer in *The Knight's Tale*, and afterwards in Beaumont and Fletcher's romantic play *The Two Noble Kinsmen*.* In 1578 was published *Promos and Cassandra*, written by GEORGE WHETSTONE, which is chiefly curious as having furnished the subject of Shakespeare's *Measure for Measure*. All these plays are marked by a general similarity of style and treatment, and belong to about the same period.

In the department of Comedy the first English works which made their appearance were very little anterior to the above pieces, but offer a most striking contrast in their tone and treatment. The earliest work of this kind in the language was *Ralph Royster Doyster*, acted in 1551 (?), and written by NICHOLAS UDALL, for some time Master of Eton College. This was followed, about fourteen years later, by *Gammer Gurton's Needle*, composed by JOHN STILL, afterwards Bishop of Bath and Wells, who had previously been Master of St. John's and Trinity Colleges in Cambridge ; by the students of which society the play was probably acted. Both these works are highly curious and interesting, not only as being the oldest specimens of the class of literature to which they belong, but in some measure from their intrinsic merit. The action of the former comedy, which is unquestionably superior to the other, takes place in London; and the principal characters are a rich and pretty widow, her lover. and an irrepressible suitor, the foolish personage who gives the title to the play. This ridiculous pretender to gaiety and love is betrayed into all sorts of absurd and humiliating scrapes ; and the piece ends with the return of the favoured lover from a voyage which he had undertaken. The manners represented are those of the middle class of the period ; and the picture given of London citizen life in the middle of the sixteenth century is curious,

* It is next to certain that a large portion of this play came from Shakespeare's pen.

animated, and natural. The language is lively; and the dialogue is carried on in a sort of loose doggrel rhyme, very well adapted to represent comic conversation. In general the intrigue of this drama is deserving of approbation; the plot is well imagined, and the reader's curiosity well kept alive. *Gammer Gurton's Needle* is a composition of a much lower and more farcical order. The scene is laid in the humblest rustic life, and all the *dramatis personæ* belong to the uneducated class. The principal action of the comedy is the sudden loss of a needle with which Gammer (*Good Mother*) Gurton has been mending the inexpressibles of her man Hodge, a loss comparatively serious when needles were rare and costly. The whole intrigue consists in the search instituted after this unfortunate little implement, which is at last discovered by Hodge himself, on suddenly sitting down, sticking in the garment which Gammer Gurton had been repairing.

As yet there were neither regular theatres nor recognised professional actors, the place of the first being supplied by town-halls, court-yards of inns, cock-pits, noblemen's dining-halls, and other places; that of the second by amateurs of various kinds. The Court plays were frequently represented by the children of the royal chapel, and placed, as the dramatic profession in general was for a long time, under the peculiar supervision of the Office of the Revels, which was obliged also to exercise the duties of a dramatic censor. Soon, however, bodies of actors, singers, tumblers, &c., calling themselves the servants of some nobleman whose livery they wore, were formed; and were frequently in the habit of wandering about the country, performing wherever they could find an audience, generally in some one of the above-mentioned places. Protected by the letters-patent of the livery of their master against the severe laws which qualified strollers as vagabonds, they generally began their proceedings by begging the countenance and protection of the authorities; and the accounts of the ancient municipal bodies, and the household registers of the great families of former times, abound in entries of permissions given to such strolling parties of actors, tumblers, and musicians, and of sums granted to them in recompense of their exertions. By far the most interesting of these entries is that found in the municipal records of Stratford-upon-Avon under the year 1569, from which we learn that in this, the year of office of Shakespeare's father, the players visited Stratford for the first time; and gave their performances, in all probability, under the patronage of the High-bailiff of the town.

At length, in the year 1576, James Burbadge, a Warwickshire man, under the powerful patronage of the Earl of Leicester, built in the precincts of the Blackfriars, where Printing-house Square now

stands, the earliest English theatre. This was followed next
year by the Curtain, which owed its existence to the same enterprising spirit; and these adventures proved so successful, that
at one time during this period London and its suburbs contained
at least twelve different theatres, of various degrees of size and
convenience. Of these the most celebrated was undoubtedly
the *Globe*, for at that time each playhouse had its sign, which
belonged to the same company that owned Burbadge's original
playhouse at Blackfriars. It was called the Globe, from its
sign bearing the effigy of Atlas supporting the globe, with the
motto "Totus Mundus agit Histrionem," and was situated on
the Bankside in Southwark, near the Surrey extremity of London
Bridge. In fact, the great majority of the London theatres was
on the southern or Surrey bank of the Thames, in order to be
out of the jurisdiction of the municipality of the City, which,
being strongly infected with the gloomy spirit of Puritanism,
carried on against the players and the playhouses a constant
war. Some of these theatres were cockpits or arenas for bull-
baiting and bear-baiting, (the word *pit* still preserves the memory of the former of these); and they were all very poor and
squalid, as compared with the magnificent theatres of the present
day, retaining in their form and arrangement many traces of the
ancient model—the inn-yard. Most of the theatres were entirely
uncovered,* excepting over the stage, where a thatched roof protected the actors from the weather; and this thatched roof was,
in 1613, the cause of the total destruction of the Globe, in consequence of the wadding of a *chamber*, or small cannon, lodging in it,
fired during the representation of Shakespeare's Henry VIII. The
boxes or *rooms*, as they were then styled, were of course arranged
nearly as in the present day; but the musicians, instead of being
placed, as now, in the orchestra, or place between the pit and the
stage, were established in a lofty gallery over the scene.

The most remarkable peculiarities of the ancient English theatres
were the total absence of painted or moveable scenery, and the
necessity that female parts should be performed by men or
boys, actresses being as yet unknown. Both these improvements
were introduced soon after the Restoration, when the golden
prime of the stage had passed away for ever. A few *traverses*,
or screens of cloth or tapestry, gave the actors the opportunity
of making their exits and entrances ; a placard, bearing the

* The Blackfriars Theatre, which was much smaller than the Globe, was entirely
roofed over; the company were in the habit of performing there in the winter,
whereas during the summer their representations were given on the Bankside, the
inclemency of the weather being then less inconvenient.

name of Rome, Athens, London, or Florence, as the case might be,
intimated to the audience the place of action. Besides these they
employed certain typical articles of furniture; a bed on the stage
suggested a bedroom; a table covered with tankards a tavern; a
gilded chair surmounted by a canopy, and called a *state*, a palace;
an altar, a church; and the like. A permanent wooden construction, like a scaffold or a high wall, erected at the back of the stage,
represented an infinity of objects according to the requirements of
the piece, such as the wall of a castle or besieged city, the outside
of a house, as when a dialogue is to take place between one
person at a window and another on the exterior; and it enabled one
of the *dramatis personæ* to overhear others without being himself
seen.

In one department, however, of the stage-economy the companies
of the early theatre were singularly lavish—that of costume, which
was invariably costly and splendid. They differed from the present
usage in employing the style of dress of the time (with the exception
of the Prologue, who appeared in the long flowing robe of the middle
ages), but this being highly picturesque did not at all impair the
effect, or mar the illusion. But this employment of the contemporary
costume in plays whose action was supposed to take place in Greece,
Rome, or Persia, naturally led into amazing anachronisms and absurdities, such as arming the assassins of Cæsar with Spanish rapiers, or
furnishing Carthaginian senators with watches; which after all did
not strike in a very offensive manner the mixed and uncritical
spectators of those times. Certain conventional attributes were
always associated with particular supernatural personages, such as
angels, devils, ghosts, and so on. Thus "a roobe for to goo in-
visibell" is one of the items in an old list of properties; and in all
probability the spectral armour of the Ghost in *Hamlet* was to be
found in the wardrobe of the ancient theatres. The curtain is supposed to have opened perpendicularly in the middle; and besides
this principal curtain there seem to have been others occasionally
drawn so as to divide the stage into several apartments, and withdrawn to exhibit one of the characters as in a tent or closet.

Though several of the companies of actors were under the
immediate patronage of the sovereign, of different members of
the royal family, and other great personages of the realm, it was
long before any of our sovereigns deigned to witness their performances in the theatres. But their patronage protected them
against interlopers and rivals, and above all against the implacable
hostility of the Puritanical municipality of London. And they were
frequently summoned to furnish entertainment to their patrons at
Court.

The performance, which generally began at three o'clock in the afternoon, was announced by three flourishes of a trumpet, and commenced with the declamation of the Prologue, at first by the author himself arrayed in the poetical costume of the middle ages, and subsequently by a proxy, who assumed the same garb. Black drapery hung round the stage intimated the performance of a tragedy; and rushes were strewn over the floor to enable the fine gentlemen who patronised the company to take their seats upon it without fear of the consequences. Dancing and singing took place between the acts; and, as a rule, a *jig* wound up the entertainment. This was a kind of comic ballad, professedly an improvisation, sung by a clown, with accompaniment of tabor and pipe and farcical dancing. A flag remained floating at the summit of the theatre during the entire performance.

The social position of an actor and playwright, even at the end of the sixteenth century, was far from being an enviable one; it was still regarded by many as scarcely a shade removed above that of the " rogues and vagabonds" of former generations; but this drawback seems to have been fully compensated for by its extraordinary profits. That these were unusually great is proved not only by historical evidence, such as the frequent allusions made by the over-rigid preachers and moralists of the day to the pride, luxury, and magnificence in dress of the successful performers, but also by the rapidity with which many of them, as Shakespeare, Burbadge, and Alleyn, amassed considerable fortunes.

Notwithstanding this social discredit that in these times attached to the actor's profession, the Drama had reached such popularity, and the employment was so lucrative, that it soon became the common receptacle of irregular genius in search of a livelihood. Indeed nothing is more remarkable than the marvellously rapid growth of this department of our literature, which indeed passed from infancy to manhood in a single generation. Not much more than twenty years after the appearance of the first rude tragedy, our Theatre entered upon the most glorious period of its history, bursting forth into a majesty and strength without parallel perhaps in the literature of any country. This was mainly the work of a small band of poets, seven in number, whose careers all began about the same time, and who were in all essential respects the creators of the English stage. Most of them were men of liberal education, but of dissolute lives, whom the new profession naturally attracted into its ranks; one or two left rustic homes to seek their fortunes in the great world of London, and were lured by the prospect of swift gain into the same employment; and all possessed abilities of a very high order, though but one of the very highest. This one, WILLIAM

SHAKESPEARE, is the giant of the group, beside whom the others dwindle into comparative insignificance, and but for whom they would have sunk into utter oblivion. It is usual indeed to call these men—CHAPMAN, LYLY, PEELE, GREENE, MARLOWE, and KYD—*predecessors* of Shakespeare, but as none of them preceded him by more than a year or two, and some actually followed him, whilst all were in a sense fellow-workers with him for a time, it would seem more proper to style them the contemporaries of his early period. But intemperance and debauchery carried off many of them before their great associate reached the maturity of his powers, and hence they are generally placed earlier in the roll of our dramatists.

Perhaps the most remarkable peculiarity of the dramatic profession at this period was the frequent combination, in one and the same person, of the qualities of player and dramatic author. This circumstance obviously exerted a mighty influence in modifying the dramatic productions of the time ; and it powerfully contributed to give to them that strong and individual character which renders them so inimitable. A dramatic writer, however great his genius, unacquainted practically with the mechanism of the stage, will frequently fail in giving to his work that directness and vivacity, that *dramatic effect* which is the essential element of popular success. Thus in the French drama Molière succeeded where Racine and Corneille failed utterly ; himself a skilful actor, as well as an un-equalled painter of comic character, he was able to give to his pieces the element of *scenic effect ;* an element in which the others, despite their perhaps higher literary qualities, having no practical acquaint-ance with the stage, were entirely deficient. Though not an unmixed benefit—coarseness, buffoonery, bombast, and bad taste, were perhaps unavoidable under the circumstances—at the same time it is the reason why the writings of these actor-authors invariably possess intense dramatic interest, and an effectiveness which literary merit alone could never give. The careers of these men, at least in their commencements and general outlines, were the same. They attached themselves, in the double quality of actors and poets, to one of the numerous companies then existing ; and after a short apprentice-ship passed in rewriting and rearranging plays already exhibited to the public, they gradually rose to original works written either alone or in partnership with some brother playwright. There being no dramatic copyright at this time, the troops of actors had the very strongest motive for taking every precaution that their pieces should *not* be printed, publication instantly annihilating their monopoly and allowing rival companies to profit by their labours ; and this is the reason why comparatively so few of the dramas of this period, in spite of their unequalled merit and their great popularity, were committed to the press during the lives at least of their authors. It also explains the singularly careless execution of such copies as were printed, these having been given to the public in many cases surreptitiously, and in direct contravention to the wishes and interests of the author.

A short sketch of the subordinate members of this remarkable group of playwrights will now be given. JOHN LYLY (1553-1601 ?) composed several court plays and pageants, of which most were written upon classical, or rather mythological subjects, as the story of *Endymion, Sappho and Phaon,* and *Alexander and Campaspe.* He has a rich and fantastic imagination; and his writings exhibit genius and elegance, though strongly tinctured with a peculiar kind of affectation with which he infected the language of the Court, the aristocracy, and even to a considerable degree literature itself, till it fell under the ridicule of Shakespeare. This consisted in a kind of exaggerated vivacity of imagery and expression; the remotest and most unexpected analogies were sought for, and crowded into every sentence. The reader may form some notion of this mode of writing, (which was called Euphuism, from Lyly's once fashionable book which appeared in two parts, the first entitled *Euphues: The Anatomy of Wit,* the second *Euphues and his England*), by consulting the caricature of it which Scott has introduced in the character of the courtier Sir Piercy Shafton in *The Monastery.* The first part of the *Euphues* appeared in 1578 or 1579. Lyly was a man of considerable classical acquirements, and had been educated at Oxford. His lyrics are extremely graceful and harmonious; and even as a playwright his merits are rather lyrical than dramatic.

GEORGE PEELE, (1552-1598?) like Lyly, had received a liberal education at Oxford. He was one of Shakespeare's fellow-actors and fellow-shareholders in the Blackfriars Theatre. His earliest work, *The Arraignment of Paris,* was printed anonymously in 1584. His most celebrated dramatic works were the *David and Bethsabe,* and *Arraignment of Paris,* just mentioned, containing great richness and beauty of language, and occasional indications of a high order of pathetic and elevated emotion. His *Edward I.* is supposed to be our first historical play, and is, though monotonous, declamatory, and stiff, in some sense the forerunner of Shakespeare's *Richard II.* and *Henry V.*

THOMAS KYD, the "sporting Kyd" of Ben Jonson, lived about the same time, and was possibly the author of the famous play called *Jeronimo,* to which, in consequence of the many recastings it received, so many authors have been ascribed. The *Spanish Tragedy,* which is a continuation of *Jeronimo,* was undoubtedly his; and this fact is now believed to be fatal to his claim to the authorship of the more remarkable work.

ROBERT GREENE (1560-1592) was a Cambridge man, and the author of a multitude of tracts and pamphlets on the most miscellaneous subjects. Sometimes they were tales, often translated or expanded from the Italian novelists; sometimes amusing exposures of the various arts of *coney-catching, i. e.*, cheating and swindling, practised at that time in London, and in which, it is to be feared, Greene was personally not unversed; sometimes moral confessions, like the *Groatsworth of Wit*, or *Never too Late*, purporting to be a warning to others against the consequences of unbridled passions. The only dramatic work we need specify of Greene's was *George-a-Green*, the legend of an old English popular hero, recounted with much occasional vivacity and humour.

But by far the most powerful genius among them was CHRISTOPHER MARLOWE (1564-1593), who was born at Canterbury in 1564. On leaving the University of Cambridge he joined a troop of actors, among whom he was remarkable for a vice and debauchery even exceeding professional limits; and he was strongly suspected by his contemporaries of being an Atheist. His career was as short as it was disgraceful: he was stabbed in the head with his own dagger, which he had drawn upon one Francis Archer, whilst playing with him at backgammon in a tavern at Deptford; and he died of this wound at the age of thirty. His works are not numerous; but they are strongly distinguished from those of preceding and contemporary dramatists by an air of astonishing power, energy, and elevation—an elevation, it is true, which is sometimes exaggerated into bombast, and an energy which occasionally degenerates into extravagance. His first work was the tragedy of *Tamburlaine;* and the rants of the declamation in this piece furnished rich materials for satire and caricature; but in spite of this bombast the piece contains many passages of great power and beauty. Marlowe's best work is incontestably the drama of *Faustus*, founded upon the very same popular legend which Goethe adopted as the groundwork of his tragedy; but the point of view taken by Marlowe is far simpler than that of Goethe; and though the German poet's work is on the whole vastly superior, there is certainly no passage in the tragedy of Goethe in which terror, despair, and remorse, are painted with such a powerful hand as the great closing scene of Marlowe's piece, when Faustus, after the twenty-four years of sensual pleasure which were stipulated for in his pact with the Evil One, is waiting for the inevitable arrival of the Fiend to claim his bargain. The tragedy of the *Jew of Malta*, though inferior to *Faustus*, is characterised by similar merits and defects. The hero, Barabas, is the type of the Jew as he appeared to the bigoted ideas of the fifteenth century— a monster half terrific, half ridiculous, impossibly rich, inconceivably bloodthirsty, cunning, and revengeful, the bugbear of an age of ignorance and persecution. The intense expression of his rage, however, his triumph and his despair, give occasion for many noble bursts of Marlowe's powerful declamation. The tragedy of *Edward II.*, which was the last of this great poet's works, shows that in some departments of his art, and particularly in that of moving terror and pity, he might, had he lived, have become no insignificant rival of Shakespeare himself. The scene of the assassination of the unhappy king is worked up to a very lofty pitch of tragic pathos.

Marlowe is honourably known in other departments of poetry also. His two *Sestiads* of *Hero and Leander*, and his translation of the first book of Lucan, are respectively written in the heroic couplet and in blank verse, and are not without merit; whilst his charming poem of *The Passionate Shepherd* had the rare distinction of being quoted by Shakespeare, and of being answered in " The Nymph's Reply " by Sir Walter Raleigh.

The merits of GEORGE CHAPMAN (1557-1634) as a translator* have so entirely eclipsed his dramatic fame, that but few of his plays are now ever referred to. His *Bussy d'Amboise* is perhaps the best known of those.

* See p. 59.

CHAPTER IX.

SHAKESPEARE.

WILLIAM SHAKESPEARE (1564–1616) was born, probably on the 23rd of April, 1564, in the small town of Stratford-on-Avon, Warwickshire, and was baptised on the 26th of the same month. His father, John Shakespeare, in all probability a fellmonger, wool-dealer, and glover, had married in 1557 an heiress of ancient and even knightly descent, Mary Arden or Arderne, whose family had figured in the courtly and warlike annals of preceding reigns; and thus in the veins of the great poet of humanity ran blood derived from both the aristocratic and popular portions of the community. Mary Arderne had brought her husband in dowry a small freehold property; but this acquisition seems to have tempted him to engage, without experience, in agricultural pursuits, which ended disastrously in his being obliged at different times to mortgage and sell, not only his farm, but even one of the houses in Stratford of which he had been owner. He at last retained nothing save that small, but now venerable dwelling, consecrated to all future ages by being the spot where the greatest of poets first saw the light. That John Shakespeare had been originally in flourishing circumstances is amply proved by his having long been one of the Aldermen of Stratford, and his having served the office of Bailiff or Mayor in 1569. His distresses appear to have become severe in 1579; and he was unable to extricate himself from his manifold embarrassments, until his son had raised himself to a position of competence, and even of affluence.

That William Shakespeare could have derived even the most elementary instruction from his parents is impossible; for we know that neither John nor Mary Shakespeare could write—an accomplishment, however, which, it should be remarked, was comparatively rare in Elizabeth's reign. But there existed at that time, and there exists at the present day, in the borough of Stratford, one of those endowed " free grammar-schools " in which provision is always made for the children of the burgesses of the town; and it is inconceivable that John Shakespeare, Alderman and Past

Bailiff as he was, should have neglected to avail himself of so useful a privilege. This circumstance, coupled with the extensive though irregular reading of which his works give evidence, and with the vague tradition that he had been " in his youth a school-master in the country," renders it more than probable that the young poet enjoyed a higher degree of culture than some would give him credit for.

The most celebrated and romantic of the legends connected with his early life is that which represents his youth as wild and irregular; and in particular recounts his deer-stealing expedition, in company with other riotous young fellows, to Sir Thomas Lucy's park at Charlcote, near Stratford. For this escapade he is said to have been seized, brought before the indignant justice of the peace, and treated with so much severity by Sir Thomas, that he revenged himself by affixing a doggrel pasquinade to the gates of Charlcote. At this the wrath of the magistrate is said to have blazed so high that Shakespeare was obliged to escape to London; where, continues the legend, the young poet was reduced to earn his livelihood by holding horses at the doors of the theatres, until, " his pleasant wit " attracting the notice of the actors, he ultimately obtained access " behind the scenes," and by degrees became a celebrated actor and valuable dramatic author. But, though the deer-stealing story may very possibly be not altogether devoid of foundation, his leaving Stratford and embracing the theatrical career is to be explained in a different and much less improbable manner. It is probable that he left his native town in 1585, at the age of twenty-two; but the motive for this step was in all probability supplied by his marriage, contracted in 1582, when he was only eighteen, with Anne Hathaway, the daughter of a small farmer, little above the rank of a labouring man, who resided at the hamlet of Shottery, about one mile from Stratford. Anne Hathaway was seven years and a half older than her boy-husband; and the marriage appears to have been pressed on with eager haste, probably by the relatives of the bride. Indeed the whole of this important episode in the poet's life bears strong trace of a not over-reputable family mystery. The fruits of this union were, first a daughter Susanna, the poet's favourite child, born in 1583, and in the following year twins, Judith and Hamnet. The latter, the poet's only son, died at twelve years of age; his two daughters survived him. After these he had no more children; and there are several facts which seem to point to the conclusion that the married life of the poet was not marked by that love and confidence which is the usual result of well-considered and well-assorted unions. During the long period of his residence in London, his wife seems to have never resided with him; bitter allusion to marriages like his own are frequent in his works; and in his will he leaves her only " his second-best bed, with furniture,"—the significance of which slighting bequest, however, is somewhat diminished by the fact that as his property was chiefly freehold, she was entitled to dower.

Concerning the boyhood and youth of the great painter of nature and of man we know little or nothing. It is not improbable that at one period of his youth he had been placed in the office of some country practitioner of the law : in all his works he shows an extraordinary knowledge of the technical language of that profession, and frequently draws his illustrations from its vocabulary. Besides, such terms as he employs he almost always employs correctly; which would hardly be possible but to one who had been professionally versed in them.

However this may be, at the age of twenty-two, Shakespeare, now the father of three children, and without means of support, determined upon the great step of leaving Stratford altogether, and embarking on the wide ocean of London theatrical life. The motives that induced him to adopt this profession are not far to seek. The companies of actors were always glad to enlist among them such men of ready genius as could render themselves useful as performers and dramatists; they had often visited Stratford in their summer peregrinations; and the greatest tragic actor of that day, Richard Burbadge, was a Warwickshire man, whilst Thomas Greene, a distinguished member of the troop of the Globe, then the first theatre in London, was a native of Stratford. With this company, therefore, it was natural for the young adventurer to throw in his lot. Like other young men of that time, he rendered himself useful to his company in the double capacity of *actor and arranger of pieces;* and his professional career differed from that of Marlowe, Jonson, and others, in no respect save in the industry and success with which he pursued it, and the prudence with which he accumulated its pecuniary results. He began, in all probability, by adapting old plays to the exigencies of his theatre, and thus acquired that consummate knowledge of stage effect which distinguished him, and which first struck out the spark of that inimitable dramatic genius which places him above all other poets in the world. His professional career continued from 1586 to his retirement, which probably took place in 1611, a period of twenty-five years, embracing the splendour of his youth and the vigour of his manhood.

Though many attempts have been made to establish the dates and sequence of Shakespeare's thirty-seven plays, none of them even approaches to a satisfactory chronology of his dramatic history. The notices of the first performances, the scanty historical allusions, the order of their sequence in the first complete edition of the plays, that of 1623, and internal evidence itself, founded upon shades of style and a higher or lower degree of artistic perfection in treatment, are alike inadequate to the solution of the great problem. From the employment of all these methods combined we may indeed sometimes class the plays of Shakespeare into certain great, but not very accurately-marked periods; but we can never hope to attain anything like an exact chronological order. During the whole of his literary career our great dramatic master-workman in all likelihood continued to adapt and arrange old plays as well as to compose original pieces; which consideration will explain the extraordinary difference in point of merit, literary as well as theatrical, between such specimens of the most consummate perfection both in style and construction as *Hamlet* and *Othello*, and such strikingly inferior compositions as *Titus Andronicus* and parts of *Henry VI*.

The company to which Shakespeare belonged possessed two theatres,—the *Globe* in Southwark, and *The Theatre* in Blackfriars, of which an account has already been given (see p. 66). This company was undoubtedly the most respectable as well as the most prosperous of the then theatres; and partly by prudently avoiding to give offence by political allusion, and partly by securing powerful protection at Court—as, for instance, that of Lord-Keeper Egerton and the accomplished Earl of Southampton, the liberal patron and personal friend of Shakespeare himself,—this society enjoyed a freedom from the interference of the authorities never conceded to the others, and many rare privileges as well. In this company our great dramatist seems to have reached a high, though not the highest, position.

That he was profoundly acquainted with the theoretic principles of his art is clear from the inimitable "directions to the players" put into the mouth of Hamlet, which, in incredibly few words, contain its whole system. We have good authority for supposing that he acted the Ghost in his tragedy of *Hamlet*; the secondary, but graceful and touching character of Adam, the faithful old servant, in his *As You Like It*; the deeply pathetic impersonation of grief and despair in the popular tragedy of *Hieronymo*; and the sensible citizen, Old Knowell, in Ben Jonson's *Every Man In His Humour*. Such parts, it is plain, belong to a particular and perhaps secondary type; and a contemporary reference ascribes to him some degree of excellence in the performance of kingly characters. There

is reason to believe that Shakespeare, like Byron, laboured under
the personal defect of lameness, to which allusion is made in two of
his sonnets; and this in itself would fully account for his imperfect
success as an actor.   In any case it was Richard Burbadge who was
the original and most popular performer of his great tragic creations,
—Richard III., Hamlet, Othello, and the like.

Shakespeare's first original poems were not dramatic; he must be
regarded as the creator of a peculiar species of narrative composition
which was destined to achieve an immediate and immense popularity.   *Venus and Adonis*, which, in his dedication to Lord Southampton, he calls "the first heir of his invention," was published in
1593.   It is highly probable that this poem—exhibiting all the
luxuriant sweetness, the voluptuous tenderness of a youthful genius
—was conceived, if not composed, at Stratford.   The *Rape of
Lucrece*, a somewhat similar but inferior work,—written in rhyme
royal,—enjoyed a great but inferior popularity.   The former of
these works was reissued in five several editions between the
years 1593 and 1602; while the *Lucrece*, during nearly the same
lapse of time, appeared in three.   At what period he began to
be fully conscious of his own vast powers, and abandoned the
adaptation of old plays for original dramatic composition, it is quite
impossible to ascertain; for some of the works which bear the
strongest impress of his wondrous genius were undoubtedly based
upon productions by former hands, and had undergone repeated
recastings by himself and others.   As examples of this may be mentioned *Hamlet*, *Henry V.*, and *King John*.   Shakespeare must have
speedily risen to so much importance in the Globe Company as
sufficed to call down upon him the attacks of envious or disappointed rivals; for in 1592 the witty but disreputable Greene makes
bitter allusions to his name and alleged want of learning, as
well as to his activity in " bombasting out a blank verse."   He is
" Johannes Factotum," and on the strength of a few blustering
common-places fancies himself " the only Shakescene in a country."
These phrases are found in the scurrilous pamphlet entitled Greene's
Groatsworth of Wit, published by Chettle after its author's death,
and are evidently dictated by the envy of a disappointed rival;
but the publisher speedily apologised in terms which bear high
testimony not only to the great poet's genius as a writer, but also
to his stainless integrity.   "Divers of worship," says Chettle,
"have reported his uprightness of dealing, which argues his
honesty, and his facetious (elegant) grace in writing, that ap-
proves his art."   Such did Shakespeare appear to his contemporaries in 1592.

It is almost certain too, that the accomplished Pembroke and the generous Southampton were his admirers and patrons. The latter, indeed, is related to have made the poet a present of 1000*l.*; but though this princely gift was in all probability merely a generous contribution to the support of the drama as represented by Shakespeare's company, the action nevertheless shows the high respect which the poet had inspired. That Shakespeare, in his business relations with the theatre and the public, exhibited great good sense, prudence, and knowledge of the world, seems proved by the skill with which, during the time of his connection with it, the actors of the Globe managed to steer clear of the various dangers in which the puritanic opposition of the London Corporation and the susceptibility of the Court involved almost all the other companies of players. For no sooner had he retired from the theatre than repeated causes of complaint arose from the petulance of his comrades, and were severely punished. Shakespeare's worldly prosperity seems to have gone on steadily increasing; for in 1597, when he was aged thirty-three, he purchased New Place in Stratford, and either built entirely or reconstructed this house, long considered the most considerable in the town. During the whole of his London life he no doubt made frequent visits to his native place; and he was able to afford a tranquil asylum to his parents, who appear to have closed their lives under his roof. The death of his only son Hamnet, in 1596, when the boy was in his twelfth year, must have been a severe shock to so loving a heart; but in general his life seems to have been one of continued prosperity. In 1602 he purchased 107 acres of land; and about the same time he paid 440*l.* for a share in the tithes of Stratford, as a means of securing a safe revenue. In 1607 his favourite daughter Susanna married Dr. Hall; and in the following year she brought into the world a grand-daughter to the dramatist. In 1611 the poet, having disposed of most of his interest in the Globe, finally withdrew to New Place, but did not long enjoy the retirement for which he had laboured so long. He died two months after the marriage of his second daughter, Judith, to Thomas Quincy, on the 23rd April, 1616, probably the anniversary of his birthday, having just completed his fifty-second year. There exists a tradition that the great poet rose prematurely from a sick-bed to entertain Ben Jonson and Drayton, and brought on a relapse by "drinking too hard." He was buried in the parish church of Stratford; and over his grave is erected a mural monument in the Italianised taste of that day, which is chiefly remarkable as containing a bust of the poet—an authentic though not very well executed portrait. This, and the coarse engraving by Droeshout, prefixed to the first folio edition of his works in 1623, the accuracy of which is vouched for by Ben Jonson's eulogistic verses, seem to be the most trustworthy of his portraits.

But few relics of Shakespeare still remain; the house of New Place has long been destroyed; but the garden in which it stood, as well as the house where the poet was born, are still preserved. His will, which was made a month before his death, testifies to his kind and affectionate disposition; to each of his old comrades and " fellows " he leaves some token of regard, generally " twenty-six shillings and eight pence a piece to buy them rings." The three autographs attached to this document, and one or two more, are literally the only specimens that have been preserved of the writing of that immortal hand.

It now becomes absolutely necessary to employ some method of classifying the works of the great dramatist into groups. The most valuable principle of classification would be the chronological, which would furnish us with a complete history of the growth of Shake-speare's mind; but this mode, though it has exercised the ingenuity and research of many laborious and acute investigators, has furnished no results which can be depended upon—a fact evidenced by their extreme discrepancy. Upon the order of the pieces as given in the first folio edition, published in 1623 by Heminge and Condell, Shakespeare's friends and " fellows," it is evident no reliance can be placed. The most superficial examination is sufficient to prove that, in spite of the assurances of the editors as to its having been based upon the " papers " of their immortal colleague, this publication must be regarded as little better than a hasty speculation, entered into for the sake of profit and without much regard to the literary reputation of the great poet. And though the system of grouping them as Tragedies, Comedies, and Histories, has at all events the advantage of clearness, and is that upon which are based most of the editions of the dramas, it also is in some measure open to objection. Some of the pieces indeed (such as *Othello, Lear, Hamlet*) are distinctly tragedies, in the ordinary sense of that word, and others (*As You Like It*, or *Twelfth Night*) are as evidently comedies; but there exists a considerable number of the plays which, from their tone and incidents, might be ranged equally under both heads. Indeed, in almost all, the tragic and comic elements are more or less intermixed, and it is precisely this mixture of the two in the same piece which constitutes the peculiar distinguishing trait of the noble romantic drama of England in the Shakespearian Age; as well as its peculiar excellence and title of superiority, as a picture of life and nature, over the national drama of every other country.

—

A third mode of classification is based upon the *sources* from which Shakespeare drew the materials for his dramatic creations. These will naturally divide themselves first into the two great genera —History and Fiction; while the former of these two genera will naturally subdivide into different classes or degrees of historical authenticity, ranging from vague and half-poetical legend to the comparatively firm ground of recent historical events. Again, the legendary category may be referred to the different countries from whose chronicles the events were borrowed: thus *Hamlet* is taken from the Danish chronicler Saxo-Grammaticus; *Macbeth*, *Lear*, and *Cymbeline*, refer respectively to the legends, more or less fabulous, of Scottish and British history; while *Coriolanus*, *Julius Cæsar*, and *Antony and Cleopatra*, are derived from the annals of ancient Rome. The purely historical dramas of Shakespeare are intended to depict the events of the more recent and consequently more reliable details of the history of his own country; and for these, beginning with *King John* and terminating with *Henry VIII.*, he mainly drew his materials from the old annalist Hollinshed. These may be described as grand panoramas of national glory or national distress, embracing often a very considerable space of time, even a whole reign, and re-tracing—with apparent irregularity in their plan, but with an astonishing unity of general feeling and sentiment—great epochs in the life of the nation. Examples of such will be found in *Richard II.*, *Richard III.*, the two unequalled dramas on the reign of *Henry IV.*, and the glorious chant of patriotic triumph embodied in *Henry V.*, in which Shakespeare has completed the type of the Hero-King. To such pieces is applied the particular designation of Histories; and of such histories Shakespeare, though not the inventor, was certainly the most prolific author.

The second general category, that of pieces derived from fiction, need not detain us long. The materials for this—the largest—class of his dramas, Shakespeare derived from the Italian novelists and their imitators, who supplied the chief element of light literature in the sixteenth century. The short tales of these writers were most singularly adapted to furnish an appropriate groundwork for the poet's humorous or pathetic actions. They were exceedingly short; they depended for their popularity entirely upon amusing and surprising incidents; and the playwright, therefore, enjoyed full liberty for the exercise of his peculiar talent of portraying human character, having ready-prepared to his hand a series of striking events which he could compress or expand as best suited his purpose. It is exceedingly likely, though not fully proved, that Shakespeare never took the trouble of inventing the plot of a piece for himself; it was certainly his usual practice to appropriate without hesitation materials already prepared, and to direct all his energies to the exhibition of human nature and human passion. The number of his pieces derived from fiction amounts to nineteen: by far the majority of these are traceable to the Italian novelists and their French imitators. We are not, however, to infer that the great poet necessarily consulted the tales in the original language. A careful examination of his works seems to prove that he has rarely made use of any ancient or foreign materials *not then existing in English translations;* a fact which lends some sort of corroboration to the well-known statement of Ben Jonson that he had "small Latin and less Greek."

The following general classification endeavours to combine, with an indication of the class to which each piece belongs, the particular origin whence Shakespeare drew his materials:—

I. History.

I. Legendary:—

Titus Andronicus (Tragedy). Possibly *Titus and Vespatia.*

Timon of Athens (Tragedy). North's Plutarch; Lucian; Paynter's *Palace of Pleasure.*

Hamlet (Tragedy). An older play: *The Historie of Hamblet,* translated from the French of Belleforest: the Chronicle of Saxo-Grammaticus.

Lear (Tragedy). An older play; Hollinshed. (The Episode of Gloster and his sons is partly taken from Sidney's *Arcadia.*)

Cymbeline (Tragi-comedy). Partly Boccacio's *Decameron* (Day 2, Nov. 9).

Macbeth (Tragedy). Hollinshed.

II. Authentic:—

(*a*) Roman

Julius Cæsar (Tragedy, ...⎫
Antony and Cleopatra (Tragedy) ⎬ North's Plutarch.
Coriolanus (Tragedy). . . . .⎭

(*b*) English

King John. An older play on the same subject.

Henry VI., Part I. Hollinshed, and perhaps Hall.

Henry VI., Part II. Older play, entitled *The First Part of the Contention.*

Henry VI., Part III. Older play, entitled *The True Tragedie of Richard, Duke of York.*

Richard III. Hollinshed: Sir Thomas More; Hall; (?) *The True Tragedie of Richard III.*

Richard II. Hollinshed.

Henry IV., Part I. ⎫
Henry IV., Part II. ⎬ Hollinshed; an old play, entitled *The Famous Victories of Henry V.*
Henry V. . . . ⎭

Henry VIII. Hollinshed; Hall; Cavendish's *Life of Wolsey.*

II. FICTION.

Love's Labour's Lost (Comedy). Source unknown.

Comedy of Errors (Comedy). The *Menaechmi* and *Amphitrio* of Plautus.

Two Gentlemen of Verona (Comedy). Perhaps *La Diana*, by Jorge de Montemayor (? translation of Bartholomew Young) ; (?) an older play, entitled " *The History of Felix and Philiomena* " (1584).

Midsummer Night's Dream (Comedy). Chaucer, *Knighte's Tale, Wif of Bath's Tale*, and *Legend of Good Women* ; Golding's *Ovid*.

Romeo and Juliet (Tragedy). Arthur Brook's *Tragicall Historye of Romeus and Juliet* ; Paynter's *Palace of Pleasure*.

Merchant of Venice (Comedy). *Il Pecorone*, by Giovanni Florentino, and *Gesta Romanorum*.

Taming of the Shrew (Comedy). An older piece, " *The Taming of a Shrew ;*" " *Supposes*" translated from Ariosto by Gascoigne.

Merry Wives of Windsor (Comedy). " *The Two Lovers of Pisa*," in Tarleton's *Newes out of Purgatorie ; Il Pecorone ; Le tredici piacevoli notti del S. Gio. Francesco Straparola*.

Much Ado About Nothing (Comedy). The Episode of *Ariodant and Genevra* in Ariosto's *Orlando Furioso;* (?) an older play ; Bandello's 22nd Novel.

As You Like It (Comedy). Lodge's *Rosalynde*, and the *Coke's Tale of Gamelyn*.

Twelfth Night (Comedy). A novel of Bandello (imitated in Rich's *Farewell to the Military Profession*); Two Italian comedies, (1) *Gl' Inganni*, (2) *Gl' Ingannati*.

All's Well that Ends Well (Comedy). The story of *Giletta of Narbona* in Paynter's *Palace of Pleasure* (taken from Boccacio's *Decameron*, Day 3, Nov. 9).

Measure for Measure (Comedy). Whetstone's play, " *The Historie of Promos and Cassandra* " (derived from Giraldo Cinthio's *Hecatommithi* ii., viii., 5).

Othello (Tragedy). Giraldo Cinthio's *Hecatommithi* i., iii., 7.

Troilus and Cressida (Tragi-comedy). Chaucer, *Troylus and Creseyde ;* Lydgate, *Troy Book ;* Caxton, *Recuyles, or Destruction of Troy ;* Chapman's *Homer.*

Pericles (Comedy). Gower's *Confessio Amantis; Gesta Romanorum,* Twine's *Pattern of Painfull Adventures.*

The Tempest (Comedy). Source unknown.

The Winter's Tale (Comedy). Greene's " *Pandosto, the Triumph of Time*," 1588.

Two Noble Kinsmen (Tragi-comedy). Chaucer's *Knighte's Tale.*

From this classification it will be seen that many plays were based upon preceding dramatic works treating of the same or nearly the same subjects; and in some few cases we possess the more ancient pieces themselves, exhibiting different degrees of imperfection and barbarism. In one or two examples we have more than one edition of the same play in its different stages towards complete perfection under the hand of Shakespeare, of which *Hamlet* is the most notable instance. A careful collation of such various editions furnishes us with precious materials for the investigation of the most interesting problem that literary criticism can approach—the tracing of the different phases of elaboration through which every great work must pass. The first impression produced on the reader by the Historical category of Shakespeare's dramas, is the astonishing force and completeness with which the poet seized the general and salient peculiarities of the age and country which he undertook to reproduce. With the limited scholarship that he probably possessed, this power is the more extraordinary. Jonson, indeed, has shown a far more accurate and extensive knowledge of the details of Roman manners, ceremonies, and institutions; but his personages, admirable as they are, are entirely deficient in that intense human reality which Shakespeare never fails to communicate to his *dramatis personæ*. In the crowd of personages necessarily introduced into each play of this kind, from the most prominent down to the most obscure, every one clearly had, in the mind of the author, a separate and distinct individuality, equally true to universal and to particular nature. The English historical plays supply the best illustrations of this, as will plainly be seen on comparing *King John*, for example, with *Henry IV.* or *Henry V.* This power of throwing himself into a given epoch is, in Shakespeare, carried to a degree which cannot be justly qualified as anything short of superhuman. His anachronisms, too, of which so much has been said, are mere external excrescences, which do not affect for a moment the sense of verisimilitude. A hero of the Trojan War may quote Aristotle, or Cæsar's Romans may wield the Spanish rapier of the sixteenth century ; but the language and sentiments of classical times are never infected with the conceits of gallant and courtly compliment that were current in the age of Louis XIV. The delicate task of giving glimpses into the private life of great historical personages, which we find generally evaded in all other authors who have treated such subjects, and the boldness with which he has introduced comic incidents amid the most solemn events of history, are proofs of the supremacy of Shakespeare's genius.

But of these thirty-seven plays some bear evident marks of an inferior hand. Thus the three parts of *Henry VI.* were in all probability older dramas which Shakespeare retouched and revivified here and there with some of his inimitable strokes of nature and poetic fancy. So, too, the last of the English historical plays, at least the l test in the date of its action, *Henry VIII.*, bears many traces of having been in part composed by a different hand; 'n the diction, the turn of thought, and in particular in the peculiar mechanism of the versification, there is much to lead to the conclusion that Shakespeare. in its composition was associated with another poet, probably John Fletcher. Such partnership was common in that age.

In the mode of delineating passion and feeling, Shakespeare proceeds differently from all other dramatic authors. They, even the greatest among them, create a personage by accumulating in it all such traits as usually accompany the fundamental elements which go to form its constitution; and thus they all, more or less, fall into the error of making their personages embodiments of certain moral peculiarities, such as ambition, avarice, hypocrisy, and the like. Moreover, such characters almost universally *describe* their sensations, which men and women in real life never do, but indicate what they feel rather by what they suppress than by what they utter. And so it is with the men and women of Shakespeare. Nor has he ever fallen into the common error of forgetting the infinite complexity of human character. No one of his personages is a mere incarnation of some predominant vice, or passion, or oddity, as most of Jonson's are. Thus, as Macaulay justly observes, the *primary* characteristic of Shylock is revengefulness; but a closer insight shows a thousand other qualities in him, the mutual play and vary-- ing intensity of which go to compose the complex being that Shake- speare has drawn in the terrible Jew. Othello is no mere imperso- nation of jealousy, nor Macbeth of ambition, nor Falstaff of selfish gaiety, nor Timon of misanthropy, nor Imogen of wifely love: in each of these personages the more closely we analyse them, the deeper and more multiform will appear the infinite springs of action which make up their personality. And this wonderful power of con- ceiving complex character is at the bottom of another distinguishing peculiarity of our great poet, namely, the total absence in his works of any tendency to self-reproduction. From the dramas of Shakespeare we learn nothing whatever of what were the sympathies and ten- dencies of the author. He is absolutely impersonal, or rather he is all persons in turn; for no poet ever possessed to a like degree the porten- tous power of successively identifying himself with a multitude of the most diverse individualities, and of identifying himself so com- pletely that we cannot detect a trace of preference. Shakespeare, when he has once thrown off such a character as Othello, never recurs to it again. Othello disappears from the stage as completely as a real Othello would have done from the world, and leaves behind him no similar personage. Not that he has not given us other pictures of jealous men : Leontes, Ford, Posthumus, all are equally jealous; but how differently is the passion manifested in each of these! In the female characters, too, what a wonderful range, what an inex- haustible variety! Perhaps in no class of his impersonations are the depth, the delicacy, and the extent of Shakespeare's creative power more visible than in his women; for we must not forget that in writing these exquisitely varied types of female character, he knew that they would be entrusted in representation to boys or young men

—no female having acted on the stage till long after the age which
witnessed such creations as Hermione, Lady Macbeth, Rosalind, or
Juliet. The author must have felt what has been so powerfully
expressed in the language of his own Cleopatra:

> " The quick comedians
> Extemporary shall stage us: Antony
> Shall be brought drunken forth, and I shall see
> Some squeaking Cleopatra *boy* my greatness."

Surely the power of ideal creation has never undergone a severer
ordeal.

In the expression of strong emotion, as well as in the delineation
of character, Shakespeare is superior to all other dramatists, superior
to all other poets. He never produces the effect he desires by violent
or declamatory rhetoric, or by unusual or abnormal combinations of
qualities. In him we meet with no sentimental assassins, no moral
monsters,

> " Linked with one virtue and a thousand crimes; "

but he is always able to interest or to instruct us with the exhibition
of general passions and feelings, manifesting themselves in the way
we generally see them in the world. In the expression, too, he uniformly draws, at least in his finest passages, his illustrations from the
most simple and familiar objects. He has too often, indeed, allowed
his taste for intellectual subtleties to get the better of his judgment ;
and his passion for playing upon words—a passion which was the
literary vice of his day, and the effects of which are traceable in the
writings of Bacon as well, often manifests itself most unreasonably.
But this indulgence in conceits generally disappears in the great culminating moments of intense passion. The much-talked of obscurity
of his style too, is not to be attributed, except in some instances, to the
corrupt state in which his writings have descended to us, and still
less to the archaism of his diction. The writings of many of the
great dramatists his contemporaries are as remarkable for the limpidity and clearness of expression as his are occasionally for its complexity. The cause of this is found in the enormously developed
intellectual and imaginative faculty in the poet, leading him to
make metaphor of the boldest kind the ordinary tissue of his style.
In all figurative writing the metaphor, the image, is an ornament,
something extraneous to the thought it is intended to illustrate, and
may be detached from it, leaving the fundamental idea intact : in
Shakespeare the metaphor is the very fabric of the thought itself,
and entirely inseparable from it. This intimate union of the reason
and the imagination is a peculiarity common to Shakespeare with
Bacon, in whose writings the severest logic is expressed in the boldest
metaphor ; and the very titles of whose books and the very definitions

of whose philosophical terms are frequently images of the most figurative character. From the writings of no poet, ancient or modern, may there be extracted such a number of profound and yet practical observations, expressed indeed with the simplicity of a casual remark, yet pregnant with the condensed wisdom of philosophy.

The *Sonnets* of Shakespeare possess a peculiar interest, not only from their intrinsic beauty, but from the circumstance of their evidently containing carefully veiled allusions to the personal feelings of their author, allusions which point to some deep disappointment in love and friendship suffered by the poet. They were first printed in 1609, though, from allusions in contemporary writings, it is clear that many of them, if not all, had been composed previously. They are 154 in number, and some are evidently addressed to a person of the male sex, while others are as plainly intended for a woman; and throughout all there runs a deep undercurrent of sorrow, self-discontent, and wounded affection, which bears every mark of being the expression of a real sentiment. No clue, however, has as yet been discovered by which we may hope to trace the persons to whom these poems are addressed, or the painful events to which they allude. The volume was dedicated, on its first appearance, by the publisher Thomas Thorpe, to "Mr. W. H.," who is qualified as the only begetter of these sonnets; and some hypotheses suppose that this mysterious "Mr. W. H." was no other than William Herbert, Earl of Pembroke, one of Shakespeare's most powerful patrons, and a man of great splendour and accomplishments. It is, however, difficult to suppose that a personage so high-placed could easily have interfered to destroy the happiness of the comparatively humble player and poet of the Globe; or, if he had, that a bookseller would have ventured to allude to him under so familiar a designation as " W. H." In fact, the whole production is shrouded in mystery—a mystery which no critical sagacity has ever yet been able to penetrate.

Of Shakespeare's plays but sixteen were printed in his lifetime, and those, so far as can be ascertained, without his sanction. One more, *Othello*, was published separately after his death, before the first folio edition of his complete works, which appeared in 1623. A second followed in 1632, and a third in 1663—which last contained *Pericles* for the first time, as well as the six apocryphal plays. One more issue of the folio, that of 1685, sufficed the English reading public, until Nicholas Rowe produced the earliest critical edition in 1709. There were, however, several issues of his Poems during the same time.

CHAPTER X.

THE SHAKESPEARIAN DRAMATISTS.

THE age of Elizabeth and James I. produced a galaxy of great dramatic poets, the like of whom, whether we regard the nature or the degree of excellence exhibited in their works, the world has never seen. In the general style of their writings they bear a strong family resemblance to Shakespeare; and indeed many of the peculiar merits of their great prototype may be found scattered among his various contemporaries, and in some instances carried to a height little inferior to that found in his writings. Thus, intensity of pathos hardly less touching than that of Shakespeare may be found in the dramas of Ford; gallant animation and dignity in the dialogues of Beaumont and Fletcher; deep tragic emotion in the sombre scenes of Webster; noble moral elevation in the graceful plays of Massinger; but in Shakespeare, and in Shakespeare alone, do we see the consummate union of all the most opposite qualities of the poet, the observer, and the philosopher.

The name which stands next to that of Shakespeare in this list is that of BEN JONSON (1573–1637), a vigorous and solid genius, built high with learning and knowledge of life. He was born in 1573, and though compelled by a stepfather to follow the humble trade of a bricklayer, he succeeded, by the generous patronage of Camden, whose pupil and assistant he was at Westminster, in making himself one of the most learned men of the age. After a short service as a soldier in the Low Countries, where he distinguished himself by his courage in the field, he began his theatrical career at about twenty years of age, when we find him attached as an actor to one of the minor theatres called the Curtain. His success as a performer is said to have been very small, owing most probably to his want of grace and beauty of person. Having killed a fellow-actor in a duel while still a very young man, he was (to use his own words) "brought near the gallows." Whilst lying in prison awaiting his trial, he was converted by a Jesuit to the Roman Catholic faith; but twelve years afterwards he returned to the bosom of his mother-Church.

His first dramatic work, the comedy of *Every Man in his Humour*, is assigned to the year 1596. This piece failed in its first representa-

tion; but by Shakespeare's advice. it is said, it was remodelled; and
two years afterwards was brought out at the Globe with triumphant
success, the great poet himself taking a part. Thus was probably
laid the foundation of that warm friendship between Jonson and
Shakespeare, the existence of which is proved not only by many
pleasant anecdotes, but by the enthusiastic, and yet discriminating,
eulogy in which Jonson has described the genius of his friend.
From the moment of this second representation of his comedy Ben
Jonson's literary reputation was established; and henceforward he
became the most prominent figure in the literary society of that
day. His " wit-combats" at the famous taverns of the Mermaid.
the Devil, and the Falcon, have been commemorated by contemporary
poets and in many anecdotes; and he came even to be regarded as
a sort of intellectual king, like Samuel Johnson afterwards.

His first comedy was followed in the succeeding year by *Every Man
Out of his Humour*, and in 1603 he gave to the world his tragedy of
Sejanus. The frank and violent character of Jonson involved him in
almost continual quarrels and disputes—Dekker, Marston, and Inigo
Jones, the Court architect and arranger of festivities and masques,
being the special objects of his dislike. Many of these literary
quarrels may be traced in his dramatic works, as in *The Poetaster* and
the *Tale of a Tub*. In rapid succession between 1603 and 1619 followed some of Jonson's finest works—*Volpone*, *Epicene*, the *Alchemist*, and the tragedy of *Catiline*. In the latter year he was
appointed Laureate; and was frequently employed by the Court in
getting up those splendid and fantastic entertainments called
masques, in which he exhibited all the stores of his invention and
all the resources of his vast and elegant scholarship. Many of
Jonson's later pieces were entirely unsuccessful; and in one of the
last, the *New Inn*, acted in 1630, the poet complains bitterly of the
hostility and bad taste of the audience. Disappointment, poverty,
ill-health, and a too great fondness for sack, made the latter years
of his life very unhappy. He died in 1637, and was buried in a
vertical position in Westminster Abbey; the stone over his grave
having been inscribed with the excellent and laconic words, " O
rare Ben Jonson!"

The dramatic works of this great poet are of various degrees
of merit, ranging from an excellence not surpassed by any
contemporary excepting Shakespeare, to the lowest point of
laborious mediocrity. His tragedies, the *Fall of Sejanus* and
the *Conspiracy of Catiline*, contain extracts from the Latin literature, reproduced with consummate vigour and fidelity. But
notwithstanding the minute accuracy with which all the details
of the Roman manners, religion, and sentiments are reproduced,

the effect of the whole is singularly stiff and unpleasing, partly perhaps from the absence of pathos and tenderness, and partly from the unmanageable nature of the subjects, the hero in both cases being so odious that no art can secure for his fate the sympathy of the reader. Of comedies properly so called, Jonson composed fifteen, the best of which are incontestably *Every Man in his Humour, Volpone, Epicene* or the *Silent Woman,* and the *Alchemist.* The plots or intrigues of Jonson are far superior to those of the generality of his contemporaries; he always constructed them himself, and with great care and skill. Those of *Volpone* and the *Silent Woman,* for example, though some of the incidents are extravagant, are admirable for the constructive skill they display, and for the art with which each detail is made to contribute to the catastrophe. The general effect, however, of Jonson's plays is unsatisfactory. He dissected the vices, the follies, and the affectations of society; he loved to dwell rather upon the eccentricities and monstrosities of human nature, than upon those universal features with which all can sympathise as all possess them. His mind was singularly deficient in what is called *humanity;* his point of view is invariably that of the satirist; and this tendency induced him to take his materials, both for intrigue and character, from odious or repulsive sources: thus the subject of two of his finest pieces, *Volpone* and the *Alchemist,* turns entirely upon a series of ingenious cheats and rascalities—all the persons, without exception, being either scoundrels or their dupes. Nevertheless his knowledge of character is so vast, the force and vigour of his expression is so unbounded, the tone of his morality is so high and manly, that his comedies cannot fail to retain a high place in literature. His admirable type of coward-braggadocio in Bobadill will always deserve to occupy a place in the great gallery of human folly.

It is singular that while Jonson in his plays should be distinguished for that hardness and dryness which we have endeavoured to point out, this same poet, in another large and beautiful category of his works, should be remarkable for the elegance and refinement of his invention and his style. In the *Masques* and *Court Entertainments,* which, to the number of about thirty-five, he composed for the amusement of the king and the great nobles, as well as in the charming fragment of a pastoral drama entitled the *Sad Shepherd,* Jonson appears quite another man. Everything that the richest and most delicate invention could supply, aided by extensive, elegant, and recondite reading, is lavished upon these courtly compliments, the gracefulness of which almost makes us forget their adulation and servility. Among the most beautiful of these masques we may mention *Pan's Anniversary,* the *Masque of Oberon,* and the

Masque of Queens. Besides his dramatic works, Jonson left literary remains in both prose and verse. The former portion, called *Discoveries*, contains many valuable notes on books and men—those on Shakespeare and Bacon being the most interesting; and the latter consists chiefly of *epigrams*, written in the manner of Martial. In his *Underwoods* is found his famous copy of verses to " The Memory of his beloved Master, William Shakespeare."

Superior to Ben Jonson in variety and animation, though hardly equal to him in solidity of knowledge, were FRANCIS BEAUMONT (1586–1616) and JOHN FLETCHER (1576–1625), both men of a higher social status, by birth and by education, than their fellow-dramatists, Beaumont being the son of a Judge, and Fletcher of a Bishop. Concerning the details of their lives and characters we possess but vague and scanty information ; it is, however, evident from their works that they were accomplished men, possessing a degree of scholarship amply sufficient to furnish their writings with rich allusions and abundant ornaments. The dramatic works of these brilliant fellow-labourers are extraordinary not only for their excellence and variety, but also for their number, their collected dramas—which were not printed in a complete form till 1647—amounting to 52. The common tradition ascribed to Beaumont more of the sublime and tragic genius, to Fletcher gaiety and comic humour; but so intimately interwoven is their glory, that neither in their names nor in their writings does biography or criticism ever separate them. Even those plays that were produced after Beaumont's death may possibly have profited by earlier sketches to which he contributed. According to Dryden, who himself owed so much to them, their first successful piece was the charming romantic drama of *Philaster ;* besides which, among the pieces performed anterior to 1616, may be mentioned the *Maid's Tragedy, A King and No King,* the *Laws of Candy,* all of a lofty or tragic character ; while the *Woman-hater,* the *Knight of the Burning Pestle* (one of their richest and most popular extravaganzas), the *Honest Man's Fortune,* the *Captain,* and the *Coxcomb,* exhibit their comic genius. Of those attributed to Fletcher alone, a large proportion possess a predominant comic tone—as the excellent comedies of the *Chances,* the *Spanish Curate, Beggars' Bush,* and *Rule a Wife and Have a Wife.* The first quality which strikes the reader in making acquaintance with these poets is the singularly airy, free, and animated manner in which they exhibit incident, sentiment, and action. Their dialogue is singularly vivacious, their style wonderfully limpid, and they often attain, in their more poetical and declamatory passages, a high elevation both of tragic and romantic eloquence. In the delineation of character and passion they are inferior to the great artist with whom they have not seldom

ventured to measure their strength; and if they are to be compared
with him at all, it is only in his secondary pieces, such as *Much
Ado About Nothing, Measure for Measure*, or the *Tempest*—works
in which the graceful, fantastic, and romantic elements predomi-
nate. In this department Beaumont and Fletcher are no unworthy rivals to the greatest of dramatists. Careless in the
construction of their plots, they keep alive the curiosity of the
reader by striking situations and amusing turns of fortune.
Though they never once attempt the English historical drama, they
freely use materials derived from Roman chronicles—as in their
tragedy of the *False One*, in which they apparently try their strength
against *Julius Cæsar*—and from the legendary history of the Middle
Ages, as in *Rollo, Thierry and Theodoret*, and other pieces. They
are singularly happy in the delineation of noble and chivalrous
feeling, the love and friendship of young and gallant souls; and
their numerous portraits of valiant veterans may be pronounced
unequalled. Their pathos, though frequently exhibited, is rather
tender than deep : but in the *Maid's Tragedy* the grief of Aspasia and
the despair of Evadne are worked up to a high pitch of tragic emotion.
In the *Two Noble Kinsmen*, the subject of which is borrowed from
the *Knight's Tale* of Chaucer, the dignity of chivalric friendship is
portrayed with the highest and most heroic spirit. But it is now an
almost universal opinion that a large portion of this play is Shakespeare's. It is perhaps in their pieces of mixed sentiment, containing comic matter intermingled with romantic and elevated incidents, that Beaumont and Fletcher's genius shines out in its full
effulgence ; of which class no better examples can be selected than
the comedies of the *Elder Brother, Rule a Wife and Have a Wife,
Beggars' Bush*, and the *Spanish Curate*. In the more violently
farcical intrigues and characters, such as are to be found in the *Little
French Lawyer*, the *Woman-hater*, the *Scornful Lady*, the eccentricity or even absurdity of the idea is forgotten in consideration of
the laughable extravagances in which it is made to develop itself;
which are very different from those "humours" which Jonson so
delighted to portray. Their fools are " lively, audible, and full of
vent ;" and the authors seem to enjoy the amusement of heaping up
absurdity upon absurdity out of the very abundance of their humorous conception. Some of the pieces of Beaumont and Fletcher
furnish us with a store of curious antiquarian and literary materials;
thus *Beggars' Bush* contains valuable illustrations of that singular subject the *slang* dialect; and the fantastic extravaganza of
the *Knight of the Burning Pestle* is an absolute storehouse of ancient
English ballad poetry. Fletcher occasionally imitates Shakespeare ;
in the *Bloody Brother* he reproduces, but by no means improves on.

the famous scene between Richard Crookback and Lady Anne; sometimes he was associated with him in a kind of dramatic partnership : and to this we undoubtedly owe *Henry VIII.* and the *Two Noble Kinsmen.* The pastoral drama of the *Faithful Shepherdess,* which is the composition of Fletcher alone, is unquestionably one of the most exquisite combinations of delicate and tender sentiment with description of nature and lyrical music, that any literature can boast ; and it is not the least glory of Fletcher that in this exquisite poem he is the victorious rival of Ben Jonson, whose delicious fragment of the *Sad Shepherd* was undoubtedly suggested by this drama ; which also furnished to Milton the prototype of his *Comus.*

PHILIP MASSINGER (1584-1640), a gentleman by birth, after a stay of two years in the University of Oxford,—where he acquired, as his works prove, an intimate knowledge of the great classical writers of antiquity,—began his theatrical life in 1606, which appears to have been an uninterrupted succession of struggle, disappointment, and distress. Like most of his fellow-dramatists, Massinger frequently wrote in partnership with other playwrights, the names of Dekker, Field, Rowley, Middleton, and others, being often found in conjunction with his. We possess the titles of about thirty-seven plays either entirely or partially written by Massinger, of which number, however, only nineteen are now extant, the remainder having been lost or destroyed. These works are tragedies, comedies, and romantic dramas partaking of both characters. The finest of them are the following : the *Fatal Dowry,* the *Unnatural Combat,* the *Roman Actor,* and the *Duke of Milan,* in the first category ; the *Bondman,* the *Maid of Honour,* and the *Picture,* in the third ; and the *Old Law,* and *A New Way to Pay Old Debts,* in the second. The qualities which distinguish this noble writer are an extraordinary dignity and elevation of moral sentiment, a singular power of delineating the sorrow of pure and lofty minds exposed to unmerited suffering, cast down but not humiliated by misfortune. Massinger had no aptitude for pleasantries ; but a desire to please the mixed audiences of those days necessitated such an amount of stupid buffoonery, and loathsome indecency, that we are driven to the supposition of his having had recourse to other hands to supply this obnoxious matter. His style and versification are singularly sweet and noble. No writer of that day is so free from archaisms and obscurities ; and perhaps there is none in whom more constantly appear all the force, harmony, and dignity of which the English language is susceptible. If we desire to characterise Massinger in one sentence, we may say that dignity, tenderness, and grace, are the qualities in which he excels.

To JOHN FORD (1586-1639) the passion of unhappy love, viewed under all its aspects, has furnished almost exclusively the subject-matter of his plays.   He began his dramatic career by joining with Dekker in the production of the touching tragedy of the *Witch of Edmonton*, in which popular superstitions are skilfully combined with a deeply-touching story of love and treachery; and the works attributed to him are not numerous.   Besides the above piece he wrote the tragedies of the *Brother and Sister*, the *Broken Heart* (beyond all comparison his most powerful work), a graceful historical drama on the subject of *Perkin Warbeck*, and the following romantic or tragi-comic pieces: the *Lover's Melancholy, Love's Sacrifice*, the *Fancies, Chaste and Noble*, and the *Lady's Trial*.   His personal character, if we may judge from slight allusions found in contemporary writings, seems to have been sombre and retiring; and in his works sweetness and pathos are carried to a higher pitch than in any other dramatist.   His lyre has but few tones; but his music makes up in intensity for what it wants in variety; and at present we can hardly understand how any audience could ever have borne the harrowing up of their sensibilities by such repeated strokes of pathos.   His verse and dialogue are even somewhat monotonous in their sweet and plaintive melody, and are marked by a great richness of classical allusion.   His comic scenes are even more worthless and offensive than those of Massinger.

But perhaps the most powerful and original genius among the Shakespearian dramatists of the second order is JOHN WEBSTER. His literary physiognomy has something of that dark, bitter, and woful expression which makes us thrill in the portraits of Dante. The number of his known works is very small; the most celebrated among them is the tragedy of the *Duchess of Malfy* (1619); but others are not inferior to that strange piece in intensity of feeling and savage grimness of plot and treatment.   Besides the above we possess *Guise, or the Massacre of France*, in which the St. Bartholomew is, of course, the main action; the *Devil's Law-Case;* the *White Devil*, founded on the crimes and sufferings of Vittoria Corombona; *Appius and Virginia;* and we thus see that in the majority of his subjects he worked by preference on themes which offered a congenial field for his portraiture of the darker passions and of the moral tortures of their victims.   Like many of his contemporaries, he knew the secret of expressing the highest passion through the most familiar images; and the dirges and funeral songs which he has frequently introduced into his pieces possess, as Charles Lamb eloquently expresses it, that intensity of feeling which seems to resolve itself into the very elements they contemplate.

As we pass on to the lower grades of dramatic talent, we are almost bewildered by the number and variety of manifestations.   A few writers, however, deserve a distinct notice. THOMAS DEKKER, one of the most inexhaustible of these, though he generally appears as a fellow-labourer with other dramatists, yet in the few pieces attributed to his unassisted pen shows great elegance of language and deep tenderness of sentiment. THOMAS MIDDLETON, best known as the author of the *Witch*, is admired for a certain wild and fantastic fancy which delights in portraying scenes of supernatural agency. JOHN MARSTON, on the contrary, is distinguished mainly by a lofty and satiric tone of invective, in which he lashes the vices and follies of mankind. THOMAS HEYWOOD exhibits a graceful fancy, and one of his plays, *A Woman Killed with Kindness*, is among the most touching of the period.

The dramatic era of Elizabeth and James closes with JAMES SHIRLEY (1594-1666), whose comedies, though in many respects bearing the same general character as the works of his great predecessors, still seem the earnest of a new period. He excels in the delineation of gay and fashionable society; and his dramas are more laudable for ease, nature, and animation, than for profound tracings of human nature, or for vivid portraiture of character. But the glory of the English drama had almost departed; and its extinction by external violence in 1642 but precipitated what was inevitable. The breaking out of the civil war in this year closed the theatres; and this suspension of the dramatic profession became perpetual by an ordinance of the Commons in 1648. From that date until the Restoration all dramatic performances were illegal; but already, with the connivance of Cromwell, Davenant had given entertainments of this kind at Rutland House in 1656; and upon the great Protector's death in 1658 he ventured to reopen a public theatre in Drury Lane. With this event begins an entirely new chapter in the history of the English stage.

The Elizabethan drama is the most wonderful and majestic outburst of genius that any age has yet seen. It is characterised by marked peculiarities; an intense richness and fertility of imagination, combined with the greatest force and vigour of familiar expression; an intimate union of the common and the refined; the boldest flights of fancy and the most scrupulous fidelity to actual reality. The great object of these dramatists being to produce intense impressions upon a miscellaneous audience, they sacrificed everything to strength and nature. Their writings reflect not only the faithful images of human character and passion under every conceivable condition, not only the strongest as well as the most delicate colouring of fancy and imagination, but the profoundest and simplest precepts derived from the practical experience of life.

CHAPTER XI.

THE PROSE LITERATURE OF THE ELIZABETHAN PERIOD

THE object of the present chapter is to trace the nature and the results of that immense revolution in philosophy brought about by the immortal writings of Bacon ; as well as to give a general view of the prose literature of the great Elizabethan era. Much of the peculiarly *practical* character, which distinguishes the political and philosophical literature of this time, is traceable to the general *laicising* of the higher functions of the public service which resulted from the Reformation. But this department of letters, it must be confessed, makes but a poor figure beside the unparalleled splendour of its more august sister. Hooker, Raleigh, and Bacon, alone redeem it from insignificance ; and Bacon's greatest triumphs were gained through the medium of the Latin language.

In the humble but useful department of historical chronicles a few words must be said on the labours of JOHN STOW (1525-1605), whose *Summary of English Chronicles, Annals,* and *Survey of London* all appeared before the end of the sixteenth century; and of RAPHAEL HOLLINSHED (d. 1580), who undertook a somewhat similar task. From the latter, Shakespeare drew the materials for many of his half-legendary, half-historical pieces, such as *Macbeth, King Lear,* and the like, as well as for most of his purely historical plays.

The most extraordinary and meteor-like personage in the literary history of this time is SIR WALTER RALEIGH (1552-1618), whose chequered career belongs rather to the political than the literary history of England. He highly distinguished himself in the wars in Ireland, where he visited Spenser at Kilcolman, and was consulted by the great poet on the *Faery Queen ;* and no less as a navigator and adventurer in the colonization of Virginia and the conquest of Guiana. On the accession of James I. he was involved in an accusation of high treason connected with the alleged plot to place the unfortunate Arabella Stuart upon the throne; and he was confined for many years in the Tower under sentence of death. During his imprisonment of twelve years Raleigh devoted himself to literary and scientific occupations; he produced, with the aid of many learned friends, among whom Jonson was one, a *History of the World,* which will ever be regarded as a masterpiece of English prose. It was never completed, and reaches only the second Macedonian war.

Of the various Christian sects generated by the great break-up of the Catholic Church at the Reformation, the Church of England is essentially a compromise between opposite extremes; and as such it was assailed with almost equal virulence by Roman Catholics and Calvinists. The great champion of the principles of Anglicanism against the encroachments of the Genevan school of theology was RICHARD HOOKER (1553-1600), a man of evangelical piety and of vast learning—though sprung from the humblest origin—and educated in the University of Oxford. His eloquence and erudition obtained for him the eminent post of Master of the Temple in London; where his colleague in the ministry, Walter Travers, propounded doctrines in church government which, being similar to those of the Calvinistic confession, were incompatible with Hooker's opinions. The mildness and modesty of Hooker's character urged him to implore his ecclesiastical superior to remove him to the more congenial duties of a country parish: and it was here that he executed that great work which has placed him among the most eminent of the Anglican divines, and among the best prose-writers of his age. The title of this work is *A Treatise on the Laws of Ecclesiastical Polity*; and its object is to investigate and define the fundamental principles upon which is founded the right of the Church to the obedience of its members, and the duty of the members to pay obedience to the Church. But, though the principal object of this book is to defend the organization of the English Church against the attacks of the Roman Catholics on the one hand, and the Calvinists on the other, Hooker has dug deep down into the eternal granite on which are founded all law, all obedience, and all right, political as well as religious. The *Ecclesiastical Polity* is a monument of close and cogent logic, supported by immense and varied erudition, and is written in a style entirely free from pedantry,—clear, vigorous, and unaffected. It is to be regretted that the last three books have not descended to us as Hooker seems to have left them, the existing Sixth Book clearly belonging to a different subject, and the Seventh and Eighth having been apparently put together from the rough draughts found among the author's papers after his death.

The political life of FRANCIS BACON (1561-1626) forms with his purely intellectual or philosophical career a contrast so striking, that it would be difficult to find, in the records of biographical literature, anything so vividly opposed. He was the son of Sir Nicholas Bacon, for twenty-one years Keeper of the Great Seal to Queen Elizabeth, and was consequently the nephew of Burleigh, —Sir Nicholas and the great Treasurer having married two sisters;

and the boy gave earnest, from his tenderest childhood, of those
powers of intellect and that readiness of mind which afterwards
distinguished him among men. While studying at Cambridge,
it is reported that he was struck with the defects of the philosophical methods, founded upon the scholastic or Aristotelian
system, then universally adopted in the investigations of science.
Then, perhaps, first dawned upon his mind the dim outline of that
great reformation in philosophy which he was destined afterwards
to bring about. After a residence of about four years on the
Continent, whither he had been sent to prepare himself for a
public career, he was recalled home by the death of his father in
1579, and found himself under the necessity of entering upon some
active employment. He appears to have been treated with great
harshness and indifference by his kinsfolk, the Cecils, who are said
to have refused him the means of devoting himself to his favourite
scientific pursuits, and insisted on his embracing the profession of
the law. He became a student of Gray's Inn; and that wonderful
aptitude, to which no labour was too arduous and no subtlety too
refined, very soon made him the most distinguished advocate of
his day, and an admired teacher of the legal science. But the
countenance which was refused to Bacon by his uncle, he obtained
from the generous friendship of Essex, who, after a prolonged but
useless effort to obtain for him the place of Solicitor-General, con-
soled him by the gift of a considerable estate. Bacon now rose
rapidly, both in professional reputation as a lawyer, and in fame
for philosophy and eloquence. He sat in the House of Commons,
and gave evidence not only of unequalled powers as a speaker,
but also of that cowardly and interested subservience to the Court
which was the great blot upon his glory. After submitting for a
time to the haughty reproaches of the Cecils, he abandoned their
faction for that of Essex, whom he flattered and betrayed. On the
unhappy Earl's trial for high treason in 1601, Bacon in his capacity
of Queen's Counsel took an active part in his prosecution, and employed his immense powers, as an advocate and a pamphleteer, to
precipitate his ruin and to blacken his memory.

On the accession of James I. in 1603, Bacon attached himself
first to Carr, the ignoble favourite of that prince, and afterwards to
Carr's successor, the haughty Buckingham. He had been knighted
at the coronation; and at the same time married Alice Barnham, a
young lady of considerable fortune, the daughter of a London
alderman. He sat in more than one parliament, and was successively made Solicitor-General, Attorney-General, and at last, in
1617, Lord Keeper and Baron Verulam; which titles were further
augmented shortly afterwards by those of Lord Chancellor and

Viscount St. Albans. Bacon exhibited, in the discharge of his great functions, the wisdom and eloquence which characterised his mind, and the servility and meanness which disgraced his conduct; and on the assembling of Parliament in 1621, the House of Commons, then filled with just indignation against insupportable abuses, ordered a deliberate investigation into various acts of bribery of which the Chancellor was accused. The King and the favourite, though ready to do all in their power to screen a devoted servant, were not bold enough to face the indignation of the country. Bacon was impeached; he made a full acknowledgment of his guilt; he lost his place as Chancellor, and was condemned to pay a fine of 40,000*l.*, to be imprisoned during the King's pleasure, to be ever after incapable of holding any office in the State, and to be incapacitated from sitting in Parliament or coming within twelve miles of the Court. But not only was a full remission of these penalties soon after conceded by the Court, but a pension of 1200*l.* a year was granted him for life.

The life of the fallen Minister was prolonged for five years after his severe but merited disgrace; and these years were the most fruitful of his life to posterity, in spite of the incessant distractions and pecuniary embarrassments that harassed him. His death took place, after a few days' illness, on the 9th April, 1626, and was caused by a cold and fever caught near Highgate, while he was engaged in stuffing a fowl with snow in the open air. And so, to use the words of Lord Macaulay, "the great apostle of experimental philosophy was destined to be its martyr." Bacon was buried, at his own desire, by his mother's side in St. Michael's Church, St. Alban's, near which place was the magnificent seat of Gorhambury, constructed by himself.

In order to appreciate the services which Bacon rendered to the cause of truth and knowledge, we must dismiss from our minds that common and most erroneous imagination that Bacon was an inventor or a discoverer in any specific branch of knowledge. His mission was not to teach mankind a philosophy, but to teach them how to philosophise. To devise a new and more effectual method of attaining truth, not to build up a new system of philosophy, was Bacon's prime object; and the excellence of this method can be nowhere more clearly seen than in the instances in which he has himself applied it to facts which in his day were imperfectly known or erroneously explained. The most brilliant name among the ancient philosophers is incontestably that of Aristotle; throughout the Middle Ages his authority was supreme; to question his judgment on a matter of science was a crime only second to heterodoxy in religion. But the instrumental or mechanical part of his system,

the mode by which he taught his followers that they could arrive
at true deductions in scientific investigation, on falling into inferior
hands, was singularly liable to be abused. And so completely
had this ancient deductive method been transformed in its
passage through the Middle Ages, that its uselessness for the
attainment of truth had become apparent; and a great reform was
soon to be inevitable long before Bacon's time. To the errors
arising from the abstract and excessive refinements of the cloister
had been added those proceeding from the unfortunate alliance
between the philosophical system of the Schools and the authority
of the Church; which eventually proved as fatal to the authority
of the one as ruinous to the value of the other. Moreover, the Aristotelian method of investigation, even in its pure and normal state,
had been always obnoxious to the charge of infertility, and of
being essentially stationary and unprogressive. The ultimate aim
and object of its speculations was the attainment of abstract truth ;
practical utility was regarded as an end which, whether attained
or not, was below the dignity of the true sage.

The great object which Bacon proposed to himself, in proclaiming
the advantages of the Inductive Method, was *fruit:* the improvement of the condition of mankind. From an early age he had been
struck with the defects, with the stationary and unproductive character, of the Deductive Method: and during the whole of his
brilliant, agitated, and, alas ! too often ignominious career, he had
constantly and patiently laboured, adding stone after stone to that
splendid edifice which will enshrine his name when his crimes and
weaknesses, his ambition and servility, shall be forgotten. His
philosophical system is contained in the great work, or rather series
of works, to which he intended to give the general title of *Instauratio Magna*, or Great Institution of True Philosophy. The whole
of this neither was, nor ever could have been, executed by one man,
or by the labours of one age; for every new addition to the stock of
human knowledge would, as Bacon plainly saw, modify the conclusions, though it would not affect otherwise than by confirming
the soundness, of the philosophical method he propounded. The
Instauratio was to consist of six separate parts or books, of which
the following is a short synoptical arrangement :—

I. *Partitiones Scientiarum:* a summary or classification of all
    knowledge, with indications of those branches which had
    been more or less imperfectly treated.

II. *Novum Organum :* the New Instrument— an exposition of the
    methods to be adopted in the investigation of truth, with

indications of the principal sources of human error, and the remedies against that error in future.

III. *Phenomena Universi:* a complete body of well-observed facts and experiments in all branches of human knowledge, to furnish the raw material upon which the new method was to be applied, in order to obtain results of truth.

IV. *Scala Intellectus:* rules for the gradual ascent of the mind from particular instances or phenomena, to principles continually more and more abstract.

V. *Prodromi:* anticipations or forestallings of the New Philosophy, *i. e.,* such truths as could be, so to say, provisionally established, to be afterwards tested by the application of the New Method.

VI. *Philosophia Secunda:* the result of the just, careful, and complete application of the methods previously laid down to the vast body of facts to be accumulated and observed, in accordance with the rules and precautions contained in the IInd and IVth parts.

Let us now inquire what portion of this project Bacon was able to execute. The first portion was published in 1605, in an English treatise, bearing the title of *The Proficience and Advancement of Learning,* which was afterwards much altered and extended, and republished in Latin, in 1623, under the title *De Augmentis Scientiarum.* The *Novum Organum,* the most important portion of the work—in short, a compendium of the Baconian logic—was published, in Latin, in 1620. Of the Third Book, Bacon has given only a specimen, consisting of a History of the Winds, of Life and Death, written in Latin ; and a collection of experiments in Physics, or, as he calls it, Natural History, in English. This portion of the work is alone sufficient to show how small are Bacon's claims or pretensions to the character of a *discoverer* in any branch of natural science, and how completely he was under the influence of the errors of his day; but at the same time it proves the innate merit of his method, and the power of that mind which could legislate for the whole realm of knowledge, and for sciences yet unborn. To the English fragment he gives the title of *Silva Silvarum,* i.e., a collection of materials. Of the Fourth Book, *Scala Intellectus,* Bacon has given us but a brief abstract; of the Fifth only a preface ; and of the Sixth nothing at all.

To prove the soundness and the fertility of Bacon's method of investigation, we have only to compare the progress made by humanity in all the useful arts during the two centuries and a half since induction has been generally employed in all branches of science, with the progress made during the twenty centuries which elapsed between Aristotle and the age of Bacon. It is no exaggeration to say, that in the shorter interval that progress has been ten times greater than in the longer. Nor is this in any degree attributable to any superiority of the human intellect in modern times; never did humanity produce intellects more vast, more penetrating, and more active, than the series of great men who wasted their powers in abstract questions which never could be solved, or in the sterile subtleties of scholastic disputation. In those sciences, too, which are independent of experiment — as theology for instance, or pure geometry—the ancients were fully as far advanced as we are at this moment. The glory of Bacon is founded upon a union of speculative power with practical utility, which were never so combined before. He neglected nothing as too small, despised nothing as too low, by which our happiness could be augmented; in him above all were combined boldness and prudence, the intensest enthusiasm and the plainest common sense. It is probable that Bacon generally wrote the first sketch of his works in English, but afterwards caused them to be translated into Latin, which was at that time the language of science, and even of diplomacy. He is reported to have employed the services of many young men of learning as secretaries and translators; among these the most remarkable is Hobbes, afterwards so celebrated as the author of the *Leviathan*. The style, in which the Latin books of the *Instauratio* were given to the world, though certainly not a model of classical purity, is weighty, vigorous, and picturesque.

Bacon's English writings are very numerous; among them unquestionably the most important is the little volume entitled *Essays*, the first edition of which, consisting of only ten, he published in 1597, and the last in 1625, by which time the number had grown to fifty-eight. These are short papers on an immense variety of subjects, from grave questions of morals and policy down to the arts of amusement and the most trifling accomplishments; and in them appears, in a manner more appreciable to ordinary intellects than in his elaborate philosophical works, the wonderful union of depth and variety which characterises Bacon. The intellectual activity they display is literally portentous, the immense multiplicity and aptness of unexpected illustration is only equalled by the originality with which Bacon manages to treat the most worn-out and commonplace subject,—such, for instance, as friendship or gardening. No author was ever so concise as Bacon: and in his mode of writing there is that remarkable quality which gives to the style of Shakespeare such a strongly-marked individuality—that is, a combination of the intellectual and imaginative, the closest reasoning in the boldest metaphor, the condensed brilliancy of an illustration identified with the development of thought. It is this that renders both the dramatist and the philosopher at once the richest and the most concise of writers. Many of Bacon's essays, as that inimitable one on *Studies*, are absolutely oppressive from the power of thought compressed into the smallest possible compass. His Latin treatise *De Sapientia Veterum*—afterwards translated into English as the *Wisdom of the Ancients*—was an attempt to explain the political and moral truths concealed in the classical mythology. He also wrote an unfinished Romance, the *New Atlantis*, which was intended to embody the fulfilment of his own dreams of a philosophical millennium : a *History of Henry VII.*, and a vast number of state-papers, judicial decisions, and other professional writings. All these are marked by the same vigorous, weighty, and somewhat ornamented style which is to be found in the *Instauratio*, and are among the finest specimens of the English language at its period of highest majesty and perfection.

It is by his *Essays* that Bacon is most widely known. "Coming home," as he says himself, "to men's business and bosoms," they gained, even in his own time, an extensive popularity, which they still retain. As a natural consequence, this success attracted others into the same path ; and in no long time it came to be recognised as a distinct walk in literature. One of the first to venture into it to some purpose was SIR THOMAS OVERBURY (1581-1613), the victim of the infamous Countess of Somerset; whose *Characters*, if somewhat different in form, possess all the material features of this kind of composition, and are an attempt to throw off, in a few bold strokes, certain remarkable types of humanity. Of these characters the "Fair and Happy Milkmaid" is the best. The *Micro-cosmographie* of JOHN EARLE (1600-1665), Dean of Westminster and a Bishop after the Restoration, which was first published in 1628, is a work exactly similar to Overbury's ; and though inferior to it in originality, is much superior in style and literary finish. A prominent place in the same province is generally assigned to OWEN FELTHAM (1610-1678?), the first part of whose *Resolves*, or attempted solution of difficult problems in morals, appeared in 1627; but Mr. Hallam pronounces him to be "not only a laboured and artificial, but a shallow writer."

But the most notable of the contemporary writers of this class was ROBERT BURTON (1576-1640), distinguished by eccentricity alike in life and works. The principal of these, the *Anatomy of Melan-*

choly, which purported to be written by " Democritus, junior," is a strange combination of the most extensive and out-of-the-way reading with just observation and a peculiar kind of grave saturnine humour. The object of the writer was to give a complete monography of Melancholy, and to point out its causes, its symptoms, its treatment, and its cure; but the descriptions given of the various phases of the disease are written in so curious and pedantic a style, accompanied with such an infinity of quaint observation, and illustrated by such a mass of quotations from a crowd of authors, principally the medical writers of the fourteenth and fifteenth centuries, of whom not one reader in a thousand in the present day has ever heard, that the *Anatomy* possesses a charm which no one can resist who has once fallen under its fascination. The greater part of Burton's laborious life was passed in the University of Oxford, where he died, not without suspicion of having hastened his own end, in order that it might exactly correspond with the astrological predictions which he is said, being a firm believer in that science, to have drawn from his own horoscope.

LORD HERBERT OF CHERBURY (1581-1648), an elder brother of " holy George Herbert," was a man of great learning and rare dignity of personal character; and was employed in an embassy to Paris in 1616. There he first published his principal work, the treatise *De Veritate*, an elaborate pleading in favour of Deism, of which Herbert was one of the earliest partisans in England. He also left a *History of Henry VIII.*, not published until after his death, and which is certainly a valuable monument of grave and vigorous prose; though the historical merit of the work is diminished by the author's strong partiality in favour of the character of the king.

Two of the minor historians of this age, RICHARD KNOLLES and SAMUEL DANIEL, the latter the well-known poet, deserve a passing notice. The first published, in 1610, a copious *History of the Turks*, which has won the emphatic approval of Dr. Johnson, who finds in it " all the excellences that narrative can admit. His style, though somewhat obscured by time, and vitiated by false wit, is pure, nervous, elevated, and clear." The second, in 1618, gave to the world a *History of England*, from the Conquest to the reign of Edward III., in which Mr. Hallam discovers many merits in language, style, and diction. The *Britannia* of WILLIAM CAMDEN (1551-1623), founder of the first chair of History at Oxford, is still quoted as a trustworthy authority on the topography of Great Britain from the earliest times.

CHAPTER XII

THE SO-CALLED METAPHYSICAL POETS.

In its literary aspect the agitated epoch of the seventeenth century, though not marked by any marvellous outburst of creative power, has yet left deep traces on the turn of thought and expression of the English people; and confining ourselves to the department of poetry, and excluding the solitary example in Milton of a poet of the first class, we may say that this period introduced a class of excellent writers in whom the intellect and the fancy play a greater part than sentiment or passion. Ingenuity predominates over feeling; and while Milton owed much to many of these poets, whom Johnson has styled the *metaphysical* class, nevertheless we must allow that they had much to do with generating the so-called correct and artificial manner which distinguishes the classical writers of the age of William, Anne, and the first George.

The founder of this fantastic school was undoubtedly JOHN DONNE (1573-1631), who has been already mentioned (p. 59) as one of our first satirists. A tendency to intellectual subtlety had set in early in the reign of Elizabeth, infecting prose and verse alike; and after a time the fashion became so universal that no man of genius, not even Shakespeare himself, escaped its influence. But what was in the great dramatist merely an occasional infirmity, became in John Donne the law of his literary nature, the essential feature of his verse. To run every thought that entered his brain through a series of the most remote, and in many cases most repulsive, analogies, generally physical and almost invariably inappropriate, seemed to him to be all that was necessary to constitute poetry. Donne's youth and early manhood were passed in the society of the wits of the Mermaid; and besides his satires, already spoken of, the chief products of his muse at this period were the *Metempsychosis*, and a series of amatory poems, which afterwards he would fain have suppressed. Entering the Church in later life he eventually became Dean of St. Paul's, when he not only wrote his *Divine Poems*, but became famous as a theologian and pulpit-orator. Donne's reputation in his own time was almost the highest; "rare Ben" pronounced him "the first poet in the world in some things;" but with unerring prophetic insight declared that "for not being understood he would perish."

GEORGE WITHER (1588-1667) and FRANCIS QUARLES (1592-1644) are a pair of poets whose writings have a considerable degree of resemblance in manner and subject, and whose lives were similar in misfortune. Wither took an active part in the Civil War, attained command under the administration of Cromwell; but had previously undergone severe persecution and long imprisonment. His most important work is a collection of poems, of a partially pastoral character, entitled the *Shepherds' Hunting*, in which the reader will find frequent rural descriptions of exquisite fancifulness and beauty, together with a sweet and pure tone of moral reflection. The vice of Wither, as it was generally of the literature of his age, was a passion for ingenious turns and unexpected conceits, which bear the same relation to really beautiful thoughts that plays upon words do to true wit. Many of his detached lyrics —as *The Steadfast Shepherd*, *The Shepherd's Resolution*—are extremely beautiful, and the verse is generally flowing and melodious. He was perhaps the most prolific versifier of the day, throwing off all manner of composition with amazing facility. His *Hymns and Songs of the Church*, and his *Hallelujah*, possess considerable merit; and of his innumerable satires, the *Abuses Stript and Whipt*, for which he was imprisoned, was the most popular. Quarles, though a Royalist as ardent as Wither was a devoted Republican, exhibits many points of intellectual resemblance to Wither; to whom, however, he was far inferior in poetical sentiment. One of his most popular works is a collection of *Divine Emblems*, in which moral and religious precepts are inculcated in short poems of a most quaint character, and illustrated by engravings filled with what may be called allegory run mad.

GEORGE HERBERT (1593-1633) and RICHARD CRASHAW (circa 1620 1650) exhibit the highest exaltation of religious sentiment; and are both worthy of admiration, not only as Christian poets, but as good men and pious priests. George Herbert was born in 1593, and at first rendered himself remarkable by the graces and accomplishments of the courtly scholar; but afterwards entering the Church, he exhibited, as parish priest at Bemerton in Wiltshire, all the virtues which can adorn the country parson—a character he has beautifully described in a prose treatise under that title. His poems, principally religious, are generally short lyrics, combining pious aspiration with frequent and beautiful pictures of nature. He decorates the altar with the sweetest and most fragrant flowers of fancy and of wit. Though not devoid of that perverted ingenuity which deformed Quarles and Wither, he has almost attained the perfection of devotional poetry—a calm and yet ardent glow, a well-governed fervour which seems peculiarly to belong to the Church of which he was a minister. His collection of sacred lyrics is entitled the *Temple, or Sacred Poems and Private Ejaculations.*

Crashaw was brought up in the Anglican Church, and received a learned education at Oxford; but during the Puritan troubles he embraced the Romish faith, in whose communion he died, as a canon of Loretto. The mystical tendency of his mind was increased by his misfortunes and by his change of religion. That he possessed an exquisite fancy, great melody of verse, and that power over the reader which nothing can replace, and which springs from deep earnestness, no one can deny. The most favourable specimens of his poetry are the *Steps to the Temple*, and the beautiful description entitled *Music's Duel.*

Love, romantic loyalty, and airy elegance, find their best representatives in four charming poets whose works may be examined under one general head. These are ROBERT HERRICK (1591-1674), SIR JOHN SUCKLING (1609-1641), SIR RICHARD LOVELACE (1618-1658), and THOMAS CAREW (1589-1639). The first of these writers, after beginning his career among the brilliant but somewhat debauched literary society of the town and the theatre, took orders; but still continued to exhibit in some of his writings the same graceful but voluptuous spirit which distinguished his early works. His poems, which were published in 1648 under the name of *Hesperides* and *Noble Numbers*, are all lyric; the former generally songs upon love and wine, the latter upon sacred subjects. In Herrick we find the most unaccountable mixture of sensual coarseness with exquisite refinement; yet in fancy, in genius, in power over the melody of verse, he is never deficient. Suckling and Lovelace are the types of the Cavalier poet; both suffered in the King's cause; and both exemplify the spirit of loyalty to their king, and gallantry to the ladies. Many of Suckling's love songs are equal, if not superior, to the most beautiful examples of that mixture of gay badinage and tender if not very deep-felt devotion which characterises French courtly and erotic poetry in the seventeenth century. His most exquisite production is his *Ballad upon a Wedding*, in which, assuming the character of a rustic, he describes the marriage of a fashionable couple, Lord Broghill and Lady Margaret Howard. Lovelace is more serious and earnest than Suckling; his lyrics breathe rather devoted loyalty than the half-passionate, half-jesting love-fancy of his rival. Such are the beautiful lines to Althea, composed when the author was closely confined in the Gate-house at Westminster. Carew's lyrics reflect the same spirit as Suckling's; his *Inquiry, Primrose*, and his " He that loves a rosy cheek," have all the grace and airy elegance that characterise such works.

The writings of WILLIAM HABINGTON (1605–1654) are principally devoted to love. He celebrates, with much ingenuity and occasional grace, the charms and virtues of a lady whom he calls Castara—she was Lucy, daughter of William Herbert Lord Powis—and who was not only his ideal mistress, but his wife. Habington, like Crashaw, was a Catholic; and his poems are free from that immorality which so often stains the graceful fancies of the poets of this age.

But the most prominent and popular figures of this period, and the writers who exerted the strongest influence on their own time, are Waller and Cowley; to which may be added the secondary but still important names of Denham and Davenant.

EDMUND WALLER (1605–1687) was of ancient and dignified family, of great wealth, and a man of varied accomplishments and fascinating manners; but his character was timid and selfish; and he exhibited repeated indications of tergiversation in those difficult times, professing adherence to Puritan and Republican doctrines while really sympathising with the Court party. Even his consummate adroitness did not always succeed in securing impunity; and in 1643, being convicted by the House of a plot to betray London to the King, it was only by an abject submission that he narrowly escaped capital punishment, being imprisoned, fined 10,000*l.*, and obliged to exile himself for some time, which he passed in France. Though the first cousin of Hampden, and so a family connexion of Oliver Cromwell himself, whom he has celebrated in one of his finest poems, Waller was ready to hail with enthusiasm every new change in the political world; and he panegyrised Cromwell and Charles II. with equal fervour, though not with equal effect. He lived to see the accession of James II., whose policy he prophesied would lead to the fatal results that afterwards occurred. In his own day, and in the succeeding generation, Waller's poetry enjoyed the highest reputation. He was said to have carried to perfection the art of expressing graceful and sensible ideas in the clearest and most harmonious language; and his example acted powerfully on Dryden and Pope, both of whom confessed their obligations to him. Regular, reasonable, well-balanced, well-proportioned, the lines of Waller always gratify the judgment, but never touch the heart or fire the imagination. Most of his poems are love verses, written mainly in honour of Lady Dorothy Sidney, whom he long wooed in vain under the name of Saccharissa, but his panegyric on Cromwell, as well as the lines on his death, contain many passages of great dignity and force. He was less felicitous in his longer work, the *Battle of the Summer Islands*, in which, in a half-serious, half-comic strain, he described an attack upon two stranded whales in the Bermudas.

Sir WILLIAM DAVENANT (1605–1668) is principally interesting to us at the present day as being connected with the revival of the theatre at the termination of the severe Puritan rule; and though a most ardent and sincere worshipper of the genius of Shakespeare, he was obliged—such was the debased taste of the age—in attempting to revive his works, to alter their spirit so completely, that every honest reader must regard the adaptations with absolute disgust. Already before the rout of the Cavaliers he had succeeded Ben Jonson as laureate, and was long connected with the Court Theatre; and both in the dramas which he composed himself, and in those which he adapted and placed upon the stage, we see how far the taste for splendour of scenery, dances, music, and decoration, had usurped the passion of the earlier public for truth and intensity in the picturing of life and nature. Principally through the influence of French tastes, the mechanical accessories of the stage had been immensely improved; and actresses, young, beautiful, and skilful, had usurped the place of the boys of the Elizabethan age. Davenant was a most prolific author, not only in the dramatic department,—in which his most popular productions were *Albovine*, the *Siege of Rhodes*, the *Law against Lovers*, the *Cruel Brother*, and many others,—but also as a narrative poet. His incomplete poem of *Gondibert* narrates a long series of lofty and chivalric adventures in a dignified but somewhat monotonous manner; and is written in a peculiar four-lined stanza with alternate rhymes, afterwards employed by Dryden in his *Annus Mirabilis*.

Sir JOHN DENHAM (1615–1668), the " majestic Denham " of Pope, was the son of the Chief Baron of the Exchequer in Ireland, and a supporter of Charles I. One work of his, *Cooper's Hill*, will always occupy an important place in English Literature; a place which it owes not only to its specific merits, but also to the circumstance that it was the first work in that peculiar department, called local or topographic poetry, in which the writer chooses some individual scene as the object round which he is to accumulate his descriptive or contemplative passages. Denham selected for this purpose a beautiful spot near Windsor on the Thames, and in the description of the scene itself, as well as in the reflections it suggests, he has risen to a noble elevation.

One of the most accomplished and influential writers of the period was ABRAHAM COWLEY (1618–1667). He was a remarkable instance of intellectual precocity, for in 1633 he published his first poems, filled with enthusiasm by the *Faery Queen* of Spenser, when only

15 years of age. After residing at Cambridge for seven years he was, in 1643, expelled for his Royalist sympathies, and went to St. John's College, in Oxford. He bore among his contemporaries the reputation of being one of the best scholars and most distinguished poets of his age. Notwithstanding his devotion to, and sufferings in, the Royal cause, he was disappointed in obtaining at the Restoration such a provision as he thought his services had deserved; but receiving a grant of some Crown leases, producing a moderate income, he quitted London and went to reside near Chertsey, with the intention of passing the rest of his life in literary ease. A few years afterwards he died of a fever caused by imprudence and excess, but not before he had learned the melancholy truth that annoyances and vexations pursue us even into the recesses of rural obscurity.

Cowley is highly regarded among the writers of his time both as a poet and an essayist. Immense and multifarious learning, well digested by reflection, renders his prose works, in which he frequently intermingles passages of verse, most delightful reading. As a poet, the reputation of Cowley, immense in his own day, has much diminished; he has very little passion or depth of sentiment; and in his love-verses, collectively called *The Mistress*, he substitutes the play of the intellect for the unaffected outpouring of the feelings. He paraphrased the *Odes of Anacreon;* and his *Pindarics* were " written in imitation of the Stile and Manner of Pindar;" but these odes have only an external resemblance to those of the " Theban Eagle." Cowley seems always on the watch to seize some ingenious and unexpected parallelism of ideas or images; and when the illustration is so found, the shock of surprise which the reader feels is rather akin to a flash of wit than to an electric stroke of genius. In the mighty movement to which the Royal Society owed its foundation Cowley deeply sympathised : and perhaps the finest of his lyric compositions is the *Ode to the Royal Society*, in which, with a grave and well-adorned eloquence, he proclaims the genius, and predicts the triumph, of Bacon and his disciples in physical science.

One long epic poem of great pretension Cowley meditated, but left unfinished. This is the *Davideis*, the subject of which is the sufferings and glories of the King of Israel. But this work is now completely neglected. The genius of Cowley was far more lyric than epic; and in his shorter compositions he exerted an influence upon the style of English poetry which is especially traceable in the writings of Dryden, Pope, and subsequent poets.

CHAPTER XIII.

THEOLOGICAL WRITERS OF THE CIVIL WAR AND THE COMMONWEALTH.

THE Civil War of the seventeenth century was in many respects a religious as well as a political contest; and the prose literature of this time, therefore, exhibits a strong religious or theological character. The most glorious outburst of theological eloquence which the Church of England has exhibited, in the writings of Jeremy Taylor, Barrow, and the other great Anglican Fathers, was responded to by the appearance, in the ranks of the sectaries, of many remarkable men, hardly inferior to them in learning and genius, and fully equal in earnestness and enthusiasm.

JOHN HALES (1584–1656), surnamed "the ever-memorable John Hales," was a man who enjoyed among his contemporaries an immense reputation for the vastness of his learning and the acuteness of his wit. The greater part of his writings are controversial, treating on the politico-religious questions that then agitated men's minds. He had been present at the Synod of Dort, as an agent of the English Church, and has given an interesting account of the questions debated in that assembly. Both in his controversial writings and in his sermons he exhibits a fine example of that rich yet chastened eloquence which characterises the great English divines of the seventeenth century.

WILLIAM CHILLINGWORTH (1602–1644), also an eminent defender of Protestantism against the Church of Rome, was converted to the Roman Catholic faith while studying at Oxford, and went to the Jesuits' College at Douay. But he subsequently returned to Oxford, renounced his new faith, and published in 1637 his celebrated work against Catholicism, entitled *The Religion of the Protestants a Safe Way to Salvation*. "His chief excellence," says Mr. Hallam, "is the close reasoning which avoids every dangerous admission, and yields to no ambiguousness of language. In later times his book obtained a high reputation; he was called the immortal Chillingworth; he was the favourite of all the moderate and the latitudinarian writers, of Tillotson, Locke, and Warburton."

The writings of Sir THOMAS BROWNE (1605–1682), though not exclusively theological, belong, chronologically as well as by their style and manner to this department. He was an exceedingly learned man, and passed the greater part of his life in practising physic in the ancient city of Norwich.   Among the most popular of his works are the treatise entitled *Hydriotaphia, or Urn-Burial*, and the Essays on *Vulgar Errors*, which bear the name of *Pseudoxia Epidemica*.   The first of these treatises was suggested by the digging up in Norfolk of some Roman funeral urns; and the other is an attempt to overthrow many of the common superstitions and erroneous notions on various subjects.   They are the frank and undis- guised outpourings of one of the most eccentric and original minds that ever existed.   At every step the author starts some extraor- dinary theory, which he illustrates by the most singular and unex- pected analogies, and all this in a style absolutely bristling with quaint Latinisms, which in another writer would be pedantic, but in Browne were the natural garb of his thought.   All this makes him one of the most amusing of writers ; and he very frequently rises to a sombre and touching eloquence.   The book, in which he communicates his own personal opinions and feelings most un- reservedly, is the *Religio Medici*, a species of Confession of Faith ; in which, however, he by no means confines himself to theological matters.

THOMAS FULLER (1608–1661) is another great and attractive prose-writer of this period, and has in some respects a kind of intel- lectual resemblance to Browne.   Educated at Cambridge, he en- tered the Church, and soon rendering himself conspicuous in the pulpit, he was nominated preacher at the Savoy in London.   At the outbreak of the Civil War, he excited the dissatisfaction of both factions by his studied moderation ; but was for a time attached, as chaplain, to the army commanded by Sir Ralph Hopton in the West of England.   During his campaigning Fuller industriously collected the materials for his most popular work, the *Worthies of England and Wales*, which, however, was not published until after the author's death.   This, more than his *Church History*, is the production with which posterity has generally associated the name of Fuller : but his *Sermons* frequently exhibit those singular pecu- liarities of style which render him one of the most remarkable writers of his age.   His writings are eminently *amusing ;* not only from the multiplicity of curious and anecdotic details which they contain, but from the odd and yet frequently profound reflections suggested by those details.   The *Worthies* contain biographical notices of eminent Englishmen, as connected with the different counties, and furnish an inexhaustible treasure of curious stories and observations : but whatever the subject Fuller treats, he places it in such a number of new and unexpected lights, and introduces in illustration of it such a number of ingenious remarks, that the attention of the reader is incessantly kept alive. He was a man of a pleasant as well as an ingenious turn of mind: there is no sourness in his way of thinking; flashes of fancy are made to light up the gravest subjects, and the sparkle of his wit is warmed by a glow of sympathy and tenderness. One great source of his picturesqueness is his frequent use of antithesis; not a bare opposition of *words*, but the juxtaposition of apparently discordant *ideas*, from whose sudden contact there flashes forth the spark of wit. In a word, he was essentially a wise and learned humourist.

But by far the greatest theological writer of the Anglican Church at this period was JEREMY TAYLOR (1613–1667). The son of a barber at Cambridge, he received a sound education at the Grammar-School of that town, and afterwards studied at Caius College, where his talents and learning soon made him conspicuous. He took holy orders at an unusually early age, and is said to have attracted by his youthful eloquence the notice of Laud, who, struck with a sermon of Taylor's, made him one of his chaplains, and procured for him a fellowship in All Souls' College, Oxford. During the Civil War he stood high in the favour of the Cavaliers and the Court; and, whilst serving as chaplain in the Royalist army, was taken prisoner in 1644 at the action fought under the walls of Cardigan Castle. The King's cause growing desperate, Taylor placed himself under the protection of his friend Lord Carbery, and resided for some time at the seat of Golden Grove, belonging to that nobleman, in Carmarthenshire. Taylor was twice married; first to Phœbe Langdale, who died early, and afterwards to Joanna Bridges, a natural daughter of Charles I., with whom he received some fortune. He was unhappy in his children, his two sons having been notorious for their profligacy; and he had the sorrow of surviving them both. He underwent many hardships and persecutions during the Commonwealth period; but on the Restoration he was made Bishop of Down and Connor, and during the short time he held that preferment he exhibited the brightest qualities that can adorn the episcopal dignity. He died at Lisburn of a fever, in 1667, and left behind him a high reputation for courtesy, charity, and zeal—all the virtues of a Christian Bishop.

In the controversial department Taylor's best-known work is the treatise *On the Liberty of Prophesying* (*i. e.*, Preaching), published in 1647, which is the first complete and systematic defence of the great principle of religious toleration: and though intended by Taylor to secure indulgence for the then persecuted Episcopal Church, is of course, equally applicable to all forms of religion. An *Apology for Fixed and Set Forms of Worship* was an elaborate defence of the noble ritual of the Anglican Church. Among his

works of a disciplinary and practical tendency may be mentioned
his *Life of Christ, the Great Exemplar*, in which the details scattered
through the Evangelists and the Fathers are co-ordinated in a continuous narrative. But the most popular of Taylor's writings are
the two admirable treatises, *On the Rule and Exercise of Holy Living*,
and *On the Rule and Exercise of Holy Dying*, which mutually correspond to and complete each other, and which form an Institute of
Christian life and conduct, adapted to every conceivable circum
stance and relation of human existence. The least admirable of his
numerous writings is the *Ductor Dubitantium*, a treatise on questions
of casuistry. His *Sermons* are very numerous, and are among the
most eloquent, learned, and powerful, that the whole range of Protestant—nay, the whole range of Christian—literature has produced.
As in his character, so in his writings, Taylor is the ideal of an
Anglican pastor, exhibiting in both the union of consummate learning with practical simplicity and fervour.

Taylor's style, though occasionally overcharged with erudition, and
marked by that abuse of quotation which disfigures a great deal of
the prose of that age, is uniformly magnificent; his periods roll on
with a soft yet mighty swell, which has often something of the enchantment of verse. He has been called by the critic Jeffrey "the
most Shakespearian of our great divines;" but it would be more
appropriate to compare him with Spenser. He has the same pictorial
fancy, the same voluptuous and languishing harmony, as the latter:
though, like Shakespeare, he draws his illustrations from the simplest
and most familiar objects, and knows how to paint the terrible and
the sublime no less than the tender and the affecting. Nevertheless,
with Spenser's sweetness, he has occasionally something of the lus-
cious and enervate languor of Spenser's style. He had studied the
Fathers so intensely that he had become infected with something of
that lavish and Oriental imagery which many of those great writers
exhibited.

Many men eminent for learning, piety, and zeal, appeared in the
ranks of the Nonconformists; but if we omit the grandest names of
all—Milton and Bunyan—who are reserved for subsequent chapters
the only writer claiming a distinct notice here is Richard Baxter.

RICHARD BAXTER (1615–1691) was the consistent and unconquerable defender of the right of religious liberty; and in the evil
days of James II. was exposed to all the virulence and brutality of
the infamous Jeffreys and his worse than inquisitorial tribunal. He
was a man of vast learning, the purest piety, and the most indefatigable industry. His works are little known in the present day, with
the exception of *The Saints' Everlasting Rest*, and *A Call to the
Unconverted*.

CHAPTER XIV

JOHN MILTON.

ABOVE the seventeenth century towers, in solitary grandeur, the sublime figure of JOHN MILTON (1608–1674). He was born on the 9th December, 1608, in Bread-street, London, and was sprung from an Oxfordshire family. His father, an ardent Puritan, from whom the great poet seems to have inherited his political and religious sympathies, had quarrelled with his relations; and embracing the profession of a money-scrivener, had amassed a considerable fortune, so as to be able to retire to a pleasant country-house at Horton, near Colnbrook, in Buckinghamshire. The son was most carefully educated, first at home under Thomas Young, then at St. Paul's School, London, whence, in his seventeenth year, he entered Christ's College, Cambridge. He left Cambridge in 1632, after taking his Master's degree, and there are many allusions in his works which prove that the doctrines and discipline of the University at that time contained much that was distasteful to his haughty and uncontrolled spirit. His first attempts in poetry were made as early as his thirteenth year, so that he is as striking an instance of precocity as of power of genius; and his sublime *Hymn on the Nativity*, in which may plainly be seen all the characteristic features of his intellectual nature, was written in his twenty-first year. On leaving the University he resided for six years at his father's seat at Horton, where he passed his time in a course of study that seems to have embraced the whole circle of human knowledge. During this period of his life he wrote the pastoral drama, or Masque, of *Comus*, the lovely elegy on his friend King entitled *Lycidas*, and in all probability the descriptive gems *L'Allegro* and *Il Penseroso*. At this epoch his mind seems to have exhibited that exquisite susceptibility to all refined, courtly, and noble emotions which is so faithfully reflected in these works—emotions not incompatible in him with the severest purity of sentiment and the loftiest dignity of principle.

In 1638 the poet, now about thirty, set out upon his travels on the Continent—the completion of a perfect education. He visited the most celebrated cities of Italy, France, and Switzerland. He was received everywhere with marked respect and admiration, and appears

to have made acquaintance with all who were most illustrious for
learning and genius; with Galileo, "then grown old, a prisoner in the
Inquisition;" with John Diodati, a celebrated professor of theology
at Geneva, and uncle to his bosom-friend, Charles Diodati; with
Manso, Marquis of Villa, the distinguished poet and well-known friend
of Torquato Tasso. These friendships were in some degree the suggesting motive of many of his Italian and Latin poems; for in the
former language he wrote at least as well as the majority of the contemporary poets of any but the first class, and in the latter his compositions have never been surpassed by any modern writer of Latin
verse. But in spite of his eager desire to visit Greece, he was recalled to England in 1639 by the first mutterings of that political
tempest which was for a time to overthrow the Monarchy and the
Church. Into this momentous conflict he threw himself with all the
ardour of his temperament and convictions; and from this period
begins the second phase of his many-sided life.

To this, the most active period of Milton's career, belong almost
all his prose writings, which were mainly controversial; and for
twenty years he was the advocate of republican principles in the
State, and the most uncompromising enemy of the Episcopal Church.
His fortune being small, he opened a school in 1640; but among
those who had the honour of his instructions only two persons are
at all celebrated—his nephews, John and Edward Phillips, who have
contributed some details to the history of English Poetry.

In 1643 he married Mary Powell, the daughter of a ruined
country gentleman of strong Royalist sympathies; but soon dis-
gusted with the austerity of Milton's life, she fled to her father's
house, and was only recalled to the conjugal roof by a report that
her husband, basing his determination upon the Levitical law, was
meditating a new marriage with another person. The lady was for-
given by her husband; but the remaining years of her marriage were
probably not happy, though three daughters were the fruit of the
union. It is to this unfortunate incident in the poet's life that we
owe his writings on Divorce. The finest of the prose compositions
produced at this epoch was the *Areopagitica* (1644), an oration after
the antique model, addressed to the Parliament of England in defence
of the Liberty of the Press.

In 1649 Milton received the appointment of Latin Secretary to
the Council of State, a post which he retained under the administration of Cromwell; though, probably in consideration of his rapidly-
increasing infirmity of sight, were joined with him in his office first
Meadowes, and afterwards the excellent and accomplished Marvell.
In 1652 the loss of his sight became total; which calamity, in one of
his finest sonnets, he proudly attributes to his having overtasked it n

the defence of liberty; and in the character of the blinded Samson he undoubtedly shadows forth his own infirmity and his own feelings. It is noteworthy that in many passages, both in prose and verse, he expresses his sympathy with the glorious administration and great personal qualities of Cromwell; the faults of whose career he probably excused in consideration of the benefits which accompanied and the patriotic spirit which animated it.

Milton's most celebrated controversy was that with Salmasius (de Saumaise), one of the most learned men of his day, who had been employed by Charles II. to write what may be called a ponderous Latin pamphlet, invoking the vengeance of Heaven upon the regicide Parliament of England. Milton replied in his *Defensio Populi Anglicani*, maintaining the right and justifying the conduct of his countrymen in making war upon, dethroning, and decapitating, their king. His invectives are not less violent than those of his antagonist, his Latinity is not less elegant, but the controversy is as little honourable to the one as to the other combatant. The subjects of Milton's prose writings, for the most part, had only a temporary interest; but among those written in English we may note the *Apology for Smectymnuus*, in which Milton defends the pamphlet against episcopacy written by Smectymnuus;* in these writings he occasionally rises to a massive high-toned eloquence in those outbursts of enthusiasm that are intermingled with drier matter; the book called *Iconoclastes* or the *Image-breaker*—intended to neutralise the effect of the celebrated *Icon Basilike*, written by Dr. (afterwards Bishop) Gauden, in the character of Charles I.; *The Reason of Church Government Urged against Prelaty;* and *A Ready and Easy Way to Establish a Free Commonwealth;* which exhibit in their titles the nature of their subjects. In his *Tractate on Education*, which appeared in 1644, he has drawn up a beautiful, but entirely Utopian, scheme for remodelling the whole system of training, and reducing it to something like the antique pattern.

The Restoration, in 1660, was naturally the signal of distress and persecution to one who by his writings had shown himself the most consistent, persevering, and formidable enemy of monarchy and episcopacy, and who had attacked, with particular vehemence, the character of Charles I. He concealed himself; but a proclamation was issued against him, and for a time his fate was uncertain. After a few months, however, the Act of Indemnity was passed without his name appearing in the list of exceptions; and the great

---

* This strange name is a kind of anagram composed of the initials of its five authors, the chief of whom was Thomas Young, Milton's deeply-venerated Puritan preceptor.

poet was safe. It is said that Sir W. Davenant successfully used his influence in his favour. From this period till his death he lived in close retirement, busily occupied in the composition of *Paradise Lost* and *Paradise Regained.* The former of these works was finished in 1665, and had been his principal employment during about seven years. The companion epic, a work of much shorter extent, as well as the noble and pathetic tragedy of *Samson Agonistes,* were published in the year 1671. On the 8th of November, 1674, Milton died, at the age of sixty-six, and was buried in Cripplegate churchyard. His first wife had died about 1652, leaving him three daughters; his second, Katharine Woodcock, in 1658, after little more than a year's marriage; but his third, Elizabeth Minshull, whom he espoused about 1664, survived him for thirty years.

Milton's literary career divides itself naturally into three great periods—that of his youth, that of his manhood, and that of his old age. The first may be roughly stated as extending from 1623 to 1640; the second from 1640 to 1660, the date of the Restoration; and the third from the Restoration to the poet's death in 1674. During the first of these he produced the principal poetical works marked by a graceful, tender character, and on miscellaneous subjects; during the second he was chiefly occupied with his prose controversies; and in the third we see him slowly elaborating the *Paradise Lost,* the *Paradise Regained,* and the *Samson Agonistes.*

(i.) The chief qualities that distinguish his early poems,—of which the most notable are *The Hymn on the Nativity, L'Allegro, Il Penseroso, Arcades, Comus,* and *Lycidas*—are a peculiar majesty of conception, combined with consummate though somewhat austere harmony and grace. Above all there is visible, in even the least elaborate of Milton's poems, a peculiar solemn weighty melody of versification, that fills and satisfies the ear like the billowy sound of a mighty organ; of which quality the *Hymn on the Nativity* is the most brilliant example. This magnificent ode is a fitting prelude to the *Paradise Lost.*

In the Masque of *Comus,* Milton communicated to what was originally a mere vehicle for elegant adulation a pure and lofty ethical tone, that soars into the very empyrean of moral speculation. This drama was written in 1634, to be performed at Ludlow Castle, in the presence of the Earl of Bridgewater, lately appointed Lord President of Wales. It seems to have been composed at the request of Henry Lawes, then a well-known musician and composer in the service of the Earl, and an intimate friend of Milton. The characters are few, consisting of the lady, a part played by the Lady Alice Egerton, the two Brothers, Comus (a wicked enchanter, the

allegorical representative of vicious and sensual pleasure), and the
Attendant Spirit, disguised as a shepherd, which part was acted by
Lawes (alluded to in v. 68 of the poem). The plot is exceedingly
simple, rather lyric than dramatic. The delineation of passion forms
no part of the poet's aim; but the dialogues are inexpressibly noble—
not however as dialogues, for they must rather be regarded as a series
of exquisite soliloquies setting forth, in pure and musical eloquence,
like that of Plato, the loftiest abstractions of love and virtue; and
the songs interspersed are of consummate melody. For instance,
the drinking chorus of Comus's rout, the Echo-song, and the admirable passages with which the Attendant Spirit opens and concludes
the piece. The general character of this production Milton undoubtedly borrowed, so far as it was borrowed at all, from Fletcher's
Faithful Shepherdess, and from Jonson's *Masques* and his delicious
fragment of a pastoral drama. In a somewhat similar strain to
Comus, Milton had before composed a fragment entitled *Arcades*,
performed at Harefield in honour of the Countess of Derby by her
grandchildren, the daughter and two sons of the Earl of Bridgewater. Though the portion contributed by the poet is comparatively
inconsiderable, it exhibits all his usual characteristics.

Lycidas was a tribute of affection to the memory of his friend
and fellow-student, Edward King, a youth of great promise, lost at
sea in a voyage to Ireland, where he was about to undertake the
duties of a clergyman. The pastoral form is adopted in the poem;
and throughout we meet with a mixture of rural description,
classical and mythological allegory, and theological allusions borrowed from the Christian system; but the shock given to the
reader's taste by this apparent incongruity is in a great measure
softened away by the abstract and poetical air of the whole, and by
the art with which the transitions are managed. Even the apparition of St. Peter among the sea-nymphs is forgotten by the reader
amid the exhaustless beauty of imagery which is displayed throughout. From a solemn and psalm-like grandeur to the airiest and
most delicate playfulness, every variety of music may be found in
Lycidas; and the poet has shown that our Northern speech, though
naturally harsh and rugged, may be made to echo the softest melody
of the Italian lyre. The two descriptive poems, *L'Allegro* and *Il
Penseroso*, are of nearly the same length, and written in the same
metre, consisting, with the exception of a few longer and irregular
lines of invocation at the beginning of each, of the short-rhymed
octosyllabic measure. In the *Allegro* the poet describes scenery,
and various occupations and amusements as contemplated by a man
of joyous and cheerful temperament; in the *Penseroso* not dissimilar
objects viewed by a person of serious, thoughtful, and studious

character. The individuality of the poet is seen in the calm and somewhat grave cheerfulness of the one, as well as in the tranquil, though not sombre, meditativeness of the other. His joy is without frivolity, as his thoughtfulness is without gloom. The Cheerful Man is awakened by the lark, the cock, and the hunter's horn; and walks out, "by hedge-row elms on hillocks green," to see the gorgeous sunrise. After a charming picture of rustic life, and a village festival, the day terminates with ghost stories and fairy legends related over the "nutbrown ale," round the farm-house fire. The poem ends with one of the most admirable of those many passages in which Milton has at once celebrated and exemplified the charms of music. Music was his favourite art: he inherited from his father an intense love for and no mean skill in it; it was afterwards his best—perhaps his highest—consolation in his poverty and blindness; and assuredly no poet in any language has shown such a deep sensibility to its enchantments. In the *Penseroso* we have the contemplative wandering in the moonlit forest; the song of the nightingale, and the solemn sound of the curfew, "over some wide-watered shore, swinging slow with sullen roar;" and the meditation over the glowing embers in some solitary chamber. The long watches of the night are passed in penetrating the sublime mysteries of philosophy with Plato, in studying the solemn scenes of the great dramatists of Greece, and in following the wild and wondrous legends of chivalric tradition and poetry. The poem ends with an aspiration after an old age of hermit-like repose and contemplation.

The Latin poems of Milton belong principally to his youth; and in felicity of diction have never been equalled by modern writers of Latin verse. The *Elegies*, however, graceful as they are, are less interesting than the *Epistolæ* addressed to his literary friends: as, for example, the exquisite *Mansus*, and the Latin verses to Charles Diodati. These, from their personal and intimate character, possess the charm of bringing us nearer to the thoughts, the tastes, and the individual occupations of the poet. In many passages, too, of these poems we see striking examples of that powerful conception which distinguishes Milton; as in his verses on the *Gunpowder Plot* there are impersonations which give us a foretaste of the *Paradise Lost*.

Though a few of Milton's sonnets are playful and almost ludicrous in their subject, the majority are of that lofty, grave, and solemn character which seems most congenial to his spirit. Sidney, Spenser, Shakespeare, and a host of inferior poets, had written sonnets, some of a very high degree of beauty; but it was reserved to Milton to transport into his native country the Italian sonnet in its highest form. Religion, patriotism, domestic affection, are his themes; and among the finest of them may be specified those *To the Nightingale; To Cromwell; To Cyriac Skinner, on his blindness; On his Blindness; On the Late Massacre in Piemont;* and *When the Assault was Intended on the City.*

(ii.) The second period of Milton's literary life is filled with political and religious controversy. Of these prose works we have already spoken. Those who are unacquainted with them are incapable of forming an idea of the entire personality of Milton. Whether written in Latin or in English, these productions bear the stamp of his mind. They are crowded with vast and abstruse erudition; and the learning is, as it were, *fused* into a burning mass by the fervour of enthusiasm. The prose style of Milton is remarkable for a weighty and ornate magnificence, under the burden of which he moves with as much ease as did the champions of the Round Table under their ponderous panoply. When lashed to anger by the calumnies directed against the purity of his personal life, he gives us, in majestic eloquence, a picture of his own studies, labours, and literary aspirations, interesting in themselves, and striking from the beauty of the language.

(iii.) There is no spectacle in the history of literature more touching and sublime than Milton blind, poor, persecuted, and alone, "fallen upon evil days and evil tongues, in darkness and with dangers compassed round," retiring into obscurity to compose those immortal Epics, *Paradise Lost* and *Paradise Regained*, which have placed him among the greatest poets of all time. The *Paradise Lost* was originally composed in Ten Books, which were afterwards so divided as to make twelve. Its composition, though the work was probably meditated long before, occupied about seven years, that is, from 1658 to 1665; and it was first published in 1667. Its subject is the grandest that ever entered into the heart of man to conceive. It differs from the great Epic poems of Antiquity in that the supernatural portion is not merely accessory and subsidiary to the development of the main plot; but the entire action moves among celestial and infernal personages and scenes; and the poet does not hesitate to usher us into the awful presence of Deity Itself. This subject is so intensely interesting to all, that no sketch so full could be given here, which would satisfy the reader, or to any extent assist him in comprehending it. Nothing but an acquaintance with the work itself would suffice.

The peculiar form of blank verse in which it, as well as the *Paradise Regained*, is written, was, if not absolutely invented by Milton, at least first employed by him in the narrative or epic form

of poetry; and acquires, in his hands, a distinctive tone and
rhythm. It is exceedingly solemn, dignified, and varied with such
inexhaustible flexibility, that the reader will hardly ever be able to
find two verses of the same structure and rhythm—at least, except
at a considerable distance from each other. In the incidents and
personages of the poem we find extreme simplicity united with the
richest complexity and inventiveness. Where it suited his purpose,
Milton closely followed the severe condensation of the Scriptural
narrative, where the whole history of primitive mankind is related
in a few sentences; and where his subject required him to give a
loose rein to his invention, he showed that no poet ever surpassed him
in fertility of conception. The description of the fallen angels, the
splendour of Heaven, the horrors of hell, the ideal yet natural
loveliness of Paradise, exhibit not only a perception of all that is
awful, sublime, or attractive, in landscape and natural phenomena,
but the power of overstepping the bounds of our earthly experience,
and so realising scenes of superhuman beauty or horror, that they
are presented to the reader's eye with a vividness rivalling that of
the memory itself. The characters introduced, the Deity and His
celestial host, Satan and his infernal followers, and, perhaps above
all, the ideal and heroic, yet intensely human personages of our first
Parents in their state of innocence, bear witness alike to the fertility of Milton's invention, the severity of his taste, and the loftiness of what we may style his artistic morality. Milton's Satan is
no caricature of the popular demon of vulgar superstition; he is
not less than Archangel, though archangel ruined; and in him, as
well as in his attendant spirits, the poet has given sublimity as
well as variety to his infernal agencies, by investing them with
the most lofty or terrible attributes of the divinities of classical
mythology. Milton is pre-eminently the poet of the learned: for
however imposing may be his pictures even to the most unculti-
vated intellect, it is only to a reader familiar with a large extent of
classical and Biblical reading that he displays his full powers. In
the personages and characters of Adam and Eve he has solved
perhaps the most difficult problem presented by his undertaking—
that of representing two human beings in a position which no other
human beings ever did or ever can occupy; and endowed with such
feelings and sentiments as they alone could have experienced. There
is nothing more admirable than the intense humanity with which
Milton has clothed them; while at the same time they are truly
ideal impersonations of love, innocence, and worship. It has been
objected that Adam is only the nominal hero of *Paradise Lost*, the real
one being Satan; and it is certainly true that the necessarily inferior
nature of man, as compared with the tremendous agencies of which

ho is the sport, reduces him, apparently at least, to a secondary part in the drama; but this difficulty is surmounted by the dignity and *moral* elevation which Milton has given to his human personages, and by his making them the central pivot round which revolves the whole action.

The companion-poem to the great Epic, the Odyssey to the Christian Iliad, is the *Paradise Regained*. It is much shorter than the first work, and consists of only Four Books or Cantos. The subject is the Temptation of Christ by Satan in the Wilderness; and the poet has closely followed the narrative of that incident, as recorded in the fourth chapter of St. Matthew's Gospel. It is, however, evident that the only event comparable in importance to the Fall of Man was the Redemption of Man through the voluntary sacrifice of the Saviour; but the poet, for reasons that cannot now be ascertained, shrank from that awful subject. The universal consent of readers places the *Paradise Regained*, in point of interest and variety, very far below the *Paradise Lost*. This inferiority is, of course, attributable to its want of action; the whole poem being occupied with the arguments carried on between Christ and the Tempter, and the description of the kingdoms of the earth as contemplated from the summit of the mountain. But in *Paradise Regained* the genius of Milton appears in its ripest and completest development: the self-restraint of consummate art is everywhere apparent; and in the descriptions of Rome and Athens, and the state of society and knowledge, the great poet has reached a height of solemn grandeur which shows him to have lost nothing either of imagination or of learning; though, in brilliancy of colouring and intensity of interest, the later poem is inferior. It may be said that the beauties of *Paradise Regained* will generally be more perceptible as the reader advances in life, and to those minds in which the contemplative faculty is more developed than the imagination.

To this, the closing period of Milton's literary career, belongs the Tragedy of *Samson Agonistes*, constructed according to the strictest rules of the Greek classical drama. In the character of the hero, his blindness, his sufferings, and his resignation to the will of God, Milton has given a most touching embodiment of himself. The whole piece breathes the somewhat harsh but lofty patriotism and religion of the Old Testament; and the lyric-choruses are sometimes inexpressibly sublime. So closely has Milton copied all the details, literary as well as mechanical, of the ancient dramas, that there is no exaggeration in saying that a modern reader will obtain a more exact impression of what a Greek tragedy was, from the study of *Samson Agonistes*, than from the most faithful translation of Sophocles or Euripides.

CHAPTER XV.

THE AGE OF THE RESTORATION.

THE most illustrious literary representative of the Cavaliers is SAMUEL BUTLER (1612-1680), who indeed resembles the great Puritan poet in an almost universal erudition, and in the immense quantity of *thought* which is embodied in his writings. He was born of respectable but not wealthy parentage in 1612, and began his education at Worcester Free School. Lack of means seems to have deprived him of any lengthened opportunity of acquiring, at either University, any portion of that immense learning which his works prove him to have possessed. As a young man he performed the office of clerk to Jeffries, a country Justice of the Peace; after wards—most likely by the protection of John Selden—he was preferred to the service of the Countess of Kent; where he enjoyed one of the few gleams of sunshine that cheered his unhappy lot. Thence he passed into the employment—in the capacity of tutor or clerk—of Sir Samuel Luke, a powerful county magnate, and an extreme Presbyterian member of the Long Parliament, in whose house Butler accumulated those traits of bigotry and absurdity which he afterwards interwove into his great satire on the Puritans; and Luke himself was undoubtedly the original of the hero. His great work, the burlesque satire of *Hudibras*, was published in detached portions and at irregular intervals; the first part, containing the first three cantos, in 1663, the second part in the following year, and the third not until 1678. The poem instantly became the most popular book of the age. Charles II. carried about *Hudibras* in his pocket, was incessantly quoting and admiring it; and Butler's poem became the rage at Court. Very little solid recompense, however, accrued to Butler. He was named Secretary to Lord Carbury, and in that capacity held for some time the office of Steward of Ludlow Castle; but he soon after lost this place. A sort of fatality combined with the usual ingratitude of that profligate Court to leave him in his former poverty; and the great wit is reported to have died in extreme poverty, in a miserable lodging in Rose Street, Covent Garden, and to have been indebted to his friend Longueville for a grave in the neighbouring churchyard of St. Paul's.

Butler's principal title to immortality is his burlesque poem of

Hudibras, a satire upon the vices and absurdities of the two dominant sects of the Presbyterians and Independents. Its plan is perfectly original, though the leading idea may be in some measure referred to the *Don Quixote* of Cervantes; but Butler's hero differs from his really loveable prototype in being a combination of all that is ugly, cowardly, pedantic, selfish, and hypocritical; and is on the very verge of being an object, not of ridicule, but of hatred and detestation. The poem describes the adventures of a fantastic Justice of the Peace called Hudibras—a name borrowed from Spenser—and his clerk Ralph, who sally forth to put a stop to the amusements of the common people, against which the Rump Parliament had in reality passed many violent and oppressive acts. Not only were the theatres suppressed, and all cheerful amusements proscribed during that gloomy time, but the rougher pastimes of the lower classes, among which bear-baiting was one of the most favourite, were prohibited by authority. Sir Hudibras, a caricature, as already remarked, of Sir Samuel Luke, is the representative of the Presbyterian party; whilst Ralph is the satiric portrait of the more enthusiastic Independent sect. Sallying forth to stop the popular amusements, Sir Hudibras and his Squire encounter a procession of ragamuffins conducting a bear to the place of combat. They refuse to disperse at the summons of the knight; when a furious mock-heroic battle ensues, in which, after varying fortunes, Hudibras is victorious, and succeeds in incarcerating in the parish stocks the principal delinquents. Their comrades return to the charge, liberate them, and place in durance in their stead the Knight and Squire; who are in their turn liberated by a rich widow, to whom Sir Hudibras, purely from interested motives, is paying his court. Hudibras afterwards visits the lady, and receives a sound beating from her servants disguised as devils; and he afterwards consults a lawyer to obtain revenge and satisfaction. Here, like its own story of the Bear and Fiddle, the poem breaks off in the middle and was never completed.

But the pleasure given by *Hudibras* is quite independent of the gratification of that kind of curiosity which finds its aliment in a well-developed intrigue. Astonishing fertility of invention, analysis of character, the vivid and animated painting of the incidents, and, above all, the immeasurable flood of witty and unexpected illustration which is poured forth throughout the whole poem—these are the qualities which have made Butler one of the great classics of the English language. Wit is the power of tracing unexpected analogies, whether of difference or resemblance: the faculty of bringing together ideas, apparently incongruous, but between which, when so brought together, even the ordinary mind at once perceives the relation; and this perception, suddenly excited, is accompanied by a flash of pleasure and surprise. This power no author ever possessed in so high a degree as Butler; his learning was portentous in its extent and variety; and he appears to have accumulated his vast stores, not only in the beaten tracks, but in the most obscure corners and out-of-the-way regions of books and sciences. The effect of the whole is augmented by the easy, rattling, conversational tone of his language, in which the most colloquial, familiar, and even vulgar expressions are found side by side with the pedantic terms of art and learning. The metre, too, is singularly happy; the short octosyllable verse carries us on with unabating rapidity; and the perpetual recurrence of odd and fantastic rhymes produces a series of pleasant shocks that awaken and satisfy the attention.

Butler's miscellaneous writings were published after his death; among which the most interesting are sketches in prose of a series of characters somewhat in the manner of Feltham. They are marked by that extreme pregnancy of wit and allusion which is so characteristic of his genius. The poems are in many instances bitter ridicule of the puerile pursuits which he attributes to the physical investigations of that day; and he is particularly severe upon the then recently-founded Royal Society, which he ridicules in his *Elephant in the Moon.*

JOHN DRYDEN (1631–1700), the greatest name in the latter part of the seventeenth century, was born of an ancient county family in 1631; and was solidly educated, first under the famous Busby at Westminster School, and afterwards at Trinity College, Cambridge. Sprung from a Puritan family, he naturally, on his entrance into life, attached himself to his kinsman Sir Gilbert Pickering, then in high favour with the Lord Protector; and Dryden's earliest considerable effort was an elegy upon England's greatest ruler. At the Restoration he abandoned his Puritanism, and sang the praises of the worthless Charles with as much zeal as he ever had that of his heroic predecessor. The whole life of Dryden is filled with vigorous and unremitting literary labour, and presents but few events unconnected with the composition of his successive works. Theatrical pieces were then the best-rewarded form of intellectual labour; and, therefore, though conscious of his own deficiency in dramatic genius, Dryden principally devoted himself to the stage, making a legal engagement with the King's Company of Players to supply them regularly with three dramas every year. His dramatic works constitute a very large portion of his entire compositions; and both in their merits and their faults they are at once strikingly characteristic of the peculiar genius of their author, and of the state of taste at the period when they were written. His dramatic career began about the year 1662, with the *Wild Gallant*, the *Rival Ladies*, the *Indian Emperor*, and many other pieces—tragic, comic, and romantic.

In 1663 the poet married Lady Elizabeth Howard, daughter of the Earl of Berkshire, a union which is not supposed to have much contributed to his happiness. In 1667 he produced his first great narrative poem, the *Annus Mirabilis*, intended to commemorate the great events of the preceding year, the terrible Fire of London and the War with the Dutch; which work gave abundant proof of the vigour, majesty, and force of his style. At this time he wrote his *Essay on Dramatic Poetry*, in which he formally maintains the superiority of rhyme in theatrical dialogues; a theory which for a time he exemplified in practice by composing many pieces, as *Tyrannic Love*, in rhyme; though he afterwards saw reason to return to the far finer and more national system of blank verse. In 1670 he succeeded Davenant as Poet Laureate, and was also made Historiographer to the King, and for some time enjoyed the salary of 200*l.* attached to these offices.

During the whole of his life Dryden was engaged in literary and political squabbles, sometimes with envious rivals, as with Settle—a bad poet, whom the public and patrons sometimes preferred to him; sometimes with more powerful and dangerous adversaries, as with the Duke of Buckingham, who with the assistance of at least *one* man of genius, Butler, caricatured him on the stage in the famous burlesque of the *Rehearsal*. In 1679 the Earl of Rochester, imputing to Dryden the *Essay on Satire*—the authorship of which is still undecided—caused the poet to be waylaid by night and severely beaten by a number of bravoes, such as were often in the pay of the great men in those times.

In 1681 appeared the first part of one of Dryden's noblest and most original works, the political satire of *Absalom and Achitophel*, in which, under a transparent disguise of Hebrew names and allusions, he attacks the factious policy of the Ex-Chancellor Shaftesbury, and his intrigues with the Duke of Monmouth on the subject of the succession of the Duke of York. The second part of this poem was published one year after, but was principally written by Tate, Dryden having contributed only 197 lines. To the same period belongs also the *Medal*, directed against the same bold and unscrupulous politician. The purely literary satire, *Mac-Flecknoe*, in which Dryden takes a terrible revenge upon his rival Shadwell, belongs to the year 1682. Dryden's fertility was almost inexhaustible. In 1682 he produced the *Religio Laici*, an eloquent and vigorous defence of the Anglican Church against the Dissenters, and one of the finest controversial poems in any language. In 1686 he embraced the Catholic doctrines, which change most suspiciously coincides with the efforts made by the King, James II., to convert everyone to the faith of which he was himself a professor. But, whether sincere or not, he produced in defence of his new faith a poem called *The Hind and Panther*, which in spite of the fundamental absurdity of its plan exhibits in a high degree his unequalled power of combining vigorous reasoning with sonorous verse and rich illustration. It was published in 1687. In the following year the Revolution deprived Dryden, not only of Court favour, but of his valuable official appointments; but this event was incapable of arresting the activity or chilling the fire of the great poet. He continued to write dramatic pieces until 1693; and during this period gave to the world his excellent translation of Juvenal and Persius. His translation of Virgil appeared in 1697, and seems to have been one of his most profitable literary ventures; it has been said that he gained 1200*l.* by this publication. At the same time he composed his *Alexander's Feast*, one of the noblest lyrics in the English language. Old age and broken health seem not to have been able to interrupt his career; for in 1700 he produced his *Fables*, a collection of tales either borrowed and modernised from Chaucer or versified from Boccacio, in which his invention, fire, and harmony appear in their very highest power. In this year he died of a mortification in the leg combined with dropsy, and was buried in Westminster Abbey, followed to the grave by the admiration of his countrymen, who saw that in him they had lost incomparably the greatest poet of the age.

In the drama, Dryden is the chief representative of that great revolution in taste which followed the Restoration, when the sweet and powerful style of the romantic drama of the Elizabethan type was supplanted by an imitation of French models. The comic pieces of Dryden are marked by all the profound immorality which corrupted fashionable society at that period; and at the same time his deficiency in humour renders his pieces dull in spite of their extravagance, giving the reader no pleasantry to compensate for their grossness. Dryden, in yielding to this detestable tendency, merely followed the prevailing fashion; and showed, by the submission with which he received Jeremy Collier's well-merited rebuke on the indecency and irreligion of his plays, that he had the grace to be ashamed of faults which he had not the virtue to avoid.

The tragedy of this period forms a most amusing contrast to the comedy, affecting a tone of romantic enthusiasm and superhuman elevation far removed from nature and common sense. The heroes are supernaturally brave; self-sacrifice is pushed to the verge of caricature; and all the ordinary feelings of nature are violated to attain a sort of impossible ideal of heroic and amorous perfection. In the *Rival Ladies*, the *Indian Emperor*, *Tyrannic Love*, *Aurengzebe*, *All for Love*, *Cleomenes*, *Don Sebastian*, and similar pieces, wo see Dryden's dramatic genius as we see the dramatic spirit of the age, in its power and in its weakness. Dryden had very little mastery over the tender emotions, and very little skill in the delineation of character; and he tried to compensate for these deficiencies by striking and picturesque incidents, by powerful declamatory dialogue, and by majesty, ease, and splendour of versification. Nor in his eagerness to gratify the vulgar taste of the day did Dryden spare the most venerated names. In *Troilus and Cressida*, and *The Tempest*, he debased to the level of the gross appetites of his audience the grand and pure creations of Shakespeare; and he did not scruple to transform the *Paradise Lost* into an operatic entertainment, styled the *State of Innocence*. His *Prologues* and *Epilogues*, however, are in general masterpieces both in the comic and the elevated style; though in many of the comic productions of this nature he unfortunately panders to the prevailing taste for loose allusion and equivoque.

Even in his *Heroic Stanzas* in praise of Cromwell it is easy to perceive that force, vigour, and majestic melody of style which distinguish him above all the writers of his age, above all the writers of any age perhaps, in the English literature. The heroic couplet was his favourite metre; and he wielded it with singular force and mastery; whether he reasons, or describes, or declaims, or narrates, he moves with perfect freedom; and the regularity of the structure of his verse, and the recurrence of the rhyme, so far from appearing to shackle his movements, seem only to give majesty and impetus to his march. Perhaps the greatest among his longer poems are those in which the subject is half-polemic and half-satirical. The *Absalom and Achitophel* contains a multitude of admirably-drawn portraits, among which those of Shaftesbury, the Duke of Buckingham, Settle, Shadwell, and the infamous Titus Oates, remain in the memory of every reader. Though a minute knowledge of the history of the time is necessary to the full appreciation of this powerful poem, yet even the general student will find in it the noblest examples of moral painting, always vigorous though not always just, and will perceive all the highest qualities of the English language as a vehicle for reasoning and description.

He has also given us, in *Mac-Flecknoe*, the first example of purely literary and personal satire. Its object was his rival Shadwell; whom the poet supposes to be the successor in the supremacy of stupidity to an Irish scribbler named Flecknoe, giving him for this purpose the title of Mac, the Irish form of the patronymic.

The two great controversial poems, *Religio Laici* and the *Hind and Panther*, exhibit in its highest perfection Dryden's consummate mastery in perhaps the most difficult species of writing, namely, poetry in which close reasoning on an abstract subject like theology should be combined with rich illustration and picturesque imagery. In the latter work we very soon get over the absurdity of the fable, in which the two animals that give the title to the poem are represented as engaging in an elaborate argument in favour of the two churches whose emblems they are—the "milk-white Hind" typifying the Catholic, and the Panther the Anglican Church—as well as the representation of the other sects under the guise of wolves, bears, and a whole menagerie of animals.

The lyric productions of this poet are not numerous in proportion to their excellence. Interspersed among the scenes of his romantic dramas are many beautiful and harmonious songs; but his most celebrated production of this kind is his *Alexander's Feast*, written for music, and celebrating the powers and the triumph of the art. This poem he is said to have written at a single jet, and in the space of a few hours. It will always be regarded as one of the most energetic lyrics in the English language.

In translation Dryden's chief merit consists in the power of transferring to his own language, not perhaps the exact sense of his originals, but their general spirit. There was a considerable similarity between the tone of Dryden's mind and that of Juvenal—the same force, the same somewhat declamatory character, and the same unscrupulous boldness in painting what was odious and detestable. Though his version of Virgil will always be regarded as one of the great standard monuments of our literature, it may be regretted that the author he selected was not one more accordant with his peculiar genius; for Dryden was certainly deficient in the grace and elegance characteristic of Virgil. Two of our most illustrious poets, Dryden and Pope, have respectively translated Virgil and Homer: their glory would have been greater had they exchanged subjects.

The highest qualities of Dryden's literary genius never blazed out with greater splendour than in his last publication, the *Fables*, of which we have already spoken. The flowing ease of the composition, the frequent occurrence of beautiful lines and happy expressions, will ever make them the most favourable specimens perhaps of Dryden's peculiar merits.

The form of Dryden's prose works was generally that of *Essays or Prefaces* prefixed to his various poems, and discussing some subject in connexion with the particular matter in hand. Thus in his

Essay on Dramatic Poetry he investigates the then hotly-argued question as to the employment of Rhyme in Tragedy; his Juvenal was accompanied with a most amusing treatise on Satire; in fact few of his poetical works appeared without some prose disquisition. Indeed Dryden must be regarded as the first enlightened critic who appeared in the English language. His judgments concerning Chaucer, Shakespeare and his mighty contemporaries, Milton and a multitude of other authors, do equal honour to the catholicity of his taste and his courage. These works, besides, are admirable specimens of lively, vigorous, idiomatic English, of which no man, when he chose to avoid the occasional pedantic employment of fashionable French words, was a greater master.

Associated with Milton, in both a political and literary relation, was the excellent ANDREW MARVEL (1620–1678). For a time he assisted the great poet in discharging the duties of Latin secretary; and the only copy of English verses prefixed to ‘Paradise Lost’ came from his pen. He represented his native town of Hull in Parliament from the year 1660 until his death; and many stories, apparently authentic, are told of his incorruptible integrity and resolute attitude towards both the caresses and menaces of the Ministers, of the day. His rough, vigorous, masculine satire did excellent service to the popular cause in the dark period that followed the Restoration—in this he hesitated not to assail Royalty itself; his poem on the death of the Lord Protector will not lose by a comparison with the effusions of his more distinguished contemporaries on the same subject—it is, at least, a genuine outspoken utterance from the heart, which can hardly be said of any of the others—and many of his minor works are marked by a simple grace and unaffected elegance, which the bluntness of his more ambitious compositions would hardly lead us to expect. His *Lamentation of a Nymph on the Death of her Fawn*, his *Song of the Emigrants to Bermuda*, his *Thoughts in a Garden*, are excellent specimens of this happier manner. Few men have left behind them a more stainless name than Marvel.

Next to Bacon, incomparably the greatest name in philosophy of the seventeenth century is that of THOMAS HOBBES, the “ philosopher of Malmesbury” (1588–1679). His theories exercised a notable influence on the opinions, not only of English, but also of Continental thinkers for nearly a century; and many of the principles affirmed by him still remain unshaken. His earliest literary work, a translation of Thucydides, was published in 1628; and almost his latest was an English version of the ‘ Iliad ’ and ‘ Odyssey,’ which appeared in 1675, but is generally represented as being almost beneath criticism. He did not produce his first original work, the *De Cive*, until

1642; which was followed by the *Human Nature* and *De Corpore Politico* in 1650. The *Leviathan*, his most elaborate and most celebrated composition, was published in 1651. A few months before his death he finished his *Behemoth*, an account of the late civil wars, which embraces the period between 1640 and 1660. The style of Hobbes is perhaps the most perspicuous ever employed by any author; clear, nervous, forcible, it conveys the exact meaning and produces the exact impression intended with greater success than has been attained by any English writer who has treated subjects of equal depth. Both in his metaphysical and political speculations this writer has encountered much hostile criticism. In the first he is charged with advocating Atheism; and he is certainly open to the accusation of having degraded the spiritual nature of man by representing self-interest as the prime impelling motive of all his actions. In the second he seems distinctly to advocate pure despotism as the only form of authority possessing a philosophical basis, his theory being that human nature is essentially ferocious, and requires the iron restraint of arbitrary power to control its unbridled passions. In the eyes of the orthodox, Hobbism has become a term expressive of all that is obnoxious in morals and politics.

The most energetic assailant of Hobbes's conclusions in Philosophy was Dr. Ralph Cudworth (1617–1688), Regius Professor of Divinity at Cambridge, a writer of extraordinary vigour, and a polemic of almost incredible candour. So fairly did he put the arguments of the Atheists, that he brought down on himself—most unjustly indeed—the imputation of Atheism. His great work is the *True Intellectual System of the Universe*. He was the contemporary at the University of the celebrated Henry More (1614–1687), known as the Platonist, whose principal works are *The Mystery of Godliness*, *the Mystery of Iniquity*, and *Philosophical Poems*. He is a writer of great power, but a mystic.

Literature presents no more original personality than that of John Bunyan (1628–1688), the greatest master of allegory that ever has existed. He was born at the village of Elstow, near Bedford, in 1628. His father was a tinker, and the son in his youth followed the same humble calling; but at about the age of eighteen he entered the military service in the Parliamentary army. In the strange and interesting religious autobiography which he wrote under the title of *Grace Abounding in the Chief of Sinners*, Bunyan has given a curious picture of his internal struggles, his despair, his conversion, and his acceptance by God; and the whole range of mystical literature does not offer a more touching confession. But it is certain that the irregularities he so deeply deplores were venial, if not altogether trifling, and that his conduct had always in the main been virtuous and moral. After experiencing the fearful internal struggles usual when strongly imaginative minds are first brought under religious conviction, he joined, in 1655, the sect of the Baptists, and he gradually attracted notoriety by the fervour of his piety and the rude eloquence of his discourses. At the Restoration, after undergoing some minor persecutions, he was convicted of frequenting and holding conventicles, and imprisoned for upwards of twelve years in the gaol of Bedford, where he supported himself by making tagged laces. It was during this confinement that he composed his immortal allegory the *Pilgrim's Progress*. On the proclamation of Charles's second Declaration of Indulgence, Bunyan was at last liberated; and in 1672 he had become a venerated and influential leader in his sect, preaching frequently both in Bedford and London. His sufferings, his virtues, his genius as a writer, and his eloquence as a pastor, contributed to his fame. He died in 1688, in London, it is said in consequence of a cold caught in a journey undertaken by him in inclement weather with the object of reconciling a father and a son. His character appears to have been essentially mild, affectionate, and animated by a truly evangelical love to all men.

The works of Bunyan are numerous; but there are only three among them upon which it will be necessary for us to dwell. These are the religious autobiography entitled *Grace Abounding in the Chief of Sinners*, already referred to; and the two religious allegories, the *Pilgrim's Progress* and the *Holy War*.

The *Pilgrim's Progress*, which is in two parts, the first beyond comparison the finer, narrates the struggles, the experiences, and the trials of a Christian in his passage from a life of sin to everlasting felicity. "Mr. Christian," dwelling in a city, is incited by the consciousness of his lost state, typified by a heavy burthen, to take a journey to the New Jerusalem—the city of eternal life. All the adventures of his travel, the scenes which he visits, the dangers which he encounters, the enemies he combats, the friends and fellow-pilgrims he meets upon his road, typify, with a strange mixture of literal simplicity and powerful imagination, the vicissitudes of religious experience. Shakespeare is not more essentially the prince of dramatists than Bunyan is the prince of allegorists. So intense was his intellectual vision, that abstract qualities are instantly clothed by him with personality, and we sympathise with his shadowy personages as with real human beings—a result which is indeed in some degree to be ascribed to the simple, direct, unadorned style in which Bunyan wrote. Moreover a great many scenes and characters in Bunyan's books are evidently drawn from real life. The description of Vanity Fair, many of the landscapes so beautifully and vividly painted, and a large number of the personages and dialogues, bear all the marks of being transcripts from Bunyan's actual experience; and we may accept, for example, the lifelike scene of the accusation before the court of justice as a faithful picture of the incredible brutality and corruption of the tribunals of those evil days. Bunyan's knowledge of books was very small; but the English version of the Bible had been studied by him so intensely that he was completely saturated with its spirit.

The *Holy War* is an allegory typifying, in the siege and capture of the City of Mansoul, the struggle between sin and religion in the human spirit. Diabolus on the one hand, and Immanuel on the other, are the leaders of the opposing armies. The narrative, viewed as a tale, is far less interesting than the *Pilgrim's Progress*, our sympathies not being excited by the dangers and escapes of a single hero; and in many points the allegory is too refined and complicated to be always readily followed. The style, though similar in its masculine vigour to that of the former allegory, is less fresh and animated.

One of the most prominent figures in the Long Parliament and the Restoration was EDWARD HYDE, afterwards Chancellor, better known by his title of EARL OF CLARENDON (1608-1674). Descended from a gentle stock, and educated at Oxford, he soon abandoned the profession of a barrister for the more exciting struggles of political life. He sate in the Short Parliament of 1640; and was also a conspicuous orator in the Long Parliament, at first supporting Opposition principles; but after a violent quarrel with the more advanced adherents of the national cause, he gradually passed over to the Royalist side; and on the breaking out of civil war he fled from London, and joined the King at York. From this time Clarendon must be regarded as one of the most faithful, though certainly one of the most moderate, adherents of the Royalist cause. In 1644 he was appointed member of the Council named to advise and take charge of the Prince, whom he accompanied to Jersey, and whose exile and vicissitudes he shared from the execution of Charles I. to the Restoration in 1660. During this time Hyde had frequently, like many of his companions, and like the King himself while wandering in France and Holland, to support extreme poverty and privation. But the Restoration took place; and Hyde reaped the reward of his services. He was made Chancellor, created first a Baron, and afterwards, in 1661, Earl of Clarendon, and for some time was among the most powerful advisers of the Court. His popularity, however, as well as his favour with the King, soon began to decline; for both his virtues and his faults were such as to render him disliked. The first made him offensive to the King and his licentious Court, the second to the people. The marriage of his daughter Anne to the Duke of York, by which he became the progenitor of two queens of England, Mary and Anne, augmented the general odium. He was impeached for high treason in 1667; went into exile, and passed the remainder of his life in France, where he died, at Rouen, in 1674.

Clarendon's great work is the *History of the Rebellion*, as ho naturally, in his quality of a Royalist, designated the Civil War; to which he afterwards added his *Life* and *Continuation* of that History. This review of events embraces a detailed account, rather in the form of Memoirs than regular history, of the proceedings from 1625 to 1633, together with a narrative of the incidents which led to the Restoration. As the materials were derived from the author's personal experience, the work is of high value, and places Clarendon among the leading historical writers of his age; while the dignity and liveliness of the style, in spite of occasional obscurity, will ever rank him among the great classical English prose-writers. Impartial he cannot be expected to be; but his partiality is less frequent and less flagrant than could fairly have been anticipated. Above all, he is excellent in the delineation of character. These are the parts of his work most carefully elaborated, and in them we often find penetration in judging and skill in portraying varieties of human nature.

IZAAK WALTON (1593-1683) was born at Stafford, and passed his early manhood in London, where he carried on the humble business of a "sempster" or linendraper. At about 50 he was able to retire from trade, probably with such a competency as was sufficient for his modest desires; and lived to the great age of 90 in ease and tranquillity, enjoying the friendship of many of the most learned and accomplished men of his time, and amusing himself with literature and his beloved pastime of the angle. He produced at different times the *Lives* of five persons, all distinguished for their virtues and accomplishments—namely, Donne, Wotton, Hooker, Herbert, and Bishop Sanderson, with the first, second, and last of whom he had been intimate. These biographies are unlike anything else in literature; they are written with such a tender and simple grace, with such an unaffected fervour of personal attachment and simple piety, that they will ever be regarded as masterpieces. But Walton's great work is the *Complete Angler*, a treatise on his favourite art of fishing, in which the precepts for the sport are combined with such inimitable descriptions of English river-scenery, such charming dialogues, and so prevailing a tone of gratitude for God's goodness, that the book is absolutely *unique* in literature. The treatise, with a quaint gravity that adds to its charm, is thrown into a series of dialogues, first between Piscator, Venator, and Auceps, each of whom in turn proclaims the superiority of his favourite sport, and afterwards between Piscator and Venator, the latter of whom is converted by the angler, and becomes his disciple. No other literature possesses a book similar to the *Complete Angler*, the popularity of which seems likely to last as long as the language. A second part was added by CHARLES COTTON, (1630-1687), a clever poet, author of *The Voyage to Ireland*, the friend and adopted son of Izaak, and his rival in the passion for angling. The continuation, though inferior, breathes the same spirit, and, like it, contains many beautiful and simple lyrics in praise of the art.

One of the most charming, as well as solid and useful, writers of this period was JOHN EVELYN (1620-1706), a gentleman of good family and considerable fortune, who was one of the founders of the delightful art, so successfully practised in England, of gardening and planting. His principal works are *Sylva*, a treatise on the nature and management of forest-trees, to the precepts of which, as well as to the example of Evelyn himself, the country is indebted for its abundance of magnificent timber; and *Terra*, a work on agriculture and gardening. In his feeling for the art of gardening he is the worthy successor of Bacon, and predecessor of Shenstone. Evelyn has left also a Diary, giving a minute account of the state of society in his time, and pictures of the incredible infamy and corruption of the Court of Charles II., through the abominations of which the pure and gentle spirit of Evelyn passed, like the Lady in *Comus*, amid the bestial rout of the Enchanter.

An original and even comic personality of this era is SAMUEL PEPYS (1632-1703), whose individual character was as singular as his writings. Though the cadet of an ancient family he was born in very humble circumstances; but by the protection of a distant connexion, Sir Edward Montagu, he was placed in a subordinate office in the Admiralty; and by his punctuality, honesty, and knowledge of business, he gradually rose to the important post of Secretary in that department. He remained many years in this office, and must be considered as almost the only honest and able public official connected with the Naval administration during the reigns of Charles II. and James II.; contributing by his honesty and activity to the reconstruction of the navy that took place in the latter king's reign. During a considerable part of his active career, Pepys had amused himself, for the eternal gratitude of posterity, in writing down, day by day, in a sort of cypher or shorthand, a *Diary* of everything he saw, did, or thought. After having been preserved for about a century and a half, this composition has been deciphered and given to the world in the present century; and the whole range of literature does not present a record more curious in itself, or exhibiting a more singular and laughable type of human character. Pepys was not only by nature a thorough gossip, curious as an old woman, with a strong taste for occasional jollifications, and a touch of the antiquary and curiosity-hunter; but he was necessarily brought into contact with all classes of persons, from the King and his Ministers down to the poor half-starved sailors whose pay he had to distribute. The *Diary* is a complete scandalous chronicle of a society so gay and debauched that the simple description of what took place is equal to the most dramatic picture of the novelist. The statesmen, courtiers, players, and demireps, actually live before our eyes; and there is no book that gives so lively a portraiture of one of the extraordinary states of society that then existed. Pepys' own character—an inimitable mixture of shrewdness, vanity, good sense, and simplicity—infinitely exalts the piquancy of his revelations; and his book possesses the double interest of the value and curiosity of its matter, and of the colouring given to that matter by the oddity of the narrator.

The political commotions of this century naturally awakened a keen interest in the philosophy of government, and started many eager minds on the investigation of the principles on which civil authority and civil society are based. High monarchical notions were advocated by Sir ROBERT FILMER (d. 1688), who, in his *Patriarcha*, published in 1680, arrived, though by a different process of reasoning, at the same results as Hobbes. His fundamental principle is, that the paternal authority is absolute, and that the first kings being fathers of families have transmitted their power to their descendants. This principle was first combated by the illustrious Algernon Sidney (1621-1683), whose *Discourses on Government* is a formal refutation of Filmer's theory. JAMES HARRINGTON also (1611-1677), in his *Oceana*, attempted a solution of the same ever-interesting problem. This work, like Bacon's 'New Atlantis,' contains an elaborate scheme for the establishment of a pure republic upon philosophical principles, carried out to those minute details that are so frequently found in paper constitutions. Harrington was the founder of the famous Rota Club, a Society of political enthusiasts who met to discuss their pet theories, to which belonged most of the philosophical republicans of the day

CHAPTER XVI.

THE new drama that followed the Restoration differed from the old both in moral tone and literary form. As to the first, it is marked by that profound corruption which distinguishes the reign of Charles II.; and as to the second, the artificial distinction between tragedy and comedy was strongly marked, and generally maintained with the same severity as upon the stage of France, which had become the chief model of imitation. In the place of the Romantic Drama arose the exaggerated, heroic, and stilted tragedy on the one hand, and on the other the Comedy of artificial life, which, drawing its materials not from nature, but from society, took for its aim the delineation not of character, but of *manners*—which is indeed the proper object of what is correctly termed Comedy in the strictest sense. Wit, therefore, now supplanted Humour; and England produced, during the seventeenth and part of the eighteenth centuries, a constellation of splendid dramatists; whose works, however, owing to their abominable profligacy, are now become almost unknown to the general reader.

Though this class of writers may be said to begin with SIR GEORGE ETHEREGE (1636-1689)—whose principal work, the *Man of Mode*, or *Sir Fopling Flutter*, was produced in 1676—yet the earliest of any eminence was WILLIAM WYCHERLEY (1640-1715). Born of a good Shropshire family, he was educated in France, where he embraced Catholicism; but upon his return to England he once more became a member of the national church. Adorned with all the graces of French courtliness, and remarkable for the beauty of his person, Wycherley, while nominally studying the Law, became a brilliant figure in the gay and profligate society of the day. His first comedy, *Love in a Wood*, was not acted until he had reached the age of about 32; which was followed, in 1673, by the *Gentleman Dancing-Master*, the plot of which was borrowed from Calderon. His two greatest and most successful comedies are the *Country Wife*, acted in 1675, and the *Plain Dealer*, in 1677. His union with the Countess of Drogheda, which commenced in an accidental and even romantic manner, was not such as to secure either his happiness or his interest; and after her death he re-

mained several years in confinement for debt. He was at last liberated, partly by the assistance of James II.; and about this time he
rejoined the Catholic church. The remainder of Wycherley's life
is melancholy and ignoble. In 1704, with the assistance of Pope,
then a mere boy, he concocted a huge collection of stupid and
obscene poems, which fell dead upon the public. The momentary
friendship and bitter quarrel of the old man and the young critic
form a curious and instructive picture. On his very death-bed he
married a young girl of 16, with the sole purpose of injuring his
family.

It is by the *Country Wife* and the *Plain Dealer* that posterity
will judge the dramatic genius of Wycherley. Of the first, the
leading idea is evidently borrowed from the *École des Femmes* of
Molière, and that of the second from the same author's *Misanthrope*.
Nothing can more clearly indicate the unspeakable moral corruption
of that epoch in our drama, and the degree in which that corruption was exemplified by Wycherley, than to observe the way in
which he has modified, while he borrowed, the data of the Great
French dramatist. Nevertheless the intrigue of the piece is animated and amusing; and the dialogue, as is invariably the case in
Wycherley's productions, is elaborated to a high degree of liveliness
and repartee. In the *Plain Dealer* the writer's total want of sensibility to moral impressions is still more painfully apparent. The
tone of sentiment in Molière, as in all creators of the highest order,
is invariably pure in its general tendency. Alceste, in spite of his
faults, is a truly respectable—nay, a noble character. But Wycherley borrowed Alceste; and in his hands the virtuous and injured
hero of Molière has become, to use Macaulay's words, "a ferocious
sensualist, who believes himself to be as great a rascal as he thinks
everybody else."

The second prominent name in this group of brilliant comic
writers is that of Sir John Vanbrugh (1666-1726), who united in
his person the rarely combined talents of architect and dramatist.
Of his skill as an architect, Castle Howard and Blenheim are enduring monuments; the latter being the splendid palace constructed
at the national expense for the Duke of Marlborough. Vanbrugh
was appointed King-at-Arms; and was employed, both in this function, and as an architect, in many honourable posts.

Vanbrugh's comedies, the production of which commenced in 1697,
are the *Relapse*, the *Provoked Wife*, *Æsop*, the *Confederacy*, and the
first sketch of the *Provoked Husband*, left unfinished, and afterwards
completed by Colley Cibber. It still keeps possession of the stage,
and is one of the best and most popular comedies in the language.
Vanbrugh's principal merit is inexhaustible liveliness of character

and incident. His fops, his booby squires, his pert chamber-maids, and valets, his intriguing ladies, his romps, and his blacklegs, are all drawn from the life, and delineated with great vivacity: though there is a good deal of exaggeration in his characters. In the *Relapse*, Lord Foppington is an admirable impersonation of the pompous and suffocating coxcomb of those days; Sir Tunbelly Clumsy, the dense, brutal, ignorant country squire, a sort of prototype of Fielding's Western, forms an excellent contrast with him; and in Hoyden, Vanbrugh has given the first specimen of a class of characters which he drew with peculiar skill, that of a bouncing rebellious girl, full of animal spirits, and awaiting only the opportunity to break out of all rule. The most striking character in the *Provoked Wife* is Sir John Brute, whose drunken uproarious blackguardism was one of Garrick's best impersonations. The *Confederacy* is perhaps Vanbrugh's finest comedy in point of plot. All the sentimental portions of the *Provoked Husband* were the additions of Colley Cibber, who lived at a time when the moral or sermonising element was thought essential in comedy. This part of the intrigue, however, had the honour of being the prototype of Sheridan's delightful scenes between Sir Peter and Lady Teazle in the *School for Scandal*. In brilliancy of dialogue Vanbrugh is inferior to Wycherley; but his high animal spirits, and his extraordinary power of contriving sudden incidents, more than compensate for the deficiency.

GEORGE FARQUHAR (1678–1708) was born at Londonderry; and having received some education at college he joined the stage; which, after a time, he quitted, and served for a short period in the army. His military experience enabled him to give very lively and faithful representations of gay, rattling officers; and furnished him with materials for one of his pleasantest comedies. His dramatic productions consist of seven plays: *Love and a Bottle*, the *Constant Couple*, the *Inconstant*, the *Stage Coach*, the *Twin Rivals*, the *Recruiting Officer*, and the *Beaux' Stratagem*. These were produced in rapid succession, for the literary career of poor Farquhar was compressed into a short space of time—between 1698, when the first of the above pieces was acted, and the author's early death about 1708.

The works of Farquhar are a faithful reflection of his gay, loving, vivacious character; and it appears that down to his early death, not only did they go on increasing in joyous animation, but exhibited a constantly augmenting skill and ingenuity in construction, his last works being incomparably his best. Among them the best are the *Constant Couple* (the intrigue of which is extremely animated), the *Inconstant*, the *Recruiting Officer*, and the *Beaux' Stratagem*. The *Beaux' Stratagem* is decidedly the best-constructed of our author's plays; and the expedient of the two embarrassed gentlemen, whe come down into the country disguised as a master and his servant, though not perhaps very probable, is extremely well conducted, and furnishes a series of lively and amusing adventures. Throughout Farquhar's plays the predominant quality is a gay geniality, which more than compensates for his less elaborate brilliancy in sparkling repartee. He seems always to write from his *heart;* and therefore, though we shall in vain seek in his dramas for a very high standard of morality, his writings are free from that inhuman tone of black-guard heartlessness which disgraces the comic literature of the time.

WILLIAM CONGREVE (1670–1729) will always stand at the very head of the comic dramatists; while he certainly occupies no undistinguished place among the tragedians. He was born in Yorkshire of an ancient and honourable family, in 1670; and received his education, first at a school in Kilkenny, and afterwards at the University of Dublin; where he acquired a considerable amount of scholarship, particularly in the department of Latin literature. During his whole life he seems to have thirsted after fame both as a man of elegance and as a man of letters; but he was all his life tormented by the difficulty of harmonising the two incompatible aspirations. Congreve's career was singularly auspicious: the brilliancy of his early works received instant recompense in solid patronage; he obtained many lucrative sinecures; he associated on equal terms with the greatest and most splendid of his time, and accumulated a large fortune. He was regarded by the poets, from Dryden to Pope, with enthusiastic admiration: the former hailed his entrance upon the literary arena with fervent praise, and in some very touching lines named Congreve his poetical successor; and the latter, when publishing his great work of the translation of Homer, passed over the powerful and the illustrious to dedicate his book to him. In his old age Congreve became the intimate friend of the eccentric Henrietta, Duchess of Marlborough, daughter and inheritress of the great Duke; to whom at his death he bequeathed the bulk of his fortune.

The literary career of Congreve begins with a novel of insignificant merit, which he published under the pseudonym of Cleophil; but the real inauguration of his glory was the representation, in 1693, of his first comedy, the *Old Bachelor.* This work, the production of a young man of twenty-three, was received by the public and by the critics with a tempest of applause. The chief merit is the unrivalled ease and brilliancy of the dialogue. Congreve's scenes are one incessant flash and sparkle of the finest repartee; the dazzling rapier-thrusts of wit and satiric pleasantry succeed each

other without cessation; but the quality in which he stands alone
is his skill in divesting this brilliant intellectual sword-play of
every shade of formality and constraint. His conversations are an
exact copy of refined and intellectual conversation, though of course
containing far more brilliancy than any real conversation ever
exhibited. The characters in the *Old Bachelor*, though conventional, are exceedingly amusing: for example, Captain Bluff is a
reproduction of the bullying braggadocio almost deserving of a place
beside Parolles, Bessus, and Bobadill.

Congreve's second theatrical venture, the *Double Dealer*, acted in
1694, was much less successful than its predecessor; but *Love for
Love*, which was acted in 1695, is a masterpiece. The intrigue is
effective, and the characters exhibit infinite variety, and relieve each
other with unrelaxing spirit. Valentine, Angelica, Sir Sampson
Legend, the doting old astrologer Foresight, Mrs. Frail, Miss Prue,
and above all the inimitable Ben—the first attempt to portray on
the stage the rough, unsophisticated sailor—the whole *dramatis
personæ*, down to the most insignificant, are a crowd of picturesque
and well-contrasted oddities. Sir Sampson Legend is one of those
big blustering characters that make their way by noise and confidence; and was the model whence Sheridan afterwards copied his
Sir Anthony Absolute.

Two years after this triumph Congreve produced his one tragedy,
the *Mourning Bride*, which was received with no less ardent en-
comiums than the comedies. This piece is written in that pompous,
solemn, and imposing strain which the adoption of French models
had rendered universal. Its chief merits consist in dignified passages of declamation; and there are several descriptive ones of
considerable power and melody, though their merit is rather that of
narrative than dramatic poetry. Of this kind is the perpetually
quoted description of a temple, which Dr. Johnson so extravagantly
eulogizes.

In 1698, JEREMY COLLIER (1650-1726), an ardent nonjuring clergyman, published his *Short View of the Profaneness and Immorality
of the English Stage*. This pamphlet was written with extraordinary
fire, wit, and energy; and the evil which it combated was so general, so inveterate, and so glaring, that he immediately ranged upon
his side all moral and thinking men in the nation. He anatomized
with a vigorous and unsparing scalpel the foul ulcer of theatrical
immorality, and cauterised it with such merciless satire that Dryden,
powerful as he was in controversy, remained silent out of shame.
The gauntlet, however, was taken up by Congreve; but the defence
he made was poor, and the victory remained, both as regards
morality and wit, on the side of Collier. The controversy had the

effect of inaugurating a better tone in the drama and in lighter literature in general; and from that period dates the gradual but rapid improvement which has ended in rendering the literature of England the purest and healthiest in Europe.

Congreve's last dramatic work was the *Way of the World*, performed in 1700. Its success was not great, although its dialogue exhibits the rare charm which never deserted him, and though it contains in Millamant one of the most delicious portraits of a gay triumphant beauty, coquette, and fine lady, ever placed upon the stage. In his old age the poet produced a volume of fugitive and miscellaneous trifles, which do not much rise above the level of a class of composition extremely fashionable at that period.

Among the exclusively tragic dramatists of the age of Dryden, the first place belongs to THOMAS OTWAY (1651–1685), who died, after a life of wretchedness and irregularity, at the early age of thirty-four. He received a regular education at Winchester School and Oxford, but very early embraced the profession of the actor; in which part of his career he produced three tragedies,—*Alcibiades, Don Carlos*, and *Titus and Berenice*. After a brief service in the army he returned to the stage; and in the years extending from 1680 to his death he wrote four more tragedies,—*Caius Marius, The Orphan, The Soldier's Fortune*, and *Venice Preserved*. All these works, with the exception of *The Orphan* and *Venice Preserved*, are now nearly forgotten; but the glory of Otway is so firmly established upon these latter, that it will probably endure as long as the language itself. The life of this unfortunate poet was an uninterrupted series of poverty and distress: and his death has frequently been cited as a striking instance of the miseries of a literary career.

As a tragic dramatist, Otway's most striking merit is his pathos. The distress in his pieces is carried to an intense and almost hysterical pitch; the sufferings of Monimia in *The Orphan*, and the moral agonies inflicted upon Belvidera in *Venice Preserved*, are carried to an almost intolerable height; but we see tokens of the essentially second-rate quality of Otway's genius the moment he attempts to delineate madness. The frequent declamatory scenes are worked up to a high degree of excellence; and Otway, with the true instinct of dramatic fitness, has introduced many of those familiar and domestic details from which the high classical dramatist would have shrunk as too ignoble. Otway's style is vigorous and racy; and in reading his best passages we are perpetually struck by a sort of flavour of Ford, Beaumont, and other great masters of the Elizabethan era.

NATHANIEL LEE (d. 1692), known generally as "the mad poet,"

not only assisted Dryden in the composition of several of his pieces, but produced many original dramatic works, the most celebrated of which is the *Rival Queens, or Alexander the Great.* THOMAS SOUTHERNE (1659–1746) was the author of ten plays, the most conspicuous of which are the tragedies of *Isabella, or the Fatal Marriage,* and the pathetic drama of *Oroonoko.* The latter is founded upon the true adventures of an African prince: the subject is said to have been given to Southerne by Aphra Behn, who being the daughter of a governor of Surinam, where the events took place, was personally acquainted both with the incidents and the individuals which form the groundwork of the story. Among the seventeen pieces produced by JOHN CROWNE (d. 1703?) may be mentioned the tragedy of *Thyestes* and the comedy entitled *Sir Courtly Nice.* Both of these works possess considerable merit.

NICHOLAS ROWE (1673–1718) was born in 1673, and studied in the Temple, employing his leisure hours in writing for the stage. He was cordially received in the brilliant and literary circles of his day, and was a member of that intellectual society which surrounded Pope, Swift, Arbuthnot, and Prior, and which was bound together by such strong ties of intimacy and friendship. His career was most brilliant. He was not only in possession of an independent fortune, but was splendidly rewarded for his literary exertions by the gift of many lucrative places in the patronage of Government. Thus he was Poet-Laureate and Surveyor of the Customs, Clerk of the Council in the service of the Prince of Wales, and Clerk of the Presentations. The profession of letters enjoyed a transient gleam of prosperity and consideration; the period preceding and that following this epoch being remarkable for the want of social consideration—nay, the degradation attaching to the author's profession. Rowe was the first who undertook an edition of Shakespeare upon true critical and philological principles; and his edition has, at all events, the merit of exhibiting a profound and loyal admiration of the great poet's genius. His dramatic productions amount to seven, the principal being *Jane Shore,* the *Fair Penitent,* and *Lady Jane Grey,* all of course tragedies. Tenderness is Rowe's chief dramatic merit; in the diction of his works we incessantly trace the influence of his study of the manner of the great Elizabethan playwrights. But this imitation is often only superficial. In the *Fair Penitent,* which is simply the *Fatal Dowry* of Massinger in another form, we have an almost intolerable load of sorrow accumulated on the head of the heroine. It is curious that the character of the seducer in this play, " the gallant, gay Lothario," should have become the proverbial type of the faithless lover—just as Don Juan has been in our own time—and should have furnished

Richardson with the outline which he filled up so successfully in his masterly portrait of Lovelace.

The only other names that need be cited among the dramatists of this period are those of Shadwell and Lillo. THOMAS SHADWELL (1640–1692) wrote seventeen plays, but is now chiefly known by Dryden's satire as the hero of *Mac-Flecknoe*, and the Og of *Absalom and Achitophel*. On the Revolution, he succeeded Dryden as Poet-Laureate. GEORGE LILLO (1693–1739) is in many respects a remarkable and singular literary figure. His dramatic works consist of a peculiar species of what may be called tragedies of domestic life; and the principal of them are *George Barnwell*, the *Fatal Curiosity*, and *Arden of Faversham*. In *George Barnwell* is traced the career of a London shopman—a real person—who is lured by the artifices of an abandoned woman and the force of his own passion first into embezzlement, and then into the murder of an uncle; and finally expiates his offences on the scaffold. The subject of the *Fatal Curiosity*, Lillo's most powerful work, is far more dramatic in its interest. A couple, reduced by circumstances, and by the absence of their son, to the lowest depths of distress, receive into their house a stranger, who is evidently in possession of a large sum : while he is asleep, they determine to assassinate him for the purpose of plunder, and afterwards discover in their victim their long-lost son. It will be remembered that the tragic story of *Arden of Faversham*, a tissue of conjugal infidelity and murder, was an event that really took place in the reign of Elizabeth, and had furnished materials for a very popular drama, attributed, but on insufficient evidence, to Shakespeare among other playwrights of the time.

It is remarkable how many of the non-dramatic poetical writers of this time were men of rank and fashion : their literary efforts were regarded as the elegant accomplishment of amateurs; and, though their more ambitious productions are generally didactic and critical, and their lighter works graceful and harmonious songs, they must be regarded less as the deliberate results of literary labour than as the pastime of fashionable dilettanti. EARL of ROSCOMMON (1634–1685), the nephew of the famous Strafford, produced a poetical *Essay on Translated Verse* and a version of the *Art of Poetry* from Horace, which were received by the public and the men of letters with an extravagance of praise attributable to the respect then entertained for any intellectual accomplishment in a nobleman. EARL of ROCHESTER (1647–1680), so celebrated for his insane debaucheries and the witty eccentricities which made him one of the most prominent figures in the profligate court of Charles II., produced a number of poems, chiefly songs and fugitive lyrics, which proved how great were the natural talents he had wasted in the most insane extravagance. To the same category may be ascribed the DUKE of BUCKINGHAM (Sheffield) (1649-1721), and the EARL of DORSET (1638-1706), perfect specimens of the aristocratic literary dilettanti of those days. The former is best known by his *Essay on Poetry*, written in the heroic couplet; the latter by his charming, playful song—*To all you ladies now on land*, said to have been written at sea on the eve of an engagement with the Dutch fleet under Opdam. It is addressed by the courtly volunteer to the ladies of Whitehall, and breathes the gay and gallant spirit that animates the *chanson militaire*, in which the French so much excel.

The only poets of any comparative importance, not belonging to the higher classes of society, were Philips and Pomfret, both of whom lived in the latter part of the seventeenth century. JOHN PHILIPS (1676-1708) is the author of a half-descriptive, half-didactic poem on the manufacture of *Cider*, written upon the plan of the Georgics of Virgil; and of *Blenheim*, an heroic poem on the exploits of Marlborough; but he is now known to the general reader by his *Splendid Shilling*, a pleasant *jeu d'esprit*, in which the learned and pompous style of Milton is agreeably parodied, by being applied to the most trivial subject. JOHN POMFRET (1667-1703) was a clergyman; and the only work by which he is now remembered is his poem of *The Choice*, giving a sketch of such a life of rural and literary retirement as has been the *hoc erat in votis* of so many.

CHAPTER XVII.

THE SECOND REVOLUTION.

THE period of the great and beneficent revolution of 1688 was characterised by the establishment of constitutional freedom in the state, and no less by a powerful outburst of practical progress in science and philosophy. It was this period that produced Newton in physical, and Locke in intellectual science. JOHN LOCKE (1632-1704) was born in 1632, educated at Westminster School and Christ-Church, Oxford, where he particularly devoted himself to the study of the physical sciences, and especially of medicine. There is no question also that his investigations during the thirteen years of his residence at Oxford had been much turned to metaphysical subjects, and that he had seen the necessity of applying to this branch of knowledge that experimental or inductive method of which his great master Bacon was the apostle. After declining an offer from the Duke of Ormond of high preferment in the Irish Church, he in 1666 became acquainted with Lord Ashley, afterwards Earl of Shaftesbury, to whom he is said to have rendered himself useful by his medical skill. He attached himself intimately both to the domestic circle and to the political fortunes of this statesman, in whose house he resided several years, having undertaken the education first of the Chancellor's son and afterwards of his grandson; the latter of whom has left no unworthy name as an elegant, philosophical, and moral essayist. He was nominated, on his patron becoming Chancellor in 1672, Secretary of the Presentations, with which he combined another appointment; but he lost these offices on the first fall of his patron. In 1675 he visited France for his health; and his journals and letters are not only valuable for the accurate but very unfavourable account they give of the then state of French society, but are exceedingly amusing, animated, and gay. In 1679 Locke returned to England and rejoined Shaftesbury on his second accession to power, but soon shared in the final fall of that statesman.

He now sought an asylum in Holland, was deprived of his Studentship at Christ-Church, and denounced as a factious and rebellious agitator, and as a dangerous heresiarch in philosophy. At the Revolution of 1688 he returned to England in the same fleet which conveyed Queen Mary from Holland to the country whose crown she was called to share. From this period his career was eminently useful. He was appointed Commissioner of Appeals, and some years afterwards a member of the Council of Trade; and in that capacity took a prominent part in carrying out Montague's difficult operation of calling in and reissuing the silver coinage; but after a short service he resigned the latter post, and resided during the remainder of his life with his friend Sir F. Masham at Oates, in Essex. Lady Masham, an accomplished and intellectual woman, and the daughter of the philosopher Cudworth, was tenderly loved and respected by her illustrious guest, who enjoyed under her roof the ease and tranquillity he had so nobly earned. Locke died in 1704; and his personal character seems to have been one of those which approach perfection as nearly as can be expected from our fallible and imperfect nature.

The writings of this excellent thinker are numerous, varied in subject, all eminently useful, and breathing a constant love of humanity. In 1689 he published the *Letters on Toleration*, originally composed in Latin, but immediately translated into French and English; in which work he goes over somewhat the same ground that had been occupied by Jeremy Taylor in his *Liberty of Prophesying*, and by Milton in the immortal *Areopagitica*. The *Treatises on Civil Government* was undertaken to overthrow those slavish theories of Divine Right which were then so predominant among the extreme monarchical parties, and nowhere carried to such extravagance as in the University of Oxford. Locke's more special object was the refutation of Sir Robert Filmer's once famous book entitled *Patriarcha*, already referred to. Locke combats and overthrows his monstrous theory, and seeks for the origin of government in the common interest of society; showing that any form of polity which secures that interest may lawfully be acquiesced in, while none that does not secure it can claim any privilege of exemption from resistance.

The greatest, most important, and most universally known of Locke's works is the *Essay on the Human Understanding*. In this book, which contains the reflections and researches of his whole life, and which was in the course of composition during eighteen years, Locke shows all his powers of close deduction and accurate observation. His object was to give a rational and clear account of the nature of the human mind, of the real character of our ideas, and of the mode in which they are presented to the consciousness. Locke is eminently an inductive reasoner, and was the first to apply the method of experiment and observation to the obscure phenomena of the mental operations; and he is thus to be regarded as the most illustrious disciple of Bacon. The most striking feature in this, as in all Locke's philosophical works, is the extreme clearness, plainness, and simplicity of his language, which is always such as to be intelligible to an ordinary understanding.

The *Essay on Education* has, like the book just examined, a practical tendency, and may be said to have mainly contributed to bring about that beneficial revolution which has taken place in the training of the young. Much of what is humane and philosophical in Rousseau's celebrated *Emile* is plainly borrowed from Locke, who is not responsible for the absurdities and extravagances engrafted upon his plans by the Genevese theorist. His treatise *On the Reasonableness of Christianity* is distinguished by calm piety and benevolence; and a small but admirable little book *On the Conduct of the Understanding*, which was not published until after the author's death, contains a kind of manual of reflections upon all those natural defects or acquired evil habits of the mind, which unfit it for the task of gaining and retaining knowledge.

To this period belongs a series of excellent writers who will always retain the place of classics in English prose, and who are equally worthy of admiration as Protestant theologians and as models of logical and persuasive eloquence. At the head of them stands ISAAC BARROW (1630-1677), a man of almost universal acquirements, whose sermons are still studied as the most powerful and majestic prose compositions that the seventeenth century produced. He was born in 1630, educated at the Charterhouse, whence he passed to Trinity College, Cambridge, of which he was one of the most illustrious alumni. Of his personal courage he gave a striking proof in a sea-fight against an Algerine pirate, when returning from his travels in the East. At the University his studies seem to have embraced every branch of knowledge—not only philology, but all the range of the mathematical sciences, together with Anatomy, Chemistry, and Botany. After some time he travelled through the greater part of Europe to the East, returning home by way of Germany and Holland in 1659. On his return he was appointed Professor of Greek at Cambridge, to which he added the chair of Geometry in Gresham College, and afterwards the Lucasian professorship of Mathematics in the University. He was one of the ablest and profoundest mathematicians of his day, and cultivated with distinguished success those same departments of science in which his illustrious pupil and successor, Newton, gained his undying glory—as Optics, Mechanics, and Astronomy. Newton was, indeed, a pupil of Barrow, who warmly appreciated and befriended him; and it was to Newton that he resigned his Lucasian professorship. He had already taken orders,

and his sermons, many of which were preached in London, now
became famous. He was named one of the King's chaplains, and in
1672 was elected Master of Trinity College; and having in his turn
filled the high office of Vice-Chancellor of the University, he died
of a fever at the early age of forty-six, in 1677.

Barrow's pulpit orations are not only filled and almost overladen
with thought, so that even the most powerful intellect must use all
its force and employ all its attention to follow his reasoning, but
they were, as compositions, elaborated with the greatest care, and
revised and rewritten with scrupulous anxiety before he was satisfied with his work. His sermons are numerous; and many of the
most valuable of them form series, devoted to the exhaustive explanation of some particular department of religious knowledge or
belief: thus there is an excellent series of discourses commenting
upon the Lord's Prayer, which is anatomized, clause by clause;
each article forming the text of a separate discourse. A similar
set of sermons is devoted to the Creed, another to the Decalogue,
another to the Sacraments, and so on. The predominant quality
of Barrow's style is a weighty majesty of thought and diction;
every line that he produced bears a peculiar stamp of unconscious
power—the vigour of a mind to which no subtlety was too arduous,
no deduction too obscure. There is perhaps no English prose
writer, the study of whose works would be more invigorating to the
mind, and more adapted to the formation of a pure taste, than
Barrow; nor can there be a better proof that the most capable
critics have agreed in this opinion, than the fact that Chatham
recommended Barrow to his son as the finest model of eloquence,
and the accomplished Landor has not hesitated to place him above
all the greatest of the ancient thinkers and philosophers.

JOHN PEARSON (1613-1686), originally Professor of Theology and
Master of Trinity College, Cambridge, and afterwards Bishop of
Chester, is a theologian of great merit. His most celebrated work
is his *Exposition of the Creed*, which is still regarded as one of the
most complete and searching treatises investigating the great
fundamental principles of our faith. But next after Barrow JOHN
TILLOTSON (1630-1694) perhaps enjoys the highest and most durable
popularity among the pulpit orators of this time; though he was a
man of a calibre far inferior to Barrow. He studied at Cambridge,
where he at first rendered himself conspicuous for his decided
Puritan sympathies. He, however, afterwards made no difficulty in
conforming to the rules and discipline of the Anglican Church,
and ultimately, in the reign of William and Mary, rose to the
dignity of Archbishop of Canterbury. He was a person of easy,
good-natured, and amiable character; as a pastor and as a prelate

he exhibited much zeal in correcting the abuses which had crept into the Church, and gave a notable example of liberal charity and episcopal virtue.   He was renowned as a preacher ; and his sermons, though falling far short of Barrow's in grasp of mind and vigour of expression, are precisely of such a nature as is most likely to command popularity.   But it was not to the mere vulgar that Tillotson commended himself.   Dryden did not hesitate to own that his own prose style was formed after Tillotson's.   " If I have any talent for English," he said, " it is owing to my having often read the writings of the Archbishop Tillotson."

ROBERT SOUTH (1633-1716) enjoyed in his day the reputation of being the " wittiest Churchman " of the time.   Though he wrote, when at Oxford, a copy of Latin verses congratulating Cromwell upon having made peace with the Dutch, he had embraced even then the extreme Tory opinions prevalent in that University; where he filled the post of Public Orator.   He often preached before Charles II., and was much admired by the courtly audiences of those days for the animation and even gaiety of his manner, and the pleasant stories and repartees which he sometimes introduced into his sermons.   The gross adulation with which he was not ashamed to address Charles II., and in which he lauded the virtues of Charles I., and his unmeasured denunciations of the principles and convictions of the popular party, have deservedly laid South open to the attacks of the opposite side in politics and religion ; but there is no reason to question his sincerity.   It is of more importance to our purpose to remark that he was a perfect master of English prose, and that his style combines ease, vigour, and rhythm, beyond that of any of his contemporaries.

Our limited space will not permit us to do more than mention the names of EDWARD STILLINGFLEET (1635-1699), and WILLIAM SHERLOCK (1641-1707) ; the first a celebrated controversialist, the victorious adversary of Dryden, but the defeated assailant of Locke ; the second, author of a Practical *Discourse concerning Death*, still in some repute.

THOMAS SPRAT (1636-1713), Bishop of Rochester, was a man renowned in his time for the brilliancy and variety of his talents.   He was an ardent cultivator of physical science ; and was one of the members of the Royal Society, then recently founded.   He was distinguished as a poet, though his writings in this department are now little read ; and as a biographer of poets was the author of an excellent and interesting *Life of Cowley*.   Besides these he was a theologian and preacher of no mean ability, and a very active contributor to the polemical and political literature of his day.

There are few episodes in the history of human knowledge more surprising than the sudden and dazzling progress made in the physical sciences towards the end of the seventeenth century; which was mainly due to the vivifying effect produced by the writings and the method of Bacon. A very prominent part in this great movement, especially in the branches of physics and natural history, was played by the Royal Society; that illustrious body which, originating in the meetings of a few learned and ingenious men at each other's houses, was incorporated by Charles II. in 1662 into the Society to the labours of which human knowledge owes so much.

Among its founders one of the most active was DR. JOHN WILKINS (1614-1672), Bishop of Chester, a most energetic and ingenious man, whose vivacious inventiveness sometimes bordered upon extravagance; but who rendered great services, both in his writings and his conversation, to the cause of science. His principal contribution to literature is *An Essay towards a Real Character and a Philosophical Language*, which was printed in 1668. He was a theological writer and a preacher of high reputation; but his name is now chiefly associated with his projects and inventions, and in particular with the prominent part he took, together with Boyle and others, in the organization of the Royal Society. He married the sister of Oliver Cromwell; and his stepdaughter was married to Tillotson.

SIR ISAAC NEWTON (1642-1727) was born in 1642, of a respectable but not opulent family, at Woolsthorpe, in Lincolnshire. From his earliest boyhood he showed the greatest taste and aptitude for mechanical invention; and entering the University of Cambridge in 1660, he made such rapid progress in mathematical studies that in nine years Barrow resigned in his favour the Lucasian professorship. The greater part of Newton's life was passed within the quiet walls of Trinity, of which college he is the most glorious ornament; and it was here that he elaborated those admirable discoveries and demonstrations in Mechanics, Astronomy, and Optics, which have placed his name in the very foremost rank of the benefactors of mankind. He sat in more than one parliament as member for his university; but he appears to have been of too reserved and retiring a character to take an active part in political discussion: he was appointed Master of the Mint in 1695, and presided over that establishment at the critical period of Montagu's bold recall and reissue of the specie. He then promptly abandoned all those sublime researches in which he stands almost alone among mankind, and devoted all his energy and attention to the public duties that had been committed to his charge. In 1703 he was made president of the Royal Society, and knighted two years afterwards by Queen Anne. He died in 1727. His character, the only defect of which appears to have been a somewhat cold and suspicious temper, was the type of those virtues which ought to distinguish the scholar, the philosopher, and the patriot. His modesty was as great as his genius; and he invariably ascribed the attainment of his discoveries rather to patient attention than to any unusual capacity of intellect. His English writings, which are chiefly discourses upon the prophecies and chronology of the Scriptures, are composed in a manly, plain, and unaffected style, and breathe an intense spirit of piety; though his opinions seem to have in some measure inclined towards the Unitarian type of theology. His glory, however, will always mainly rest upon his purely scientific works, the chief of which are so well known that it is almost superfluous to enumerate them, the *Philosophiæ Naturalis Principia Mathematica;* and the invaluable treatise on *Optics,* of which latter science he may be said to have first laid the foundation.

JOHN RAY (1628–1705), together with Derham and Willoughby, combined the descriptive department of Natural History with moral and religious eloquence of a high order; they seem never to be weary of proclaiming the wisdom and goodness of that Providence whose works they had so attentively studied. Ray was the first who elevated Natural History to the rank of a science. ROBERT BOYLE (1627–1691) was an able writer as well as a distinguished philosopher. "No Englishman of the seventeenth century, after Lord Bacon," observes Mr. Hallam, "raised to himself so high a reputation in experimental philosophy as Robert Boyle; it has even been remarked that he was born in the year of Bacon's death, as the person destined by nature to succeed him. . . . . . His works occupy six large volumes in quarto. They may be divided into theological or metaphysical, and physical or experimental. The metaphysical treatises, to use that word in a large sense, of Boyle, or rather those concerning Natural Theology, are very perspicuous, very free from system, and such as bespeak an independent lover of truth."

One of the most extraordinary writers of this period—at least in a purely literary sense—was THOMAS BURNET (1635–1715), Master of the Charter-house, author of the eloquent and poetic declamation *Telluris Theoria Sacra,* a work written in both Latin and English, and giving a hypothetical account of the causes which produced the various irregularities and undulations which we see in the earth's surface. The geological and physical theories of Burnet are fantastic in the extreme; but the pictures which he has drawn of the devastation caused by the great unbridled powers of Nature are grand

and magnificent, and give Burnet a claim to be placed among the most eloquent and poetical of prose-writers.

This writer must not be confounded with GILBERT BURNET (1643-1715), born in Edinburgh in 1643, who was one of the most active politicians and divines during the latter part of the seventeenth century. By birth and personal predilections he occupies a middle space between the extreme Episcopalian and Presbyterian parties; and though a man of ardent and busy character, he was possessed of rare tolerance and candour. He was much celebrated for his talents as an extempore preacher, and was the author of a very large number of theological and political writings. Among these his *History of the Reformation* is still considered as one of the most valuable accounts of that important revolution. The first volume of this was published in 1679, and the last in 1714. He also gave to the world an account of the *Life and Death* of the witty and infamous *Rochester*, whose last moments he attended as a religious adviser, and whom his pious arguments recalled to a sense of repentance. He at one time enjoyed the favour of Charles II., but soon forfeited it by the boldness of his remonstrances against the profligacy of the king, and by his defence of Lord William Russell. Burnet also published an *Exposition of the XXXIX. Articles.* On falling into disgrace at Court he travelled on the Continent; and afterwards attached himself closely to the service of William of Orange at the Hague, where he became the religious adviser of the Princess Mary, afterwards Queen. At the Revolution, Burnet accompanied the deliverer on his expedition to England, took a very active part in controversy and political negociation, and was raised to the Bishopric of Salisbury, in which function he gave a noble example of the zeal, tolerance, and humanity which ought to be the chief virtues of a Christian pastor. He died in 1715, leaving the MS. of his most important work, the *History of My Own Times*, which he directed to be published after the lapse of six years. This work, consisting of Memoirs of the important transactions of which Burnet had been contemporary, is of a similar nature and not inferior value to Clarendon's, which represents the events of English history from a nearly opposite point of view. Burnet is minute, familiar, and gossiping, but lively and trustworthy in the main as to facts; and no one who desires to make acquaintance with a very critical and agitated period of our annals can dispense with the materials he has accumulated

CHAPTER XVIII.

THE SO-CALLED AUGUSTAN POETS.

Sense, vigour, harmony, and a kind of careless yet majestic regularity, were the characteristics of that powerful school of poetry which was introduced into England at the Restoration, and of which Dryden is the most eminent type. These qualities were, in the so-called Augustan reign of Queen Anne, succeeded by a still higher polish, and an elegance sometimes degenerating into effeminacy. Far above all the poets of this epoch shines the brilliant name of ALEXANDER POPE (1688-1744). He was born in London of a respectable Catholic family of good descent, in 1688. His father had been engaged in trade as a linendraper, and had retired to a pleasant country house at Binfield, near Windsor; so that the childish imagination of the future poet imbibed impressions of rural beauty from the lovely scenery of the Forest. The boy was of almost dwarfish stature, and so deformed that his after life was "one long disease." He exhibited an extraordinary precocity of intellect; "I lisped in numbers, for the numbers came," he says of himself; and his earliest attempts at poetry were made when he was very young. His father had acquired a competent fortune, which enabled the boy-poet to indulge that taste for study and poetical reading which continued to be the passion of his life. At sixteen he commenced his literary career by composing a collection of *Pastorals*, and by translating portions of *Statius*, published in 1709 and 1712 respectively. From this period his activity was unremitting; and an uninterrupted succession of works, equally varied in their subjects and exquisite in their finish, placed him at the head of the poets of his age. His *Essay on Criticism*, published in 1711, and highly praised by Addison, was perhaps the first poem that fixed his reputation, and gave him a foretaste of that immense popularity which he enjoyed during his whole life. It is to this period of his career that we must ascribe the conception and first sketch of the most charming production not only of Pope, but of the century in which he lived; a perfect gem, or masterpiece, equally felicitous in its plan and in its execution. This was the mock-heroic poem *The Rape of the Lock*, justly described by Addison as "*merum sal*, a delicious little thing," which is the victorious rival of Boileau's *Lutrin*, and is indeed incomparably superior to every heroic-comic composition that the world has hitherto seen. In 1713 appeared his pastoral eclogues entitled *Windsor Forest*, in which beauty of versification and neatness of diction do all they can to compensate for the absence of that deep feeling for nature which the poetry of the eighteenth century did not possess. The plan of this work is principally borrowed from Denham's *Cooper's Hill*. He likewise published several modernised versions from Chaucer, as if he were desirous in all things to parallel his great master Dryden. These consist of the not over-moral story of *January and May*, which is in substance the *Merchant's Tale*, and *The Prologue to the Wife of Bath's Tale*. The *Temple of Fame* is an imitation of the same poet's *House of Fame*.

At this time, too, Pope undertook the laborious enterprise of translating into English verse the Iliad and the Odyssey. The work was to be published by subscription; and Pope was at first reduced almost to despair when brought face to face with the vastness of his undertaking: but with practice came facility, and the whole of the Iliad was successfully given to the world by the year 1720. In a pecuniary sense this was a most successful venture; Pope thereby laid the foundation of that competence which he enjoyed with good sense and moderation. The Odyssey did not appear till five years later; and of this he himself translated only twelve of the twenty-four books, employing for the remaining half the assistance of the respectable contemporary poets WILLIAM BROOME (1689-1745) and ELIJAH FENTON (1683-1730), to whom he paid a certain share of the proceeds. Mechanically these translations are far from unfaithful; but in the spirit, the atmosphere, so to say, of the original, the ballad-like version of Chapman is far superior. Bentley's criticism is, after all, the best and most comprehensive that has yet been made on this work: "it is a pretty poem, Mr. Pope, but you must not call it Homer." It will nevertheless be always regarded as a noble monument of our national literature.

Other compositions of Pope belonging to this early period of his life, are the *Elegy on an Unfortunate Lady*, the *Epistle from Sappho to Phaon*, borrowed from the *Heroïdes* of Ovid, and the *Epistle of Eloisa to Abelard*, a poem on a similar plan, but taking its subject from the romantic and touching story of mediæval times. These works, though somewhat artificial, express a passion so intense, and are illustrated with such beautiful imagery, that they will ever be considered masterpieces. During this part of his life Pope was living, with his father and mother, to whom he always showed the tenderest affection, at Chiswick; but on the death of the former parent he removed with his mother to a villa he had purchased at

Twickenham, on a most beautiful spot on the banks of the Thames.
Here he passed the remainder of his life, in easy, if not opulent
circumstances; his taste for gardening, and his grotto and quin-
cunxes, in which he delighted, amused his leisure; and he lived
in familiar intercourse with almost all the most illustrious statesmen, orators, and men of letters of his day,—Swift, Atterbury,
Bolingbroke, Prior, Gay, and Arbuthnot. In 1725 he published
an *Edition of Shakespeare* in six volumes, in the compilation of
which he exhibited a deficiency in that peculiar kind of knowledge
which is absolutely indispensable to the commentator on an old
author. This work was but too justly criticised by Theobald in his
Shakespeare Restored, an offence deeply resented by the sensitive
poet; and we shall see by-and-by how savagely he revenged himself. During the three following years he was engaged, together
with Swift and Arbuthnot, in putting together that famous collection
of *Miscellanies* to which each of the friends contributed. The principal project of the fellow-labourers was the extensive satire on the
abuses of learning and the extravagances of philosophy, entitled
Memoirs of Martinus Scriblerus. Pope's admirable satiric genius,
however, would seem to have instantly deserted him when he
abandoned verse for prose; and perhaps, with the exception of
Arbuthnot's inimitable burlesque *History of John Bull*, these Miscellanies are hardly worthy of the fame of their authors.

The brilliant success of Pope, his steady popularity, the tinge of
vanity and malignity in his disposition, and, above all, the supercilious tone in which he speaks of the struggles of literary existence,
raised around him a swarm of enemies, animated alike by envy and
revenge. Determining, therefore, to inflict upon these gnats and
mosquitoes of the press a memorable castigation, he composed in
1726 the satire of the *Dunciad*, the primary idea of which may
have been suggested by Dryden's Mac-Fleckno, but which is incomparably the fiercest, most sweeping, and most powerful literary
satire that exists in the whole range of literature. Most of the
persons attacked are so obscure that their names are now rescued
from oblivion by being embalmed in Pope's satire; but in the
latter part of the poem, and particularly in the portion added in
the editions of 1742 and 1743, the poet has given a sketch of the
gradual decline of taste and learning in Europe, which is one of the
noblest outbursts of his genius. In the original form of the poem
the palm of stupidity was given to Theobald; but in the new
edition of 1743 the distinction is transferred to the then poet
laureate, Colley Cibber, an actor, manager, and dramatic author of
the time, who, whatever were his vices and frivolity, certainly was
in no sense an appropriate King of the Dunces. But in this, as in

numberless other instances, Pope's bitterness of enmity entirely
ran away with his judgment.

In the four years extending from 1731 to 1735 Pope was engaged
in the composition of his *Epistles*, addressed to Burlington, Cobham,
Arbuthnot, Bathurst, and other distinguished men. These poems,
half satirical and half familiar, were in their manner a reproduc
tion of the charming productions of Horace. At the same period
was composed the *Essay on Man*, in four epistles, addressed to
Bolingbroke, a work of more pretension, and aiming at the illustration of important ethical and metaphysical principles. This poem
is an incomparable example of the highest skill in the art of so
treating an abstract philosophical subject as to render it neither dry
nor unpoetical. About the same time he gave to the world his
highly-finished and brilliant *Imitations of Horace*, in which, like so
many previous writers of his own and other countries, from Bishop
Hall down to Boileau, he adapted the topics of the Roman satirist
to the persons and vices of modern times.

On the 30th of May, 1744, this great poet died, unquestionably
the most illustrious writer of his age, hardly inferior to Swift in the
vigour, the perfection, and the originality of his genius. As a man
he was a strange mixture of selfishness and generosity, malignity
and tolerance : he had a peculiar tendency to indirect and cunning
courses; and his intense literary ambition sometimes showed itself
in personal and sometimes in literary meannesses and jealousies.
Among his works few of any importance have been left unnoticed.
We should perhaps mention his Eclogue of the *Messiah*, a happy
adaptation of the Pollio of Virgil to a sacred subject, the *Ode on
St. Cecilia's Day*, in which he was bold enough to try his strength
with Dryden, and, though defeated, yet without disgrace. He composed a considerable number of *Epitaphs*, some of which are
remarkable as exemplifying his consummate skill in the art of
paying a compliment, one of the most perfect instances of which is
in the closing lines of the Epitaph on young Harcourt. But
perhaps the most inimitable of Pope's productions is the *Rape of
the Lock*, the subject of which is the rather cavalier frolic of Lord
Petre, a man of fashion at the court of Queen Anne, in cutting off
a lock of hair from the head of Arabella Fermor, a beautiful young
maid of honour. This incident Pope treated with so much grace
and delicate mock-heroic pleasantry, that on consulting Addison on
the first sketch of the poem, the latter strongly advised him to
refrain from altering a "delicious little thing," that any change
would be likely to spoil. Pope, however, fortunately for his glory,
incorporated into his poem the delicious supernatural agency of the
Sylphs and Gnomes, beings which he borrowed from the Rosicru-

eian philosophers; the action of which miniature divinities is exquisitely proportioned to the frivolous persons and events of the poem.

The most original genius as well as the most striking character of this period was JONATHAN SWIFT (1667-1745), who occupies a foremost place in the literary and political history of the time. He was born in Dublin, in 1667, of English family and descent; but his father having died in embarrassed circumstances, Swift, a posthumous child, became a dependent upon the charity of relations. He passed three years of his infancy in England, and was afterwards sent to a school at Kilkenny, whence he proceeded, in 1682, to Trinity College, Dublin. Here he occupied himself with irregular and desultory study, and at last received his degree with the unfavourable notice that it was conferred "speciali gratiâ," indicating that his conduct had not satisfied the academical authorities. In 1688 he entered the household of Sir William Temple, a distant connexion of his family; in whose service he remained as secretary and literary subordinate for some years. Temple was frequently visited and consulted by King William, who is said to have offered Swift a commission in a troop of horse and taught him the Dutch way of cutting and eating asparagus. Swift's residence at Moor Park continued down to Temple's death in 1699, with, however, one interruption in 1694, when he entered into holy orders on the Irish Church establishment, having obtained the small prebend of Kilroot. This temporary absence was caused by a quarrel with his patron, whose supercilious condescension his haughty spirit could not brook. During this period of his life he was industriously employed in study; and steady and extensive reading corrected the defects of his earlier education. On Temple's death he became the literary executor of his patron, and prepared for the press the numerous works he left; which he presented, with a preface and dedication written by himself, to William III.

Failing to obtain any preferment from that sovereign, Swift went to Ireland in 1699 as chaplain to Earl Berkeley, the Viceroy; and received the small livings of Laracor and Rathbeggan, altogether amounting to about 400l. a year. At Laracor he lived till 1710, amusing himself with gardening, and with repairing his church and parsonage, and making yearly visits to England, where he became the familiar companion of the most illustrious men of the time,—Halifax, Godolphin, Somers, and Addison. His connexion with William III. and Temple, as well as the predominance at that moment of Whig policy, naturally caused Swift to enter public life under the Whig banner, under which all these great statesmen fought.   And it was in the interests of this party that he wrote his first work, the *Dissensions in Athens and Rome*, a political pamphlet in favour of the Whig ministers who were impeached in 1701.

But his first important works were the *Battle of the Books* and the *Tale of a Tub*, which were published in 1704.   The latter is a savage and yet exquisitely humorous pasquinade ridiculing the Roman Catholics and Presbyterians, and for the exaltation of the High Anglican party, the three churches being impersonated in the ludicrous and not very decorous adventures of his three heroes, Peter, Jack, and Martin.   The *Battle of the Books*, though first published in 1703, appears to have been written as early as 1697, to support his patron, Sir William Temple, in the celebrated Boyle and Bentley controversy on the letters of Phalaris.   This dispute, originating in a mere personal squabble with Bentley, (who had been, though unjustly, accused of discourtesy in his capacity of librarian to the University of Cambridge), arose out of the then violently-contested question of the relative superiority of the Ancients and the Moderns, which was first started in England by Sir William Temple in 1692.   Swift became a champion of the Boyle faction, and in this work gave a striking foretaste of those tremendous powers of sarcasm and vituperation which made him the most formidable pamphleteer that ever existed.

But his advocacy of Whig principles, never very hearty, came to an end in 1710.   His hopes of preferment in England were not fulfilled; and this was the more galling, as he had long regarded Ireland with a mixture of contempt and detestation, and was eager to escape from that country for ever.   He accordingly unceremoniously abandoned his former party, and began to write, to intrigue, and to satirize, with even greater force, vehemence, and success, on the side of the Tories.

In this year, too, Harley, afterwards Earl of Oxford, and St. John, better known as the brilliant but unprincipled Bolingbroke, had reached the head of affairs.   Swift was received with open arms; he became more useful to his present than he had ever been to his former party, and was caressed and flattered by the great, the fair, the witty, and the wise.   He poured forth with unexampled rapidity squib after squib and pamphlet after pamphlet, employing all the stores of his unequalled fancy and powerful sophistry to defend his party and to blacken and ridicule his antagonists.   The great object of his ambition was an English bishopric, and the ministers would have been willing enough to gratify him; but his authorship of the *Tale of a Tub*, and a lampoon of his on the Duchess of Somerset, proved fatal to him, and he was obliged to content himself with the deanery of St. Patrick's, Dublin, to which he was nominated, to his extreme disappointment, in 1713. This was the most active period of Swift's life. His *Public Spirit of the Whigs*, his *Conduct of the Allies*, and his *Reflections on the Barrier Treaty*, the ablest political pamphlets ever written, not only reconciled the nation to the peace policy of the Tory ministry, but also kindled a feeling of enthusiasm for the Tory statesmen among the people. Evil days, however, were at hand. Harley and St. John tore asunder their party with their dissensions, and, in spite of all Swift's efforts, the breach became irremediable. St. John, combining with Mrs. Masham, the Queen's favourite, succeeded in turning out Harley. But his triumph was short. The death of Anne and the accession of the Elector of Hanover recalled the Whigs to power. The ministry were accused of a plot for bringing back the Pretender; Oxford was committed to the Tower; Bolingbroke fled beyond the sea; and Swift retired to Ireland, where he was received with a universal yell of contempt and execration.

From 1714 to 1726 Swift resided constantly in Ireland, and from being an object of detestation raised himself to a height of popularity which has never been surpassed. The condition of Ireland was just then unusually deplorable; the manufacturing industry and the commerce of the country were paralysed by the protective statutes of the English Parliament; while the agricultural classes were reduced to the lowest abyss of degradation. In a pamphlet recommending to the Irish the use of their own manufactures, Swift boldly proclaimed the misery of the country; and his force and bitterness soon drew down the persecution of the Ministers. But the highest point of Swift's Irish popularity was attained by the seven famous letters which he wrote in 1724. signed *M. B. Drapier* (draper), and published as separate pamphlets. The occasion was the attempt, on the part of the English ministry, to force on Ireland the circulation of a large sum of copper money, the contract for coining which had been undertaken by William Wood, a Birmingham speculator. This money Swift endeavoured to persuade the people was enormously below its nominal value; and he counselled all true patriots not only to refuse to take it, but to refrain from using any English manufactures whatever. The force of his arguments, and the skill with which he wore his mask of a plain, honest tradesman, excited the impressionable Irish almost to frenzy. Swift was known to be the real author of the letters, and his defence of the rights of the Irish people made him from this moment the idol of that warm-hearted race.

In 1726 Swift once more visited England for the purpose of bringing out his famous *Gulliver's Travels*, which at once excited a universal burst of delight and admiration. The death of Stella, one of the few beings that he ever really loved, happened in 1728; and the loss of many friends further contributed to darken and intensify the gloom of this proud and sombre spirit. He had from an early period suffered occasionally from giddiness; and his fearful anticipations of insanity were destined to be cruelly verified. In 1741 he was afflicted with a painful inflammation which necessitated restraint, and which gradually merged into a state of idiocy that lasted without interruption till his death in 1745. He is buried in his own cathedral of St. Patrick's; and over his grave is inscribed that terrible epitaph composed by himself, in which he speaks of resting "ubi sæva indignatio ulterius cor lacerare nequit."

Any account of Swift would be imperfect without some mention of the two unhappy women whose love for him was the glory and the misery of their lives. While residing in Temple's family he became acquainted with Esther Johnson, a beautiful young girl, brought up as a dependent in the house, to whom, while hardly in her teens, Swift gave instruction; and the bond between master and pupil ripened into the deepest and tenderest passion on the part of both. On his removal to Ireland, Swift induced Stella— such was the poetical name he gave her—to settle with her friend Mrs. Dingley in that country; and he maintained with both of them that long, curious, and intimate correspondence which has since been published as his *Journal to Stella*. The journal is full of the most affectionate aspirations after a tranquil retreat in the society of "little M. D.;" and there can be hardly any doubt that Swift anticipated marrying Stella, while Stella's whole life was filled with the same hope. During one of his visits to London, Swift became intimate with the family of a rich merchant named Vanhomrigh, whose daughter Hester, to whom he gave the name of Vanessa, he unconsciously succeeded in inspiring with a deep and intense passion, which the difference of age only makes more difficult to explain. On the death of her father, Miss Vanhomrigh, who possessed an independent fortune, retired to a villa at Celbridge in Ireland, where Swift continued his visits, but without clearing up to one of these unhappy ladies the nature of his relations with the other. At last Vanessa, driven almost to madness by suspense and irritation, wrote to Stella to inquire into the nature of Swift's position with regard to her. The letter was given by Stella to Swift, and brought back by him and thrown down without a word, but with a terrible countenance, before poor Vanessa, who died a few weeks afterwards (1723). Swift, however, was already in all probability the husband of Stella; in 1716, it is said, the ceremony of marriage was privately performed in the garden of the Deanery, though Swift never either recognised her in public, or changed his strange rule of never living in the same house with her, or even seeing her otherwise than in the presence of a third person.

The greatest and most characteristic of Swift's prose works is the *Voyages of Gulliver*, a vast and all-embracing satire upon humanity itself, though many of the strokes were at the time intended to allude to particular persons and contemporary events. This admirable fiction consists of four parts or voyages: in the first Gulliver visits the country of Lilliput, whose inhabitants are about six inches in stature, and where all the objects, houses, trees, ships, and animals, are in exact proportion to the miniature human beings. The invention displayed in the droll and surprising incidents is as unbounded as the natural and *boná-fide* air with which they are recounted; and the strange scenes and adventures are recorded with an air of simple straightforward honesty altogether inimitable. The second voyage is to Brobdingnag, a country of enormous giants, about sixty feet in height; and here Gulliver plays the same part as the pigmy Lilliputians had played to him. As in the first voyage, the contemptible and ludicrous side of human things is shown, by exhibiting how trifling they would appear in almost microscopic proportions, so in Brobdingnag we are made to perceive how odious and ridiculous would appear our politics, our wars, and our ambitions, to the gigantic perceptions of a more mighty race. The third part carries Gulliver to a series of strange and fantastic countries. The first is Laputa, a flying island, inhabited by philosophers and astronomers; whence he passes to the Academy of Lagado; thence to Glubbdubdrib and Luggnagg; which latter episode introduces the terrific description of the Struldbrugs, wretches who are cursed with bodily immortality without preserving at the same time their intellects or their affections.

Gulliver's last voyage is to the country of the Houyhnhnms, a region in which horses are the reasoning beings; and where men, under the name of Yahoos, are degraded to the rank of noxious, filthy, and unreasoning brutes. The satire goes on deepening as it advances; playful in the scenes of Lilliput, it grows bitterer at every step, till in the Yahoos it reaches a pitch of almost insane ferocity, which there is but too much reason to believe faithfully embodied Swift's real opinion of his fellow-creatures.

Besides the purely political pamphlets already mentioned, Swift wrote many others of a partly religious character, such as his *Sentiments of a Church of England Man*, his remarks on the *Sacra-*

mental Test, and a multitude of others, which being written on local and temporary subjects, are now little consulted; but they all exhibit the vigour of his reasoning, the admirable force and directness of his style, and his unscrupulous ferocity of invective. Of all his occasional productions it may be said, that they are party pamphlets of the most virulent kind, in which the author was never restrained by any feeling of his own dignity, or of candour and indulgence for others, from overwhelming his opponents with ridicule and abuse. Many of his smaller prose writings are purely satirical, as his *Polite Conversation* and *Directions to Servants*. In the former he has combined in a sort of comic manual all the vulgar repartees, nauseous jokes, and *selling of bargains*, that were at that time common in smart conversation; and in the latter, under the guise of ironical precepts, he shows how minute and penetrating had been his observations of the lying, pilfering, and dirty practices of servants. Perhaps the pleasantest, as they are the most innocent, of his prose pleasantries, are the papers written in the character of Isaac Bickerstaff, where he shows up, with exquisite drollery, the quackery of the astrologer Partridge His letters are very numerous; and those addressed to his intimate friends, as Pope and Gay, and those written to Sheridan, half-friend and half-butt, contain inimitable specimens of his peculiar humour.

Swift will not only be ever regarded as one of the greatest masters of English prose, but his poetical works will give him a prominent place among the writers of his age. Yet they have no pretension to loftiness of language, but are written in the *sermo pedestris*, in a tone studiously preserving the familiar expression of common life. In nearly all of them Swift adopted the short octosyllable verse that Prior and Gay had rendered popular. The poems show the same wonderful acquaintance with ordinary incidents as the prose compositions, the same intense observation of human nature, and the same profoundly misanthropic view of mankind. The longest of the narrative writings, *Cadenus* (Decanus, an anagram indicating the Dean himself) *and Vanessa*, is at the same time the least interesting. It gives an account, though not a very clear one, of the love-episode which terminated so fatally for poor Hester Vanhomrigh. The most likely to remain popular are the *Verses on my own Death*, describing the mode in which that event, and Swift's own character, would be discussed among his friends, his enemies, and his acquaintances; and perhaps there is no com position in the world which gives so easy and animated a picture, at once satirical and true, of the language and sentiments of ordinary society. He produced an infinity of small pleasantries, in prose and verse : as, for example, *The Grand Question Debated*, in which he has, with consummate skill and humour, adopted the maundering style of a vulgar servant-maid. Many of his verses are slight toys of the fancy, but they are toys executed with the greatest perfection ; and in some, as the *Legion Club*, the verses on Bettesworth and on Lord Cutts, the ferocious satire of Swift is seen in its full intensity.

No member of the brilliant society of which Pope and Swift were the chief luminaries, deserves more respect, both for his intellectual and personal qualities, than DR. JOHN ARBUTHNOT (1667-1735). He was of Scottish origin, and enjoyed high reputation as a physician, in which capacity he remained attached to the Court from 1709 till the death of Queen Anne. He is supposed to have conceived the plan of that extensive satire on the abuses of learning, embodied in the *Memoirs of Martinus Scriblerus*, and to have indeed executed the best portions of that work, and in particular the description of the pedantic education given to his son by the learned Cornelius. It is entirely impossible, however, to distinguish between the different contributions of the brilliant wits who formed the club. But the fame of Arbuthnot is more intimately connected with the inimitable *History of John Bull*, in which the intrigues and Wars of the Succession are so drolly caricatured. The object of the work was to render the prosecution of the war by Marlborough unpopular with the nation ; but the adventures of Squire South (Austria), Lewis Baboon (France), Nic. Frog (Holland), and Lord Strutt (the King of Spain), are related with fun, odd humour, and familiar vulgarity of language. Arbuthnot is always good-natured ; and he shows no trace of that fierce bitterness and misanthropy which tinges every page of Swift. The characters of the various nations and parties are conceived and maintained with consummate spirit ; and perhaps the popular ideal of John Bull, with which Englishmen are so fond of identifying their personal and national peculiarities, was first stamped and fixed by Arbuthnot's amusing burlesque.

MATTHEW PRIOR (1664-1721) was a poet and diplomatist of this time, who played a prominent part on the stage of politics as well as on that of literature. He was of humble origin ; but by the generous liberality of the splendid Dorset, he was enabled to pursue his studies at St. John's College, Cambridge, where he distinguished himself and obtained a small fellowship. He took part with Charles Montagu in the composition of the *Country Mouse and City Mouse*, a poem intended to ridicule Dryden's *Hind and Panther* ; and the door of public employment was soon opened to him. After acting as Secretary of Legation at the Peace of Ryswick, he twice resided at Versailles in the capacity of envoy, and by his talents in negotiation, as well as by his wit and accomplishments in society appears

to have been very popular among the French. On returning to
England he was made a Commissioner of Trade, and in 1701
became a member of the House of Commons. Though he had
entered public life as a partisan of the Whigs, he now deserted
them for the Tories, on the occasion of the impeachment of Lord
Somers; and he again went to Paris, where he lived in great
splendour during the negotiations in which Bolingbroke acceded to
the disgraceful Treaty of Utrecht. In 1715 he was ordered into
custody by the Whigs, on a charge of high treason, and remained
two years in confinement. But for his College Fellowship, which
he prudently retained throughout the period of his prosperity, he
would now have been reduced to entire poverty. Moreover, with
the assistance of his friends, he published by subscription a collection of his works, the proceeds of which amounted to a considerable
sum. His longer and more ambitious poems are *Alma*, a metaphysical discussion carried on in easy Hudibrastic verse, exhibiting a
good deal of thought and learning disguised under an easy conversational garb, and the Epic entitled *Solomon*, a poem somewhat in
the manner, and with the same defects, as the *Davideis* of Cowley.
A work of considerable length, and ambitious in its character, is the
dialogue entitled *Henry and Emma*, modernised, and spoiled in the
modernising, from the exquisite old ballad of the *Nutbrowne Maide*.
Prior's claim to admiration rests mainly upon his easy, animated,
half-tender, half-libertine love-songs, exhibiting the union of natural
though not profound sentiment with a sort of philosophic gaiety.

JOHN GAY (1688-1732) was one of those easy, amiable, good-
natured men who are the darlings of their friends, and whose
talents excite admiration without jealousy, while their characters
are the object rather of fondness than respect. He entered life as a
linendraper's shopman, but soon exchanged this occupation for a
dependence upon the great, and for a vain pining after public
employment, for which his indolent and self-indulgent habits rendered him singularly unfit. His most important poetical productions at the beginning of his career were the collection of Eclogues
entitled *The Shepherd's Week*, originally intended as a parody on
the pastorals of Ambrose Philips, and the original and charmingly
executed mock-didactic poem *Trivia, or the Art of Walking the
Streets of London*. He has shown great address in applying the
topics of Theocritus and Virgil to the customs, employments, and
superstitions of English peasants, and he has endeavoured to
heighten the effect by the occasional employment of antiquated and
provincial expressions. The *Trivia* is interesting, not only for its
ease and quiet humour, but for the curious details it gives us of the
street scenery, costume, and manners of that time. Gay's dramatic

pieces generally contained, or were supposed to contain, occasional political allusions, the piquancy of which greatly contributed to their popularity. His most successful venture was the *Beggars Opera*, the idea of which is said to have been first suggested by Swift when residing, in 1726, at Pope's villa at Twickenham. The conception is eminently happy: it was to transfer the songs and incidents of the Italian Opera—then almost a novelty in England, and in the blaze of popularity—to the lowest class of English life. To use Swift's expression, it was a kind of Newgate pastoral, and was a sort of parody of the opera then in vogue, while it became the origin of the English Opera. It proved an unparalleled success; and Gay acquired from the performance of his piece the very large sum of nearly 700*l.* Encouraged by this he produced a kind of continuation called *Polly*, which, though far inferior, was even more profitable, for on its being prohibited by the Lord Chamberlain, the opposition party contributed so liberally to its publication that Gay is said to have cleared about 1100*l.* After losing the bulk of his property in the South Sea mania, he was received into the family of the Duke and Duchess of Queensberry, where he remained till his death in 1732. He was the author of a collection of *Fables* in easy octosyllable verse, written to contribute to the education of William Duke of Cumberland, which still retain a kind of popularity from their figuring in every collection of poetry for the young; their style rendering them peculiarly adapted for reading and learning by heart. Gay's songs and ballads, whether those introduced into the *Beggars' Opera* and other dramatic works, or those written separately, are among the most musical, touching, playful, and charming, that exist in the language.

Our space will only permit a cursory mention of SIR SAMUEL GARTH (died in 1719), a Whig physician of eminence, whose poem of *The Dispensary*, written on occasion of a squabble between the College of Physicians and the Apothecaries' Company, was half satirical and half a plea in favour of giving medical assistance to the poor; of THOMAS PARNELL (1679-1717), a friend of Pope and Swift, who held a living in Ireland, and is known chiefly by his graceful but somewhat feeble tale of *The Hermit*, a versified parable founded on a striking story originally derived from the *Gesta Romanorum*; and of THOMAS TICKELL (1686-1740), celebrated for his friendship with the accomplished Addison, whose death suggested a noble elegy, the only work of Tickell which rises above the elegant mediocrity that marks the general tone of the minor poetry of that age.

EDWARD YOUNG (1681-1765) began his career in the unsuccessful pursuit of fortune in the public service. Disappointed in his hopes he entered the church; and serious domestic losses still further intensified a natural tendency to morbid and melancholy reflection. He obtained his first literary fame by his satire entitled the *Love of Fame, the Universal Passion*, written before he had abandoned a secular career. But Young's place in the history of English poetry is due to his striking and original poem *The Night Thoughts*. This work, consisting of nine *nights* of meditations, is in blank verse, and is made up of reflections on Life, Death, Immortality, and all the most solemn subjects that can engage the attention of the Christian and the philosopher. The general tone of the work is sombre and gloomy, perhaps in some degree affectedly so; for the author perpetually parades the melancholy personal circumstances under which he wrote, overwhelmed by the rapidly-succeeding losses of many who were dearest to him; and the reader can never get rid of the idea that the grief and desolation were purposely exaggerated for effect. The epigrammatic nature of some of his most striking images is best testified by the large number of expressions which have passed from his writings into the colloquial language of society, such as "procrastination is the thief of time," "all men think all men mortal but themselves," and a multitude of others.

The poetry of the Scottish Lowlands found an admirable representative at this time in ALLAN RAMSAY (1686-1758), born in a humble class of life, who was first a wigmaker, and afterwards a bookseller in Edinburgh. He was of a happy, jovial, and contented humour, and rendered great services to the literature of his country by reviving the taste for the excellent old Scottish poets, and by editing and imitating the incomparable songs and ballads current among the people. He was also the author of an original pastoral poem, the *Gentle* (or Noble) *Shepherd*, which grew out of two eclogues he had written, descriptive of the rural life and scenery of Scotland. The complete work appeared in 1725, and consists of a series of dialogues in verse, written in the melodious and picturesque dialect of the country, and interwoven into a simple but interesting love-story.

CHAPTER XIX.

THE ESSAYISTS.

THE class of writers who form the subject of this chapter are
identified with the creation of a new and peculiar form of English
literature, which was destined to exert a powerful and most beneficial influence on the manners and intellectual development of
society. The mode of publication was periodical; and a kind of
journals made their appearance, many of them enjoying an immense
popularity, combining a small modicum of public news with a
species of short essay or lively dissertation on some subject connected with morality or criticism, and inculcating principles of
virtue in great, and good taste and politeness in small things. The
first establishment of the periodical essay is due to Sir Richard
Steele; but the most illustrious representative of this department
of literature is JOSEPH ADDISON (1672-1719). This great writer
and excellent man was the son of Lancelot Addison, a divine of
some reputation for learning, and was born in 1672. He was educated at the Charter-house, from whence he passed to Queen's and
ultimately to Magdalen College, Oxford; and here he distinguished
himself by the regularity of his conduct, the assiduity of his application, and his exquisite taste in Latin verse. His first essays in
English verse, at the age of 22, were some lines in praise of
Dryden, followed by an eulogistic poem on the King (William III.).
Addison continued his trial-flight, under Dryden's wing, translating
the greater part of the IVth Georgic of Virgil. Lord Somers procured for the rising neophyte a pension of 300*l.*, which enabled him
to travel in France and Italy; but the death of King William having
deprived him of his pension, he returned to England; and he passed
some time in London, very poor in purse, but exhibiting that dignified
patience and quiet reserve which made his character so estimable.
But his period of obscuration was very brief. In 1704 the great Marlborough won the memorable victory of Blenheim; Godolphin, eager
to see the event celebrated in some worthy manner, applied, on Halifax's recommendation, to Addison, and the poem of the *Campaign* was
the result. The verses are stiff and artificial enough; but Addison,
abandoning the absurd custom of former poets, who paint a military hero as slaughtering whole squadrons with his single arm,

places the glory of a great general on its true basis—power of conceiving and executing profound intellectual combinations, and calmness and imperturbable foresight in the hour of danger. From this moment the career of Addison was a brilliant and successful one. He was appointed Under-Secretary of State, and afterwards Chief Secretary for Ireland; besides which high posts he at different times received various other places both lucrative and honourable. The publication of the *Campaign* had been followed by that of his *Travels in Italy*, exhibiting proofs not only of Addison's graceful scholarship, but also of his delicate humour, his benevolent morality, and his deep religious spirit. In 1707 he gave to the world his pleasing and graceful opera of *Rosamond*; and about this time he in all probability sketched the comedy of the *Drummer*, which however was not published till after his death, when it was brought out by his friend Steele, who is said to have had some share in its composition.

It was in the year 1711 that Addison embarked in that remarkable literary venture, the *Spectator*, first launched by Steele, a short account of whom will not perhaps be out of place here. SIR RICHARD STEELE (1675-1729) was of Irish origin, and as the schoolfellow of Addison, had come to regard him with the deepest veneration and love. Passionately fond of pleasure, and always ready to sacrifice his own interest to the whim of the moment, he caused himself to be disinherited by enlisting in the Horse-Guards as a private; and when afterwards promoted to a commission, he wrote a moral and religious treatise entitled the *Christian Hero*, breathing the loftiest sentiments of piety and virtue. Being an ardent partisan pamphleteer, he was rewarded by Government with the place of Gazetteer, which gave him a sort of monopoly of official news at a time when newspapers were still in their infancy. In 1709 he determined to profit by the facilities this post afforded him, and to found a new species of periodical which should combine ordinary intelligence with a series of light and agreeable essays upon topics of universal interest, likely to improve the taste, the manners, and the morals of society. To this he gave the name of the *Tatler*, a small sheet which appeared thrice a week at the cost of a penny, each number containing a short essay, generally extending to about a couple of octavo pages, and the rest filled up with news and advertisements. Addison, who was in Ireland at the time, did not at first take any part in the project; and the work had already gone through several numbers before he even became aware that Steele was the principal author; but on learning the fact, he gave him valuable assistance, and the extent of his later contributions are well known. After a fairly successful run of almost two years, it was succeeded by the more celebrated *Spectator*, which was carried on upon the same plan, with the difference that it appeared every day, and reached 555 numbers before it was discontinued.   A third journal, the *Guardian*, was commenced in 1713, and reached 175 numbers, but was strikingly inferior to the *Spectator* both in talent and success.   On its failure the old *Spectator* was resumed, but never got beyond the 80th number.   Though master of a singularly ready and pleasant pen, Steele was of course obliged to obtain as much assistance as he could from his friends: and many writers of the time furnished hints or contributions— Swift, Berkeley, Budgell, and others.   But the most constant and powerful aid was supplied by Addison, who to the *Tatler* contributed about one-sixth, to the *Spectator* nearly one-half, and to the *Guardian* one-third of the whole quantity of matter.   Steele died at Caermarthen, in Wales, in 1729.

In 1713 Addison brought out his tragedy of *Cato*, which, from many causes, partly political, and partly personal, enjoyed an enormous popularity.   It is a solemn, cold, and pompous series of tirades in the French taste, and is written in scrupulous adherence to the classical unities; but the intrigue is totally devoid of interest, and the characters are mere frigid embodiments of patriotic and virtuous rhetoric.   In 1716 he married the Dowager Countess of Warwick, to whose son he had in former days been tutor; but this union does not seem to have added much to his happiness.   He then took up his residence in Holland House, to which historic abode he has bequeathed the glory of his presence.   Neither as a member of the House of Commons, nor as a Government official, can Addison be said to have won any great distinction; his invincible timidity prevented him from speaking with effect; and his powers of conversation quite deserted him in the presence of more than one or two hearers.   To this may be ascribed the most marked blemish in his character, for to conquer his natural diffidence, and to give flow and vivacity to his ideas, he had recourse to wine.   We must not forget, however, that excessive drinking was rather the fashion, than regarded as the vice, of the age in England.

In 1717 Addison reached the highest point of his political career: he was made Secretary of State, and in this eminent position exhibited the same liberality, modesty, and genuine public spirit, that had characterized his whole life.   Even in his political journals, the *Freeholder* and the *Examiner*, he never departed from a tone of candour, moderation, and good breeding, which he was almost the first to introduce into political discussion.   He did not retain his post of Secretary of State for a long period; but soon retired,

with a handsome pension of 1500*l.* a year, and determined to devote
the evening of his days to the composition of an elaborate work
on the evidences of the Christian religion. In this task he was
interrupted by death, which cut short his career in 1719. His
celebrated quarrel with Pope was of too complicated a nature to
be described here; but however painful it may be to find the
highest spirits of the age embittered against each other, we can
hardly regret it, for we owe to it one of the finest passages of Pope's
works, the unequalled lines drawing the character of Atticus, which
was unquestionably meant for Addison. Of all the accusations so
brilliantly launched against him, Addison might plead guilty to
none save the very venial one of loving to surround himself with
an obsequious circle of literary admirers; but the blacker portions
of the portrait are traceable to the pure malignity of the sparkling
satirist.

It is the prose portion of Addison's works which gives him the
right to the very high place he holds in the English Literature of
the eighteenth century; and among them, almost exclusively those
Essays which he contributed to the *Tatler*, *Spectator*, and *Guardian*.
The immense fertility of invention displayed in these charming papers, the variety of their subjects, and the singular felicity
of their treatment, will ever place them among the masterpieces of fiction and of criticism. Their variety is indeed extraordinary. Nothing is too high, nothing too low, to furnish matter
for amusing and yet profitable reflection; from the patched and
cherry-coloured ribbons of the ladies to the loftiest principles of
morality and religion, everything is treated with appropriate yet
unforced appositeness. Addison was long held up as the finest
model of elegant yet idiomatic English prose: and even now the
student will find in him some qualities that never can become
obsolete—a never-failing clearness and limpidity of expression, and
a singular harmony between the language and the thought. To
Steele is due the invention of the Club in the *Spectator*, consisting of representatives of the chief classes of town and rural
society. Thus we have Sir Andrew Freeport as the type of the
merchants, Captain Sentry of the soldiers, Sir Roger de Coverley
of the old-fashioned country-gentlemen, and Will Honeycomb of
the men of fashion and pleasure; while linking them all together
is Mr. Spectator himself, the short-faced gentleman, who looks
with a somewhat satirical yet good-humoured interest on all that
he sees going on around him. The inimitable personage of Sir
Roger de Coverley is a perfectly finished picture, worthy of Cervantes
or of Walter Scott; and the manner in which the foibles and the
virtues of the old squire are combined is a proof that Addison,

who added most of the subtle strokes to the character, possessed
humour in its highest and most delicate perfection. And the
inimitable sketches of his dependents, the chaplain, the butler, and
Will Wimble, the poor relation—all these traits of character and
delicate observation of nature must ever place Addison very high
among the great painters of human nature.

Addison's poetry, though very popular in his own time, has
since fallen in public estimation to a point very far below that
occupied by his prose. The songs in *Rosamond* are pleasing and
musical; and, had Addison continued to write in that manner,
he would undoubtedly have left something which rival authors
would have found it very difficult to surpass. His *Hymns* not only
breathe a fervent and tender spirit of piety, but are in their diction
and versification stamped with great beauty and refinement; especially the verses beginning, "When all Thy mercies, O my God,"
and the well-known adaptation of the noble psalm, "The Heavens
declare the Glory of God." The earlier and more ambitious poems
of Addison, even including the once-lauded *Campaign*, have little
to distinguish them from the vast mass of regular, frigid, irre-
proachable composition popular in that time.

Sir William Temple (1628-1698), whose name is more famous in
politics than in literature, produced a number of graceful though
superficial *Essays*, which were extravagantly lauded at a time
when the rank of a writer much increased the public admiration of his works; but which are now read with interest principally on account of their easy good sense, and the agreeable style
in which they are written. One of these, that on *Ancient and
Modern Learning*, will long be remembered as having originated
the notorious controversy respecting the authenticity of the
"Epistles of Phalaris." Even in letter-writing, said Temple, the
Ancients are superior to the Moderns; witness the Epistles of
Phalaris, which are still unapproached and unapproachable. A
new edition of these invaluable productions was published by the
Christ-Church Wits, containing a severe reflection on Bentley, the
great scholar; who, stung by the injustice of the attack, replied
with an argument to prove the spuriousness of these much-lauded
letters. Thus began the great *Boyle and Bentley Controversy;*
which terminated in the complete triumph of Bentley.

No name among the brilliant circle which surrounded Pope and
Swift, is more remarkable than that of Bishop Atterbury (1662-
1732). A Tory and Jacobite of the extreme Oxford type, he played
a prominent part both on the political and literary scene. He was
a man of great intellectual activity, of considerable, though by no
means profound learning, and of a violent, imperious, and restless

temper. He took an active part in the controversy between Boyle
and Bentley, and was for a time considered, by the people of
fashion who knew nothing of the subject, to have completely
demolished the dull, ill-bred Cambridge pedant. He was the
principal author of the reply written in the name of Boyle, whose
tutor he had been at Christ Church, of which illustrious college
Atterbury was for some time Dean. He was in 1713 raised to the
see of Rochester, and became conspicuous not only as a controversialist, but for the force and eloquence of his speeches in Parliament. His plot for the restoration of the exiled Stuarts, his banish-
ment in 1723, and the remaining events of his feverish life, belong
to the history of the country. The private and personal side of
Atterbury's character is far more attractive and respectable than
his public conduct. His friendship for Pope was tender and sincere;
and he was not only the great poet's most affectionate companion,
but guided him with wise and valuable literary counsel. His taste
in literature appears to have been sound: and the intense admiration he always showed **for** the genius of Milton is the more honourable to his judgment, as his extreme Tory opinions must have made
it difficult for him to sympathise with the Puritan and Republican
poet.

LORD SHAFTESBURY (1671-1713), grandson of the famous chancellor, and pupil of Locke, stands very high both as a moralist and
metaphysician, and also as an elegant and classical model of
English prose. His collected works bear the title of *Characteristics*,
and may still be read with interest. Shaftesbury's style is refined
and regular, though somewhat ambitious and finical; but he sometimes, as in his dialogue entitled the *Moralists*, rises to a lofty
height of limpid eloquence. His delineations of character show
much acuteness and observation, and have obtained for him the
honour of comparison with La Bruyère, to whose neat antithetical
mode of portrait-painting the thoughts and language of Shaftesbury
bear no inconsiderable resemblance.

HENRY ST. JOHN, VISCOUNT BOLINGBROKE (1678-1751), remarkable for his extraordinary career as a statesman and orator, was
a prominent member of the brilliant coterie of Pope and Swift.
After many strange vicissitudes, he amused the declining years of
life in the composition of many political, moral, and philosophical
essays. One of these, the *Idea of a Patriot King*, he gave in MS.
to Pope, and exhibited great anger when he discovered, after the
poet's death, that the latter had caused a large impression to be
printed, contrary to a solemn promise. Of his other works, his
Letter to Sir William Windham in defence of his political conduct,
and his *Letters on the Study and Use of History*, are the most im-

portant. The language of Bolingbroke is lofty and oratorical; but the tone of philosophical indifference to the usual objects of ambition generally strikes the reader as affected. It was to Bolingbroke that Pope addressed the *Essay on Man*, and some of the not very orthodox positions maintained in that poem are supposed to have been suggested by him. Bolingbroke's writings against revealed religion were bequeathed by him to his friend DAVID MALLET, an unbeliever, who brought them out, together with Bolingbroke's other works, in 1754. Mallet, who died in 1765, was himself an author, but he is now chiefly known by his *Ballads*, of which *William and Margaret* is the most striking and beautiful.

The most celebrated work of BERNARD MANDEVILLE (1670-1733) is the *Fable of the Bees*, a poem with notes, in which the author endeavours to prove that private vices may be public benefits; or, in other words, that the play of human passions and propensities, however immoral some of them may be in the relations between man and man, works unconsciously towards the welfare of that complex body which we call society. His doctrines were vigorously assailed by the accomplished and almost ideally virtuous BISHOP BERKELEY (1684-1753), equally famous for the evangelic benevolence of his character and the acuteness of his genius, whose mind was ever full of projects for increasing the virtue and happiness of his fellow-creatures. As Bishop of Cloyne in Ireland, he presents one of the rare instances of a prelate, out of pure love for his flock and an unaffected contentment with his lot, obstinately refusing any further promotion. His writings are exceedingly numerous, and embrace a wide field of moral and metaphysical discussion. He is one of the most brilliant, as well as one of the earliest maintainers of the extreme spiritualistic theory; and thus is in some degree an opponent of Locke. Berkeley frequently wrote in the form of dialogue; and one of the most characteristic and popular of his works is entitled *The Minute Philosopher*. In the connexion between the physical and metaphysical branches of investigation, Berkeley's writings occupy an important place: thus his *Theory of Vision* established several valuable facts; and he drew conclusions from several striking phenomena, concerning that subtle subject. In all his arguments his aim was to refute the materialists.

LADY MARY WORTLEY MONTAGU (1690-1762) was the most brilliant letter-writer of this period, when Pope and many other distinguished men of letters assiduously cultivated the epistolary form of composition. She was the daughter of the Duke of Kingston, and celebrated, even from her childhood, as Lady Mary Pierrepont, for the vivacity of her intellect, her precocious mental acquirements, and the beauty and graces of her person. Her

education had been far more extensive and solid than was then
usually given to women : her acquaintance with history, and even
with Latin, was considerable, and her studies had been in some
degree directed by Bishop Burnet. In 1712 she married Mr.
Edward Wortley Montagu, a grave and saturnine diplomatist, with
whose character the sprightly and airy woman of fashion and
literature could have had nothing in common. She accompanied
her husband on his embassy to the court of Constantinople, and
described her travels over Europe and the East in those delightful
Letters which have given her in English literature a place
resembling that of Madame de Sévigné in the literature of France.
Admirable common sense, observation, vivacity, extensive reading
without a trace of pedantry, and a pleasant tinge of half-playful
sarcasm, are the qualities which distinguish her correspondence.
The style is perfection : the simplicity and natural elegance of the
high-born and high-bred lady, combined with the ease of the
thorough woman of the world. The moral tone, indeed, is far from
being high, for neither the character nor the career of Lady Mary
had been such as to cherish a very scrupulous delicacy. But she
had seen so much, and had been brought into contact with so many
remarkable persons, and in a way that gave her unusual means of
judging of them, that she is always sensible and amusing. The
successful introduction of inoculation for the smallpox is mainly to
be attributed to the intelligence and courage of Lady Mary
Montagu, who not only had the courage to try the experiment upon
her own child, but with admirable constancy resisted the furious
opposition of bigotry and ignorance against the bold innovation
She was at one time the intimate friend of Pope, and the object of
his most ardent adulation ; but a violent quarrel occurred between
them, and the spiteful poet pursued her for a time with an almost
furious hatred. She is the Sappho of his satirical works.

CHAPTER XX.

Most departments of literature were cultivated earlier in England than that of Prose Fiction. We have, it is true, the romantic form of this kind of writing in the *Arcadia* of Sydney, and the philosophical form in the *Utopia* and the *Atlantis;* but the exclusive employment of prose narrative in the delineation of the passions, characters, and incidents of real life was first carried to perfection by a constellation of great writers in the eighteenth century, among whom the names of Defoe, Richardson, Fielding, Smollett, Sterne, and Goldsmith, are the most brilliant luminaries. In England, where the genius of the nation is eminently practical, and where the immense development of free institutions has tended to encourage individuality of character, and to give importance to private and domestic life, the literature of Fiction divided into two great but correlative branches, to which our language alone has given specific and distinct appellations—the Romance and the Novel. Of the former the characters and incidents are of a lofty, historical, or supernatural tone ; the latter expresses a recital of the events of ordinary or domestic life, generally of a contemporary epoch. It is the latter department in which English writers, from the time of its first appearance in our literature down to the present time, have encountered few rivals and no superiors.

The founder of the English Novel is Daniel Defoe (1661-1731), a man of extraordinary versatility and energy as a writer ; for his complete works are said to comprise upwards of 200 separate compositions. Of humble origin, he was educated for the ministry in a dissenting sect, but embraced a mercantile career, having at various periods carried on the business of a hosier, a tile-maker, and a woollen-draper. He carried his devotion to Protestant principles so far as to join the abortive insurrection under the Duke of Monmouth ; though from this danger he escaped with impunity. In spite of the pillory, of fines and imprisonment, to which he was condemned more than once, he continued fearlessly to pour forth pamphlet after pamphlet, full of irony, logic, and patriotism. Among the most celebrated of his works in this class are his

Trueborn Englishman, a poem in singularly tuneless rhymes, but full of strong sense and vigorous argument, in which he defends William of Orange and the Dutch against the prejudices of his countrymen; the *Hymn to the Pillory*, and the famous pamphlet *The Shortest Way with the Dissenters*, written in 1702, in which, to show the folly and cruelty of the recent Acts persecuting the Sectarians, he with admirable sarcasm adopts the tone of a violent persecutor, and advises Parliament to employ the stake, the pillory, and the halter, with unrelenting severity. For this he was thrice pilloried, and lay in Newgate for more than a year, during which imprisonment he commenced the *Review*, a literary journal which may be regarded as the prototype of our modern semi-political, semi-literary periodicals. It appeared thrice a week, and was written with great force and ready vigour of language. During the negotiations which preceded the union of Scotland to the British crown, he was employed as a confidential agent in Edinburgh, and acquitted himself with ability.

In 1719 Defoe published the first part of *Robinson Crusoe*, the success of which, among that comparatively humble class of readers which Defoe generally addressed, was instantaneous and immense. The primary idea of this famous work may have been derived from the authentic narrative of Alexander Selkirk, a sailor who had been *marooned*, as the term then was, by his captain on the uninhabited island of Juan Fernandez, where he passed several years in complete solitude. The intense interest of *Robinson Crusoe* arises partly from the simplicity and probability of the events, the *unforeseenness* of many of which completely annihilates the reader's suspicion of the truth of what he is perusing, and partly from the skill with which Defoe identifies himself with the character of his Recluse, who is always represented as a commonplace man, without any pretensions to extraordinary knowledge or intelligence. It is perhaps somewhat injurious that this book is generally read when we are very young; for the impressions it leaves upon the memory and the imagination are so deep and permanent that we do not return to the work when increased intellectual development would make us better able to appreciate Defoe's wonderful art. The second part, which the success of the first encouraged Defoe to produce, is inferior to the first: indeed, the moment the solitude of the island is invaded by more strangers than Friday, the charm is evidently diminished. Scott has well remarked that a striking evidence of Defoe's skill in this kind of fiction is the studiously low key, both as regards style and incidents, in which the whole is pitched.

Among Defoe's numerous other works of fiction may be mentioned the *Memoirs of a Cavalier*, supposed to have been written by one who had taken part in the great Civil War, which so far deceived even the great Lord Chatham that he cited it as an authentic narrative. A not less remarkable narrative is the *Journal of the Great Plague in London*, where the imaginary annalist, a respectable London shopkeeper—a character which Defoe assumed with consummate skill—describes the terrible sights of that fearful time. Nothing can exceed the vividness with which episodes of the city life during the great calamity are set before us; and in some passages, as in the description of the maniac fanatic Solomon Eagle, the 'Great Pit in Aldgate, and the long line of anchored ships stretching far down the Thames, Defoe rises into a very lofty and powerful strain of description. A number of stories,—the *Adventures of Colonel Jack, Moll Flanders, Roxana, Captain Singleton*,—show the same quiet power of imitating reality. In a remarkable tract he has described the *Apparition of one Mrs. Veal to her friend Mrs. Bargrave at Canterbury*; and this is one of the boldest experiments ever made upon human credulity. It was composed to help off the sale of a dull book of Sermons, and had the effect of instantly causing the whole edition to quit the bookseller's shelves; for *Drelincourt on Death* was powerfully recommended by the visitor from another world.

But SAMUEL RICHARDSON (1689-1761) must be regarded as the real founder of the romance of private life. He was born of very humble rustic parentage, and came to London when a lad to be apprenticed to a printer. In this calling he distinguished himself by so much diligence that he gradually rose to the highest place in his business, having at last become the purchaser of a half share in the lucrative patent office of Printer to the King. Having accumulated an easy fortune, he retired to a pleasant suburban house at Parson's Green, near London, where he passed an honourable old age in literary employment, surrounded by a little knot of female worshippers, whose adulatory incense his intense vanity made him greedily receive. The works of Richardson are three in number: *Pamela*, published in 1740, *Clarissa Harlowe*, in 1748, and *Sir Charles Grandison*, in 1753. These three novels are all written upon one plan; that is, the story is entirely told in letters which are supposed to be written by the various persons in the action, a mode of fictitious composition which is attended with advantages and disadvantages of a very evident kind. It was in any case eminently suited to the peculiar genius of Richardson, which is seen rather in the evolution of character by slow and delicate touches of self-betrayal, than by any vigour of description of persons or events.

Pamela describes the sufferings, trials, and vicissitudes undergone by a poor, but beautiful and innocent, country girl who enters the

service of a rich gentleman. She triumphantly resists all the
seductions, and all the violence by which he essays to overcome her
virtue, and even the promptings of her own heart in his favour; for
Richardson represents her as passionately attached to her unworthy
master, to whom, by way of a moral inculcating the reward of
virtue, she is ultimately married. *Pamela* originally sprang from
a collection of familiar letters which Richardson, at the request of
his publishing firm, had undertaken to write as a manual to
improve the style and the morality of the middle classes of readers:
and while engaged on it he was struck with the happy idea of
making his letters tell a continuous story. The popularity of the
work was so great that five editions were exhausted in one year;
although this, like all Richardson's works, is extremely voluminous.

Clarissa Harlowe is incontestably Richardson's greatest work.
Whether we consider the interest of the story, the variety and truth
of the characters, or the intense pathos of the catastrophe, to which
every incident artfully leads, we must not only accord it a decisive
superiority over his other productions, but must give it one of the
foremost places in the history of prose fiction. It is the story of a
young lady who falls a victim to the treachery and profligacy of a
man of splendid talent and attractions, but of complete and almost
diabolical corruption. Though Richardson, both by natural disposition and circumstances, is far more successful in the delineation of
female than of male characters, Lovelace, the seducer, is one of the
most perfect and finished portraits that literature has to show.
There is no better proof of this than the fact that the name has
become in all languages the synonym of the brilliant and unprincipled seducer; which circumstance also gives us a record of the
immense popularity which Richardson still enjoys throughout
Europe.

The last work in this famous trilogy is *Sir Charles Grandison*, in
which the author, who never relinquished the idea of incorporating
a moral in his fictions, intended to give an ideal portrait of a
character which should combine consummate ethical and religious
perfection with the graces and accomplishments of a man of fashion.
In his three successive novels Richardson essayed to portray three
different orders in the social scale: in *Pamela* the lower, in *Clarissa*
the middle, and in *Grandison* the aristocratic class of society. But
he was, from education and position, totally unacquainted with the
real manners and modes of thought and feeling prevalent in the
fashionable world; and in describing what he so imperfectly guessed
at he fell into the error natural to men of imperfect education and
inexperienced in the manners of the great world. He is perpetually
straining after fine language, which forms a ludicrous contrast with

the really easy unaffected tone of the higher circles. It is said that Richardson consulted a great lady as to the tone and language of high life; and that she found so many errors and inconsistencies that he abandoned in despair the hope of correcting them. The distinguishing characteristics of Richardson are patient analysis of the human mind and passions, particularly in the female sex, a tendency to accumulate minute incident and microscopic description, and a sickly and morbid tone of sentiment, combined with a pathetic force rarely found in writers of any nation.

The second great name among the novelists of this period is that of HENRY FIELDING (1707-1754), qualified by Byron as " the prose Homer of human nature." In his personal character, as well as in his literary career,—in everything, indeed, but the power of his genius,—he was the exact opposite of Richardson. Of noble birth, being a descendant of the illustrious house of Denbigh, and son of General Fielding, he early in life succeeded to a ruined inheritance, and betook himself to the stage, becoming a dramatic author and a lively writer in the *Covent Garden Journal*. He produced a considerable number of pieces, now entirely forgotten, which show that his talent was in no way adapted to the theatre. His career for some years was a continuous struggle with fortune and his own extravagance. He married an excellent lady, and squandered her not inconsiderable portion; he speculated in the Haymarket Theatre and failed utterly; he then tried the law, and was called to the bar, but without any immediate advantage. He also took an active part in political controversy, and in numerous pamphlets and articles for journals maintained liberal and anti-Jacobite principles. But it was not until the year 1742 that he struck out that vein of humorous writing in which he never had, nor is ever likely to have, a rival; when he produced his first novel, *Joseph Andrews*, which was in some sense intended as a parody or caricature, ridiculing the timid and fastidious morality, the shopkeeper tone and the somewhat preaching *good-boy* style of *Pamela*, just then in the full blaze of success. Fielding's novel at once received the honour due to a great original creation; and in pretty rapid succession he produced his *Journey from this World to the Next*, full of political allusions that have now lost their piquancy, and his truly remarkable satirical tale *The Life of Jonathan Wild the Great*. In 1749 he was appointed to the laborious and then far from respectable post of a London police magistrate: and while engaged in this occupation he composed the finest, completest, and profoundest of his works, the incomparable *Tom Jones;* which was followed after a brief interval by *Amelia*, in which he unquestionably intended to portray some of his own follies and irregularities, but with the principal object of paying a tribute to the virtues and affection of his first wife. Ruined in health by labour and excesses, he sailed for Lisbon in 1754; and after a short time died in that city, and was buried in the Protestant cemetery there towards the end of the same year.

The qualities which distinguish Fielding's genius are accurate observation of character, and an extraordinary power of deducing the actions and expressions of his personages from the elements of their nature, a constant sympathy with the vigorous unrestrained characters, in all ranks of society, but especially in the lowest, which he loved to delineate. In the construction of his plots he is masterly. That of *Tom Jones* is perhaps the finest example to be met with in fiction of a series of events probable yet surprising, each of which inevitably leads to the ultimate catastrophe. He combined an almost childish delight in fun and extravagantly ludicrous incident, with a philosophic closeness of analysis of character and an impressive tone of moral reflection, the latter often masked under a pleasant air of satire and irony. His novels breathe a sort of fresh *open-air* atmosphere, a strong contrast to the close artificial medium which pervades the romances of Richardson.

The most attractive character in *Joseph Andrews* is Parson Adams, one of the richest, most humorous, and truly genial conceptions of this great artist. Adams's learning, simplicity, and courage, together with his innumerable and always consistent oddities, make him as truly humorous a character as Sancho Panza himself. In the adventures of *Jonathan Wild the Great* the exploits of a consummate scoundrel are related in a tone of ironical admiration; and the story contains some powerful and many humorous scenes.

In *Tom Jones* it is difficult to know what most to admire,—the artful conduct of the plot, the immense variety, truth, and humour of the personages, the gaiety of the incidents, or the acute remarks which the author has copiously introduced. The character of Squire Western, the type of the violent, brutal rural magnate of those days, is one which remains for ever fixed on the memory. Tom Jones himself and the fair Sophy, though elaborated by the author with peculiar care, as types of all that he thought attractive, are tinged with much coarseness and vulgarity; but the time when Fielding wrote was remarkable for the low tone of manners and sentiment.

The interest of *Amelia* is entirely domestic and familiar: the errors and repentance of Captain Booth, and the inexhaustible love and indulgence of the heroine, are strongly contrasted. Fielding had little power over the pathetic emotions; there are, however, in this novel several episodes and strokes of character which are touching, and which exhibit that peculiar characteristic of truly humorous conceptions, namely the power of touching the heart while exciting the sense of the ludicrous.

TOBIAS GEORGE SMOLLETT (1721-1771) was descended from an ancient and respectable family in Scotland. After remaining a short time in the service of a medical practitioner in Glasgow, he proceeded to London when only nineteen years of age with the MS. of a tragedy, entitled the *Regicide*, in his pocket. Failing in his attempt to bring out this work he entered the naval service as surgeon's mate, and was present at the unfortunate expedition to Carthagena in 1741. Here he had the opportunity of studying the oddities of sea-characters, which he afterwards so admirably reproduced in his fictions, and of learning by experience the atrocious cruelty, corruption and incompetency which then reigned in the naval administration. In 1748 he began his career as a novelist with *Roderick Random;* in which, as indeed in all his novels, he relied for success rather on a lively series of grotesque adventures than on any elaboration of intrigue or deep analysis of character. *Peregrine Pickle* was published in 1751; and Smollett now devoted himself to the career of a writer and politician. In 1753 he produced his third great romance, *The Adventures of Ferdinand, Count Fathom,* describing, with a higher moral intention than is usually found in his works, the career of an unprincipled scoundrel, cheat, and swindler. A few years afterwards the violence of Smollett's political opinions brought him in collision with the law. He was prosecuted for an attack on Admiral Knowles, was fined 100*l.* and imprisoned for three months, during which time he continued the management of the *Critical Review*, and in his editorial capacity managed to raise up against himself a whole swarm of angry politicians, writers, and doctors. He now produced his novel of *Sir Lancelot Greaves*, a most unfortunate and feeble effort to adapt the plot and leading idea of *Don Quixote* to English contemporary life; and wrote, with extraordinary rapidity, his *History of England,* of which the ardent and partial judgments are the most remarkable features. In a *Tour in France and Italy,* which he undertook to divert his grief under the loss of a beloved child, Smollett exhibits a painful and almost ludicrous incapacity to appreciate the beautiful, sublime, or interesting objects he met with: he "travelled from Dan to Beersheba, and found all barren." In a now-forgotten tale, *The Adventures of an Atom*, he attacked Bute, who had formerly been his patron. Completely broken in health by incessant labour and continual agitation, he at last retired to die at Leghorn; where, in spite of weakness, exhaustion, and suffering, the dying genius gave forth its most pleasing flash of comic humour. This was the novel of *Humphrey Clinker*, the only fiction in which Smollett adopted the epistolary form, and the most cordial, comic, and laughable of them all.

In the structure of his fictions Smollett is manifestly inferior to both Richardson and Fielding: his novels are simply a series of striking, grotesque, farcical, and occasionally pathetic scenes, which have little other bond of union than the fact of their being threaded, so to say, on the life of a single person. Yet his books are eminently *amusing*; the reader's attention is kept awake by a lively succession of persons and events, some of which, though they may be coarse and low-lived, are invariably vivid and life-like. There can be no doubt that Smollett was frequently in the habit of transferring to his novels real adventures of his own life, which is specially true of his inimitable and exquisitely varied sailor-characters, from Lieutenant Bowling and Ap Morgan in the first novel, through the rich gallery of oddities in his later works, particularly Commodore Trunnion and Pipes in *Peregrine Pickle*. As a rule his heroes have but little to attract the reader's sympathy, being generally hard, impudent, selfish, and ungrateful adventurers; but in the subordinate persons, and especially in those of grotesque but faithful followers, like Strap or Pipes, Smollett shows a greater warmth of sentiment. In *Humphrey Clinker*, though running over with fun and grotesque incident, there is a riper and mellower tone of character-painting than is to be found in his preceding works. The personages of Lismahago and Tabitha Bramble are inimitably carried out: the latter is indeed perhaps the most finished portrait in Smollett's whole gallery.

Smollett possessed considerable poetical talents. He wrote the powerful verses entitled the *Tears of Scotland*, which breathed the patriotic indignation of a generous mind, horrorstruck by the cruelties inflicted by the orders of the Duke of Cumberland after the battle of Culloden; a poem equally honourable to his civil courage and to his genius.

LAURENCE STERNE (1713–1768), whose character was as eccentric as his works, was born in Ireland, but educated, with the assistance of some relations of his mother's, at Cambridge. Entering the Church, he long held the living of Sutton, to which he afterwards added a prebendal stall in the Cathedral of York; and he was ultimately advanced to the rich living of Coxwold. The first two volumes of his novel of *Tristram Shandy* were published in 1761, and the novelty and oddity of his style instantly raised him to the summit of popularity: two more volumes appeared in the following year, and Sterne became for a time the pet and lion of fashionable London society. He made two tours on the Continent, the first in

France, and the second in France and Italy, where he accumulated the materials incorporated in his delightful *Sentimental Journey*, intended to form a part of his romance, but which is generally read as an independent work. In this book he personates his favourite character Yorick, a mixture of the humorist and the sentimental observer. He died alone and friendless in a Bond-street lodging-house, attended in his last illness by mercenaries, who are said to have plundered him of such trifles as he possessed—a comfortless and gloomy ending, which he had himself desired.

His works consist of the novel of *Tristram Shandy*, of the *Sentimental Journey*, and of a collection of *Sermons*, written in the odd and fantastic style which he brought into temporary vogue. *Tristram Shandy*, though nominally a romance in the biographical form, is intentionally irregular and capricious, the imaginary hero never making his appearance at all, and the story consisting of a series of sketches and episodes introducing us to the interior of an English country family, one of the richest collections of oddities that genius has ever delineated. The narrative is written partly in the character of Yorick (Sterne himself), supposed to be a clergyman and a humorist, and partly in that of the phantom-like Tristram; and the most prominent persons are Walter Shandy, a retired merchant, the father of the supposed hero, his mother, his uncle Toby Shandy (a veteran officer), and his servant Corporal Trim. These are all conceived and executed in the finest and most Shakespearian spirit of humour, tenderness, and observation; and they are supported by a crowd of minor yet hardly less individual portraitures — Obadiah, Dr. Slop, the Widow Wadman, Susanna, nay down to the "foolish fat scullion." Mr. Shandy, the restless crotchety philosopher, is delineated with consummate skill, and admirably contrasted with the simple benevolence and professional enthusiasm of the unequalled Uncle Toby, a personage belonging to the same category of creative genius as Sancho or as Parson Adams. In all Sterne's writings there is a great parade of obscure and quaint erudition, which tends powerfully to give an original flavour to his style. His humour and his pathos are often truly admirable; and he possesses in a high degree that rare power, found only in the greatest humorists, of combining the ludicrous and the pathetic; though both his humour and his pathos are very often false and artificial. His episodes, as the often-quoted *Story of Le Fevre*, are related with consummate art and tenderness; but in Sterne—probably from his vanity and deficiency of discrimination — there is no medium between excellence and failure. He is an acute and just observer of the little turns of gesture and expression, and makes his characters *betray* their idiosyncrasies by involuntary touches, just as men do in real life.

The most charming and versatile writer of the eighteenth century is OLIVER GOLDSMITH (1728-1774), whose works bear a peculiar stamp of gentle grace and elegance. Born at the village of Pallas in the county of Longford, the son of a poor curate of English extraction, in 1745 he entered the University of Dublin in the humble quality of sizar. His career there was one of the strangest; and after many disheartening attempts to make his way into some honourable profession, he began those travels—for the most part on foot, and subsisting by the aid of his flute and the charity given to a poor scholar—which successively led him to Leyden, through Holland, France, Germany, and Switzerland, and even to Padua, where he boasted that he received a medical degree. In 1756 he found his way back to his native country; and his career during about eight years was a succession of desultory struggles with famine; sometimes he acted as a chemist's shopman in London; sometimes as an usher in boarding-schools; sometimes as a practitioner of medicine among "the beggars in Axe Lane," as he expressed it himself; but most generally as a bookseller's hack. His literary apprenticeship was passed in writing to order schoolbooks, tales for children, prefaces, indexes, and reviews of books; and in contributing to the Monthly, Critical, and Lady's Review, the British Magazine, and other periodicals. In this period of obscure drudgery he composed some of his most charming works, or at least formed that inimitable style which makes him the rival of Addison. He produced the *Letters from a Citizen of the World*, the plan of which is imitated from Montesquieu's Lettres Persanes, giving a description of English life and manners in the assumed character of a Chinese traveller; a *Life of Beau Nash;* and a short and gracefully-narrated *History of England*, in the form of Letters from a Nobleman to his Son, the authorship of which was ascribed to Lyttelton. It was in 1764 that the publication of his beautiful poem of the *Traveller* caused him to emerge from this slough of obscure literary drudgery; and from this period Goldsmith's career was one of uninterrupted literary success, though his folly and improvidence kept him in constant debt. In 1766 appeared the *Vicar of Wakefield*, that masterpiece of gentle humour and delicate tenderness; and in the following year his first comedy, the *Goodnatured Man*, which comparatively failed upon the stage—in some measure from its very merits. In 1768 Goldsmith composed, as taskwork for the booksellers, the *History of Rome*, distinguished by its extreme superficiality of information and want of research, no less than by ex chanting grace of style and vivacity of narration. In 1770 he published the *Deserted Village*, the companion poem to the *Traveller*, written in some measure in the same manner, and not less touching and perfect: and in 1773 was acted his comedy *She Stoops to Conquer*, one of the gayest, pleasantest, and most amusing pieces that the English stage can boast. Goldsmith was now one of the most popular authors of his time; his society was courted by the wits, artists, statesmen, and writers, who formed a brilliant circle round Johnson and Reynolds; and he became a member of the famous Literary Club. His unconquerable improvidence, however, still kept him the slave of booksellers, who obliged him to waste his exquisite talent on works hastily thrown off, and for which he neither possessed the requisite knowledge nor could make the necessary researches; thus he successively put forth as taskwork the *History of England*, the *History of Greece*, and the *History of Animated Nature*, the two former works being mere compilations of second-hand facts, and the last an epitomized translation of Buffon. He died at the age of forty-six, deeply mourned by the brilliant circle of friends to which his very weaknesses had endeared him, and followed by the tears and blessings of many wretches whom his inexhaustible benevolence had relieved.

In everything Goldsmith wrote, prose or verse, serious or comic, there is a peculiar delicacy and purity of sentiment, tinging, of course, the language and diction as well as the thought. No quality in his writings is more striking than the union of grotesque humour with a sort of pensive tenderness which gives to his verse a peculiar character of gliding melody and grace. The two poems of the *Traveller* and the *Deserted Village* will ever be regarded as masterpieces of sentiment and description. The light yet rapid touch with which, in the former, he has traced the scenery and the natural peculiarities of various countries, will be admired long after the reader has learned to neglect the false social theories embodied in his deductions; and in the latter the reader lingers over the delicious details of human as well as inanimate nature which the poet has combined into the lovely pastoral picture of "sweet Auburn." The touches of tender personal feeling which he has interwoven with his description are all characterised by a sweet pensive grace; while, when the occasion demands, he can rise with easy wing to the height of even sublime elevation.

The *Vicar of Wakefield*, in spite of the extreme absurdity and inconsistency of its plot, is one of those works that the world will not willingly let die. The gentle and quiet humour embodied in the simple Dr. Primrose, the delicate yet vigorous contrasts of character in the other personages, the atmosphere of purity, cheerfulness, and gaiety, which envelopes all the scenes and incidents, insure it immortality. Goldsmith's two comedies are written in two different manners, the *Goodnatured Man* being a comedy of character, and *She Stoops to Conquer* a comedy of intrigue. The merit of the first piece chiefly consists in the truly laughable personage of Croaker, and in the excellent scene where the disguised bailiffs are passed off on Miss Richland as the friends of Honeywood, whose house and person they have seized. But in *She Stoops to Conquer* we have a first-rate specimen of the comedy of intrigue, where the interest mainly depends upon a tissue of lively and farcical incidents, and where the characters, though lightly sketched, form a gallery of eccentric pictures.

Of Goldsmith's lighter fugitive poems the *Haunch of Venison* is a model of easy narrative and accurate sketching of commonplace society; and *Retaliation* consists of a series of slight yet delicate portraits of some of the most distinguished literary friends of the poet thrown off with a hand at once refined and vigorous.

CHAPTER XXI.

HISTORICAL, MORAL, POLITICAL, AND THEOLOGICAL WRITERS OF
THE EIGHTEENTH CENTURY.

In accordance with that peculiar law which seems to govern the appearance, at particular epochs, of several great names in one department of art or literature, like the sculptors of the Periclean age, the romantic dramatists in that of Elizabeth, and the novelists who appeared in England in the days of Richardson and Fielding, the eighteenth century was signalised by a remarkable wealth of historical genius, and gave birth to Hume, Robertson, and Gibbon.

DAVID HUME (1711-1776) was born of an ancient Scottish family, and received his education in the University of Edinburgh. His desires and ambition were set upon literary fame, and after reluctantly trying the profession of law and the pursuit of commerce, he lived abroad some years, devoting himself to the cultivation of moral and metaphysical science, and to the preparation of his mind for future historical labours. In 1737 he returned to England, and was so much discouraged with the coldness of the public towards his first moral and metaphysical productions, that he at one time meditated changing his name and expatriating himself for ever. In 1746 and the following year a gleam of success shone upon him; he entered the public service, and was employed as secretary to General St. Clair in various diplomatic missions. In 1752 he accepted the post of Librarian to the Scottish Faculty of Advocates, and there began his great work, the *History of England* from the accession of the Stuart Dynasty to the Revolution of 1688; to which he afterwards added in successive volumes the earlier history from the invasion of Julius Cæsar to the reign of James I. Though far from successful at first, the work soon overcame the indifference of the public, and rapidly rose to the highest popularity. Hume's reputation was now solidly established; he accompanied as secretary the embassy of General Conway to Paris, where he became one of the lions of the fashionable society of the French capital. He fulfilled for a short time the still higher functions of Under-Secretary of State; and retiring with a pension passed the evening of his life in philosophic tranquillity, enjoying the respect and affection which his virtuous and amiable qualities attracted, and which not even his scepticism could repel. He died in 1776.

As a moral and metaphysical writer Hume certainly deserves a high place in the history of philosophy. The prominent feature of his *Treatise on Human Nature*, published in 1738, was the attempt to deduce the operations of the mind entirely from the two sources of impressions and ideas, which he looks upon as distinct, and his denying the existence of any fundamental difference between such actions as we call virtuous and vicious, other than as they are practically found to be conducive to or destructive of the advantage of the individual or the species.

The *History of England* is a book of very high value. In a certain exquisite ease and vivacity of narration it has certainly never been surpassed; and in the analysis of character and the appreciation of great events Hume's singular clearness and philosophic elevation of view give him a right to one of the foremost places among modern historians. But its defects are no less considerable. Hume's indolence induced him to remain contented with taking his facts at second-hand from preceding writers, without troubling himself about accuracy. He shows a strong leaning to the Stuart dynasty, and even to the Catholic church as opposed to Protestantism; for he belonged to the aristocratical section of the Scottish people, who were almost uniformly Jacobites; and thus the sceptical reasoner was inclined from personal sympathies to opinions precisely contrary to those which he might have been expected to maintain.

Contemporary with Hume was his countryman WILLIAM ROBERTSON (1721-1793), distinguished, like him, by the eloquence of his narrative, by the picturesque power of delineating characters and events, and also by a singular dignity and purity of style. As a Presbyterian pastor he was highly celebrated for his eloquence in the pulpit; and in 1762 was elected Principal of the University of Edinburgh. He produced three great historical works, the *History of Scotland*, embracing the reigns of the unfortunate Mary and her son James VI. down to the accession of the latter to the throne of England, the *History of the Reign of Charles V.*, and the *History of the Discovery*, and first Colonisation by the Spaniards, *of America*. In all of them we perceive a rich and melodious though somewhat artificial style, great though not always accurate research, and a strong power of vivid and pathetic description. Yet though many of the general disquisitions prefixed to or introduced in Robertson's history, are marked by largeness of view and lucidity of arrangement, his account of many episodes of the life of Charles V., and in particular that of his retirement to San Yuste, contains much of the romantic and theatrical inaccuracy which recent investigations have dispelled. But in spite of these defects Robertson's name will always retain an honourable place among the historians of England.

By far the greatest name in English historical literature is that of EDWARD GIBBON (1737-1794). Descended from an ancient family, he was born at Putney near London in 1737, and was the grandson of a merchant of large fortune. In consequence of his constitutional delicacy of health his education was at first neglected ; but he gradually acquired an insatiable appetite for reading of all kinds, which at length concentrated itself upon historical literature. At the early age of fifteen he was placed at Oxford, where he remained only fourteen months. On his embracing the Catholic faith, while still at the University, his father sent him to Lausanne, where he was placed under the care of M. Pavilliard, an eminent Swiss theologian. He subsequently re-entered the Protestant Church ; though his religious belief from this time forward was little more than a sort of philosophical Deism. In Switzerland, however, he commenced that course of systematic study, which gradually filled his mind with immeasurable stores of sacred and profane learning : and here too he acquired that strong sympathy with French modes of thought that makes him the least national of all our great authors. Indeed the first-fruits of his pen actually appeared in French, an essay on the *Study of Literature.* Between 1763 and 1765 he travelled over France, Switzerland, and Italy ; and while at Rome, in 1764, the idea of writing the history of the *Decline and Fall* of the mighty empire first flashed upon his mind. Returning to England in 1765 he set strenuously to work on the composition of his history, the first volume of which did not appear, however, until 1776, when it was received not only with the applause of the learned, but with universal popularity in the fashionable world. At various intervals until the year 1787 appeared the successive volumes, each of which excited the admiration and enthusiasm which the grandeur of the work was so calculated to inspire.

As member for Liskeard, Gibbon supported Lord North with a silent vote during the whole course of the American War, and was rewarded with the post of one of the Lords Commissioners of Trade, which he held till the abolition of the office in 1782. In 1783 Gibbon established himself at Lausanne in the comfortable house which he had purchased on the lovely shore of Lake Leman. This was perhaps the happiest part of his life : he was able to devote himself in tranquillity to his mighty task, and his leisure hours were enlivened with intellectual society. At length his residence at Lausanne becoming disagreeable in consequence of the agitation

which followed the outbreak of the French Revolution, he returned
to London in 1793 and died there in the following year.

His *History of the Decline and Fall of the Roman Empire* is undoubtedly one of the greatest monuments of industry and genius.
It embraces, exclusive of the introductory sketch of Roman history
from the time of Augustus, a period of upwards of thirteen centuries,
that is, from about 180 to 1453 A.D.   This immense space included
not only the manhood and the decrepitude of the Roman Empire,
but the irruption of the Barbarian nations, the establishment of the
Byzantine power, the reorganisation of the European nations, the
foundation of the religious and political system of Mahomedanism,
and the Crusades.   Nor was the complexity of the subject less formidable than its extent: the materials for much of its treatment
were to be painfully sifted from the rubbish of the Byzantine
annalists, and the wild exaggerations of the Eastern chroniclers.
From this immense chaos were to be deduced light, order, and
regularity; and the historian was to be familiar with the whole
range of philosophy, science, politics, and war.   Gibbon is one of
the most dangerous enemies by whom the Christian faith was ever
assailed—he was the more dangerous because he was insidious.   He
does not formally deny the evidence upon which is based the structure of Christianity, but he indirectly includes that system in the
same category with the mythologies of paganism.   But the accusations of having intentionally distorted facts or garbled authorities
he has refuted in the Vindication in which he replied to his
opponents; and the deliberate opinion of Guizot, whom no one can
accuse of indifference to religion, will be conclusive as to Gibbon's
merit on this point.   His style is remarkably pompous, elaborate,
and sonorous: originally artificial, it had gradually become the
natural garb of his thoughts.   His descriptions of events, as of
battles, of nations, of individual characters, are wonderfully life-like
and animated; and his chief sin against good taste is a somewhat
too gorgeous and highly coloured tone.   His worst fault is a
peculiar and most offensive delight in dwelling upon scandalous and
immoral stories; and this tendency becomes doubly odious when
exhibited in combination with Gibbon's solemn and majestic
language.

Perhaps the most striking figure in the social and literary history
of this period is that of SAMUEL JOHNSON (1709-1784).   He was the
son of a learned but poor and struggling provincial bookseller in
Lichfield; and he exhibited, from his very childhood, the same
singular union of mental power and constitutional indolence, ambition and hypochondriacal gloom, which distinguished him through
life.   On receiving a promise of assistance from a neighbouring

gentleman, he carried to Pembroke College, Oxford an amount of scholarship very rare at his age. Here he remained about three years: but his father's affairs being in hopeless confusion, and the promises of assistance not being fulfilled, he was obliged to leave the University without a degree, and at his father's death entered upon the hard career of teacher in various provincial schools. Finally after unsuccessfully attempting to keep a school himself at Edial, near Lichfield, he began that tremendous struggle with labour and want, which continued during thirty years. His first literary undertaking was a translation of Father Lobo's *Travels in Abyssinia;* but his hopes of success meeting with little but disappointment, he determined to launch upon the great ocean of London literary life. Already encumbered with a wife, a lady old enough to be his mother, without fortune, without friends, of singularly uncouth exterior, Johnson entered upon the career—then perhaps at its lowest ebb of profit and respectability—of a bookseller's hack, or literary drudge. He became a contributor to divers journals, and particularly to the *Gentleman's Magazine,* then carried on by its founder, Cave; and as an obscure labourer for the press he furnished criticisms, prefaces, translations, in short all kinds of humble literary work, and ultimately supplied reports of the proceedings in Parliament, though the names of the speakers, in obedience to the law which then rendered it penal to reproduce the debates, were disguised under imaginary titles. He first emerged into popularity in 1738 by the publication of his *London,* an admirable paraphrase of the third satire of Juvenal, in which he adapts the sentiments and topics of the great Roman poet to the neglect of letters in London, and the humiliations which an honest man must encounter in a society where foreign quacks and native scoundrels could alone hope for success. In 1744 he published the *Life of Savage,* that unhappy poet whose career was so extraordinary, and whose vices were not less striking than his talents. Johnson had known him well, and they had often wandered supperless and homeless about the streets at midnight. Indeed, Johnson's literary life for twenty-five years was an unbroken exemplification of the truth of his own majestic line: " slow rises worth, by poverty depressed."

From 1747 to 1755 Johnson was engaged in the execution of his laborious undertaking, the compilation of his great *Dictionary of the English Language,* which long occupied the place among us of the Dictionary of the Academy in France and Spain. The etymological part of this great work, in consequence of Johnson sharing the then almost universal ignorance of the Teutonic languages, is totally without value; but the accuracy and comprehensiveness of the definitions, and, above all, the interesting quotations adduced to exemplify the different senses of the words, render it a book that may always be read with pleasure. While engaged in this task he diverted his mind by the publication of the *Vanity of Human Wishes*, a companion to his *London*, being a similar imitation of the tenth satire of his Roman prototype. This is written in a loftier, more solemn and declamatory style than the preceding poem, and is a fine specimen of Johnson's dignified but somewhat gloomy rhetoric. Instead of the fall of Sejanus, Johnson has introduced the no less impressive picture of the disgrace of Wolsey; and his episode of Charles XII. is no unworthy counterpart to the portrait of Hannibal. At about the same time he brought out upon the stage the tragedy of *Irene*, which had long been in vain awaiting the opportunity of representation. Its success was insignificant, and indeed could not have been otherwise, for the plot of the piece is totally devoid of interest and probability; there is no discrimination of character, no painting of passion, and the work consists of a series of lofty moral declamations in Johnson's laboured and rhetorical style.

Johnson founded, and carried on alone, two periodical papers in the style that Addison and Steele had rendered so popular. These were the *Rambler* and the *Idler*, the former of which continued to be published from 1750 until 1752, and the latter from 1758 until 1760. The ease, grace, pleasantry, and variety which gave such charm to the *Tatler* and *Spectator* are totally incompatible with the heavy, antithetical ponderous manner of Johnson; and his good sense, piety, and sombre tone of morality are but a poor substitute for the *mite ingenium* and knowledge of the world displayed in his models. This species of periodical essay-writing, which exerted so powerful an influence on taste and manners in the eighteenth century, may be said to terminate with the *Idler*, though continued with gradually increasing want of originality by other writers. Johnson's mother died in 1759; and he wrote with extraordinary rapidity, and for the purpose of raising funds for her funeral, his once-celebrated moral tale, *Rasselas, Prince of Abyssinia*. The manners and scenery of this story are neither those of oriental, nor of any other known country, and the book is little else but a series of dialogues and reflections, embodying the author's ideas on an immense variety of subjects connected with art, literature, society, and philosophy, and his lofty, but gloomy and discouraging principles of ethics and religion. It was not till 1762, when the philosopher had reached the age of fifty-three, that he emerged from the constant poverty which had hitherto almost overwhelmed him, and against which he had so valiantly struggled. At the accession of George III. the Government hoped to gain popularity by showing some favour to art and letters; and Johnson was gratified by Lord Bute with a pension of 300*l.* a year. He now found himself, for the first time in his life, placed above want, and was able to indulge not only his constitutional indolence, but that noble charity and benevolence which transformed his dwelling into a sort of asylum for helpless indigence.

At this period of his life Johnson became acquainted with JAMES BOSWELL (1740-1795), whose biography of the old sage is perhaps the most perfect and interesting account of a literary life and a literary epoch which the world has yet seen. Boswell was a young Scottish advocate of good family and fortune; and though he was a vain, tattling, frivolous busybody, his sincere admiration for Johnson won the old moralist's heart; and he has produced not only the most lively and vivid portrait of the person, manners, and conversation of Johnson, but the most admirable picture of the society amid which he played so brilliant a part. Among the most celebrated social meetings of that age of clubs was the society founded by Johnson, and in which his friends Reynolds, Burke, Garrick, Bishop Percy, Goldsmith, Bennet Langton, Beauclerc, and others, were prominent figures. Johnson's powers of conversation were extraordinary: he delighted in discussion, and had acquired by constant practice the art of expressing himself with pointed force and elegance; and his muscular and idiomatic expression formed an appropriate vehicle for his weighty thoughts, his apt illustrations, and his immense stores of reading and observation. This was perhaps the most brilliant and the happiest portion of his life. He made the acquaintance of the family of Thrale, a rich brewer and a member of the House of Commons, whose wife was equally famous for her own talents and for the bright intellectual society she loved to assemble round her, and under whose roof Johnson enjoyed all that friendship and respect, aided by great wealth, could give. This connection, which lasted for sixteen years, gave Johnson the opportunity of frequenting refined society; and in the company of the Thrales he made several excursions to different parts of England, and once indeed as far as Paris. His edition of Shakespeare, which after many delays appeared in 1765, cannot be said to have added to his reputation; indeed, with the exception of an occasional happy remark, and a sensible selection from the commentaries of preceding annotators, it is quite unworthy of him. In 1773 Johnson undertook, in company with his friend Boswell, an expedition to the Hebrides, which not only enabled him to make acquaintance with Scotland and the Scots, and thus to dissipate many of his old prejudices against the country and the people, but afforded him the opportunity of exercising his observation on a region entirely new to him. The volume in which he gives an account of his impressions contains many and interesting characteristic passages. His last work of any consequence, which is also unquestionably his best, was the *Lives of the Poets*, originating in the proposal made to him by several publishers that he should write a few lines of biographical and critical preface to each of the works of the English poets, of which they were preparing an edition. Johnson undertook the task, and performed it with such skill, and poured forth so abundantly the stores of his sound sense and acute reflection, that these lives are not only one of the most amusing books in the language, but contain, in spite of the narrowness of the author's literary creed, innumerable passages of the happiest and most original criticism, particularly in treating of those writers who, belonging to what is called the classical or artificial school, exhibit characteristics which Johnson was capable of appreciating. His remarks upon the poetry of Cowley, Waller, and Pope, are admirable; and his immense knowledge of life, and sharp and weighty sense, have filled his pages with striking and valuable observations. On Dec. 13, 1784, this good man and vigorous writer died, after suffering severely from dropsy and a complication of disorders; and a week afterwards his body was buried in Westminster Abbey. Johnson was a singular mixture of prejudice and liberality, of scepticism and credulity, of bigotry and candour: and with that paradoxical strangeness which pervades all his personality, we know him better, and admire him more, in the unadorned records which Boswell has given of his conversational triumphs, than in those rhetorical and elaborate writings which his contemporaries thought so magnificent, but which more recent generations seem likely to condemn to comparative oblivion.

EDMUND BURKE (1728-1797) was a man of powerful and versatile genius, carrying the fervour and imagery of a great orator into philosophical discussion, and uniting in himself the highest qualities of the statesman, the writer, and the philosopher. His predominant quality was a burning enthusiasm for whatever object attracted his sympathies, and in the service of this enthusiasm he impressed all the disciplined forces of his learning, his logic, and his historical and political knowledge. He was the son of a Dublin attorney, came early to England to study law, but commenced his career as a miscellaneous writer in magazines. He was the founder and first author of the *Annual Register*, a useful epitome of political and general facts; and gained his first reputation by his *Vindication of Natural Society*, an ironical imitation of the style and sentiments of Lord Bolingbroke; which was followed a few months afterwards by his *Essay on the Sublime and Beautiful*, a short treatise in which ingenuity is more perceptible than solidity of reasoning. He now became a leading member of the brilliant literary circle which surrounded Johnson, who, jealous as he was of his own social supremacy, confessed that in Burke he encountered a fully equal antagonist. He began his political career as Secretary to Hamilton in Ireland, and he was afterwards attached in the same capacity to Lord Rockingham. He sat in the House of Commons successively for Wendover, Bristol, and Malton, and was one of the most prominent debaters during the agitated period of the American War and the French Revolution. For a short time he held the lucrative post of Paymaster of the Forces in the second Rockingham administration. The culminating points of his political life were his share in the famous India Bill, which was to entirely change the administration of our Eastern dependencies, and the part he played in the trial of Warren Hastings, which lasted from 1788 to 1795, and terminated with the acquittal of the accused. In this majestic and solemn scene, where a great nation sat in public judgment upon a great criminal, Burke played perhaps the most prominent part : he was one of the managers of the impeachment in the name of the Commons, and his speech is one of the sublimest philippics that ancient or modern oratory can show. The Reign of Terror in France transformed Burke from a constitutional Whig into a Tory, but at the same time animated his genius to some of its most unrivalled bursts of eloquence. His finest written compositions are his *Letter to a Noble Lord*, in which he defends himself against the aspersions of the Duke of Bedford, who had attacked him for accepting a pension; his *Reflections on the French Revolution*, and his *Letter on a Regicide Peace*. In Parliament, though his speeches were perhaps unequalled for spendour of illustration, for an almost supernatural acuteness of political foresight, and for the profoundest analysis of constitutional principles, he was often less popular than many inferior debaters : he spoke *over the heads* of his audience, but he will ever be regarded as one of the greatest orators and statesmen of any age or country.

From about the beginning of 1769, and with occasional interruptions down to 1772, there appeared in the 'Public Advertiser,' one of the leading London journals, then published by Woodfall, a series of *Letters* for the most part signed Junius. Their attack was directed against the great public men of the day, more especially the Dukes of Grafton and Bedford; and they exhibited so much weight and dignity of style, and so minute an acquaintance with the details of party tactics, and breathed such a lofty tone of constitutional principle, combined with such a bitterness, and even ferocity of personal invective, that their influence was unbounded. The whole annals of political controversy show nothing so bitter and terrible as the personalities and invectives of *Junius*, which are rendered more formidable by the lofty dignity of the language, and by the moderate and constitutional principles which he professes to maintain. These letters will always be regarded as masterpieces in their particular style. Burke, Hamilton, Francis, Lyttelton, and Lord George Sackville have been successively fixed upon as the writer; but of these Sir Philip Francis appears to have the strongest suffrages.

ADAM SMITH (1723-1790) was the founder, in England, of the science of Political Economy. He was a Scotchman, and successively Professor of Logic and of Moral Philosophy in the University of Glasgow. His most important work is the *Inquiry into the Nature and Causes of the Wealth of Nations*, the fruit of ten years of study and investigation, which laid the foundation for modern economic science. It was the first systematic treatise produced in England upon this most important subject; and though not free from erroneous deductions, was the most valuable contribution ever made to a science, then almost in its infancy, which was destined. thanks in a great measure to his clear and logical reasoning and abundant and popular illustration, to exert an immense and beneficial influence on legislation and commerce. His moral and metaphysical theories are now nearly forgotten, but his *Inquiry* will ever remain the alphabet or text-book of the important science of which he was the pioneer.

The most prominent names in the English theological philosophy of the eighteenth century are those of BISHOP BUTLER (1692-1752) and WILLIAM PALEY (1743-1805). The former is more remarkable for the severe and coherent logic with which he demonstrates his conclusions, the latter for the consummate skill with which he popularised the abstruser arguments of his predecessors. Butler's principal work is *The Analogy of Religion Natural and Revealed to the Constitution and Course of Nature*, in which he examines into the resemblance between the existence and attributes of God, as proved by arguments drawn from the works of Nature, and shows that that existence and those attributes are in no way incompatible with the notions conveyed to us by Revelation. Paley's books are numerous, and all excellent : the principal of them are *Elements of Moral and Political Philosophy*, the *Horæ Paulinæ*, the *Evidences of Christianity*, and the wonderful production of his old age, the *Treatise on Natural Theology*. It will be seen from the titles of these books over what an immense extent of moral and theological philosophy Paley's mind had travelled. For clearness, animation, and easy grace, the style of Paley has rarely been equalled.

If the palm of merit is to be awarded less to the pretension of a literary work than to a universal popularity arising from a consummate charm of execution, then the fame of GILBERT WHITE (1720-1793) is to be coveted little less eagerly than that of Izaak Walton. White was educated at Oxford, where he became a fellow of Oriel College; but, declining all college livings, he resided in his native village of Selborne, in Hampshire, and there devoted his happy and tranquil life to the observation of nature. In a series of letters he has registered every phenomenon both of animal and vegetable life, as well as of scenery and meteorology, which came under the eye of a most curious, patient, and loving observer; and a thousand details so slight or so familiar as to escape the attention of previous naturalists, have been chronicled with exquisite grace, and form valuable contributions to science. Every change of weather, every circumstance in the habits of birds, beasts, and insects, were noted by him with an interest and enthusiasm that captivates the dullest reader; and the *Natural History of Selborne* has made at least as many naturalists as *Robinson Crusoe* has made sailors.

Among the vast crowd of less noticeable writers who might claim a place in this chapter, a few produced works that still possess some value, though they are comparatively but little known. In 1764 LORD LYTTELTON (1709-1773), slightly distinguished as a poet, and to some extent as a statesman, published a *History of Henry II.*, which is noteworthy as being the most elaborate and minute work yet written on one of the most momentous reigns in the English Annals, and as being one of the earliest attempts made in the direction of a sound system of historical criticism. SIR WILLIAM BLACKSTONE's *Commentaries on the Laws of England* is still the only popular compendium of our constitutional and legal principles and usages. *The Elements of Criticism* of LORD KAMES, *The Philosophy of Rhetoric* of DR. GEORGE CAMPBELL remain, in spite of many publications on the same subjects since their time, standard authorities in their respective departments. The fame of LORD CHESTERFIELD's *Letters*, which was almost unparalleled when they were first published, is not extinct even yet; nor was it altogether undeserved, let Dr. Johnson say what he will.

CHAPTER XXII.

THE DAWN OF ROMANTIC POETRY.

THE great revolution in popular taste and sentiment, which substituted what is called the romantic type in literature for the cold and clear-cut artificial spirit of that classicism which is exhibited in its highest form in the writings of Pope, was, like all powerful and durable movements, whether in politics or in letters, gradual. The mechanical perfection of the poetry of the age of Queen Anne had been imitated with such success, that every versifier had caught the trick of melody and the neat antithetical opposition of thought; and indications soon began to be perceptible of a tendency to seek for subjects and forms of expression in a wider, more passionate, and more natural sphere of nature and emotion. In MATTHEW GREEN's (1696-1737) truly original poem, called *The Spleen*, in the *Minstrel* of JAMES BEATTIE (1735-1803), in the striking meditative lines entitled *The Grave* by ROBERT BLAIR (1699-1746) this tendency is perceptible, and may be in some measure ascribed to the weariness inspired by the eternal repetition of the neat and epigrammatic ingenuity which had gradually become a mere far-off echo of Pope.

JAMES THOMSON (1700-1748), the poet who connects the age of Pope with that of Crabbe, was born in a rural and retired corner of Scotland, and after receiving his education at Edinburgh, came to London in 1725, carrying with him the unfinished sketch of his poem of *Winter*. This work appeared in 1726, and after a short time was received with great favour. *Summer* was given to the world in the succeeding year; and Thomson then without delay issued proposals for the completion of the whole cycle of poems, *Spring* and *Autumn* being still wanting to fill up the round of the *Seasons*. In 1733 the Lord Chancellor Talbot, to whose son Thomson had been for some time tutor, appointed him to a sinecure office in the Court of Chancery; and even when he lost this post on the death of the minister, its loss was supplied by the yearly pension of 100*l*. from the Prince of Wales; and his friend Mr. Lyttelton afterwards conferred on him a lucrative situation under the Crown. He now purchased a snug cottage near Richmond, and lived in modest luxury and literary ease. He was of an extremely kind and generous disposition, and his devotion to his relations is an amiable trait in his character. His death was premature; for, catching cold in a boating-party on the Thames, he died of a fever in the 48th year of his age. During the years of his happy retirement, he had time to compose his delightful half-serious, half-playful poem of the *Castle of Indolence*, the most enchanting of the many imitations of the style and manner of Spenser, and a work which at the same time possesses the finest qualities of Thomson's own natural genius. He was also the author of a somewhat declamatory and ambitious poem on the subject of *Liberty*, and of a few tragedies, some of which, as *Sophonisba*, were acted with temporary success. The *Seasons*, consisting of the four detached poems *Spring, Summer, Autumn*, and *Winter*, must be considered as the corner-stone of Thomson's literary fame. It is a work, in plan and treatment, entirely original, and gives a general, and at the same time a minute description of all the phenomena of Nature during an English year. The metre is blank-verse, which, though seldom showing anything of the Miltonic swell or tenderness, is rich and harmonious. Thomson's chief defect is a kind of pompous struggle after fine language, which sometimes degenerates into ludicrous vulgarity. In order to relieve the monotony of a poem entirely devoted to description, he has occasionally introduced episodes or incidental pictures more or less naturally suggested by the subject : though in such of these as involve the passion of love, it must be con·fessed that his mode of delineating that feeling is far more ardent than ideal. In point of literary finish the *Castle of Indolence* is superior to the Seasons. The allegory of the enchanted "Land of Drowsihead," in which the unhappy victims of Indolence find themselves hopeless captives, and their delivery from durance by the Knight Industry, are relieved with occasional touches of a sly and pleasant humour, as in those passages where Thomson has drawn portraits of himself and of his friends.

The popularity of WILLIAM SHENSTONE (1714-1763), once considerable, has now given place to oblivion; but his pleasing and original poem the *Schoolmistress* will deserve to retain a place in every collection of English verse. This is a poem in the Spenserian stanza and antique diction, which, with a delightful mixture of quaint playfulness and tender description, paints the dwelling, the character, and the pursuits of an old village dame who keeps a rustic day-school.

The career of WILLIAM COLLINS (1721-1759) was brief and unhappy. He exhibited from very early years the strong poetical powers of a genius which, ripened by practice and experience, would have made him the first lyrical writer of his age; but his ambition was rather feverish than sustained; he led a life of projects and dissipation; and the first shock of literary disappointment drove him to despondency, despondency to indulgence, and indulgence to insanity. His first publication was a series of Eclogues, transferring the usual sentiments of pastoral verse to the scenery and manners of the East. Thus a camel-driver bewailing the dangers and solitude of his desert journey takes the place of the lamentation of the shepherd expelled from his native fields; and the dialogues so frequent in the bucolics of Virgil or Theocritus are transformed into the amœbæan complaints of two Circassian exiles. But though these eclogues exhibit traces of vivid imagery and melodious verse, the real genius of Collins must be looked for in his *Odes*. Judged by these latter, he will be found entitled to a very high place : for true warmth of colour-ing, power of personification, and dreamy sweetness of harmony, no English poet had till then appeared that could be compared to Collins. Of these, that entitled *The Passions* is the most frequently quoted; nevertheless, many of the less popular ones, as those addressed to *Fear*, to *Pity*, to *Simplicity*, and that *On the Poetical Character*, contain happy strokes, sometimes expressed in wonderfully laconic language, and singularly vivid portraiture. Some of the smaller and less ambitious lyrics, as the *Verses to the Memory of Thomson*, the *Dirge in Cymbeline*, and the exquisite verses *How sleep the brave*, are perhaps destined to a more certain immortality; but all the qualities of Collins's finest thought and expression will be found united in the lovely little *Ode to Evening*, consisting merely of a few stanzas in blank verse, but so subtly harmonised that we may read them a thousand times without observing the absence of rhyme.

MARK AKENSIDE (1721-1770), like Arbuthnot, Garth, Smollett, and Blackmore, was a physician as well as a writer, and a man of considerable learning, as well as of a pure, lofty, and classical turn of genius. His chief work is the philosophical poem entitled *The Pleasures of the Imagination*, in which he seeks at once to investigate and illustrate the emotions excited by beautiful objects in art and nature upon the human mind. The philosophical merit of his theories, indeed, is very often but small; but the beauty of the imagery and the language will ever secure for this lofty, thoughtful, and noble work, the admiration of those readers who can content themselves with elevated thoughts, without looking for passages of strong human interest, in which Akenside is deficient. Few English poets since Milton have been more deeply saturated with the spirit of classical antiquity than Akenside.

The greatest of the exclusively lyrical poets that England had hitherto produced was THOMAS GRAY (1716-1771), a man of vast and varied acquirements, whose life was devoted to the cultivation of letters. He received his education at Eton, and afterwards settled in learned retirement at Cambridge, where he became Professor of History in 1768. He acquired a high poetical reputation by his beautiful *Ode on a Distant Prospect of Eton College*, published in 1747; which was followed, at pretty frequent intervals, by his other imposing and highly-finished works, the *Elegy written in a Country Churchyard*, the *Pindaric Odes*, and the far from numerous but splendid productions which make up his works. His industry was untiring, and his acquirements undoubtedly immense; for he had pushed his researches far beyond the usual limits of ancient classical philology, and was not only deeply versed in the romance literature of the Middle Ages, in modern French and Italian, but had studied the then almost unknown departments of Scandinavian and Celtic poetry. Many passages of his works are a kind of mosaic of thought and imagery borrowed from Pindar, from the choral portions of the Attic tragedy, and from the majestic lyrics of the Italian poets of the sixteenth and seventeenth centuries: but the fragments are, so to say, fused into one solid body by the intense flame of a powerful and fervent imagination. His finest lyric compositions are the Odes entitled *The Bard*, that on the *Progress of Poesy*, the *Installation Ode* on the Duke of Grafton's election to the Chancellorship of the University, and the short but truly noble *Ode to Adversity*. The *Elegy written in a Country Churchyard* is a masterpiece from beginning to end. The thoughts indeed are obvious enough, but the dignity with which they are expressed, the immense range of allusion and description with which they are illustrated, and the finished grace of the language and versification in which they are embodied, give to this work something of that inimitable perfection of design and execution which we see in an antique statue or a sculptured gem. In the *Bard*, starting from the picturesque idea of a Welsh poet and patriot contemplating the victorious invasion of his country by Edward I., he passes in prophetic review the whole panorama of English History, from the thirteenth to the sixteenth century. In the odes entitled *The Fatal Sisters* and *The Descent of Odin*, Gray borrowed his materials from the Scandinavian legends. The tone of the Norse poetry is not perhaps very faithfully reproduced; but these attempts to revive the rude and archaic grandeur of the Eddas deserve no small approbation.

The two brothers JOSEPH WARTON (1722-1800), and THOMAS WARTON (1728-1790) were the sons of a Professor of Poetry at

Oxford, and both brothers, especially the younger, deserve a place in the annals of our literature. Thomas, who was poet-laureate from 1785 until his death, rendered great service to literature by his agreeable but unfinished *History of English Poetry*, which unfortunately comes to an abrupt termination just as the author is about to enter upon the glorious period of the Elizabethan era: but the work is valuable for research and a warm tone of appreciative criticism. The best of his own original verses are sonnets, breathing a peculiar tender softness of feeling, and showing much picturesque fancy.

WILLIAM COWPER (1731-1800) is eminently the poet of the domestic affections, and the exponent of that strong religious feeling, which towards the end of the eighteenth century began to penetrate and modify all the relations of social life. His story is singularly sad. He was of ancient and even illustrious race, the grand-nephew of Lord Chancellor Cowper, and was born with an extremely tender and impressionable character. After being cowed by bullying at a private school he was sent to Westminster; whence he passed for some years into an attorney's office; but ultimately obtained the post of Clerk of the Journals to the House of Lords; where, however, his sensitive nature was so terrified at the idea of making a public appearance, that he fell into a gloomy despondency, and attempted to put an end to his existence. Madness followed; and although a short confinement in an asylum restored his intellect, he was so shaken by the attack as to be entirely unfitted for any active career. He now retired into the country, and passed the remainder of his life in privacy, being first placed under the care of the family of Mr. Unwin, a clergyman in Huntingdon. This was the beginning of that remarkable friendship with Mrs. Unwin which entered so largely into his whole subsequent life. Cowper's mind, always impressionable, became morbidly susceptible of enthusiastic religious feeling; and his occasional hallucinations took that most unhappy form of mental disease, religious despair. On the death of Unwin he removed, with the widow, to Olney, where he made the friendship of John Newton, an evangelical divine of great eloquence. He began to cultivate literature at first merely as a pastime, and as a means of escaping from himself; but the force, originality, and grace of his genius soon acquired popularity, and he pursued as a profession what he had at first taken up as a diversion. His poetical talent did not flower until late. In 1779 he contributed a large portion of the *Olney Hymns*, published by Newton; and in 1782 he gave his first volume of poems to the world. This included *Table Talk*, *The Progress of Error*, *Truth*, and one or two others. These poems did not meet with much success; whereupon his friend Lady Austen playfully gave him the Sofa as a subject. Upon this he composed, in blank verse, his fine poem of *The Task*, which, published in 1785, with *Tirocinium* as a humble companion, at once became popular. His most laborious but least successful undertaking was the translation of the Iliad into English blank verse. From Olney he removed to Weston, and thence to East Dereham, where Mrs. Unwin died, and the pain of this loss clouded the remaining days of the unhappy poet with redoubled gloom and despondency.

The pictures of life and nature drawn by Cowper, whether of rural scenery or of indoor life, have seldom been surpassed for truth and picturesqueness; and his satirical sketches of the follies and absurdities of manners, and his indignant denunciations of national offences against piety and morality, are equally remarkable, in the one case, for sharpness and humour, and in the other for a lofty grandeur of sentiment. From him the level banks of the Ouse, the most unromantic of English rivers, have caught a magic that will never pass away; the quiet home circle of middle English life, the tea-table, the newspaper, and the hearth, have derived from him a beauty and a diguity which other men have failed to communicate to the proudest scenes of camps and courts. In spite of the morbid religious system of Cowper, many of his comic and humorous delineations exhibit the full effulgence of a playful gaiety which no cloud can dim. Of all our poets Cowper is essentially the painter of domestic life; the mixture of worldly observation, delicate painting of nature, and intense religious feeling, that is found in his poems, peculiarly endears them to the great middle class in England. Many of Cowper's songs and shorter lyrics are elegant and sportive; and his beautiful lines *On Receiving my Mother's Picture* will ever be read with delight. His comic ballad *John Gilpin* is a pleasant drollery. His letters are perhaps the most charming in the language; they show the poet in his most amiable light, and invest every trifle which surrounds him with a sort of halo of purity and goodness.

Several poems have appeared in England possessing what may be called a technical character, being either devoted to the teaching of some art, or describing some special sport or amusement, such as Armstrong's *Art of Preserving Health*, Grainger's *Sugar-Cane*, Philips's *Cyder*, and Somerville's *Chase*. The most successful work, however, of this kind is the *Shipwreck* of William Falconer (1730-1769), a narrative poem in three cantos, detailing the danger and ultimate loss of a merchant-ship on a voyage to Venice, which is cast away, after experiencing a violent gale in the Greek archipelago, on the dangerous rocks of Cape Colonna, the ancient

Sunium. To the same department of poetry belongs also ERASMUS DARWIN (1731-1802), who endeavoured to clothe in dazzling and somewhat tinsel splendour the principles of the Linnæan sexual system of vegetable physiology. His principal work is the *Botanic Garden*, the first part of which was entitled the *Economy of Vegetation*, and the second the *Loves of the Plants*, which latter Canning humorously parodied in the *Loves of the Triangles*. He wrote another poem, entitled *The Temple of Nature; or, the Origin of Society*. In these compositions the elaborate and ambitious melody of his versification has not sufficed to compensate for the over-wrought and fatiguing monotony of his imagery; though many of his episodes and subordinate descriptions exhibit a great force of language, and a powerful faculty of the picturesque.

The middle of the eighteenth century was remarkable for several nearly contemporaneous attempts at literary imposture—the poetical forgeries of Macpherson, Chatterton, and Ireland. The first of these three has alone survived, in some part, the ordeal of strict critical examination; and that because, though the totality of the works palmed upon the public as Ossian's have no claim whatever to the character arrogated for them by their pretended translator, they are nevertheless filled with names, incidents, and allusions really traceable to Celtic antiquity. JAMES MACPHERSON (1738-1796), originally a country schoolmaster, and afterwards a tutor, pretended to have accumulated, in his travels through the Highlands of Scotland, an immense mass of fragments of ancient poetry composed in the Gaelic or Erse dialect common to that country and Ireland. The translations, which Macpherson professed to have made from the originals, were composed in a pompous and declamatory sort of prose; and immediately on their publication a furious war ensued on the question of their authenticity. The Highlanders, eager for the honour of their country, maintained the affirmative; while the Southern critics, among whom Johnson occupied a foremost place, expressed the strongest disbelief. Macpherson might at once have settled the question by producing the supposed originals; but this he refused to do, under the pretext that his honour had been impeached. He afterwards published two long poems in the same style, *Fingal* in six, and *Temora* in eight books, which he attributed, like the preceding fragments, to the genius of the Celtic Homer. The regularity of construction in these works, the numerous passages in them as well as in their predecessors evidently plagiarised from the whole range of literature, from the Bible and Homer down to Shakespeare, Milton, and even Thomson, the artificial and monotonous though strained and highly-wrought diction, and, above all, the sentiments in constant discordance with the real manners of the ancient Highlanders, would have sufficed, even in the general ignorance of the Gaelic language, to undeceive all except those who were ignorantly carried away by the imposing but hollow magnificence of the style. Yet in Germany the admiration for these productions has not even now altogether subsided; and perhaps the only poetry, which attracted the imagination of Napoleon, was this wild declamatory rhapsody which left no faint traces upon his bulletins.

The annals of literature hardly present a more extraordinary example of precocious genius than that of THOMAS CHATTERTON (1752-1770), nor an instance of a career more brief and melancholy. He was born in 1752, the son of a poor sexton and parish schoolmaster at Bristol; and he died, by suicide, before he had completed his eighteenth year. He produced at eleven years of age verses which will more than bear a comparison with the early poems of any author: and though he had received little education beyond that of a parish school, he conceived the project of deceiving all the learned of his age, and creating, it may almost be said, a whole literature of the past. In the muniment-room of St. Mary Redcliffe's, Bristol, of which church his father was sexton, there was a chest called Canynge's coffer (Canynge was a rich citizen, who lived in Edward IV.'s reign), in which had been preserved charters and other documents connected with Canynge's benefactions to the church. The young poet, familiarised with the sight of these antiquated writings, conceived the idea of forging a whole series of documents, which he pretended either to have found in Canynge's coffer, or to have transcribed from originals in that mysterious receptacle. After successfully producing these on several occasions, as local events appeared appropriately to suggest them, he went so far as to furnish Horace Walpole, then engaged on his Anecdotes of British Painters, with a long list of mediæval artists who had flourished in Bristol. All these documents he fathered upon a priest, Thomas Rowley, whom he represents to have been employed by the munificent Canynge as a sort of agent for collecting works of art. The poems are of immense variety and unquestionable merit; and though modern criticism will instantly detect in them, as did Gray and Mason when Walpole submitted some of them to their opinion, the most glaring marks of forgery, yet their brilliancy and their number were enough to deceive many learned scholars in an age when minute antiquarian knowledge of the Middle Ages was much rarer than at present. Yet no task is so difficult as that of successfully imitating ancient compositions, and Chatterton fell into errors which detect him at once. Thus in his eagerness to incrust his diction with the rust of antiquity, he overlays his words with such an accumulation of consonants as belong to no orthography of any age of our language. He has also, as was inevitable, sometimes made a slip in the use of an old word, as when he borrowed the expression *mortmal* which he found in Chaucer's description of the Cook, he employed it to signify, not a disease, the gangrene, but a dish. Of the same kind are his innumerable examples of impossible architecture and heraldry at variance with every principle of the art. Burning with pride, hope, and literary ambition, the unhappy lad betook himself to London, where after struggling a short time with distress, and almost with starvation, he poisoned himself with a dose of arsenic on the 25th of August, 1770. Singularly enough his acknowledged poems, though indicating very great powers, are manifestly inferior to those he wrote in the assumed character of Thomas Rowley.

WILLIAM HENRY IRELAND (1777-1835) deserves mention only on account of his Shakespearian forgeries, among which was a play entitled *Vortigern*, in which John Kemble acted in 1795. Ireland soon afterwards acknowledged his guilt.

If Cowper be rightly denominated the poet of the domestic hearth, GEORGE CRABBE (1754-1832) is eminently the poet of the passions in humble life. He was born at the little seaport-town of Aldborough in Suffolk, where his father was a humble fisherman; and after a dreamy and studious childhood, he was apprenticed to a surgeon and apothecary. Passionately fond of literature and botany, he determined to seek his fortune in London, carrying with him several unfinished poems, which he published, but which were coldly received. After some stay in London he found himself reduced to despair; when he addressed a manly and affecting letter to Edmund Burke, who immediately admitted him to his house and friendship. From this moment his fortune changed; he was assisted, both with money and advice, in bringing out his poem of *The Library*, was induced to enter the Church, and was promised the powerful influence of Lord Chancellor Thurlow. He became domestic chaplain to the Duke of Rutland; but after marriage with a young lady to whom he had been long attached, he changed the splendid restraint of Beauvoir for the humbler but more independent existence of a parish priest, and in this occupation he continued until his death.

It was not till the appearance of *The Village*, in 1783, that Crabbe struck out that path in which he had neither predecessor nor rival. The success of this poem was very great, for it was the first attempt to paint the manners and existence of the labouring class without dressing them up in the artificial colours of fiction. His next work was *The Parish Register*, in which the public saw the gradual ripening of his vigorous and original genius; and this was followed, at comparatively short intervals, by *The Borough, Tales in Verse.* and *Tales of the Hall.* These, with the striking but painful poems, written in a different measure, entitled *Sir Eustace Grey* and *The Hall of Justice,* make up Crabbe's large and valuable contribution to the poetical literature of his country. Almost all these works are constructed upon a peculiar and generally similar plan. Crabbe starts with some description, as of the Village, the Parish Church, the Borough, from which he naturally proceeds to deduce a series of separate episodes, usually of middle and humble life, appropriate to the leading idea. Thus in the *Parish Register* we have some of the most remarkable births, marriages, and deaths that are supposed to take place in a year amid a rural population; in the *Borough,* the lives and adventures of the most prominent characters that figure on the narrow stage of a small provincial town. With the exception of *Sir Eustace Grey* and the *Hall of Justice,* which are written in a peculiar rhymed short-lined stanza, Crabbe's poems are in the classical ten-syllabled heroic verse, and the contrast is strange between the neat Pope-like regularity of the metre, and the deep passion, the intense reality, and the quaint humour of the scenes which he displays. No poet has more subtly traced the motives which regulate human conduct; and his descriptions of nature are marked by the same unequalled power of rendering interesting, by the sheer force of truth and exactness, the most unattractive features to the external world. The village-tyrant, the poacher, the smuggler, the miserly old maid, the pauper, and the criminal, are drawn with the same gloomy but vivid force as that with which Crabbe paints the squalid streets of the fishing-town, or the fen, the quay, and the heath.

The greatest poet, beyond all comparison, that Scotland has produced is ROBERT BURNS (1759-1796). He was born at the hamlet of Alloway in Ayrshire, and was the son of a peasant farmer of the humblest class. Popular education was at that period very generally diffused in Scotland; and accordingly he acquired a good general acquaintance with the great masterpieces of English literature, and was able to use with perfect facility the style and diction of the great classical authors of South Britain. From a very early age he began to express in verse the impressions made upon his fancy by the beautiful and pastoral nature which surrounded him, and the outpourings of his own feelings and heart In early life Burns laboured like a peasant upon his father's farm, and afterwards endeavoured, but without success, to conduct a farm with his brothers. On the failure of these speculations, he resolved to emigrate to the West Indies; and in order to raise funds for the voyage, he was induced to publish a collection of his poems, which had long enjoyed a great local popularity. They were at once received by the highly cultivated society of Edinburgh with a tempest of enthusiasm that instantly made the " Ayrshire ploughman" the idol of the fashionable and literary world. Intoxicated by success, he abandoned his design ; and after again falling into embarrassments, rendered more inextricable by his irregularities, he obtained an humble appointment in the Excise service, the duties of which were unfortunately of a nature to still further foster habits of intemperance that had been continually growing upon him. His strong constitution was undermined by excess and excitement of all kinds, and the poet died of fever at Dumfries, in extreme poverty, in the 37th year of his age.

In Burns the highest poetical qualities were united to a degree which is rarely met with,—tenderness the most exquisite, humour the broadest and the most refined, the most delicate and yet powerful perception of natural beauty, the highest finish and the easiest negligence of style. His writings are chiefly lyric, consisting of songs of inimitable beauty, but he has also produced works either of a narrative or satirical character, in some of which, too, the lyric element is combined with the descriptive. The longest and most remarkable of his poems is *Tam o'Shanter*, a tale of popular witch-superstition, in which the most brilliant descriptive power is united to a pathos the most touching, a fancy the most wild, and a humour the quaintest, slyest, and most joyous. Another inimitable poem, half-narrative, but set thick with glorious songs, is the *Jolly Beggars*: careless vagabond jollity, roaring mirth and gipsy merriment, have never been so expressed. In his *Address to the De'il*, *Death and Dr. Hornbook, the Twa Dogs*, and the dialogue between the Old and New Bridges of Ayr, Burns combines humorous and picturesque description with reflections and thoughtful moralising upon life and society. The Dialogue between the *Twa Dogs* is an elaborate comparison between the relative degree of virtue and happiness granted to the rich and the poor. His description of the joys and consolations of the poor man's lot is perhaps even more beautiful in this poem than in the more generally popular *Cotter's Saturday Night*, written in stanzas, and in a language less provincial than the former, a circumstance which has rendered the poem better known to the general public. In the poem descriptive of rustic fortune-telling on *Halloween*, in the *Vision*, where Burns gives such a sublime picture of his own early aspirations, in the unequalled sorrow that breathes through the *Lament for Glencairn*, in *Scotch Drink*, the *Haggis*, the epistles to *Captain Grose* and *Matthew Henderson*, in the exquisite description of the death of

the old ewe Mailie, and the poet's address to his old mare, we find
the same prevailing mixture of pathos and humour, that truest
pathos which finds its materials in the common everyday objects of
life, and that truest humour which is allied to the deepest feeling
The famous lines *On Turning up a Mouse's Nest with the Plough*,
and on destroying in the same way a *Mountain Daisy*, will ever
remain among the chief gems of tenderness and beauty.

Those of Burns's *Songs* that are written in pure English have often
an artificial and somewhat pretentious air, which places them below
the Doric of the Lowland Muse. Intensity of feeling, condensed
force and picturesqueness of expression, and admirable melody of
flow, are the qualities which distinguish them. In the song *Ae fond
Kiss and then we Part* is concentrated the whole essence of a
thousand love-poems: the heroic outbreak of patriotism in *Scots wha
hae wi' Wallace bled* is a lyric of true Tyrtæan force: and in those of
a calmer and more lamenting character, as *Ye Banks and Braes*,
there is the finest union of personal sentiment with the most complete assimilation of the poet's mind to the loveliness of external
nature. The only defects with which this great poet can be re-
proached are an occasional coarseness of satire, as exemplified in the
personalities of *Holy Fair*, a tone of defiant and needless opposition
of one class against another, and now and then a vulgar and mis-
placed ornament which contrasts tawdrily with the sweet simplicity
of the general style.

The poetical movement in the direction of greater freedom and an
expansion into a larger and fuller life, and the eagerness to escape
from the paralysing influences of the so-called correct school, which
characterised the latter half of the eighteenth century, are no less
marked in the many minor poets of this time. Thus the numerous
satirical productions of CHARLES CHURCHILL (1731-1764) are distinguished by a rugged massive force and a rude strength which
strikingly contrast with the dainty elegance and refined feebleness
of the followers of Pope. His *Rosciad*, in which he mercilessly
lashed the stage and actors of the day, the *Prophecy of Famine*,
directed against the then highly obnoxious Scotch, the *Ghost*,
where the great Doctor figures as "Pomposo," are all evidences
that a nobler period of literary development was at hand.
Few writers have enjoyed a greater immediate popularity than
Churchill; but notwithstanding his merits, and they are numerous,
the interest in his works has almost entirely died out with that of
the bitter political controversy to which they mainly belong. The
Grongar Hill of DYER, and the *Clifton Grove* of KIRKE WHITE are
likely to be remembered as long as vigour of imagination and
poetic sensibility are prized in England.

In tracing the progress of the comic drama from the middle of the eighteenth century down almost to the present time, the chief names to be noted are those of Garrick, Foote, Cumberland, the two Colmans, father and son, of whom the second is by far the most considerable, and lastly Sheridan, that strange cometary genius, whose powers were so versatile, and whose life was so brilliant and so disreputable.   But with the single exception of the last, none of these authors produced anything of permanent value, though all of them enjoyed a high reputation in their day.

RICHARD BRINSLEY SHERIDAN (1751-1816) is certainly one of the most remarkable figures in the social, political, and intellectual life of the period.   Byron justly said that the intellectual reputation of Sheridan was truly enviable, that he had made the best speech— that on the Begums of Oude—written the two best comedies, the *Rivals* and the *School for Scandal*, the best opera, the *Duenna*, and the best farce, the *Critic*.   His whole life, both in Parliament and in the world, was a succession of extravagance and imprudence; and the ingenious shifts by which he endeavoured to stave off his embarrassments, and the jokes with which he disarmed even his angriest creditors, would of themselves furnish matters for a most amusing jest-book.   His two great comedies belong to the two distinct types of the drama; the *Rivals* depends for its interest upon the grotesqueness of its characters and the amusing unexpectedness of its incidents, while the *School for Scandal* is essentially a piece of witty dialogue or repartee.   The language of the latter was polished by the author with the most anxious care, and every passage sparkles with the cold and diamond-like splendour of Congreve.   In the *Critic* we have a farce, based upon the same plan as the *Rehearsal*, which gives the author the opportunity of introducing a burlesque or caricature of the imaginary piece, while at the same time he can introduce the absurdities of the author and the criticism of his friends.   It is probable that not a line of these three pieces will ever cease to be popular: whether acted or read, they are equally delightful.   A dramatic work which was immensely popular at this time, and which even Sir Walter Scott pronounced a masterpiece, is the *Douglas* of JOHN HOME (1724-1808).   The author was a minister of the Scotch Kirk, but lost this position by the success of his play.   He was, however, pensioned by Lord Bute His other works are worthless, and now entirely forgotten.

CHAPTER XXIII.

WALTER SCOTT.

The great revolution in taste, substituting romantic for classical sentiment and subjects, which culminated in the poems and novels of Walter Scott, is traceable to the labours of BISHOP PERCY (1728-1811). His publication in 1765, under the title of *Reliques of Ancient English Poetry*, of a collection of old ballads, many of which had been preserved only in manuscript, while others, having originally been printed in the rudest manner on flying sheets for circulation among the lower orders of the people, had owed their preservation only to the care of collectors, must be considered as a critical epoch in the history of our literature. Many authors before him, as, for example, Addison and Sir Philip Sydney, had expressed the admiration which a cultivated taste must ever feel for the rough but inimitable graces of our old ballad-poets; but Percy was the first who undertook an examination, at once systematic and popular, of those neglected treasures. It is true that he did not always adhere with scrupulous fidelity to the ancient texts, and where the poems were in a fragmentary and imperfect condition he did not hesitate, any more than Scott after him in the *Border Minstrelsy*, to fill up the rents of time with matter of his own invention. This, however, at a period when his chief object was to excite among general readers an interest in these fine old monuments of mediæval genius, was no unpardonable offence. Percy found, in collecting these compositions, that the majority of the oldest and most interesting were distinctly traceable, both as regards their subjects and the dialect in which they were written, to the North Countrée, that is, to the frontier region between England and Scotland which had necessarily been the scene of the most frequent and striking incidents of predatory warfare, such as those recorded in the noble ballads of *Chevy Chase* and the *Battle of Otterburn*. Besides a very large number of these purely heroic ballads, Percy gave specimens of an immense series of songs and lyrics extending down to a comparatively late period of English history, even to his own century; but the chief interest of his collection, and the chief service he rendered to literature by his publication, is concentrated on the earlier portion. It is impossible to exaggerate the influence exerted by Percy's *Reliques*: this book has been devoured with the most intense interest by generation after generation of English poets, and has undoubtedly contributed to give the first direction to the youthful genius of many of our most illustrious writers. The boyish enthusiasm of Walter Scott was stirred, "as with the sound of a trumpet," by the vivid recitals of the old Border rhapsodists; and but for Percy it is possible that we should have had neither the *Lady of the Lake* nor *Waverley*. In fact, the appearance of this work distinctly indicates the approaching advent of the great modern Romantic School of writers.

Literary history presents few examples of a career so splendid as that of WALTER SCOTT (1771-1832). A genius at once so vigorous and versatile, a productiveness so magnificent and so sustained, will with difficulty be found, though we ransack the wide realms of ancient and modern letters. He was born in 1771, the son of a respectable Writer to the Signet in Edinburgh, and was connected, both by the father's and mother's side, with several of those ancient historic Border families whose warlike memories his genius was destined to make immortal. In consequence of delicate health in early life he passed much of his time at the farm of his grandfather near Kelso, where he was surrounded with legends, ruins, and historic localities, of which he was to make in his works so admirable a use. On leaving the University, where he was altogether undistinguished, he was destined to the profession of the bar, and he practised during some time as an advocate before the Scottish tribunals. On his marriage with a young lady of French origin, called Charpentier, he took up his residence at Lasswade, where he made his first essays in literature. The direction of his mind was towards the poetical and antiquarian curiosities of the Middle Ages; but just at that time there had been awakened among the intellectual circles of Edinburgh a taste for German literature, then only just beginning to become known; and Scott contributed several translations, as that of Goethe's *Erl-König*, of the *Lenore* of Bürger, and afterwards the whole drama of *Götz of the Iron Hand*. He next conceived the plan of rescuing from oblivion the large stores of Border ballads which were still current among the descendants of the Liddesdale and Annandale mosstroopers, and for that purpose travelled for a time in those picturesque regions. The result of his researches he published as *Minstrelsy of the Scottish Border*; and the learning and taste of this work gave Scott a high reputation, and in some degree contributed to induce him to abandon the profession of the law for that of literature. He was still further confirmed in his project by receiving the appointment of Sheriff of Selkirkshire, the duties of which left much leisure at his disposal.

He now changed his residence to the pretty villa of Ashestiel on the Tweed; and in 1805 he first burst upon the world in the quality of a great original romantic poet. In this year *The Lay of the Last Minstrel* was published, which the public received with a rapture of enthusiasm. In rapid succession followed *Marmion*, the *Lady of the Lake*, *Rokeby*, and the *Lord of the Isles*; not to enumerate a number of less important and less successful works, such as the *Vision of Don Roderick*, the *Bridal of Triermain*, *Harold the Dauntless*, and the *Field of Waterloo*, the first and last of which were written with the special purpose of celebrating the triumph over Napoleon, and which, as is generally the case with such productions, are unworthy of the author's genius. These all appeared before 1817. It is certain, however, that with *Rokeby* the popularity of Scott's poetry, though still very great, began perceptibly to decline; a fact which with manly sense he fully recognised, and accordingly abandoned poetry to launch into a new career—a career in which he could have neither equal nor second.

In 1814 appeared *Waverley*, the commencement of which had been sketched out and thrown aside nine years before; and with *Waverley* began that inimitable series of romances which he poured forth with a splendour and facility surpassing even that of the poems. During the seventeen years intervening between 1814 and 1831 were written the entire series of Waverley Novels, produced with such inconceivable rapidity, that on an average about two of such works appeared in one year. Our wonder at such fertility is still further augmented, when we learn that during this period Scott succeeded in writing, independently of the above fictions, a considerable number of works in the departments of history, criticism, and biography. The *Life of Napoleon*, the *Tales of a Grandfather*, the amusing Letters on *Demonology and Witchcraft*, and the *History of Scotland*, belong to the latter part of this period. Spurred on by the desire of founding a territorial family, Scott went on purchasing land, planting and improving, and transforming the modest cottage of Abbotsford on his beloved Tweed into a "romance in stone and lime," a baronial residence crowded with the rarest objects of mediæval antiquity. The very large outlay necessitated by this mode of life he supplied partly by his inexhaustible pen, and partly by engaging secretly in large commercial speculations with the printing and publishing firm of the Ballantynes, his intimate friends and schoolfellows. But by the failure of the Ballantynes in the fatal commercial crisis of 1825, Scott found himself ruined, and moreover responsible for a gigantic amount of debt. He might easily have escaped from his liabilities by taking advantage of the bankrupt law; but his sense of honour was so high and delicate, that he only asked for time, and resolutely set himself to clear off, by unremitting literary toil, the vast accumulation of nearly 120,000*l.* He all but accomplished his colossal task, but he died under the effort; nor does the history of either literature or commerce afford a brighter example of probity.

In 1820 Scott had been raised to the dignity of the baronetcy; for the enchanting series of the *Waverley Novels*, though anonymously published, were generally ascribed to him, as to the only man in Great Britain whose peculiar acquirements and turn of genius could have given birth to them. Nevertheless, the mystery of the true authorship, long a very transparent one, was maintained by Scott with great care; and it was not till the failure of Ballantynes' house rendered concealment any longer impossible that he formally avowed himself the author of these fictions. Towards the year 1830 his mind, exhausted by such incessant toil, began to show symptoms of hopeless weakness; and he was sent abroad to Italy and the Mediterranean in the vain hope of re-establishing his health. He returned home to die; and after lingering in a state of almost complete unconsciousness for a short time, this great and good man terminated his earthly career on the 21st of September, 1832, at Abbotsford. His personal character is almost perfect. High-minded, generous and hospitable to the extreme, he hardly had an enemy or a misunderstanding during the whole of a long and active career. He was the delight of society; for his conversation, though unpretending, kindly, and jovial, was filled with that union of old-world lore and acute and picturesque observation which renders his works so enchanting; and there never perhaps was a man so totally free from the pettinesses and affectations to which men of letters are prone.

The romantic narrative poems of Scott form an epoch in the history of modern literature. In their subjects, their versification, and their treatment, they were an innovation, the success of which was as remarkable as their execution was brilliant. The materials were derived from the legends and exploits of mediæval chivalry; and the persons were borrowed partly from history and partly from imagination. He seems to move with most freedom in that picturesque Border region with whose romantic legends he was so wonderfully familiar, and which furnished, from the inexhaustible stores of his memory, such a mass of striking incident and vivid detail. The greatest of these poems are unquestionably the three first—the *Lay of the Last Minstrel, Marmion,* and the *Lady of the Lake.* According to Scott's own judgment, the interest of the *Lay* depends mainly upon the style, that of *Marmion* upon the descriptions, that of the *Lady of the Lake* upon the incidents. The form

adopted in all these works, though it may be remotely referred to a
revival of the spirit and modes of thought of the ancient French
and Anglo-Norman Trouvères, was more immediately suggested, as
Scott himself has confessed, by the example of Coleridge, who in
his *Christabel* gave the key-note upon which he composed his
vigorous and varied harmony. The somewhat monotonous octo-
syllable-rhymed verse of the Trouvères Scott had the good taste to
vary and enliven by a frequent intermixture of all other sorts of
English verse, anapæstic, trochaic, or dactylic. But his principal
metrical expedient was the employment of two, three, or four verses
of octosyllabic structure, rhyming together, and relieved at frequent
intervals by a short Adonic verse of six syllables, giving at once
great vigour and exquisite melody. The plots or intrigues of these
poems are in general neither very probable nor very logically constructed, but they allow the poet ample opportunities for striking
situations and picturesque episodes. The characters are discrimi-
nated rather by broad and vigorous strokes, than by any attempt at
moral analysis or strong delineation of passion. In his descriptions of scenery, which are exceedingly varied and intensely vivid,
Scott sometimes indulges in a quaint but graceful vein of moralising
which beautifully connects inanimate nature with the sentiments
of the human heart. A charming instance of this will be found
in the opening description of *Rokeby*.

The action of the *Lay of the Last Minstrel* is drawn from the
legends of Border war; and necromantic agency, the tourney, the
raid, and the attack on a strong castle, are successively described
with unabating fire and energy. The midnight expedition of Delo-
raine to the wizard's tomb in Melrose Abbey, the ordeal of battle,
the alarm, the feast, and the penitential procession, are painted
with the force and picturesqueness of real scenes. In *Marmion* the
main action is of a loftier and more historical nature, and the catastrophe is made to coincide with the description of the great battle
of Flodden, in which Scott gave earnest of powers in this department of painting hardly inferior to those of Homer himself. It is
indeed " a fearful battle rendered you in music;" and the whole
scene, from the rush and fury of the onset down to the least heraldic
detail or minute trifle of armour and equipment, is delineated with
the truth of an eyewitness. In the *Lady of the Lake* he broke up
new and fertile ground; he brought into contact the wild half-
savage mountaineers of the Highlands and the refined and chivalrous court of James V. The exquisite scenery of Loch Katrine
became, when invested by the magic of the descriptions, the chief
object of the traveller's pilgrimage; and it is no exaggeration to
say, as Macaulay has done, that the glamour of the great poet's

genius has for ever hallowed even the barbarous tribes whose manners are here invested with all the charms of fiction. In no other of his poems is that noble and gallant spirit—the fine flower of chivalric bravery and courtesy — which so universally pervades Scott's poetry as it animated his personal character, so powerfully manifested. Though the tale of *Rokeby* contains many beautiful descriptions, and exhibits strenuous efforts to draw and contrast individual characters with force, the epoch—that of the Civil Wars of Charles the First's reign—was one in which Scott obviously felt himself less at home than in his well-beloved feudal ages.

The last of the greater poems, the *Lord of the Isles*, went back to Scott's favourite epoch; and the voyage of the hero-king, Robert Bruce, among the Isles, the scenes in the Castle of Artornish, the description of the savage and terrific desolation of the Western Highlands, show little diminution in picturesque power. The Battle of Bannockburn reminds us of the hand that drew the field of Flodden; and Scott's ardent patriotism must have found a special pleasure in delineating the great victory of his country's independence. *Harold the Dauntless* and the *Bridal of Triermain* are written in a less vigorous style than the earlier poems; the latter indeed was playfully intended to pass off upon the public as the production of Scott's friend Erskine. In *Triermain* we see a somewhat effeminate and theatrical treatment of a striking legend which figures in the cycle of the exploits of Arthur; and *Harold* strives to combine the spirit of the old Berserk sagas with Christian and Chivalric manners, and the union of the two elements is too discordant to be pleasing. The *Vision of Don Roderick*, though based upon a striking and picturesque tradition, is principally a song of triumph over the recent defeat of the French arms in the Peninsula; but the moment he leaves the mediæval battle-field Scott seems to lose half his power; in this poem, as in *Waterloo*, his combats are neither those of feudal knights nor of modern soldiers, and there is throughout a struggle painfully visible to be emphatic and picturesque.

If we apply to the long and splendid series of prose fictions generally known under the name of the *Waverley Novels*, the same rough analytical distribution as has been adopted in a former chapter for the purpose of giving a classification of Shakespeare's dramas, we shall obtain the following results. The novels are twenty-nine in number, of varied, though for the most part extraordinary degrees of excellence. They may be divided into the two main classes of Historical, or such as derive their principal interest from the delineation of some real persons or events, and Fictitious, or those which are entirely or principally founded upon Private

Life or Family Legend, and which are more remotely, if at all, connected with history. The first of these two great classes will naturally subdivide into subordinate categories, according to the epoch or country selected by the author, as Scottish, English, and Continental history. According to this rude, and merely approximative method of classification, we shall range seven works under the class of Scottish history, seven under English, also of various epochs, and three will belong to the Continental department; while the novels mainly assignable to the head of Private Life— sometimes, it is true, more or less connected, as in the cases of *Rob Roy* and *Redgauntlet*, with historical events,—are twelve in number. The latter class are for the most part of purely Scottish scenery and character. The following rough scheme or plan of the above arrangement will at least be found to assist the memory in recalling such a vast and varied cycle of works :—

I. History.

I. Scottish ... *Waverley.* The period of the Pretender's attempt in 1745.

Legend of Montrose. The Civil War in the seventeenth century.

Old Mortality. The rebellion of the Covenanters.

Monastery.⎫ The deposition and imprisonment
Abbot.⎭   of Mary Queen of Scots.

Fair Maid of Perth. The reign of Robert III.

Castle Dangerous. The time of the Black Douglas.

II. English ... *Ivanhoe.* The return of Richard Cœur de Lion from the Holy Land.

Kenilworth. The reign of Elizabeth.

Fortunes of Nigel. Reign of James I.

Peveril of the Peak. Reign of Charles II. period of the pretended Catholic plot.

Betrothed. The wars of the Welsh Marches.

Talisman. The third Crusade : Richard Cœur de Lion.

Woodstock. The Civil War and Commonwealth.

III. Continental . *Quentin Durward.* Louis XI. and Charles the Bold.

Anne of Geierstein. The epoch of the battle of Nancy.

Count Robert of Paris. The Crusaders at Byzantium.

II. Private Life and Mixed.

Guy Mannering.	*Pirate.*
Antiquary.	*St. Ronan's Well.*
Black Dwarf.	*Redgauntlet.*
Rob Roy.	*Surgeon's Daughter.*
Heart of Midlothian.	*Two Drovers.*
Bride of Lammermoor.	*Highland Widow.*

In this unequalled series of fictions, the author's power of bringing near and making palpable to us the remote and historical, whether of persons, places, or events, is equally wonderful with the skill and certainty with which he clothes with solidity, so to say, the conceptions of his own imagination. In this respect his genius has something in common with that of Shakespeare, as shown in his historical dramas. Scott was generally careless in the construction of his plots : he wrote with great rapidity, and aimed rather at picturesque effect than at logical coherency of intrigue; and his powerful imagination carried him away so vehemently, that the delight he must have felt in developing the humours and adventures of one of those inimitable persons he had invented, sometimes left him no space for the elaboration of the pre-arranged intrigue. An example of this will be found, among a multitude of others, in the case of Dugald Dalgetty, or Baillie Nicol Jarvie. His style, though always easy and animated, is far from being careful or elaborate; and a curious amount of Scotticisms will be met with in almost every chapter. Description, whether of scenery, incident, or personal appearance, is very abundant in his works; and few of his countrymen, whether North or South Britons, will be found to complain of his luxuriance in this respect, for it has filled his pages with bright and vivid pictures that no lapse of time can efface from the reader's memory.

In the delineation of character as well as in the painting of external nature, Scott proceeds objectively : his mind was a mirror that faithfully reflected the external surfaces of things. He does not show the profound analysis which penetrates into the internal mechanism of the passions and anatomises the nature of man, nor does he communicate, like Richardson and Byron, his own personal colouring to the creations of his fancy; but he sets before you so brightly, so transparently, so vividly, all that is necessary to give a distinct idea, that his images remain indelibly in the memory.

CHAPTER XXIV.

THE immense influence exerted by Byron on the taste and sentiment of Europe has not yet passed away, and, though far from being so supreme and despotic as it once was, is not likely to be ever effaced. He called himself, in one of his poems, "the grand Napoleon of the realms of rhyme;" and there is some similarity between the suddenness and splendour of his literary career, and the meteoric rise and domination of the First Buonaparte. They were both, in their respective departments, the offspring of revolution; and both, after reigning with absolute power for some time, were deposed from their supremacy, though their reign will leave profound traces in the history of the nineteenth century. GEORGE GORDON NOEL BYRON (1788-1824) was born in London in 1788, and was the son of an unprincipled profligate and of a Scottish heiress of ancient and illustrious extraction; who on being deserted by her worthless husband, retired with her boy to Aberdeen, where they lived for several years in very straitened circumstances. The future poet inherited from his mother a susceptibility almost morbid, which his early training under her capricious guidance must have still further aggravated. He was about eleven years old when the death of his grand-uncle, a strange, eccentric, and misanthropic recluse, made him heir-presumptive to the baronial title of one of the most ancient aristocratic houses in England, which had been for several generations notorious for the vices and even crimes of its representatives. With the title he inherited large though embarrassed estates, and the noble picturesque residence of Newstead Abbey near Nottingham. He was now sent first to Harrow School, and afterwards to Trinity College, Cambridge. At college he became notorious for the irregularities of his conduct. He was a greedy though desultory reader; and his imagination appears to have been especially attracted to Oriental history and travels.

It was while at Cambridge that Byron made his first literary attempt, in the publication of a small volume of fugitive poems entitled *Hours of Idleness, by Lord Byron, a Minor.* An unfavourable criticism of this work in the Edinburgh Review threw him into a frenzy of rage. He instantly set about taking his revenge in the satire *English Bards and Scotch Reviewers*, in which he involved in one common storm of invective not only his enemies of the Edinburgh Review, but almost all the literary men of the day, —Walter Scott, Moore, and a thousand others, from whom he had received no provocation whatever,—a violence of which he soon became heartily ashamed. Though written in the classical, declamatory, and regular style of Gifford, himself an imitator of Pope, the *English Bards* shows a fervour and power of expression that enables us to see in it, dimly, the earnest of Byron s intense and fiery genius, which was afterwards to exhibit itself under such different literary forms.

Byron now went abroad to travel, and filled his mind with the picturesque life and scenery of Greece, Turkey, and the East, accumulating those stores of character and description which he poured forth with such royal splendour in his poems. The two first cantos of *Childe Harold* absolutely took the public by storm, and at once placed the young poet at the summit of social and literary popularity. These were followed in rapid succession by the *Giaour, Bride of Abydos, Corsair, Lara*, in which Byron broke up new ground in describing the manners, scenery, and wild passions of the East and of Greece—a region as picturesque as that of his rival Scott, as well known to him by experience, and as new and fresh to the public he addressed. Returning to England in the full blaze of his dawning fame, the poet became the lion of the day. He at this period married Miss Milbanke, a lady of considerable expectations; but the union was an unhappy one, and in about a year Lady Byron suddenly quitted her husband. Her reasons for taking this step will ever remain a mystery. Deeply wounded by the scandal of this separation, the poet again left England; and from thenceforth his life was passed uninterruptedly on the Continent, in Switzerland, in Italy, and in Greece, where he solaced his embittered spirit with misanthropical attacks upon all that his countrymen held sacred, and gradually plunged deeper and deeper into a slough of sensuality and vice. While at Geneva he produced the third canto of *Childe Harold*, the *Prisoner of Chillon, Manfred*, and the *Lament of Tasso*. Between 1818 and 1821 he was principally residing at Venice and Ravenna; and at this period he wrote *Mazeppa*, the five first cantos of *Don Juan*, and most of his tragedies, as *Marino Faliero, Sardanapalus*, the *Two Foscari, Werner, Cain*, and the *Deformed Transformed*, in many of which the influence of Shelley's literary manner and philosophical tenets is more or less traceable; and here too he terminated *Don Juan*, at least as far as it ever was completed. In 1823 he determined to devote his fortune and his influence to the aid of the Greeks, then struggling for their independence. He arrived at Missolonghi at the beginning of 1824; where, after giving striking indications of his practical talents, as well as of his ardour and self-sacrifice, he died on the 19th of April of the same year, at the early age of thirty-six.

The earliest considerable effort of Byron, and in many respects his most remarkable composition, is *Childe Harold*, which consists of a series of gloomy but intensely poetical monologues, put into the mouth of a jaded and misanthropic voluptuary, who takes refuge from his disenchantment of pleasure in the contemplation of the lovely or historical scenes of travel. The first two cantos are somewhat feeble and tame as compared with the strength and massive power of the two later, which are the productions of his more mature faculties. The third canto contains the magnificent description of the Battle of Waterloo, and bitter and melancholy but sublime musings on the vanity of military fame. The poem is written in the Spenserian stanza; and in the beginning the poet makes an effort to give something of the quaint and archaic character of the Fairy Queen; but he soon throws off the useless and embarrassing restraint. In intensity of feeling, in richness and harmony of expression, and in an imposing tone of gloomy, sceptical, and misanthropic reflection, *Childe Harold* stands alone in our literature.

The romantic tales of Byron are all marked by similar peculiarities of thought and treatment, though they may differ in the kind and degree of their respective excellences. The *Giaour*, the *Siege of Corinth*, *Mazeppa*, *Parisina*, the *Prisoner of Chillon*, and the *Bride of Abydos*, are written in that somewhat irregular and flowing versification which Scott brought into fashion; while the *Corsair*, *Lara*, and the *Island*, are in the regular English rhymed heroic measure. These poems are, in general, fragmentary: they are made up of intensely interesting *moments* of passion and action. Neither in these nor in any of his works does Byron show the least power of delineating *variety* of character. There are but two personages in all his poems—a man in whom unbridled passions have desolated the heart, and left it hard and impenetrable; a man contemptuous of his kind, sceptical and despairing, yet occasionally feeling the softer emotions with a singular intensity. The woman is the woman of the East—sensual, devoted, and loving, but loving with the unreasoning attachment of the lower animals. These elements of character, meagre and unnatural as they are, are however set before us with such consummate power that the young and inexperienced reader invariably loses sight of their contradictions. In all these poems we meet with inimitable descriptions, tender, animated, or profound, which harmonise with the tone of the *dramatis personæ:* thus the famous comparison of enslaved Greece to a corpse in the *Giaour*, the night-scene and the battle-scene in the *Corsair* and *Lara*, the eve of the storming of the city in the *Siege of Corinth*, and the fiery energy of the attack in the same poem, the exquisite opening lines in *Parisina*, besides a multitude of others, might be adduced to prove Byron's extraordinary genius in communicating to his pictures the individuality and the colouring of his own feelings and character.

In *Beppo* and the *Vision of Judgment* Byron has ventured upon the gay, airy, and satirical. The former of these poems is not over-moral; but it is exquisitely playful and sparkling. The *Vision* is a most severe attack upon Southey, parodying the very poor and pretentious verses which the Laureate composed as a sort of apotheosis of George III.; and though somewhat ferocious and truculent, is exceedingly brilliant. The *Island* is a striking incident extracted from the narrative of the famous mutiny of the Bounty, when Captain Bligh and his officers were cast off by his rebellious crew in an open boat, and the mutineers, under the command of Christian, established themselves in half-savage life on Pitcairn's Island, where their descendants were recently living Among the less commonly read of Byron's longer poems we may mention the *Age of Bronze*, a vehement satirical declamation; the *Curse of Minerva*, directed against the spoliation of the frieze of the Parthenon by Lord Elgin; the *Lament of Tasso*, and the *Prophecy of Dante*, the latter written in the difficult *terza rima*, which Wyatt alone of English poets had previously used. The *Dream* is in some respects the most touching of Byron's minor works. It is the narrative, in the form of a vision, of his early love-sorrow for Mary Chaworth. There is hardly, in the whole range of literature, so tender, so lofty, and so condensed a life-drama as that narrated in these verses.

The dramatic works of Byron are in many respects the precise opposite of what might *à priori* have been expected from the peculiar character of his genius. In form they are cold, severe, and lofty, partaking but little of the manner of Shakespeare. Artful involution of intrigue they have not; but though singularly destitute of powerful *passion* they are full of intense sentiment. The finest of them is *Manfred*, which, however, is not so much a drama as a dramatic poem; and consists not of action represented in dialogue, but of a series of sublime soliloquies, in which the mysterious hero describes nature, and pours forth his despair and his self-pity In this work, as well as in *Cain*, we see the full expression of Byron's sceptical spirit, and the tone of half-melancholy, half-mocking misanthropy which colours so much of his writings, and which was in him partly sincere and partly put on for effect. The more exclusively historical pieces—*Marino Faliero*, the *Two Foscari*—are derived from Venetian annals; but neither in the one nor in the other has Byron clothed the events with that living reality which the subjects would have received even from Rowe or Otway. There is in these dramas a complete failure in variety of character; and the interest is concentrated on the obstinate harping of the principal personages upon one topic—their own wrongs and humiliations. In *Surdanapalus* the remoteness of the epoch chosen, and our total ignorance of the interior life of those times, removes the piece into the region of fiction. But the character of Myrrha, though beautiful, is an anachronism and an impossibility; and the antithetic contrast between the effeminacy and the sudden heroism in Sardanapalus belongs rather to satire or to moral disquisition than to tragedy. *Werner*, a piece of domestic interest, is bodily borrowed, as far as regards its incidents, and even much of its dialogue, from the German Story in Miss Lee's 'Canterbury Tales'; indeed Byron's share in its composition extends little further than the cutting up of Miss Lee's prose into tolerably regular, but often very indifferent lines.

Don Juan, written in the *ottava rima*, is the longest, the most singular, and in some respects the most characteristic, of Byron's poems. It is, indeed, one of the most significant productions of the age of revolution and scepticism which preceded its appearance. The outline of the story is the old Spanish legend of Don Juan de Tenorio, upon which have been founded so many dramatic works, among the rest the *Festin de Pierre* of Molière and the immortal opera of Mozart. The fundamental idea of the atheist and voluptuary enabled Byron to carry his hero through various adventures, serious and comic, to exhibit his unrivalled power of description, and left him unfettered by any necessities of time and place. Even in the imperfect state in which it was left, it consists of sixteen cantos, and there is no reason why it should not have been indefinitely extended. It was the author's intention to bring his hero's adventures to a regular termination, but so desultory a series of incidents have no real coherency. The merit of this extraordinary poem is the richness of ideas, thoughts, and images; its witty allusion and sarcastic reflection: and above all, the constant passage from the loftiest and tenderest tone of poetry to the most familiar and mocking style. The tone of morality is throughout very low and selfish, even materialistic; but in spite of much superficial flippancy, this poem contains an immense mass of profound and melancholy satire; and in a very large number of serious passages Byron has shown a power, picturesqueness, and pathos which in other works may indeed be paralleled, but cannot be surpassed.

THOMAS MOORE (1779-1852), the personal friend and biographer of Byron, was born in Dublin, of humble parentage. After distinguishing himself at the University of Dublin, he passed over to London, nominally with the intention of studying law in the Temple; but he soon appeared before the public as the translator of the *Odes of Anacreon*, a task for which his elegant and varied, though perhaps not very profound, scholarship rendered him sufficiently fit. This work was published by subscription, and dedicated to the Prince Regent; and immediately introduced Moore into that gay and fashionable society of which he remained all his life a somewhat too assiduous frequenter. His dignity of character, perhaps, suffered from his passion for the frivolous triumphs of fashionable circles; but Moore was during his whole life the spoiled child of popularity. In 1804 he obtained a small government post in the island of Bermuda, which, indeed, enabled him to visit America and the Antilles, and drew from him some of the most sparkling of his early poems. Neglecting the duties of his station, he became responsible, by the dishonesty of a subordinate, for a considerable sum of public money. This claim of the Crown he afterwards discharged by his literary labour; and nearly the whole of his long life was devoted to the production of a rapid succession of compositions, both in prose and verse, some of which obtained an immense and all a respectable success. As an Irishman and Catholic, Moore was naturally a Whig, "and something more;" which circumstance supplied the biting and yet pleasant sarcasm which seasons his political pasquinades. He spent the latter part of his life in a cottage near Bowood, the residence of the Marquess of Lansdowne, who had cherished his friendship.

The poetical, which is also the larger, portion of Moore's writings consists chiefly of lyrics, whether serious or comic, the most celebrated collection among them being the *Irish Melodies*. The version of *Anacreon*, though tolerably faithful in the general rendering of the original, is far too brilliant and ornamental in its language to give a correct idea of the manner of the Greek poet. In his juvenile poems, as well as in the collection published under the pseudonym of *Thomas Little*, in the productions suggested by his visit to America and the West Indies, and in the *Odes and Epistles*, we see that ingenious and ever-watchful invention which forms a prominent characteristic of Moore's genius; and also the strongly erotic and voluptuous tendency of sentiment, which is sometimes carried beyond the bounds of good taste and morality.

The *Irish Melodies*, a collection of about 125 songs, were composed in order to furnish appropriate words to a great number of beautiful national airs, some of great antiquity, which had been degraded by becoming gradually associated with lines often vulgar and not always decent. Patriotism, love, and conviviality form the subject-matter of these charming lyrics; their versification has never been surpassed for melody and neatness; the language is always clear, appropriate, and concise, and sometimes reaches a high degree of majesty, vigour, or tenderness. Though Moore is destitute of the intense sincerity of Burns, or of that exquisite sensibility to popular feeling which makes Béranger the darling of the middle and lower classes of France, yet he appeals, as they do, to the universal sentiments of his countrymen, and his popularity is proportionally great. The *National Airs*, which were intended to be set to tunes peculiar to various countries, exhibit the same exquisite musical sensibility and the same neatness of expression as the *Irish Melodies;* but they are naturally inferior to them in intensity of patriotic feeling. A small collection of *Sacred Songs* affords frequent examples both of the merits and defects of Moore's lyrical genius, though the latter are perhaps more prominent as destructive occasionally of the lofty religious tone which the subject required him to maintain. All these collections, however, exhibit a high polish, an almost fastidious finish of style, which makes them models of perfection in their peculiar manner.

The political squibs of Moore were directed against the Tory party in general, and were showered with peculiar vivacity and stinging effect upon the Regent, afterwards George IV., Lord Eldon, Castlereagh, and all those who were opposed to the granting of any relaxation to the Irish Catholics. His *Satirical and Humourous Poems*, his *Fables for the Holy Alliance*, show an inexhaustible invention of quaint and ingenious ideas, and the power of bringing the most apparently remote allusions to bear upon the person or thing selected for attack. Some of the most celebrated of these brilliant pasquinades were combined into a sort of story, as for example the *Fudge Family in Paris*, purporting to be a series of letters written from France just at the period of the Restoration of the Bourbons. Nothing can be more animated, brilliant, and humorous than the description of the motley life and the giddy whirl of amusement in Paris at that memorable moment; and the whole is seasoned with such a multitude of personal and political allusions, that the *Fudge Family* will probably ever retain its popularity, as both a social and political sketch of a most interesting episode in modern European history.

The longer and more ambitious poems of Moore are *Lalla Rookh* and the *Loves of the Angels*, the former being immeasurably the better, both as regards the interest of the story and the power with which it is treated. The plan of *Lalla Rookh* is original and happy ; it consists of a little prose love-tale describing the journey of a beautiful Oriental princess from Delhi to Bucharia, where she is to meet her betrothed husband, the king of the latter country. The prose portion of the work is inimitably beautiful; the whole style is sparkling with Oriental gems, and perfumed, as it were, with Oriental musk and roses : and the very abuse of brilliancy and of voluptuous languor, which in another kind of composition might be regarded as meretricious, only adds to the Oriental effect. The four poems to which the above story forms a setting are the *Veiled Prophet*, the *Fire Worshippers*, *Paradise and the Peri*, and the *Light of the Harem;* all, of course, of an Eastern character, and the two first in some degree historical in their subject. The longest and most ambitious is the first, which is written in the rhymed heroic couplet, while the others are composed in that irregular animated versification which Walter Scott and Byron had brought into fashion.

The *Loves of the Angels*, the only remaining poem of any length, need not detain us long. It is manifestly inferior to *Lalla Rookh*, not only in the impracticable nature of its subject, but in the monotony of its treatment. The fundamental idea is based upon that famous and much misunderstood passage of the Book of Genesis, where it is said, that in the primeval ages " the sons of God " became enamoured of " the daughters of men," the issue of which connexion was the Giants. Moore introduces three of these sons of God, who by yielding to an earthly love have forfeited the privileges of their celestial nature, and who relate, each in his turn, the story of their passion and its punishment. This poem was written during Moore's retirement to Paris, and bears some traces of the influence of Byron's somewhat similar, and not much more successful production, *Heaven and Earth*, which was in its turn generated to a certain degree by the writings of Shelley.

The chief prose works of Moore are the three biographies of Sheridan, Byron, and Lord Edward Fitzgerald, and the tale of the *Epicurean*. The last, a narrative of the first ages of Christianity, describes the conversion, under the influence of love, of a young Athenian philosopher, who travels into Egypt, and is initiated into the mysterious worship of Isis. Moore's biographies, especially that of Byron, are of great value. It is particularly valuable from consisting, as far as possible, of extracts from Byron's own journals and correspondence, so that the subject of the biography is delineated in his own words, Moore furnishing little more than the arrangement and the connecting matter.

PERCY BYSSHE SHELLEY (1792-1822) was of ancient and opulent family, the eldest son of Sir Timothy Shelley, and was born at Field Place, near Horsham, in Sussex, August 4th, 1792. At Eton his sensitive mind was shocked by the sight of boyish tyranny; and he went to Oxford full of abhorrence for the cruelty and bigotry which he fancied pervaded all the relations of civilised life. An eager and desultory student, he rapidly filled his mind with the sceptical arguments against Christianity; and having published a tract avowing atheistic principles, he was expelled from the University. This scandal, together with a marriage he contracted with a beautiful girl, his inferior in rank, caused him to be renounced by his family. After a few years he separated from his wife, who subsequently terminated her existence in a melancholy manner by suicide; and he contracted during his wife's lifetime a new connexion with the daughter of Godwin; and having induced his family to make him a considerable annual allowance, he was from thenceforth relieved from pecuniary difficulties. The delicate state of his health rendered it advisable that he should leave England for a warmer climate, and the remainder of his life was passed abroad, with only one short interruption. In Switzerland he became acquainted with Byron, and the ardour of his character and the splendour of his genius undoubtedly exerted a powerful influence on his mighty contemporary. He afterwards migrated to Italy, where he kept up an intimate companionship with Byron, still continuing to pour forth his strange and enchanting poetry in indefatigable profusion. He resided principally at Rome, and composed there many of his finest productions. His death was early and tragic. As he was returning in a small yacht from Leghorn, in company with a friend and a single boatman, his vessel was caught in a squall, and went down with all on board in the Gulf of Spezzia. Thus perished this great poet, at the age of thirty.

Shelley was all his life, both as a poet and as a man, a dreamer, a visionary : his mind was filled with glorious but unreal phantoms of the possible perfectibility of mankind. The very intensity of his sympathy with his kind clouded his reason; and he fell into the common error of all enthusiasts, of supposing that, if the present organisation of society were swept away, a millennium of virtue and happiness must ensue. As a poet he was undoubtedly gifted with genius of a very high order, an immense, though somewhat vaporous

richness and fertility of imagination, an intense fire and energy in
the reproduction of what he conceived, and a command over all the
resources of metrical harmony such as no English poet has surpassed.   His career commences with *Queen Mab*, written by the poet
when but eighteen years old, a wild phantasmagoria of beautiful
description and fervent declamation, in that irregular unrhymed
versification of which Southey's Thalaba is an example.   The defect
of this poem, as indeed of many of Shelley's other compositions, is a
vagueness of meaning which often becomes absolutely unintelligible.

Perhaps the finest, as it is the completest and most distinct, of
Shelley's longer poems is *Alastor, or the Spirit of Solitude*, in which
he depicts the sufferings of such a character as his own, a being of
the warmest sympathies, and of the loftiest aspirations, driven into
solitude and despair by the ingratitude of his kind, who are incapable of understanding and sympathising with his aims.   The *Revolt
of Islam, Hellas*, and the *Witch of Atlas*, are works which belong,
more or less, to the category of Queen Mab; violent invectives
against kingcraft, priestcraft, religion, and marriage, alternating
with airy and exquisite pictures of scenes and beings of superhuman
and unearthly splendour.   The defect of these poems is the extreme
obscurity of their general drift.   Though particular objects stand
out with the vividness and splendour of reality, and are lighted up
with a dazzling glow of imagination, the effect of the whole is sin
gularly vague and uncertain.

Two important works of Shelley are dramatic in form; the *Prometheus Unbound* and the *Cenci*.   The former, however, is rather a
lyric in dialogue than a drama, while the latter is a regular tragedy.
The *Prometheus* is one of the wildest and most unintelligible of all
this poet's works, though it contains numberless passages of the
highest beauty and sublimity.   The fundamental idea is based upon
the gigantic drama of Æschylus, of which it is intended to be the
complement; but it breathes throughout that strange union of
fierce hostility to social systems and intense love for humanity in
the abstract which forms so singular an anomaly in the writings of
Shelley.   Many of the descriptive passages are sublime; and noble
bursts of lyric harmony alternate with the wildest personifications
and the fiercest invective.   The *Cenci* is a regular tragedy on the
severe and sculptural plan of Alfieri.   It is founded on the famous
crime of Beatrice di Cenci, driven to parricide by the diabolical
wickedness of her father, for which she suffered the penalty of death
at Rome; but in spite of several powerful and striking scenes, the
piece is of a morbid and unpleasing character, though the language
is vigorous and masculine.

The narrative poem of *Rosalind and Helen* is an elaborate plead

ing against the institution of marriage, an intense and almost
amusing hostility to which was one of Shelley's pet crazes. In the
poem of *Adonais* the poet has given us a beautiful and touching
lament on the early death of Keats, whose short career gave such a
noble foretaste of poetical genius as would have made him one of
the greatest writers of his age. One of the most imaginative, and at
the same time one of the obscurest, of Shelley's poems is the *Sensitive
Plant*, which combines the qualities of mystery and fancifulness to
the highest degree, perpetually stimulating the reader with a desire
to penetrate the meaning symbolised in the luxuriant description of
the garden and the Plant, and filling him with the richest imagery
and description. Many of his detached lyrics are of inexpressible
beauty, as the *Ode to a Skylark*, which breathes the very rapture of
the bird's soaring song, and the wild but picturesque imagery of the
Cloud, besides a number of minor but not less beautiful productions.

JOHN KEATS (1796–1821) was born in Moorfields, London, and
was apprenticed to a surgeon in his fifteenth year. During his
apprenticeship he devoted most of his time to poetry, and in 1817
he published a volume of juvenile poems. This was followed in
1818 by his long poem *Endymion*, which was severely censured
by the *Quarterly Review*, an attack which has been somewhat
erroneously described as the cause of his death. But he had a constitutional tendency to consumption, which would most likely have
developed itself under any circumstances. He went for the reco-
very of his health to Rome, where he died on the 24th of February,
1821. In the previous year he had published another volume of
poems, *Lamia, Isabella*, &c., in which was included the fragment of
his remarkable poem entitled *Hyperion*.

It was the misfortune of Keats to be either extravagantly praised
or unmercifully condemned. That which is most remarkable in his
works is the wonderful profusion of figurative language, often exquisitely beautiful and luxuriant, but sometimes purely fantastical and
far-fetched. This peculiarity Keats carries to extravagance—one
word, one image, one rhyme suggests another, till we quite lose sight
of the original idea, which is smothered in its own luxuriance.
Keats deserves high praise for one very original merit : he has
treated the classical mythology in a way absolutely new, representing the Pagan deities not as mere abstractions of art, nor as mere
creatures of popular belief, but giving them passions and affections
like our own, though highly purified and idealised. In *Hyperion*,
in the *Ode to Pan* (which appears in 'Endymion'), in the verses
on a *Grecian Urn*, we find a strain of beautiful classic imagery,
combined with a perception of natural loveliness inexpressibly

luxuriant, rich, and delicate. Such of Keats's poems as are founded
on more modern subjects—*The Eve of St. Agnes* for example, or *The
Pot of Basil*, a beautiful anecdote versified from Boccacio—are, to
our taste, inferior to those of his productions in which the scenery
and personages are mythological. Keats was a true poet. If we
consider his extreme youth and delicate health, his solitary and
interesting self-instruction, the severity of the attacks made upon
him by hostile and powerful critics, and, above all, the original richness and picturesqueness of his conceptions and imagery, even when
they run to waste, he appears to be one of the greatest of the young
poets—resembling the Milton of *Lycidas*, or the Spenser of the
Tears of the Muses.

Though the *ottava rima* was employed in early times by more
than one poet of distinction, the writer whose compositions immediately suggested it to Lord Byron was JOHN HOOKHAM FRERE
(1769–1846), assistant of Canning in the management of the famous
Anti-Jacobin, and honourably known as a translator of Aristophanes.
It was in the above metre that he wrote his *Prospectus and Specimen of an intended National Work by William and Robert Whistle-
craft*, &c., a burlesque of great celebrity when it first appeared in
1817, and for some time afterwards. A writer of much the same
calibre as Frere, though perhaps superior in some respects, is
WINTHROP MACKWORTH PRAED (1802–1839), son of Mr. Serjeant
Praed, and a politician of great promise, whose premature death
was a loss alike to the nation and to literature. As a writer of *vers
de société*, a kind of composition in which the English language is
unusually rich, he has had few equals, and perhaps no superior.
His *Belle of the Ball-Room* and *Letter of Advice* are not excelled
even by Moore, whose name is perhaps the highest in this particular department. Indeed for sparkle, for airy elegance, for playful,
if not over deep, humour, and for flowing grace, he is not likely ever
to be excelled.

Our limited space will allow no more than a mention of the
Pleasures of Memory of SAMUEL ROGERS (1763–1855), and the *Rejected
Addresses* of JAMES and HORACE SMITH.

THOMAS CAMPBELL (1777–1844), who was born on the 27th of
July, 1777, at Glasgow, was educated at the University in that
city, where he distinguished himself by his translations from the
Greek poets. In 1799, when he was only in his twenty-second year,
he published his *Pleasures of Hope*, which was received with a burst
of enthusiasm as hearty as afterwards welcomed the *Lay of the Last
Minstrel* and *Childe Harold*. Shortly afterwards he travelled abroad,
where the warlike scenes he witnessed, and the battle-fields he visited,
suggested some noble lyrics. To the seventh edition of the *Pleasures*

of Hope, published in 1802, were added the magnificent verses on
the battle of *Hohenlinden*, *Ye Mariners of England*, the most popular
of his songs, and *Lochiel's Warning*. In the following year he settled
in London, married, and commenced in earnest the pursuit of
literature as a profession. His works were written chiefly for the
booksellers, and with the exception of his *Gertrude of Wyoming*,
which appeared in 1809, do not require any notice in a history of
literature. In 1843 he retired to Boulogne, where he died in the
following year. His body was brought over to England and interred
in Westminster Abbey.

In the circle of poets with Byron, Shelley, and Keats, outliving
by many years the latest of these, must be mentioned the names of
Leigh Hunt and Walter Savage Landor.

JAMES HENRY LEIGH HUNT (1784–1859) was born at Southgate,
Middlesex, and received his education at Christ's Hospital, which he
left " in the same rank, at the same age, and for the same reasons,
as Lamb." In 1805 he joined his brother in editing a newspaper
called the *News*, and shortly afterwards established the *Examiner*,
which still exists. A conviction for libel on the Prince Regent
detained him in prison for two years, the happiest portion of his
life: he was free from the worry and care which never afterwards
forsook him. Soon after he left prison he published the *Story of
Rimini*, an Italian tale in verse (1816), which contains some exquisite poetry, both as to conception and execution. About 1818 he
started the *Indicator*, a weekly paper, in imitation of the *Spectator ;*
and in 1822 he went to Italy, to assist Lord Byron and Shelley in
their projected paper called the *Liberal*. Shelley died soon after
Hunt's arrival in Italy; and though Hunt was kindly received by
Byron, and lived for a time in his house, there was no congeniality
between them. Returning to England he continued to write for
periodicals, and published various poems from time to time, of which
one of the most celebrated was *Captain Sword and Captain Pen*.
Leigh Hunt's poetry is graceful, sprightly, and full of fancy. Though
not possessing much soul and emotion, it has true life and genius :
while here and there his verse is lit up with wit, or glows with
tenderness and grace. His prose writings consist of essays, collected
under the titles of *The Indicator* and *The Companion; Sir Ralph
Esher*, a novel; *The Old Court Suburb;* his lives of *Wycherley,
Congreve, Vanbrugh*, and *Farquhar*, prefixed to his edition of their
dramatic writings, and many others.

The father of WALTER SAVAGE LANDOR (1775–1864) was a gentleman of good family and wealthy circumstances residing in Warwickshire. The son entered Rugby at an early age, and thence
proceeded to Trinity College, Oxford; but he left the University

without a degree. In 1795 his first work—a volume of poems—appeared, followed early in the present century by a translation into Latin of *Gebir*, one of his own English poems. Landor had no small facility in classical composition, and he appeared to have the power of transporting himself into the times and sentiments of Greece and Rome. This is still more clearly seen in the *Heroic Idylls* (1820), in Latin verse; and the reproduction of Greek thought in *The Hellenics* is one of the most successful attempts of its kind. Shortly after the death of his father, the poet took up his abode on the Continent, where he resided during the rest of his life, with occasional visits to his native country. The republican spirit which led him to take part as a volunteer in the Spanish rising of 1808 continued to burn fiercely to the last. He even went so far as to defend tyrannicide, and boldly offered a pension to the widow of any one who would murder a despot. Between 1820 and 1830 he was engaged upon his greatest work, *Imaginary Conversations of Literary Men and Statesmen.* This was followed in 1831 by *Poems, Letters by a Conservative, Satire on Satirists* (1836), *Pentameron and Pentalogue* (1837), and a long series in prose and poetry, of which the chief are the *Hellenics enlarged and completed, Dry Sticks Fagoted,* and *The last Fruit off an Old Tree.* He died on the 17th September, 1864, at Florence, an exile from his country, misunderstood from the very individuality of his genius by the majority of his countrymen, but highly appreciated by those who could rightly estimate the works he has left behind him.

THOMAS HOOD (1799-1845) has unfortunately been regarded only as a humourist; and as the English reader would accept from him nothing but wit and humour, the most valuable of his writings are in danger of being forgotten. He was associated with the brilliant circle who then contributed to the *London Magazine ;* among whom were Lamb, Hazlitt, the Smiths, De Quincey, and Reynolds. The latter of these was united with Hood in the publication of the *Odes and Addresses,* which appeared anonymously, and were ascribed by Coleridge to Lamb. These were followed by *Whims and Oddities.* Hood became at once a popular writer; but in the midst of his success a firm failed which involved him in its losses. The poet, disdaining to seek the aid of bankruptcy, emulated the example of Scott, and determined by the economy of a life in Germany to pay off the debt which he had thus involuntarily contracted. In 1835 the family took up their residence in Coblenz; from thence removed to Ostend (1837); and returned to London in 1840. He subsequently became editor of the *New Monthly* in 1841, and held it until 1843, when the first number of his own Magazine was issued. A pension was obtained for him, with reversion to his wife and daughter in 1844; and he died upon the 3rd of May in the following year.

Hood stands very high among the poets of the second order. He was not a creative genius. He has given little indication of the highest imaginative faculty; but his fancy was most delicate, and full of graceful play. His most distinctive mark was the thorough *humanity* of his thoughts and expressions. His poems are amongst the most valuable contributions to English literature of sympathy with, and insight into, human life and character. He possessed in a most remarkable degree the power of perceiving the ridiculous and the odd. Words seemed to break up into the most queer and droll syllables. His wit was caustic, and yet it bore with itself its remedy. It was never coarse. An impurity even in suggestion cannot be found in Hood's pages. With the humour was associated a most tender pathos. The *Deathbed* is one of the most affecting little poems in our language, and is equalled only by another of his ballads entitled *Love's Eclipse*. Amongst his larger works, the *Plea of the Midsummer Fairies*, and *Hero and Leander*, are the most sustained and elaborate. The descriptive pieces in both are full of the most careful observation of nature, and most musical expression of her beauties. The best known of his poems are *The Bridge of Sighs*, *Eugene Aram*, and the *Song of the Shirt*.

However inferior the present age may be in some respects to many of its predecessors, in one at least it is vastly superior to all others— the excellence of its female intellects. Not to speak of CARO- LINE BOWLES (the second Mrs. Southey), Mrs. HEMANS, LETITIA ELIZABETH LANDON (better known perhaps by her signature of L. E. L.), we may say of ELIZABETH BARRETT BROWNING (1809- 1861) that she has gained for herself a place among poets to which not one of her own sex has ever attained. Her first acknow- ledged work was a translation of the *Prometheus Bound*, which was published in 1833. Next appeared a collection of poems in 1844, which established her reputation as the strongest, most high-toned and most melodious of female poets. Her sympathy with Italian aspirations, which enters so largely into the character of her best works, dates from her marriage with Robert Browning, when her failing health compelled her to reside in Italy. To this circum- stance we owe her *Casa Guidi Windows*, and her *Poems before Congress*, which appeared respectively in 1851 and 1860. In- comparably her greatest work, however, and in the estimation of some the noblest poem of the present century, is *Aurora Leigh*, pub- lished in 1856. This she herself pronounces " the most mature of her works, and the one into which her highest convictions upon Life and Art have entered." In the same year she left England for the last time, dying at Florence, June 29th, 1861.

CHAPTER XXV.

THE LAKE SCHOOL.—WORDSWORTH, COLERIDGE, AND SOUTHEY.

WILLIAM WORDSWORTH (1770–1850), the founder of the so-called
Lake School of poetry, was born at Cockermouth, in Cumberland,
April 7, 1770. In his ninth year he was sent to a school at Hawks-
head, in the most picturesque district of Lancashire, where his
relish for the beauties of creation, to which he mainly owes his
place among poets, was early manifested and rapidly developed.
After taking his degree at Cambridge in 1791, he went over to
France, and eagerly embraced the ideas of the wildest champions
of liberty in that country. His political sentiments, however, became gradually modified, till in later life they settled down into
steady Conservatism in Church and State. In 1793 he produced
to the world two little poems, *An Evening Walk*, and *Descriptive
Sketches*, of which the metre and language are in the school of
Pope; but they are the work of a promising scholar, and not of a
master. In the following year he completed the story of *Salisbury
Plain, or, Guilt and Sorrow*, which did not appear entire till 1842,
but of which he published an extract in 1798, under the title of
The Female Vagrant. In regard to time it is separated from the
Descriptive Sketches by a span, but in respect of merit they are
parted by a gulf. He had ceased to write in the train of Pope; and
composed in the stanza of his later favourite Spenser. His second
experiment was the tragedy of *The Borderers*, which was considered,
when it appeared, an unqualified failure. In June, 1797, Coleridge
formed a close friendship with Wordsworth and his sister; and to
furnish funds for a journey to Germany the two friends published
their *Lyrical Ballads*, the first piece in which was Coleridge's
Ancient Mariner, but several of the remaining poems were by
Wordsworth.

On their return to England in 1799 Wordsworth and his sister
settled in the lake district, from which circumstance he and his
friends, Coleridge, Southey, De Quincey, and Wilson, received the
name of the *Lake School*. He now set himself to work, both by pre-
cept and practice, to inculcate his peculiar views of poetry, which
encountered for a long time the fierce hostility of the critics. In
1799 he commenced *The Prelude*, which was not published in full

till after his death. In 1800 he published an enlarged edition of the *Ballads*, in which thirty-seven pieces were added to the original collection.

The year 1802 was an eventful one to the poet. A considerable accession of fortune, which had been due to his father at the time of his death, enabled him to marry a lady to whom he had been long attached, Mary Hutchinson, his sister's friend. In 1807 he gave to the world two new volumes of *Poems*, which contained the *Song at the Feast of Brougham Castle*, and many more of his choicest pieces. Here appeared his first sonnets, and several of them are still ranked among his happiest efforts in that department. Wordsworth's next publication was in prose. His indignation rose at the grasping tyranny of Napoleon; and in 1809 he put forth a pamphlet against the Convention of Cintra. The sentiments were spirit-stirring, but the manner of conveying them was the reverse, and his protest passed unheeded. His great work, *The Excursion*, appeared in 1814. This is a fragment of a projected great moral epic, discussing and solving the mightiest questions concerning God, nature, and man, our moral constitution, our duties, and our hopes. Its dramatic interest is exceedingly small; its structure is very inartificial; and the characters represented in it are devoid of life and probability. On the other hand, so sublime are the subjects on which they reason, so lofty is their tone, and so deep a glow of humanity is perceptible throughout, that no honest reader can study this grand composition without ever-increasing reverence and delight.

In 1815 appeared *The White Doe of Rylstone*, the only narrative poem of any length which Wordsworth ever wrote. The incidents turn chiefly on the complete ruin of a north-country family in the "Rising of the North" in 1569. *Peter Bell* was published in 1819, and was received with a shout of ridicule. The poet stated in the dedication that the work had been completed twenty years, and that he had continued correcting it in the interval to render it worthy of a permanent place in our national literature. The work is meant to be serious, and is certainly not facetious, but there is so much farcical absurdity of detail and language that the mind is revolted. This poem was followed by *The Waggoner*, which was not more successful. Between 1830 and 1840 the flood which floated *him* into favour rose to its height. Scott and Byron had in succession entranced the world. They had now withdrawn, and no third king arose to demand homage. It was in the lull which ensued that the less thrilling notes of the Lake bard obtained a hearing. It was during this time that he published his *Ecclesiastical Sonnets* and *Yarrow Revisited;* and in 1842 he brought forth a complete collection of his poems. His fame was now firmly established. On the death of Southey in 1843 he was made Poet-Laureate.   He died on April 23, 1850, when he had just completed his eightieth year.

The poetry of Wordsworth has passed through two phases of criticism, in the first of which his defects were chiefly noted, and in the second his merits.   Already we have arrived at the third era, when the majority of readers are just to both.   Perhaps the fairest estimate that has yet appeared of Wordsworth's poetry is given by an acute critic in the *Quarterly Review*:—" It is constantly asserted that he effected a reform in the language of poetry, that he found the public bigoted to a vicious and flowery diction, which seemed to mean a great deal and really meant nothing, and that he led them back to sense and simplicity.   The claim appears to us to be a fanciful assumption, refuted by the facts of literary history.   Feebler poetasters were no doubt read when Wordsworth began to write than would now command an audience, however small; but they had no real hold upon the public, and Cowper was the only *popular* bard of the day.   His masculine and unadorned English was relished in every cultivated circle in the land, and Wordsworth was the child and not the father of a reaction, which, after all, has been greatly exaggerated.   Goldsmith was the most celebrated of Cowper's immediate predecessors, and it will not be pretended that *The Deserted Village* and *The Traveller* are among the specimens of inane phraseology.   Burns had died before Wordsworth had attracted notice.   The wonderful Peasant's performances were admired by none more than by Wordsworth himself: were they not already far more popular than the Lake-poet's have ever been—or ever will be ? and were they, in any respect or degree, tinged with the absurdities of the Hayley school?   .   .   .   Whatever influence Wordsworth may have exercised on poetic style, be it great or small, was by deviating in practice from the principles of composition for which he contended.   Both his theory, and the poems which illustrate it, continue to this hour to be all but universally condemned.   He resolved to write as the lower orders talked; and though where the poor are the speakers it would be in accordance with strict dramatic propriety, the system would not be tolerated in serious poetry.   Wordsworth's rule did not stop at the wording of dialogues.   He maintained that the colloquial language of rustics was the most philosophical and enduring which the dictionary affords, and the fittest for verse of every description . . . . When his finest verse is brought to the test of his principle, they agree no better than light and darkness.   Here is his way of describing the effects of the pealing organ in King's College Chapel, with its self-poised roof, scooped into ten thousand cells :'—

> ' But from the arms of silence—list ! O list !—
> The music bursteth into second life ;
> The notes luxuriate, every stone is kissed
> With sound, or ghost of sound, in mazy strife !'

" This is to write like a splendid poet, but it is not to write as rustics talk. A second canon laid down by Wordsworth was, that poetic diction is, or ought to be, in all respects the same with the language of prose; and as prose has a wide range, and numbers among its triumphs such luxuriant eloquence as that of Jeremy Taylor, the principle, if just, would be no less available for the advocates of ornamental verse than for the defence of the homely style of the *Lyrical Ballads*. But the proposition is certainly too broadly stated ; and, though the argument holds good for the adversary, because the phraseology which is not too rich for prose can never be considered too tawdry for poetry, yet it will not warrant the conclusions of Wordsworth, that poetry should never rise above prose, or disdain to descend to its lowest level."

SAMUEL TAYLOR COLERIDGE (1772-1834) was born at Ottery-St.-Mary, in Devonshire, and was educated at Christ's Hospital; from whence he proceeded to Jesus College, Cambridge. Leaving the University in his second year he enlisted in the 15th Dragoons, under the assumed name of Comberbacke. One of the officers, learning his real history, communicated with his friends, by whom, his discharge was at once effected. After forming a wild scheme, in conjunction with Southey, for founding a model republic in North America, to which they gave the name of " Pantisocracy," and abandoning it for want of funds, he then turned his attention to literature. He had previously written the first act of the *Fall of Robespierre*, of which Southey composed the second and third acts (published in 1794). In 1795 he married Miss Sarah Fricker of Bristol, a sister of Southey's wife. During the first three years after his marriage he lived in Wordsworth's neighbourhood, and his share in the celebrated *Lyrical Ballads*, published in 1798, has been already mentioned. At this period also his tragedy, *Remorse*, was written. In 1798 Coleridge visited Germany, where he studied the language and literature. After his return he took up his abode in the Lake District, near Wordsworth and Southey. He subsequently spent some time in Malta, where he was secretary to Sir Alexander Ball in 1804 and 1805. In 1810 he quitted the Lakes, leaving his wife and children wholly dependent upon Southey,—a striking illustration of his well-known indifference to personal and pecuniary obligations. He then took up his residence in London, finding a home in the house of Mr. Gillman at Highgate, where he died, July 25, 1834.

Coleridge began life as a Unitarian and republican; his intollectual powers were chiefly formed in the transcendental schools of Germany; but he ultimately became from conviction a most sincere adherent to the doctrines of the Anglican church, and an enthusiastic defender of our monarchical constitution. Though the lyrics to which we have alluded (the finest of which are the odes *On the Departing Year*, and that supposed to be written *At sunrise in the Valley of Chamouni*) are somewhat injured by their air of effort, they are indubitably works of singular richness and exquisitely melodised language. In his translation of Schiller's *Wallenstein* Coleridge was most successful. With almost all readers it will for ever have the charm of an original work. Indeed, many beautiful parts of the translation are exclusively the property of the English poet, who used a manuscript copy of the German text before its publication by the author. That Coleridge had no power of true dramatic creation is strongly proved by his tragedy of *Remorse*, in which he has failed to produce a drama which either excites curiosity or moves any strong degree of pity. He was, however, a consummate critic of the dramatic productions of others. Till he wrote, deep and universal as had been the admiring love of the English for Shakespeare, there still remained, in their judgment, something of that *de haut en bas* tone which characterises all the criticisms anterior to Coleridge's *Lectures on Shakespeare*. Coleridge first showed that the creator of *Hamlet* and *Othello* was not only the greatest genius, but also the most consummate artist, that ever existed. He was the first to make some approach to the discovery of those laws which, expressly or intuitively, governed the evolutions of the Shakespearian drama—the first to give us some faint idea of the dimensions, the length, and breadth, and depth, of that huge sea of truth and beauty.

The most popular of Coleridge's poems, as *The Ancient Mariner*, *Christabel*, and the fragment called *Kubla Khan*, are of a mystic, unreal character; indeed, Coleridge asserted that the last was actually composed in a dream—an affirmation which may well be believed, for it is a thousand times more unintelligible than the general run of dreams. Like everything that Coleridge ever wrote, the versification is exquisite. His language puts on every form, it expresses every sound; he almost writes to the eye and to the ear. In point of completeness, exquisite harmony of feeling, and unsurpassable grace of imagery and language, Coleridge has left nothing superior to the charming little poem entitled *Love, or Genevieve*.

Coleridge takes rank also as a psychologist, moralist, and general philosopher. The *Friend*, the *Lay Sermons*, the *Aids to Reflection*, and the *Church and State*, are works which have exercised a great influence upon the intellectual character of his generation. But his chief reputation through life was founded less upon his writings than upon his conversation, or rather what may be called his conversational oratory, which must have resembled those disquisitions of the Greek philosophers of which the dialogues of Plato give some idea. It is in his innumerable fragments, in his rich but desultory remains (published posthumously under the title of *Literary Remains*), in casual remarks scribbled like Sibylline leaves, often on the margin of borrowed books, and in imperfectly-reported conversations, that we must look for proofs of Coleridge's immense but incompletely recorded powers. From a careful study of these we shall conceive a high admiration of his genius, and a deep regret at the fragmentary and desultory manifestations of his powers.

ROBERT SOUTHEY (1774-1843) was born at Bristol, where his father carried on the business of a draper. He was sent to Westminster at the age of fourteen, but he had had no proper classical training previously, and the defect was never repaired. After spending four years at Westminster he was expelled for writing an article against flogging in public schools, which appeared in the *Flagellant*, a periodical commenced by Southey and his friend and schoolfellow, Grosvenor Bedford. The following year he went to Oxford, and was entered at Balliol. His religious opinions preventing him from entering the Church, he lingered at Oxford, until Coleridge appeared with his scheme of "Pantisocracy," already related. Quitting Oxford, Southey attempted to raise by authorship funds for the American scheme, and in 1794 published at Bath, in conjunction with Robert Lovell, a small volume of poems, which brought neither fame nor profit. His chief reliance, however, was on his epic poem *Joan of Arc*, composed in 1793, for which Joseph Cottle of Bristol, the patron of Coleridge, offered him fifty guineas. In November, 1795, Southey accompanied his uncle to Lisbon, having on the morning of his departure secretly united himself to Miss Fricker, a young lady to whom he had for some time been engaged. He returned six months afterwards, and immediately commenced that life of patient literary toil from which he never swerved again while health and intellect remained. He had from the outset an allowance of 160*l.* a year from his friend Mr. Wynn, till he had obtained for him a pension of equal value from the Government. Yet, with his talents and industry, he was constantly on the verge of poverty, and not even his philosophy and hopefulness were always proof against the difficulties of his position. In 1804 he took up his residence at Greta Hall, near Keswick, in Cumberland, where he continued to reside for the remainder of his life. From being a sceptic and a republican, he became a firm believer in Christianity, and a stanch supporter of the English Church and Constitution. In 1813 he was appointed poet-laureate, and in 1835 received a pension of 300*l.* a year from the Government of Sir Robert Peel. During the last four years of his life he had sunk into a state of hopeless imbecility. He died March 21st, 1843.

Southey's literary activity was prodigious. The list of his writings, published under his own name, amounts to *one hundred and nine* volumes. In addition to these he contributed to the *Critical Review* fifty-two articles, to the *Foreign Quarterly* three, to the *Quarterly* ninety-four. The composition of these works was a small part of the labour they involved : they are all, even to his poems, books of research, which obliged him to turn over numerous volumes for the production of one.

Joan of Arc, the earliest of his long poems, was a juvenile pro·duction published in 1795. It was received with favour by most of the critical journals on account of the republican doctrines which it espoused. *Madoc*, which was completed in 1799, was not given to the world till 1805. Upon this poem he was contented to rest his fame. It is founded on one of the most absurd legends connected with the early history of America. Madoc is a Welsh prince of the twelfth century, who is represented as making the discovery of the Western world; and his contests with the Mexicans, and ultimate conversion of that people from their cruel idolatry, form the main action of the poem, which, like *Joan of Arc*, is written in blank verse. Though the poem is crowded with scenes of more than possible splendour—of more than human cruelty, courage, and superstition—the effect is singularly languid ; and the exaggeration of prowess and suffering produces the same effect upon the mind as the extravagance of fiction in the two Oriental poems which we shall next notice.

Thalaba was published in 1801, and the *Curse of Kehama* in 1810. The first is a tale of Arabian enchantment, full of magicians, dragons, hippogriffs, and monsters; and in the second the poet has selected for his groundwork the still more unmanageable mythology of the Hindoos. The poems are written in an irregular and wandering species of rhythm—the *Thalaba* altogether without rhyme; and the language abounds in an affected simplicity, and perpetual obtrusion of vulgar and puerile phraseology.

Kehama was followed, at an interval of four years, by *Roderick, the Last of the Goths*, a poem in blank verse, and of a much more modest and credible character than its predecessors. The subject is the punishment and repentance of the last Gothic King of Spain whose vices, oppressions, and in particular an insult offered to the virtue of Florinda, daughter of Count Julian, incited that noble to betray his country to the Moors.

On being appointed poet-laureate, Southey paid his tribute of Court adulation with an eagerness which showed how complete was his conversion from the political faith of his youthful days. His laureate odes exhibit a passionate hatred of his former liberal opinions which gives interest even to the ambitious monotony of these official lyrics.

Southey's prose works are very numerous and valuable on account of their learning; but the little *Life of Nelson*, written to furnish young seamen with a simple narrative of the exploits of England's greatest naval hero, has perhaps never been equalled for the perfection of its style. In his other works—the principal of which are *The Book of the Church*, *The Lives of the British Admirals*, *The Life of Wesley*, a *History of Brazil*, and a *History of the Peninsular War* —we find the same clear, vigorous English, and no less the strong prejudice and violent political and literary partiality, which so much detract from his many excellent qualities as a writer and as a man.

CHAPTER XXVI.

THE MODERN NOVELISTS

The department of English literature which has been cultivated during the latter half of the last and the commencement of the present century with the greatest assiduity and success, is undoubtedly that of prose fiction—the romance and the novel.

To give an idea of the immense richness and fertility of this branch of our subject, it will be advisable to classify the authors and their productions into a few great general species; which plan will be found, we trust, to secure clearness and aid the memory. The divisions which we propose are as follows: I. Romances properly so called; *i.e.* works of narrative fiction, the adventures of which are generally of a picturesque and romantic character, and the personages of a lofty and imposing kind. II. The vast class of pictures of society, whether invented or not. III. Oriental novels. IV. Naval and military novels.

I. ROMANCES.—The impulse to this branch of composition was first given by HORACE WALPOLE (1717-1797), the fastidious *dilettante* and brilliant chronicler of the court scandal of his day; a man of singularly acute penetration, of sparkling epigrammatic style, but of a mind devoid of enthusiasm and elevation. He retired early from political life, and shut himself up in his little fantastic Gothic castle of Strawberry Hill, to collect armour, medals, manuscripts, and painted glass; and to chronicle with malicious assiduity, in his vast and brilliant correspondence, the absurdities, follies, and weaknesses of his day. *The Castle of Otranto* is a short tale, written with great rapidity and without preparation, in which the first successful attempt was made to take the Feudal Age as the period, and the passion of mysterious, superstitious terror as the prime mover, of an interesting fiction. The manners are totally absurd and unnatural, the heroine being one of those inconsistent portraits in which the sentimental languor of the eighteenth century is superadded to the female character of the Middle Ages—in short, one of those incongruous contradictions which we meet in all the romantic fictions before Scott.

The immense success of Walpole's original and cleverly-written tale encouraged other and more accomplished artists to follow in the same track. The great name of this class is ANN RADCLIFFE (1764-1823), whose numerous romances exhibit a surprising power over the emotions of fear and undefined mysterious suspense. Her two greatest works are *The Romance of the Forest* and *The Mysteries of Udolpho*. The scenery of her predilection is that of Italy and the south of France; the ruined castles of the Pyrenees and Apennines form the theatre, and the dark passions of profligate Italian counts the principal moving power, of her wonderful fictions. The substance of them all is pretty nearly the same; mystery is the whole spell; the personages have no more individuality than the pieces of a chess-board; but they are made the exponents of such terrible and intense fear, suffering, and suspense, that we sympathise with their fate as if they were real.

A class of writing *apparently* so easy was, of course, followed by a crowd of writers. Of these the most noteworthy are Lewis and Mrs. Shelley. MATTHEW GREGORY LEWIS (1775-1818), a good-natured, effeminate man of fashion, the friend of Byron, and one of the early literary advisers of Scott, was the first to introduce into England a taste for the infant German literature of that day, with its spectral ballads and diablerie of all kinds. He was a man of lively and childish imagination; and besides his metrical translations of the ballads of Bürger, and others of the same class, he published in his twentieth year a prose romance called *The Monk*, full of horrible crimes and diabolic agency. MRS. SHELLEY (1797-1851), the wife of the poet, and the daughter of W. Godwin, wrote in Italy, in 1816, the powerful tale of *Frankenstein*, in which a young student of physiology succeeds in constructing, out of the horrid remnants of the churchyard and dissecting-room, a kind of monster, to which he afterwards gives, apparently by the agency of galvanism, a kind of spectral and convulsive life. Some of the chief appearances of the monster, particularly the moment when he begins to move for the first time, and, towards the end of the book, among the eternal snows of the arctic circle, are managed with a striking and breathless effect, that makes us for a moment forget the childish improbability and melodramatic extravagance of the tale.

To this subdivision belong the works of that most easy and prolific writer, G. P. R. JAMES (1801-1862)—the most industrious, if not always most successful, imitator of Scott, in the revival of chivalric and Middle-Age scenes. The number of James's works is immense, but they bear among themselves a family likeness so strong, and even oppressive, that it is impossible to consider this author otherwise than as an ingenious imitator and copyist—first of Scott, and secondly of himself. He is particularly versed in the history of France, and some of his most successful novels have reference to that country, among which we may mention *Richelieu*. His great deficiency is want of real, direct, powerful human passion, and consequently of life and movement in his intrigues.

II. Our second subdivision—the *Novels of real life and society*—is so extensive that we can but throw a rapid glance on its principal productions. To do this consistently with clearness, we must begin rather far back, with the novels of Miss Burney. FRANCES BURNEY (1752-1840) was the daughter of Dr. Burney, author of the *History of Music*. While yet residing at her father's house, she composed in her stolen moments of leisure the novel of *Evelina*, published in 1778, and is related not to have communicated to her father the secret of her having written it, until the astonishing success of the fiction rendered her avowal triumphant and almost necessary. *Evelina* was followed in 1782 by *Cecilia*, a novel of the same character. In 1786 Miss Burney received an appointment in the household of Queen Charlotte, where she remained till her marriage in 1793 with Count d'Arblay, a French refugee officer. She published after her marriage a novel entitled *Camilla*; and her name has more recently come before the public by her *Diary and Letters*, which appeared in 1842, after her death.

Miss Burney was followed by a number of writers, chiefly women, among whom the names of Mrs. Charlotte Smith, Mrs. Inchbald, and Mrs. Opie, are prominent. Their fictions, like those of Miss Edgeworth in more recent times, have a high and never-failing moral aim; and these ladies have exhibited a power over the feelings, and an intensity of pathos, not much inferior to Richardson's in *Clarissa Harlowe*. But their works are very unequal, and the pathos of which we speak is not diffused, but concentrated into particular *moments* of the action; and is obtained at the expense of great preparation and involution of circumstances.

At the head of the second division of our fictions is undoubtedly WILLIAM GODWIN (1756-1836), a man of truly powerful and original genius, who devoted his whole life to the propagation of certain social and political theories—visionary, indeed, and totally impracticable, but marked with the impress of benevolence and philanthropy. He was in reality one of those hard-headed enthusiasts— at once wild visionaries and severe logicians—who abounded in the age of Marvel, Milton, and Harrington; and his true epoch would have been the first period of Cromwell's public life. His own career, extending down to his death in 1836, was incessantly occupied with literary activity: he produced an immense number of works, some immortal for the genius and originality they display, and all for an intensity and gravity of thought, for reading and erudition. The first work which brought him into notice was the *Inquiry concerning Political Justice* (1793), a Utopian theory of morals and government, by which virtue and benevolence were to be the *primum mobile* of all human actions, and a philosophical re-public was to take place of all our imperfect modes of polity. The first and finest of his fictions is *Caleb Williams* (1794). Its chief didactic aim is to show the misery and injustice arising from our present imperfect constitution of society, and the oppression of our imperfect laws, not merely those of the statute-book, but also those of social feeling and public opinion. Caleb Williams is an intelligent peasant-lad, taken into the service of Falkland, the true hero, an incarnation of honour, intellect, benevolence, and a passionate love of fame, who, however, in a moment of ungovernable passion, has committed a murder, for which he allows an innocent man to be executed. This circumstance, partly by accident, partly by his master's voluntary confession, Williams learns, and is in consequence pursued through the greater part of the tale by the unrelenting per-secution of Falkland, who is now led, by his frantic and unnatural devotion to fame, to annihilate, in Williams, the evidence of his guilt. The adventures of the unfortunate fugitive, his dreadful vicissitudes of poverty and distress, the steady, bloodhound, unre-laxing pursuit, the escapes and disguises of the victim, like the agonised turnings and doublings of the hunted hare—all this is depicted with an incessant and never-surpassed power of breathless interest. At last Caleb is formally accused by Falkland of robbery, and naturally discloses before the tribunal the dreadful secret which had caused his long persecution, and Falkland dies of shame and a broken heart. The interest of this wonderful tale is indescribable; the various scenes are set before us with something of the minute reality, the dry, grave simplicity of Defoe.

Of more modern novelists WILLIAM MAKEPEACE THACKERAY (1811–1863) is one of the greatest. He was born at Calcutta in 1811, and was educated at the Charterhouse, to which he makes loving reference in his *Vanity Fair* and *The Newcomes*, under the name of "Grey Friars." He afterwards went to Cambridge, which he left without taking his degree. His great desire at this time was to become an artist; and with a considerable fortune he started for the continent, where he studied for four or five years in France, Italy, and Germany. But though a master of the pencil, Thackeray was not destined to become a great artist. On returning to London he continued his art studies; but the loss of his fortune compelled him to throw himself with all his powers into the field of literature. He was first known by his articles in *Fraser*, to which he contributed under the names of Michael Angelo Titmarsh and George Fitzboodle, Esq. Tales, criticism, and poetry appeared in great profusion; and were illustrated by the author's own pencil. The chief of his contributions to *Fraser* was the tale of *Barry Lyndon, The Adventures of an Irish Fortune-Hunter*. This was full of humour and incident, but the reading public was not yet expecting a great future from this unknown writer. In 1841 *Punch* was commenced, to which Thackeray contributed the *Snob Papers* and *Jeames's Diary*, and many other papers in prose and verse. In 1846 and the two following years appeared *Vanity Fair*, by many supposed to be the best of his works—certainly the most original. The novel was not complete before its author took his place among the great writers of English fiction. It seized all circles with astonishment. The author of satirical sketches and mirthful poems had shown himself to be a consummate satirist, and a great novelist. *Vanity Fair* was followed by his other novels, of which we shall speak presently.

On the establishment of the *Cornhill Magazine* in 1860, Thackeray became editor, and whilst connected with it he contributed his later stories, *The Adventures of Philip, Lovell the Widower*, and a little monthly sketch, *de omnibus rebus et quibusdam aliis*, though oftener *de nihilo*, called the *Roundabout Papers*. He died suddenly in the house which he had built at Kensington on Dec. 23, 1863.

Vanity Fair, the first of Thackeray's chief works, is called a " Novel without a Hero." It is possessed, however, of two heroines —Rebecca Sharp, the impersonation of intellect without heart, and Amelia Sedley, who has heart without intellect; the first of which is without doubt the ablest creation of modern fiction. As a whole the book is full of quiet sarcasm and severe rebuke; but a careful reading will perceive the kindly heart that is beating under the bitterest sentence and the most caustic irony.

Pendennis, published in 1849 and 1850, was the immediate successor of *Vanity Fair*, and is the life of a Tom Jones of the present age. Literary life presents scope for description, and is well used in the history of Pen, who is a hero of no very great worth. As *Vanity Fair* gives us Thackeray's knowledge of life in the present day, so *Esmond*, which appeared in 1854, exhibits his intimate acquaintance with the society of the reigns of the later Stuarts and earlier Georges. Like *Vanity Fair*, it is without plot, and gives in an autobiographical form the history of Colonel Henry Esmond. The style of some hundred and fifty years ago is reproduced with marvellous fidelity. The story of *Esmond* is probably the best of Thackeray's writings.

The *Virginians* is the history of the grandsons of Esmond, and though not published till 1857, we mention it next as related to

Esmond in history. It consists of a series of well-described scenes
and incidents in the reign of George II. In 1853 was ended the
most popular and best liked of Thackeray's novels, *The Newcomes.*
" The leading theme or moral of the story is the misery occasioned
by forced and ill-assorted marriages." The noble courtesy, the
Christian gentlemanliness of *Colonel Newcome*, is perhaps a complete
reflection of the author himself. *Ethel Newcome* is Thackeray's
favourite female character. The minor personages are most life-
like, while over the whole there is a clear exhibition of the real
kindliness of heart which Thackeray possessed.

The two courses of lectures *On the English Humourists* and *The
Four Georges*, are models of style and criticism. The latter is a
clever sketch of the home and court life of the first Hanoverians.
The lectures are full of thoughts sternly abhorrent of the falsity and
rottenness which these courts presented, while admiration for the
goodness and kindness of the third George almost makes the lecturer
forget his weaknesses. The *Humourists* is a more valuable work,
containing some of the most complete criticism on those writers
which is to be found in our language.

In marked contrast with the slowness of Thackeray's rise to
literary eminence was the almost instantaneous recognition of
CHARLES DICKENS (1812-1870) as the first humorist of the day.
Dickens sprang into the place of national favourite when still very
young, and at a single bound. The son of a government clerk, whose
life was a continuous struggle with poverty and debt, he was forced
in early boyhood to undergo humiliations galling to his sensitive
nature; though he was—to use his own words—" a child of singular
abilities, quick, eager, delicate, and soon hurt," he was doomed to
drudge for some years in a blacking manufactory situated in the
worst quarter of London. Yet this cruel school supplied an admirable training for the future novelist; the manifold knowledge
that the child thus gained of city life in its lowest forms, treasured
up in a most tenacious memory, furnished materials for many of
the man's greatest works. He was afterwards office-boy to an
attorney, then reporter in Doctors' Commons, then reporter in Parliament, winning his way to comparative competence by steady
industry. His first efforts in literature were some contributions
to the ' Monthly Magazine,' which, when published in a collected
form as *Sketches by Boz*, attracted some notice, and soon reached
a second edition. But the same year (1836) distinction of
the most dazzling kind suddenly came to him. At the request of a publishing firm he began the *Posthumous Papers of
the Pickwick Club*, and before the work had half run its course he
had risen to a height of popular favour rarely exampled in literary

history.   Everybody read the *Pickwick Papers*; the sayings of Sam
Weller passed briskly from mouth to mouth; the sale of the monthly
numbers rose to 40,000 copies.

This was the beginning of a career of incessant literary activity
and unbroken literary success.   Before *Pickwick* was ended *Oliver
Twist* was begun; and when this work was finished, Dickens's large
experience of a hitherto neglected section of humanity enabled him
to give to the world, in swift succession, *Nicholas Nickleby*, the *Old
Curiosity Shop*, and *Barnaby Rudge*.   The last of these works was
published in 1841; Dickens had added five masterpieces to the
literature of humour before he had reached his thirtieth year.

There now seemed to be some danger of the early vein being
prematurely worked out; and in 1842 Dickens went to America
to gather new materials for his pen.   He was welcomed there
with a burst of applause such as few men of letters have
ever experienced; the whole nation strove its best to do him
honour.   Yet the *American Notes* and *Martin Chuzzlewit*, which
came out soon after his return home, drew a picture of Transatlantic
society which, whether true or false, deeply wounded the national
feeling; and Dickens was charged with gross ingratitude to his
generous hosts.   His defence was that the man who did not spare
his own countrymen could hardly be expected to sacrifice the truth
through tenderness for what was absurd in the ways of foreigners.
He next paid a long visit to the Continent (1844–1847), during
which he wrote the *Christmas Carol* and *Dombey and Son*, the last
number of the latter appearing in 1848.   His next work, *David
Copperfield* (1849), is usually regarded as marking the culmina-
tion of his genius; and its author would seem to have thought
so himself; "of all my books," he says, "I like this the best."
And no wonder; in the hero we must recognise Dickens himself,
and in many of the incidents of the work the events of his own
early life.

Fame and fortune were now assured; and henceforward longer
intervals separated the publications of his great serial novels.   *Bleak
House* was finished in 1853; *Little Dorrit* in 1857; *The Mutual
Friend* in 1865.   Notwithstanding the alleged decay of power in
these later works there was no decay of popular interest; Dickens
never lost the place he had early won in the national heart.   Last
came the beginnings of *The Mystery of Edwin Drood*; but death
snapped the thread of the author's life before many numbers were
given to the world.   *Edwin Drood* remains a fragment.

Dickens had more than once projected monthly or weekly periodicals.   His first enterprise of this kind, *Master Humphrey's
Clock*, lived long enough to start the *Old Curiosity Shop* and *Bar-*

naby Rudge; but his latest, *Household Words,* which was begun in 1850, struck vigorous root, was transformed, nine years later, into *All the Year Round,* and thus in a sense exists still. For this he wrote his shorter novels, *Hard Times,* the *Tale of Two Cities,* and *Great Expectations,* of which the last is hardly less excellent than the best of his greater works. Soon after his return from a second visit to America, in which the Americans nobly avenged themselves by making it a still greater triumph than the first, he was suddenly smitten down by apoplexy, the penalty of an overtasked brain, at his house of Gadshill, near Rochester, and died the next day, June 9, 1870. He was buried in Westminster Abbey.

To specify even the leading characteristics of Dickens's genius is hardly possible within the limits of a book like this. His one peerless gift was his humour, rich and inexhaustible; of this it seemed as if the fountain could never run dry; it shows itself as clearly in the *Mutual Friend* as in the *Pickwick Papers.* The file of irresistibly comic characters that he created, Sam Weller, Dick Swiveller, Micawber, Wemmick, and the others—to name them all were not easy—stretch far beyond the longest that can be drawn out for any other writer; in this respect Dickens is unapproachable. This supreme manifestation of humour was, perhaps, the product of two forces; a power of observation so marvellous as almost to suggest inspiration, and a boundless faculty of conceiving new humorous touches and strokes of character, which he added to, and thereby heightened, the laughable traits of the men and women of his experience. In this way his unthrifty father became Micawber, his mother Mrs. Nickleby. Dickens has many other merits; but his humour eclipses them all. He was fond of a peculiar kind of sentiment; but this often threatens to degenerate into maudlin sentimentality; his inborn love of dramatic effects betrayed him into an occasional striving after the sensational. But on the whole the tone of his writings is manly and sound, and their general view of life cheerful and inspiriting. He failed completely in the construction of a plot; indeed many of his works can hardly be said to have any plots at all. Their manner of publication—in monthly numbers, each of which was expected to have a unity of its own—was, perhaps, chiefly to blame for this fault; but it goes far towards vitiating their character as works of art.

The third popular master of fiction of this age, LORD LYTTON— *Edward George Earle Lytton Bulwer-Lytton*—(1805–1873), was of a totally different type of genius from either of his great contemporaries. The most striking feature in his literary character was the vast range of his intellectual activities; poet, playwright, social critic, journalist, essayist, historian, orator, statesman, and above all novelist—in each character he gained eminence, in all but one or two not far short of the highest attained in his time. The fertility of his mind was still more wonderful. He was born in 1805, and was the son of General Bulwer and Miss Lytton, of Knebworth in Hertfordshire, both whose names he ultimately united on inheriting his mother's property. His genius bloomed early; at fifteen he wrote *Ismael*, a tale; a little later, when a student at Cambridge, he won the Chancellor's prize for a poem on *Sculpture*. After two or three other youthful attempts, he made his first decided hit in *Pelham* (1827), which soon became the fashionable novel of the day. From this date till his death he toiled incessantly to win himself an honourable name in literature. Novel succeeded novel, each showing a distinct improvement on its predecessor; poem succeeded poem, that on *Milton* gaining the approbation of the judicious; and in 1838 Bulwer was made a baronet at the Queen's coronation solely because of his distinction as a man of letters. Among the many novels written by him since 1827, the most valuable are *Eugene Aram*, *The Last Days of Pompeii*, and *Rienzi*, and of these the latter two are likely to keep the public favour longest. Both seek to bring back to life past ages and extinct societies, and with more than average success; in any case they awaken in their readers a vivid interest in the men and women of bygone times.

Bulwer's greatness, however, was long in ripening. Much unfriendly criticism and not a little ridicule were directed against him for many years. He was accused of being affected, artificial, dandified; exception was taken to the morality of his works, and especially to the tinsel glitter that he was declared to have thrown over vulgar crime. Carlyle made him the butt of solemn banter in 'Sartor Resartus'; Thackeray scoffed at him in more than one of his compositions. And undoubtedly his works had many faults. But most of these gradually disappeared before the chastening influence of time and study. In what we may call the novels of his second period Bulwer clearly rose to a higher level of thought, morality, and art. The names only of the more impressive can be given here:—the *Last of the Barons*, *Harold*, and the series of the *Caxton Novels*, the latter being the best of all his works. The qualities of genius become even more marked, as we pass into the novels and romances of his third period; in *The Coming Race*—a political romance of the Utopia type—*The Parisians* and *Kenelm Chillingly*—this last published posthumously—the stream of thought, intellect, and observation, still flows in full volume.

His dramatic gifts too were of a high order. He wrote many plays; and three of them, *Richelieu*, *The Lady of Lyons*, and

Money, still hold the stage, and are great favourites with playgoers. His poems—of which, one, *King Arthur*, is an Epic—never gained the recognition that their author thought they deserved; but besides *Milton*, a goodly share of admiration has been given to *St. Stephens*, a sketch of past and present parliamentary celebrities in vigorous and harmonious verse. He was, moreover, a biting satirist; his *New Timon* had a sharp sting in it for some of his contemporaries. But his intellect grew mellower as he drew towards old age; it is remarked that even in the vicious characters of his later works there are " happy touches of a better nature."

His political career was comparatively brief. He first entered Parliament in 1831 as a Liberal, and for a time showed some zeal in promoting measures of Reform. But when, after a long exclusion from Parliament, he again returned to it as member for Hertfordshire, he was a Conservative; and he then made such telling speeches against further constitutional innovation that, in the second administration of Lord Derby, he was appointed Secretary of State for the Colonies. In 1866 his old chief raised him to the peerage as Lord Lytton. He died in 1873.

At the head of the very large class of female novelists who have adorned the more recent literature of England, we must place MARIA EDGEWORTH (about 1767-1849). Her long and useful life was chiefly passed in Ireland; and many of her earlier works were produced in partnership with her father, Richard Lovell Edgeworth, a man of eccentric character and great intellectual activity, who devoted himself to experiments in education and social ameliorations. The most valuable series of Miss Edgeworth's educational stories were the charming tales entitled *Frank, Harry and Lucy, Rosamond*, and others, combined under the general heading of *Early Lessons*. These are written in the simplest style and language, and are intelligible and intensely interesting even to very young readers; while the knowledge of character they display, the naturalness of their incidents, and the sound practical principles they inculcate, make them delightful even to the adult reader. In the *Parents' Assistant* the same qualities are applied to the moral and intellectual improvement of a more advanced age; and the common errors, weaknesses, and prejudices of boys and girls are combated in a series of stories which, in the good sense and observation they display, are as admirable as in their artistic construction. Some of these—as, for example *Simple Susan*—are little masterpieces of style and execution. But perhaps the most truly original of Miss Edgeworth's stories is the inimitable *Castle Rackrent*, giving the biographies, equally humorous and pathetic, of a series of Irish landlords. The follies and vices which have caused no small proportion of the social miseries that have afflicted Ireland are here shown up with a truly dramatic effect. In the novels of *Patronage* and the *Absentee* other social errors, either peculiar to that country or common to it with others, are powerfully delineated. Almost all these works show a delicate appreciation of the merits and the weaknesses of the Irish character, and especially of the Irish peasantry; and Miss Edgeworth has in some sense done for her humbler countrymen what Scott did with such loving genius for the Scottish people. The services rendered by Maria Edgeworth to the cause of common sense are incalculable; and the singular absence of enthusiasm in her writings, whether religious, political, or social, only makes us more wonder at the force, vivacity, and consistency with which she has drawn a large and varied gallery of characters.

JOHN GALT (1779-1839), in a long series of novels, has confined himself to the minute delineation of the interior life of the Scottish peasantry and provincial tradespeople. The *Annals of the Parish*, the supposed journal of a quaint, simple-minded Presbyterian pastor, give us a singularly amusing insight into the microscopic details of Scottish life in the lower classes. Galt's primary characteristic is a dry, subdued, quaint humour—a quality very perceptible in the lower orders of Scotland, which in his works, as in the national character of his countrymen, is often accompanied by a very profound and true sense of the pathetic. The more romantic and tragical side of the national idiosyncrasy has been exquisitely portrayed in the touching tales of PROFESSOR JOHN WILSON (1785-1854), also celebrated as a poet and the author of *Noctes Ambrosianæ*, of whom we shall speak more fully in the subsequent chapter. In his *Lights and Shadows of Scottish Life*, published in 1822, and in *The Trials of Margaret Lyndsay*, which appeared in 1823, he exhibits a deep feeling for the virtues and trials of humble life.

But the department of fiction which undoubtedly possesses not only the greatest degree of value for the English reader, but will have the most powerful attraction for foreign students of our literature, is that which depicts the manners of the middle and lower classes of the English people. The first in point of time, and the first in point of merit, in this province is MISS AUSTEN (1775-1817), whose novels may be considered as models of perfection in a new and very difficult species of writing. She depends for her effect upon no surprising adventures, upon no artfully-involved plot, upon no scenes deeply pathetic or extravagantly humorous. She paints a society which, though virtuous, intelligent, and enviable above all others, presents the fewest salient points of interest and singularity to the novelist: we mean the society of English country-gentlemen. Whoever desires to know the interior life of that vast and admirable body the rural gentry of England—a body which absolutely exists in no other country on earth, and to which the nation owes many of its most valuable characteristics—must read Miss Austen's novels, *Sense and Sensibility*, *Pride and Prejudice*, *Mansfield Park*, and *Emma*. In these works the reader will find very little variety and no picturesqueness of persons, little to inspire strong emotion, nothing to excite wonder or laughter; but he will find admirable good sense, exquisite discrimination, and an unrivalled power of easy and natural dialogue.

Among the almost countless host of female novelists that the insatiable appetite of these later times for this kind of reading has given birth to, the authoress of *Jane Eyre* is distinguished by special force and originality, and by extraordinary power in the conception and delineation of character. CHARLOTTE BRONTE (1816-1855) was the eldest of three rather remarkable sisters, daughters of the incumbent of Haworth in Yorkshire, and first appeared before the public in 1846, as joint contributor with her sisters to a volume of poems which failed to attract any attention. But her next work met with a very different fate. In 1847 *Jane Eyre* was published, and the reputation of the author, who wrote under the name of Currer Bell, was fixed as one of the highest in this department of letters; and this position it still retains. *Shirley* followed in the same style in 1849, and *Villette* in 1853—this last in some respects the greatest of her works. In 1854 she married her father's curate, Mr. Nicholls; but after a few months of happiness which contrast strangely with the many troubles of her earlier days, died in the beginning of 1855. Her life has been written by Mrs. GASKELL, herself a novelist of great merit, lately dead, and is one of the saddest and most touching of narratives.

Of the purely comic manner of fiction there are few better examples than the novels of THEODORE HOOK (1788-1842). He is greatest in the description of London life, and particularly in the rich drollery with which he paints the vulgar efforts of suburban gentility to ape the manners of the great. There is not one of his numerous novels and shorter tales in which some scene could not be cited carrying this kind of drollery almost to the brink of farce. What, for example, can be more irresistible than the Bloomsbury evening party in *Maxwell*, or the dinner at Mr. Abberley's in *The Man of Many Friends?* Hook's more exclusively serious novels are generally considered as inferior to those in which there is a mixture of the ludicrous; and for one of the last works produced by this clever writer before his death, he selected a subject admirably adapted to the peculiar strength of his talent. This was *Jack Brag*, a most spirited embodiment of the arts employed by a vulgar pretender to creep into aristocratic society, and the ultimate discomfiture of the absurd hero. Hook died in 1841, leaving a large number of works, all of them exhibiting strong proofs of humour, but mostly deprived of permanent value by the haste perceptible in their execution. The best of them are, perhaps, *Gilbert Gurney*, and its continuation, *Gurney Married*.

Very similar to Theodore Hook in the subject and treatment of her novels, and not unlike him in the general tone of her talent, is MRS. TROLLOPE, whose happiest efforts are the exhibition of the gross arts and impudent stratagems employed by the pretenders to fashion. Her best work is, perhaps, *The Widow Barnaby*, in which she has reached the ideal of a character of gross, full-blown, palpable, complete pretension and vulgar assurance. Mrs. Trollope's plots are exceedingly slight and ill-constructed, but her narrative is lively, and she particularly excels in her characters of goodnatured, shrewd old maids.

It would be a great injustice were we not to devote a few words of admiration to the charming sketches of MISS MITFORD (1786-1855), a lady who has described the village life and scenery of England with the grace and delicacy of Goldsmith himself. *Our Village* is one of the most delightful books in the language; it is full of those *home scenes* which form the most exquisite peculiarity, not only of the external nature, but also of the social life of the country. Miss Mitford describes with the truth and fidelity of Crabbe and Cowper, but without the moral gloom of the one, and the morbid sadness of the other.

III. ORIENTAL NOVELS.—There exists in our literature a class of novels which have for their aim the delineation of the manners and scenery of distant countries; and as among these works the Oriental are naturally the most splendid and prominent, we shall take three which seem the most favourable specimens of this subdivision. These are *The History of the Caliph Vathek*, by WILLIAM BECKFORD (1759-1844); the romance of *Anastasius*, by THOMAS HOPE (about 1770-1831); and the inimitable *Hajji Baba* of JAMES MORIER (d. 1849). *Vathek* is an Arabian tale, and was originally published in 1784, *in French*, being one of the rare instances of an Englishman being able to write that difficult language with the grace and purity of a native. Being afterwards translated by the author into his mother tongue, it forms one of the most extraordinary monuments of splendid imagery and caustic wit which literature can afford. It narrates the adventures of a haughty and effeminate monarch, led on, by the temptations of a malignant genie and the sophistries of a cruel and ambitious mother, to commit all sorts of crimes, to abjure his faith, and to offer allegiance to Eblis, the Mahomedan Satan, in the hope of seating himself on the throne of the Preadamite Sultans. In the concluding scene, which soars into the highest atmosphere of grand descriptive poetry, he descends into the sub-terranean palace of Eblis, where he does homage to the Evil One, and wanders for a while among the superhuman splendours of those regions of punishment. The fancy of genius has seldom con-ceived anything more terrible than the concluding portion of this strange work.

Hope's work, though very different in form from that of Beckford, was not unlike it in some points. *Anastasius*, published in 1819, purports to be the autobiography of a Greek, who, to escape the consequences of his own crimes and villanies of every kind, becomes a renegade, and passes through a long series of the most extra-ordinary and romantic vicissitudes. The hero is a compound of almost all the vices of his unfortunate and degraded nation; and in his vicissitudes of fortune we see passing before us, as in a diorama, the whole social, political, and religious life of Turkey and the Morea. The style is elaborate and passionate: and this, as well as the cha-racter of the principal personage,

"Link'd with one virtue and a thousand crimes,'

reminds us, in reading *Anastasius*, very strongly of the manner of Lord Byron.

But if the darker side of Oriental nature be presented to us in *Vathek* and *Anastasius*, the *Hajji Baba* of Morier will make us ample amends in drollery and a truly comic *verve*. This is the *Gil Blas* of Oriental life. Hajji Baba is a barber of Ispahan, who passes through a long but delightfully varied series of adventures, such as happen in the despotic and simple governments of the East, where the pipe-bearer of one day may become the vizier of the next. The hero is an easy, merry good-for-nothing, whose dexterity and gaiety it is impossible not to admire, even while we rejoice in the punish-ment which his manifold rascalities draw down upon him; and perhaps there is no work in the world which gives so vast, so lively, and so accurate a picture of every grade, every phase of Oriental existence.

IV. NAVAL AND MILITARY NOVELS.—It now remains only to speak of one species of prose fiction—that which has for its subject the manners and personages of marine or military life. It may easily be conceived that, the former service being most entwined with all the sympathies of the national heart, the subdivision of marine novels should be the richest. At the head of this class stands CAPTAIN MARRYAT (1792-1848), one of the most easy, lively, and truly humorous story-tellers we possess. One of the chief elements of his talent is undoubtedly the tone of high, effervescent, irrepressible animal spirits which characterises everything he has written. He seems half-tipsy with the gaiety of his heart, and never scruples to introduce the most grotesque extravagances of character, language, and event, provided they are likely to excite a laugh. Nothing can surpass the liveliness and drollery of his *Peter Simple, Jacob Faithful*, or *Mr. Midshipman Easy;* what an inexhaustible gallery of originals has he paraded before us! Marryat's narratives are exceedingly inartificial, and often grossly improbable; but we read on with gay delight, never thinking of the story, but only solicitous to follow the droll adventures, and laugh at the still droller characters. This author has a peculiar talent for the delineation of boyish characters: his Faithful and Peter Simple (the " fool of the family ") not only amuse but interest us; and in many passages he has shown no mean mastery over the pathetic emotions. Though superficial in his view of character, he is generally faithful to reality, and shows an extensive if not very deep knowledge of what his old waterman calls "human natur." There are few authors more amusing than Marryat; his books have the effervescence of champagne.

The tales called *Tom Cringle's Log* and *The Cruise of the Midge* are also works in this kind (although not exclusively naval) of striking brilliancy and imaginative power. In these we have a most gorgeously coloured and faithful delineation of the luxuriant scenery of the West Indian Archipelago, and the manners of the Creole and colonist population are reproduced with consummate drollery and inexhaustible splendour of language. They were the production of MR. MICHAEL SCOTT (d. 1835), a gentleman engaged in commerce, and personally familiar with the scenes he described; and the admiration they excited at their first appearance (anonymously) in *Blackwood's Magazine* caused them to be ascribed to the pen of some of the most distinguished of living writers, particularly to that of PROFESSOR WILSON.

The military novels are mostly by living authors, and are therefore excluded from our work.

ADDENDUM TO MODERN NOVELISTS.

Since the publication of the last edition of this work, three distinguished novelists have died.

George Eliot (1819–1880), is the famous name under which Mary Anne Evans chose to address the world. The daughter of a Warwickshire land-steward, she came thus from the same county, and sprang from the same social stock as Shakspeare. She was born on that border-land of English society, where the gentleman's and yeoman's conditions meet; and, partly by accident of birth, partly by a generous natural endowment, partly by an equally generous culture—mostly self-acquired—and partly by observation, she was fitted to be the interpreter of what was best and most racy in the characters of both classes.

She was already in her thirty-seventh year when her first attempt at fiction, *The Sad Fortunes of Amos Barton*, appeared in *Blackwood's Magazine* early in 1857. Other sketches soon followed in the same periodical; and by the time that these were collected into a single volume Miss Evans had fixed upon " George Eliot " as her name in literature. The clear-sighted critics of the day began slowly to recognise in the new author a genius of unusual power and breadth, and to see in the *Scenes of Clerical Life*—for such was the title of the volume—infinite promise of great things to come. In January, 1859, *Adam Bede* was published. Creations so fresh and winning as Mr. Irwin and Mrs. Poyser could not be long resisted; the ruddy tints of English life, among the green pastures, sweet-smelling country lanes, sleepy farmhouses, and village homesteads of the Midlands, were too warm and natural to fail of their effect; and in time the book made its way into the very core of the national heart, whence it is not likely to be soon dislodged. Curiosity was stimulated; but the secret of authorship was well kept, until a gentleman who lived near Nuneaton was pitched upon by the neighbourhood as the too-retiring genius, and had almost persuaded himself of his identity with George Eliot, when the veil was gradually withdrawn.

Adam Bede proved, however, to be but the beginning of an illustrious line; its immediate successor, *The Mill on the Floss*, which appeared in 1860, deservedly carried the fame of the author still higher. This we believe to be George Eliot's masterpiece, the one of her compositions pre-eminent in strokes of the noblest order of genius. Yet *Silas Marner*, which followed in 1861, seems to us the most pleasing of the series, in fact, a perfect prose idyll, breathing of the green fields, and telling of the simple lives, loves, sins, foibles, and frailties of simple country folk in a healthy, social order that progress has effaced.

Romola came next (1862-63). The design and subject of this work put the writer's powers to a severer test than anything she had attempted; but the result amply vindicated her confidence in them. If taken merely as a book, without any allowance being made for the difficulties inherent in its plan, *Romola* is, in our opinion, inferior to *The Mill on the Floss;* but if judged with a due consideration of the nature of the task imposed by its composition, and as a proof of the author's strength, it is equal, if not superior, to anything of the kind ever written. To bring back to life an extinct age, to reanimate grand historical forms of men and things—this George Eliot essayed in *Romola*, and came nearer to absolute success than any other English writer that has undertaken a similar task, nearer, we think, than even Thackeray in *Esmond*. Whether Florence in the days of the Renaissance and Savonarola really were what *Romola* depicts, it is of course impossible to say; but there is no doubt about the animation and impressiveness of the picture. In *Felix Holt* (1866) George Eliot came back again to the familiar ground of English life, but hardly succeeded in maintaining the high level of her previous works. The days of the Reform Bill failed to kindle within her the same living interest as the days of the immediately preceding generation.

By this time her pen had begun to move more slowly; it was not until 1872 that her next novel, *Middlemarch*, reached the public. In *Middlemarch* we certainly find the old power, and much more of it. We find a wonderful variety of strongly drawn characters, and abundance of calm energy, but hardly the old freshness and freedom: we seem to miss the old blithe, spontaneous movement, and with it some of the charm, of the earlier books. In *Adam Bede* and *Silas Marner* we have, as it were, the subject working through the author, in *Middlemarch* the author working through the subject. And this remark, if it be true, applies with still greater force to her last and most elaborate novel, *Daniel Deronda* (1877). Hard, though excellent, work is visible in every page; there is great display of intellectual strength; it always astonishes, often gives a keen pleasure; but the demands it makes on the attention of readers will prevent its ever becoming a popular work; the mental strain required to keep up with the train of reflection and observation is too exacting.

George Eliot now and then strayed into other paths besides that of prose fiction, but never to the same excellent purpose. Poetry attracted her; and she did all that genius and toil could do to secure a position among the great poets of her country. In 1868 she published *The Spanish Gipsy*, a volume in verse that wanted little but the gift of song to make it a great poem. Many smaller poems, valuable for their weighty matter and weightier utterances, for their softness, tenderness, and humanity, she has also given us.

Her last composition was *The Impressions of Theophrastus Such* (1879), which, as its name denotes, is a book of characters, similar in design to those of Overbury and Earle. It is a work of unequal merit. In June, 1880, she married Mr. Walter Cross. On the following 22nd December she died at Chelsea. Her life has been written by Mr. Cross.

The unique combination of a brilliant novelist and an imperial statesman of world-wide fame is found in BENJAMIN DISRAELI (1804–1881), created in 1876, Earl of Beaconsfield. This illustrious man—known in early life as "Young Disraeli," to distinguish him from his father, Isaac Disraeli, author of the *Curiosities of Literature* and several other works—had made himself a considerable name in prose fiction years before he entered Parliament. His earliest work, *Vivian Grey* (1826), is a most striking, if crude, attempt to body forth the notable men of that time, and to give utterance to singularly daring and original ideas on politics. *The Young Duke*, written in 1829, is a more mature effort "to pourtray the fleeting manners of a somewhat frivolous age," yet betrays its author's fascinated interest in the movement of public life. *Contarini Fleming* (1832), being published anonymously, missed its mark for the moment, being, in its writer's words, "almost still-born," but made its way, though slowly, after a time, and gained the hearty approval of more than one other man of genius. His next publication, *The Wondrous Tale of Alroy* (1833), an historical and oriental novel, revealed, for the first time, how tenderly and passionately the soul of the young Anglo-Israelite brooded over the history, spirit, ideas, and destiny, of the extraordinary race from which he was sprung. The very year 1837, which began the transformation of the novelist into the politician, he issued two novels, *Henrietta Temple* and *Venetia*, which have nothing whatever to do with politics. The first is what it calls itself, "a love story"; into the second the personalities of the poets Byron and Shelley are worked ; and in its action their destinies are blended with some ingenuity but doubtful felicity.

Disraeli was seven years in Parliament when his first strikingly impressive book, *Coningsby* (1844), appeared before the public. In this powerful work the author delivered his soul on "the origin and condition of political parties," with such scorching irony, humour, sarcasm, keenness of temper, and flashing wit, that it has settled into a kind of classic; its Rigby, Taper, and Tadpole, are still familiar as typical figures in the public life of the day. It was followed by the second and third portions of the great Triology, as their author names the group, *Sybil* (1845), and *Tancred or the New Crusade* (1847), in which the mounting politician's original and occasionally fantastic views were further and fully developed.

Twenty-three years later, when the man of letters was believed to have been irrecoverably lost in the statesman, the political veteran startled the world with *Lothair* (1870), of which he boasts that it " has been more extensively read...than any work that has appeared for the last half century." The freshness of spirit and thronging life of its pages, in which many of the high-placed personages of the hour are made to play their parts under thin disguises, explain to some extent its amazing popularity. The glittering file closes with *Endymion* (1881), another work of like character with *Lothair*, and making up by its absorbing personal interest,—for its hero is a reminiscence of the writer's own youthful personality,—for what it may lack of the sparkling qualities of its predecessor. Besides these, Lord Beaconsfield wrote the *Revolutionary Epick* (1834), a fragment of an ambitious poem, and *Count Alarcos*, a tragedy (1839), the *Life of Lord George Bentinck* (1851), and some minor pieces of fiction. His manner as a writer is somewhat puzzling, occasionally distracting, mixture of seriousness and jest, of the grave and the gay; stinging satire and solemn sneer alternate with generous outbursts and sincere earnestness. He shows throughout a distinct turn for the splendid, the dazzling, the gorgeous in modern life; his style is often rhetorical and heavy, a kind of literary cloth of gold. But the mark of high genius is on all his work.

With Disraeli's death died the last of the " giant brood " of English novelists. In passing to ANTHONY TROLLOPE (1815-1882) we sink to a lower level of art and faculty—to mere talent in fact. But Trollope's work is sound, wholesome, and genial; its quiet and true pictures of ordinary English life have a soft and winning, if somewhat tame and commonplace, charm peculiar to themselves. The circumstances of his life may have been largely answerable for the character of his writings. Though born of a good family, a younger son of the author of *Widow Barnaby*, and educated at Winchester and Harrow, he was driven by the misfortunes of his father to take a clerkship in the Post Office, from which, rising by slow degrees to the position of surveyor, he was compelled to travel much, to live for periods of varying length in many parts of England and Ireland, and thus to mix with and observe average insular

humanity of many forms and shades of local or individual character.
His love of the hunting field, amounting almost to a passion, added
considerably to his opportunities of noticing the ways of men. His
literary essays met with scant encouragement for several years; but
struggling on with that methodic persistence which only death
arrested, he at last contrived to make a palpable hit in *The Warden*
(1855). The favour thus gained was maintained by the still widely-
read *Barchester Towers* (1857), a sequel to the *Warden*, and was
never afterwards seriously imperilled. For a quarter of a century
from this time he was the untiring and unresting producer of modest
and well-flavoured fiction, even-flowing narratives of personal adventure, and an occasional slight biography, for readers of homely
tastes. For several years no day passed without its allotted number
of pages; no pause in the regular, almost punctual, birth of book
after book gave warning of flagging energy or failing materials.
Among the half hundred of novels thus created, perhaps the most
worthy of notice are *Doctor Thorne*, *Framley Parsonage*, *Orley
Farm*, *the Small House at Allington* and the *Last Chronicle of
Barset;* but out of such abundance and such a distinct tendency to
uniformity of merit, it is not easy to choose. He was most at home
in clerical circles: his Archdeacon Grantley, Dean Arabin, Mr.
Crawley and Mrs. Proudie are prominent in several of his novels;
and the Mr. Plantagenet Palliser of *Framley Parsonage*, with or
without Lady Glencora his wife, is, as Duke of Omnium, the central
or an important figure in *Can you Forgive Her*, *Phineas Finn*, *the
Prime Minister*, and *the Duke's Children*. Hawthorne's verdict on
Trollope is likely to be final: " His characters are just as real as if
some giant had hewn a great lump out of the earth, and put it
under a glass case, with all its inhabitants going about their daily
business, and not suspecting that they were made a show of."

CHAPTER XXVII.

PROSE LITERATURE OF THE NINETEENTH CENTURY.

THE early years of the present century were years of conflict and excitement. The public mind was wrought to the highest pitch, now of fear, and now of triumph. England fought for the liberties of Europe; at times the struggle seemed to be for her own existence. The literature of a people always reflects something of the prevalent tone of its age, and we may therefore expect that the chief compositions of the first thirty years of this century will be marked by intense feeling, passion, and emotion. Accordingly there is no age in English history which can exhibit such an array of masters of song. The most passionate states of the human mind demand an expression in song. In the "Victorian age," on the other hand, the prose element has predominated. The calmer inquiries into politics, philosophy, art, and physical science, have been prosecuted in the more tranquil period, and the first noticeable feature in the writers of the present century is the growing prevalence of our prose literature, more especially in the department of fiction.

Another feature of the present age is the growth of periodical literature. The rise of our leading reviews will be noticed presently, and together with these have sprung up the countless magazines and newspapers which form the chief part of most men's reading. The *Book* has become too laborious, too tedious a thing for the study of this overworked age. We have come to require stimulants in our reading. Everybody reads something, and few read much.

The chief external influence affecting the literature of the age has come from Germany. The thoughts and even style of this philosophical literature have done much to shape and regulate English thoughts and language. Coleridge introduced it largely, and he has been followed in the work by Thomas Carlyle.

In no department of literature has Europe made greater progress during the present century than in that of History. A new impulse was given to the study of Ancient History by the publication of the first volume of Niebuhr's *Roman History*, in Germany, in 1811. This remarkable work taught scholars not only to estimate more accurately the value of the original authorities, but to enter more fully

into the spirit of antiquity, and to think and feel as the Romans felt
and thought. In the treatment of Modern History the advance has
been equally striking. An *historical sense*, so to speak, has grown
up. A writer of any period of modern history is now expected to
produce in support of his facts the testimony of credible contemporary witnesses; while the public records of most of the great
European nations, now rendered accessible to students, have imposed
upon historians a labour, and opened sources of information, quite
unknown to Hume, Robertson, and the historical writers of the
preceding century.

The most eminent English writers upon Ancient History are
Bishop Thirlwall (1797–1875) and George Grote (1794–1871),
both of whom have produced *Histories of Greece* far superior to any
existing in other European languages. Dr. Thomas Arnold (1795–
1842), Head-Master of Rugby School, wrote a *History of Rome* in
three volumes (1838-40–42), which was broken off, by his death, at
the end of the Second Punic War. This work is chiefly valuable
as a popular exhibition of Niebuhr's views, and is written in clear
and masculine English. Dr. Arnold also published some *Introductory Lectures on Modern History* (1842), which display more
independence of thought. He was also the author of several theological works, which exercised great influence upon his generation.
The most formidable opponent of Niebuhr's views was Sir George
Cornewall Lewis (1806–1863), equally remarkable as a statesman
and a scholar. His most important historical work is *An Inquiry
into the Credibility of the early Roman History*, published in 1855.
While rejecting with Niebuhr the received narrative of early Roman
history, Sir George Lewis attacks the defective method adopted by
the German historian in attempting to reconstruct this portion of
Roman history. He was also the author of many valuable political
works, of which the most important are, *A Treatise on the Method
of Observation and Reasoning in Politics*, the *Influence of Authority in Matters of Opinion*, and the *Use and Abuse of Political
Terms*.

The most illustrious recent writer of modern history is Thomas
Babington Macaulay (1800-1859), raised to the peerage, in 1857,
as Lord Macaulay of Rothley. He was the son of Zachary Macaulay,
an ardent philanthropist, and one of the earliest opponents of the
slave trade. Educated at Trinity College, Cambridge, of which
College he became a Fellow, and called to the bar at Lincoln's Inn,
he suddenly achieved a literary reputation by an article on Milton
in the *Edinburgh Review* in 1825. This was the first of a long series
of brilliant literary and historical essays which he contributed to the
same periodical. His career as a statesman was both brilliant and

successful, but it is as a man of letters that his name will be longest remembered.

Macaulay is distinguished as a Poet, an Essayist, and an Historian. His *Lays of Ancient Rome* are the best known of his poems; but the lines which he wrote upon his defeat at Edinburgh in 1847 are the finest. His Essays and his History will, in virtue of their inimitable style, always give Macaulay a high place among English classics. His style has been well described by Dean Milman. "Its characteristics were vigour and animation, copiousness, clearness; above all, sound English, now a rare excellence. The vigour and life were unabating; perhaps in that conscious strength which cost no exertion he did not always gauge and measure the force of his own words. . . . His copiousness had nothing tumid, diffuse, Asiatic; no ornament for the sake of ornament. As to its clearness, one may read a sentence of Macaulay twice to judge of its full force, never to comprehend its meaning. His English was pure, both in idiom and in words, pure to fastidiousness; . . . every word must be genuine English, nothing that approached real vulgarity, nothing that had not the stamp of popular use, or the authority of sound English writers, nothing unfamiliar to the common ear."

Macaulay's Essays are philosophical and historical disquisitions, embracing a vast range of subjects; but the larger number and the most important relate to English History. These Essays, however, were only preparatory to his great work on the *History of England*, which he had intended to write from the accession of James II. to the time immediately preceding the French Revolution. But of this subject he lived to complete only a portion. The two first volumes, published in 1849, contain the reign of James II. and the Revolution of 1688; two more, which appeared in 1855, bring down the reign of William III. to the peace of Ryswick in 1697; while a fifth, published in 1861, after the author's death, nearly completes the history of that reign.

The other great writer on modern history in the present century, superior in judgment to Macaulay, though inferior in graces of style, is HENRY HALLAM (1777-1859). He was one of the early contributors to the *Edinburgh Review*, and his criticism in that Journal, in 1808, of Sir Walter Scott's edition of Dryden's works was marked by that power of discrimination and impartial judgment which characterized all his subsequent writings.

The result of his long-continued studies first appeared fully in his *View of the State of Europe during the Middle Ages*, published in 1818, and exhibiting, in a series of historical dissertations, a comprehensive survey of the chief circumstances that can interest a philosophical inquirer during the period usually denominated the Middle

Ages. Mr. Hallam's next work was *The Constitutional History of England from the Accession of Henry VII. to the Death of George II.*, published in 1827; and his third great production was *An Introduction to the Literature of Europe, in the Fifteenth, Sixteenth, and Seventeenth Centuries*, which appeared in 1837-39. Mr. Hallam's latter years were saddened by the loss of his two sons, the eldest of whom formed the subject of Tennyson's *In Memoriam.*

An estimate of Hallam's literary merits has been given by Macaulay, his illustrious contemporary, in a review of the Constitutional History:—" Mr. Hallam is, on the whole, far better qualified than any other writer of our time for the office which he has undertaken. He has great industry and great acuteness. His knowledge is extensive, various, and profound. His mind is equally distinguished by the amplitude of its grasp, and by the delicacy of its tact. . . . His work is eminently judicial. The whole spirit is that of the bench, not that of the bar. He sums up with a calm, steady impartiality, turning neither to the right nor to the left, glossing over nothing, exaggerating nothing, while the advocates on both sides are alternately biting their lips to hear their conflicting misstatements and sophisms exposed. On a general survey, we do not scruple to pronounce the *Constitutional History* the most impartial book that we have ever read."

The oft-repeated reproach once directed against the English people that Gibbon was its only ecclesiastical historian has been entirely removed by HENRY HART MILMAN (1791-1868), Dean of St. Paul's, one of the best-balanced and most highly-cultivated intellects that England has ever produced. To Byron, writing in 1821, he is merely —

> " The poet-priest Milman,
>   So ready to kill man ; "

author of *Fazio* and *Samor*, and a somewhat trenchant reviewer in the 'Quarterly.' To us, however, he is something more—an historian whose astonishing impartiality is perhaps not the greatest of his merits, an editor of Gibbon distinguished alike by the breadth and accuracy of his knowledge and by a high-toned liberality, and a classical scholar of singular taste and judgment. He held for many years the professorship of Poetry at Oxford, to which he was elected in 1821; and in addition to the above-mentioned works he published at different times *The Martyr of Antioch*, the *Fall of Jerusalem*, and other poems, all respectable in their way, but falling far short of supreme excellence. *Fazio* and the *Fall of Jerusalem*, both dramas, are perhaps the most meritorious. But it is upon his historical productions that his fame rests. These have already taken their place among the English classics; and it will be long before they are superseded. They consist of three great works, the *History of the Jews*, the *History of Christianity*, and last, though very far from least, the *History of Latin Christianity*, which appeared in 1829, 1840, and 1854, respectively. Certain indispensable qualities of the true historian Milman possessed in fuller perfection than any English writer that ever lived,—the keenest critical sagacity, a rare faculty of sifting and determining the exact value of evidence, a mind singularly free from prejudice, and almost unerring in its power of penetrating to the truth, wherever truth were attainable. His knowledge was enormous ; and he seems to move with the most perfect ease beneath the immense weight of his acquisitions, which never once interfered with his independence of thought. Few men have won a more honourable position in literature than Dean Milman ; he grappled with a subject which more than any other tries the historical sinew : extending over a vast period of time, embracing the widest area of human activity, and dealing with the subtlest and most intricate of phenomena, it presents difficulties which any but the boldest would naturally shrink from. It is the undying distinction of this great writer that on this subject he has produced a series of works likely to last as long as the language they are written in. His latest, which is indeed also a posthumous publication, the *Annals of St. Paul's Cathedral*, is interesting as showing that his magnificent powers remained undecayed until the end.

The theological and religious literature of this age is marked by a less metaphysical character than that of former times. Works of a controversial kind have been fewer, while greater attention has been paid to exegetical studies. The practical and homiletical works have been very numerous. The array of Sermons which the last sixty years have seen published is appalling, and if the good accomplished has been proportioned to the number of tracts and sermons issued, there must certainly have been an effect which should cheer the believer in human progress. Space forbids even a mention of the Societies whose special work is the publication of religious literature, of which many were founded in the present century, and all have received their greatest success in the present age. Many of the best-known religious writers have won their chief literary honours in the other fields of criticism, history, or philosophy, and will receive notice there. The three most distinguished theological writers are perhaps Hall, Foster, and Chalmers.

In Philosophy a large number of contributions to our literature has been made during the period under our consideration. Though perhaps there has been but little original speculation, and no great discovery in mental science, the investigation of metaphysical phenomena has been profound and accurate. The scope of this work forbids a notice of living writers; but we may refer to some names, such as WHEWELL and MILL, whose analyses and investigations, more especially in the systems of inductive science, have had none to compare with them since the great work of Bacon; while in the more direct examination of mental phenomena, the Scotch school has had some of its ablest members in the present era, and the materialist schools of different colour have found their strongest advocates and expounders in writers, many of whom are still living. The influence of Germany has been felt in no department of our literature so greatly as here. The followers of Reid owe no little to the writings of Kant, whilst the idealists of England have borrowed no little of the truth they hold from the profound though the very obscure speculations of Hegel. The study of logic in England proper has been revived almost within our own memory, and the once neglected studies have emerged from their misapprehension and obloquy, and are rapidly gaining in the universities their proper position abreast of classics and mathematics.

SIR WILLIAM HAMILTON (1788-1856), the son of Dr. Hamilton of Glasgow, was educated at Oxford, and called to the bar in 1813. He became Professor of Universal History at Edinburgh, in 1821, and in 1836 obtained the Chair of Logic and Metaphysics, which he occupied until his death. His chief works were essays in the *Edinburgh Review*, collected as *Discussions on Philosophy*, &c. (1852), and *An Edition of Reid, with Dissertations*. His *Lectures* have been published since his death, under the editorship of Mr. Mansel and Mr. Veitch. Sir William Hamilton was without doubt the greatest philosopher of his age. He founded his system on consciousness, following Reid more than any other master, and guiding his speculations by Aristotle and Kant. His style is a model of philosophical writing. It is clear, capacious, and appropriate. It neither perplexes by technicalities, nor misleads by figure and illustration.

ARCHBISHOP WHATELY (1787-1863), the son of Dr. Whately of Nonsuch Park, Surrey, was born in London, and educated at Oriel College, Oxford. Having entered the Church, he became Rector of Halesworth in 1822, Principal of St. Alban's Hall in 1825, then Professor of Political Economy, and in 1831 was raised to the archiepiscopal see of Dublin. His first publications were, in 1821, three sermons on the *Christian's Duty with respect to the Government*, followed by his *Bampton Lectures;* and, in 1826 and 1828, by his *Logic* and *Rhetoric*. To enumerate all the publications of this diligent writer would not be possible in this sketch. The chief were his essays on *New Testament Difficulties* (1828), · the *Sabbath*, and *Romanism*, which were produced together two years later. His lectures on *Political Economy* appeared in 1831; and later he published other works on social and economical questions.

Whately had a mind of great logical power, with little imagination and fancy. His views of questions are often shallow, but always practical. His style is luminous, easy, and well adorned with every-day illustrations. A moralist of much higher tone than Paley,—which fact arose from the general spirit of his time,—he is the best representative of Paley in the present age. He is, as Paley was, clear rather than profound, vigorous rather than subtle; with little speculation he unites much practical sense.

A very important portion of modern literature embraces those subjects which have reference to physical science. Our forefathers were more satisfied with reasons than with facts. The aim of modern investigators is to discover what is hidden in nature, rather than, by a course of deductive reasoning from pre-established principles, to display what ought to be found in nature. The inductive method of Bacon has never been so carefully applied and diligently followed as in the scientific researches of the nineteenth century; and the advance of physical science has therefore been more rapid than that of any other branch of human knowledge. The greatest writers on physical science are still alive; and many of them will deserve a place in English literature on account of the style of their writings, such as OWEN and HUXLEY.

We now pass on to the most extensive of the prose writings of the nineteenth century,—namely, those which are for the most part found scattered in magazines and serials, and which embrace the critical essays and other compositions on social, political, and moral subjects. The increased facilities of printing and a larger class of readers have combined to render the "periodicals" the great feature of the age. These range from the valuable quarterlies, through the various forms of magazine and review, down to the daily paper, the peculiar feature of the literature of the times. Some of the most valuable of our essays have been contributed to these magazines. Every shade of politics, every school of philosophy, every sect of religion, has its paper or its magazine. No feature is so striking in this class of writings as the real worth and ability displayed in many of the articles of the periodicals. To give a history of all these periodicals is of course impossible, but the *Edinburgh* and *Quarterly Reviews* imparted such an impulse to literature as to demand a few words.

The *Edinburgh Review* was established in 1802 by a small party of young men—Brougham, Jeffrey, Sydney Smith, Horner—obscure at that time, but ambitious and enterprising, who were all destined to attain a high degree of distinction. It founded its claim to success upon the boldness and vivacity of its tone, its total rejection of all precedent and authority, and the audacity with which it discussed questions previously held to be "hedged in" with the "divinity" of proscription. It was conducted from 1802 to 1829 by FRANCIS JEFFREY (1773-1850), a Scotch advocate, who was subsequently raised to the bench. He wrote a large number of critical articles, marked by good taste and discrimination, the most important of which were republished by him in a collected form in 1844. Another of the most important of the early contributors to the *Review*, and who indeed edited the first number, was SYDNEY SMITH (1768-1845), an English clergyman, and in the later period of his life Canon of St. Paul's. He wrote chiefly upon political and practical questions with a richness of comic humour, and an irresistible dry sarcasm, which is not only exquisitely amusing, but is full of solid truth as well as pleasantry.

To counteract the danger of those liberal opinions which were fiercely advocated by the *Edinburgh*, the late Mr. Murray in 1809 started a new periodical, called *The Quarterly Review*, which was warmly welcomed by the friends of the Government, and immediately obtained a literary reputation at least equal to that of the earlier periodical. The editorship of it was entrusted to WILLIAM GIFFORD (1757-1826), the translator of Juvenal (1802), and the author of the *Baviad* (1794) and *Mæviad* (1795), two of the most bitter, powerful, and resistless literary satires which modern days have produced. Gifford was a self-taught-man, who had raised himself, by dint of almost superhuman exertions and admirable integrity, to a high place among the literary men of his age.

Gifford was succeeded in the editorship of the *Quarterly*, after a short interregnum, by JOHN GIBSON LOCKHART (1794-1854), a man of undoubted genius, the author of several novels, which have been already mentioned, and one of the earliest and ablest contributors to *Blackwood's Magazine*. Many of the best articles in the *Quarterly* were written by himself; and those which combine the biography and criticism of distinguished authors are unsurpassed by anything of the kind in the English language. In 1820 he married the eldest daughter of Sir Walter Scott, and in 1837-39 he published the charming Life of his father-in-law. In biography he was unrivalled; and his *Life of Napoleon*, which appeared without his name, is far superior to many more ambitious performances.

Blackwood's Magazine first appeared in 1817, and was distinguished by the ability of its purely literary articles, as well as by the violence of its political sentiments. Among the many able men who wrote for it, one of the most eminent was JOHN WILSON (1785-1854), born in Paisley, May 18, 1785, the son of a wealthy merchant.

After studying at Oxford, he took up his abode on the banks
of the Windermere, attracted thither by the society of Wordsworth, Southey, and Coleridge. Wilson was an ardent admirer of
Wordsworth, whose style he adopted, to some extent, in his own
poems, the *Isle of Palms* (1812), and *The City after the Plague*
(1816). The year before the publication of the latter poem Wilson
had been compelled, by the loss of his fortune, to remove to
Edinburgh, and to adopt literature as a profession. Though Mr.
Blackwood was the editor of his own magazine, Wilson was the
presiding spirit, and under the name of Christopher North and
other pseudonyms he poured forth article after article with
exuberant fertility. His *Noctes Ambrosianæ*, in which politics,
literary criticism, and fun were intermingled, enjoyed extraordinary
popularity. In 1820 he was elected Professor of Moral Philosophy
at Edinburgh.

It would be impossible in our limits to give an account of the
many other writers who distinguished themselves by their contributions to the Reviews and Magazines: but in addition to those
already mentioned two essayists stand forth pre-eminent—Charles
Lamb and Thomas De Quincey.

CHARLES LAMB (1775-1834) was born in the Temple, where his
father was clerk to one of the Benchers, and was educated at
Christ's Hospital. He was essentially a *Londoner:* London life
supplied him with his richest materials; and yet his mind was so
imbued, so saturated with our older writers, that he is original by
the mere force of self-transformation into the spirit of the older
literature; he was, in short, an old writer, who lived by accident a
century or two after his real time. During the early and greater
part of his life, Lamb, poor and unfriended, was drudging as a
clerk in the India House; and it was not till late in life that he
was unchained from the desk. In his earliest compositions, such
as the drama of *John Woodvil*, and subsequently in the *Essays of
Elia*, although the world at first perceived a mere imitation of the
quaintness of expression of the old writers, there was in reality a
revival of their very spirit. The *Essays of Elia*, contributed by
him at different times to the *London Magazine*, are the finest things
for humour, taste, penetration, and vivacity, which have appeared
since the days of Montaigne. Where shall we find such intense
delicacy of feeling, such unimaginable happiness of expression,
such a searching into the very body of truth, as in these unpretending compositions? The style has a peculiar and most subtle
charm: not the result of labour, for it is found in as great perfection in his familiar letters—a certain quaintness and antiquity,
not affected in Lamb, but the natural garb of his thoughts. As in
all the true humourists, his pleasantry was inseparably allied with

the finest pathos; the merry quip on the tongue was but the commentary on the tear which trembled in the eye. The inspiration that other poets find in the mountains, in the forest, in the sea, Lamb could draw from the crowd of Fleet-street, from the remembrances of an old actor, from the benchers of the Temple.

Lamb was the schoolfellow, the devoted admirer and friend of Coleridge; and perhaps there never was an individual so *loved* by all his contemporaries, by men of every opinion, of every shade of literary, political, and religious sentiment, as this great wit and amiable man. His *Specimens of the Old English Dramatists* showed what treasures of the richest poetry lay concealed in the unpublished, and in modern times unknown, writers of that wonderful age, whose fame had been eclipsed by the glory of some two or three names of the same period. Indeed, Lamb's mind, in its sensitiveness, in its mixture of wit and pathos, was eminently Shakespearian; and his intense and reverent study of the works of Shakespeare doubtless gave a tendency to this: the glow of his humour was too pure and steady not to have been reflected from the sun. In his poems, as, for instance, the *Farewell to Tobacco*, the *Old Familiar Faces*, and his few but beautiful sonnets, we find the very essence and spirit of this quaint tenderness of fancy, the simplicity of the child mingled with the learning of the scholar.

One of the greatest masters of English prose in the present century is Thomas De Quincey (1785-1859). He was born of wealthy parents near Manchester; and after leaving Oxford he settled at Grasmere, but resided during the latter part of his life at Glasgow and Edinburgh.

The best known of De Quincey's writings is the *Confessions of an English Opium-Eater*, published in 1821, in which the language frequently soars to astonishing heights of eloquence. Of his historical essays and narratives, the finest is his *Flight of the Kalmuck Tartars*, which is equal, in many passages, to the *English Opium-Eater*. Some of his essays are almost exclusively humorous, among which *Murder considered as one of the Fine Arts* is the best known. An able critic thus sums up De Quincey's literary merits:—" A great master of English composition; a critic of uncommon delicacy; an honest and unflinching investigator of received opinions; a philosophic inquirer, second only to his first and sole hero (Coleridge), De Quincey has left no successor to his rank. The exquisite finish of his style, with the scholastic rigour of his logic, form a combination which centuries may never reproduce, but which every generation should study as one of the marvels of English literature."

One of the studies peculiar to the present century has been that of political economy. Ricardo, Senior, Macculloch, and Mill, are writers whose place in a history of literature would perhaps be small, but whose influence on politics and commerce have been so great, that it would be a serious omission not to call the attention of the student to their works. The most important writer upon ethics, jurisprudence, and political economy, is undoubtedly JEREMY BENTHAM (1748-1832). He was the son of a solicitor in London, was educated at Oxford, and called to the bar, but did not pursue it as a profession. For half a century Bentham was the centre of a small but influential circle of philosophical writers, and was the founder of what is called the Utilitarian school. It is, however, on his writings on jurisprudence that his fame chiefly rests ; and almost al. the improvements in English law that have since been carried into effect may be traced, either directly or indirectly, to his exertions.

ADDENDUM.

THE following writers, who have died since the publication of the last edition of this work, deserve special mention.

THOMAS CARLYLE (1795–1881) was the son of James Carlyle, Mason, of Ecclefechan, a Border village in Dumfriesshire ; and many of the singularities of this singular genius may, we suspect, be traced to the fact that, like his own Ziethen, he was "a rugged son of the moorlands, nourished, body and soul, on frugal oatmeal, with a large sprinkling of fire and iron thrown in." The proofs of special ability that he gave when still a boy tempted his father,'a man of sterling worth and much reverenced by his son, to put him in the way of getting the best education that Scotland afforded ; and at Annan School and Edinburgh University the lad and youth gathered in a supply of miscellaneous knowledge of varying degrees of value. For twenty years after leaving the college he lived an unsettled life, having declined to enter the ministry, to which his father had destined him. His first considerable literary effort was a translation (1824) of the *Wilhelm Meister* of Goethe, whose merits Carlyle never through life wearied of preaching ; and this was followed in 1825 by the *Life of Schiller*, to which succeeded in 1827 the *Specimens of German Romance*. He had now become known to Jeffrey, and was enrolled among the writers of the *Edinburgh Review*. Gradually, too, he was drifting into that eccentric style, so repellant to most educated persons, now known as Carlylese ; his articles in the *Review*, many of which were on German subjects, became, as time went on, more and more markedly characteristic and unlike those of any other contributor. For more than seventeen years review-writing formed one of his regular employments ; but his hitherto exclusive interest in things German had yielded in due course to the claims of French and English subjects; and his four volumes of *Critical and Miscellaneous Essays*, published long afterwards, are a collection of papers contributed to a variety of Magazines and Reviews, and by the characters of the subjects dealt with they make a continuous record of the greater literary designs he was engaged in from time to time.

The earliest work that stamped him in the eyes of the more sagacious as a nature of exceptional strength and intensity was *Sartor Resartus*, which, though written for publication as a book, had to be cut up (1833) for insertion in 'successive numbers of *Fraser's Magazine*, because no publisher would have anything to do with it. It was first raised to the dignity of a book in America, but had to wait until 1838 for similar distinction in England. Indeed the first clear glance of recognition and encouragement that fell upon him came from America. But his real vocation was now determined; and in 1834 he left his moorland farm of Craigenputtoch, came up to London, and fixed his abode at 5, Cheyne Row, Chelsea, where he was to live and work for wellnigh half a century. Struggle was not yet over, but he pinned his "desperate hope," as he called it, on *The French Revolution, a History*, on which he lavished, for three years' space, his whole wealth of brain and heart, of vigilance and energy. The publication was delayed by a terrible mishap; through carelessness the MS. of the first volume was allowed to be burnt; and it had to be written all over again entirely from memory. But in 1837 publication placed it beyond the reach of any similar misadventure. Social and political questions were always high, sometimes uppermost, in his thoughts; and two of his three next publications, *Chartism* (1839), *Heroes and Hero-Worship* (1841), and *Past and Present* (1843), gave utterance to sentiments and opinions in startling contrast to those held and maintained by any of the political parties. His *Heroes and Hero-Worship* are a report of a series of lectures on the characters and influence of great men, which he delivered to London audiences in 1840; and is an impressive embodiment of the splendid paradoxes on that subject, of which through life he was the consistent apostle. From the roll of heroes glorified in these lectures his heart was attracted towards one by natural affinity; and he brought out in 1846 his glorification of Cromwell in the work entitled *Oliver Cromwell's Letters and Speeches: with Elucidations*. By this time he had fallen into an attitude of pronounced antagonism to the general movement of his age; its aspirations, opinions, forms of thought, pursuits, principles, schemes, general works and ways, stirred within him what Horace and Burke call "splendid bile": what he regarded as its hollowness, unreality, dishonesty, love of shams, of windy talk, of glitter and show, filled his soul with righteous scorn. At length his rage became uncontrollable; and after a premonitory demonstration in his *Occasional Discourses on the Nigger Question* (1849), he made, in 1850, a " furious raid," as Mr. Arnold describes it, into " the field of political practice," with his *Latter Day Pamphlets*.

From these wasting denunciations his mind turned to an enterprise that proved the most laborious of his life; he valiantly buckled himself to the task of doing for the memory of Frederick the Great of Prussia the same service that he had done for Cromwell's. For a whole decade and more he toiled painfully to present to mankind a picture of the great but questionable German, that might wear the features of a hero and yet be not unfaithful to fact. The result was his largest work, the *History of Friedrich II. of Prussia*, of which the first and second volumes appeared in 1858, the third in 1862, the fourth in 1864, and the fifth and sixth in 1865. The author's mannerisms, as mannerisms are wont to do, had grown upon him with growing age. His style, peculiar, grotesque, puzzling, distracting as it is, sprang from no affectation; it is the natural clothing of such thoughts and feelings as Carlyle struggles to utter; it is the natural outcome of the man's character, and indeed an essential part of the man.

Carlyle's productive career practically ended in the same field where it had begun, for the history of the great German king proved to be his last, as the translation of a work of German genius had been his first grand literary publication. Yet the sixteen years of life that still remained to him were not eventless. In 1865 his University chose him its Lord Rector; and the address that he gave at his installation in the following year created a kind of enthusiasm for him in the popular mind which has not been altogether sustained. He died at Chelsea on the 4th of February, 1881, of mere physical decay. Not many weeks after his death his *Reminiscences* appeared, a portion of which had been written half a century before, but the greater part in 1867. His life has been written by Mr. Froude.

ARTHUR PENRHYN STANLEY, D.D. (1815-1881), Dean of Westminster, was born on December 10th, 1815, at Alderley, Cheshire, the living of his father, the Rev. Edward Stanley, younger brother of the first Lord Stanley of Alderley, and afterwards Bishop of Norwich, and a fast friend of Dr. Arnold of Rugby, of whom Arthur Stanley became a favourite pupil. Proceeding from Rugby to Baliol College in 1834, he entered on a brilliant career at Oxford, where he became Fellow and Tutor of University College, and resided for many years. His place in literature was at once gained by his *Life and Correspondence of Dr. Arnold* (1844), a biography as remarkable for literary skill as for devotion to the memory of

the master and friend, whose influence moulded his whole career.
His appointment as select preacher to the University (1845), gave
the occasion for his *Sermons and Essays on the Apostolical Age*, the
first of those works which displayed his special capacity for repro-
ducing the scenes of sacred and ecclesiastical history in their living
spirit, as he conceived it, and with the charm of pictorial vividness.
The same character was stamped on the four *Essays*, suggested by
his association with Canterbury Cathedral as Canon (1851), on St.
Augustine, Thomas Becket, and the Black Prince, published under
the title of *Historical Memorials of Canterbury*.   His peculiar
power of "picturesque sensibility" (to use one of Lord Beaconsfield's happy phrases) was still more conspicuous in his *Sinai and
Palestine* (1853), the fruit of a tour in Egypt and the Holy Land.
Returning to Oxford as Regius Professor of Ecclesiastical History,
to which chair he was appointed in 1856, he delivered his *Lectures
on the Eastern Church* (1858), in which the scenes of early Ecclesiastical History are made alive with his power of imagination and
his personal knowledge of the East.   Another fruit of his professorship was his volume of *Lectures on the Jewish Church* (1863).

In 1863 he was appointed to the Deanery of Westminster; and,
while much that made him honourably conspicuous in that office
would be out of place here, it is right to notice the wide sympathy
with literature and science which he showed on the occasion of the
funerals of such men as Grote, Herschel, and others, and the zeal
for his Minster and its historical associations displayed in his
Historical Memorials of Westminster Abbey (1868).

Foremost among the antagonists of Hamilton and Whately
(see p. 268), and perhaps a more successful leader of thought than
either, was JOHN STUART MILL (1806–1873).   Mill was the finest
type of the indomitable intellect and fearless thinker that the
current age has seen.   His father, James Mill, still known as the
historian of India and founder of an unspiritual philosophy,
fashioned him almost from his cradle to be the apostle of pure
reason, the finished incarnation of the logical faculty.   From the
hour of dawning intelligence he fed the intellect of the child with
purely secular knowledge, leaving the seeds of feeling utterly un-
tended.   In 1823 he was admitted to a clerkship at the India House,
where his father held an important post, and there showing a special
talent for the finest kind of administrative work, he reached eventually an office of the highest trust.   Mill had convinced himself
that the scientific method was as obligatory on the single-minded
inquirer into the principles of human conduct as it was in physics;
and that by the employment of this method conclusions might be
reached in morals and politics as certain, as little dashed with error,
as were those of Kepler and Newton.   His master-effort towards

this end was his powerful *System of Logic* (1843), on which he had laboured long. This, though his first, is still recognised as his greatest work. It is a miracle of stubborn and rigorous reasoning. It set upon a strong foundation its author's fame, and the principles of the philosophical school that his father had founded. This, known as the " Experience Philosophy," is the exact opposite of the intuitional system of Hamilton, for "it derives," as its expounder avows, " all knowledge from experience, and all moral and intellectual qualities from the direction given to the associations." As an exhaustive text-book of this school, Mill's *Logic* is hardly likely to be soon supplanted. It was with the same view that Mill composed his second masterly work, the *Principles of Political Economy* (1848). Clearness, courage, and originality, distinguished this in as high a degree as the work on *Logic;* it was at once widely read, and its influence has proved itself as extensive as its popularity. It still holds the first rank in the literature of economics.

Mill's later writings diffused rather than added to his fame. These are somewhat numerous; the deposition of the Company from the Government of India, in 1858, having discharged him to a well-pensioned leisure for the rest of his life, which left him free to toil exclusively at his self-appointed function. His little volume, entitled *On Liberty* (1859), is a fervent and stimulating appeal for the largest admissible measure of emancipation from restraint in the dealings of civilised men with one another. In 1860 he published *Representative Government.* In *Utilitarianism* (1861) he defends his cherished beliefs against the manifold attacks made upon them from various sides. In the *Examination of Sir W. Hamilton's Philosophy* (1865), he seeks to carry by force of a fiery and dexterous logic the vital positions of the leading adversary of his philosophical tenets. His *Subjection of Women* (1869) is a comprehensive arraignment of the existing status of the physically weaker sex, and a pleading for its elevation to an equality with that of men.

In 1865, he was drawn, by his unsolicited election for Westminster in the Liberal interest, into an active participation in public affairs, and was for three years a man of mark in Parliament. Rejected, however, in 1868, he retired to his southern home near Avignon, and lived there till his death in 1873. A comparatively brief *Autobiography,* and three essays—on *Nature, Utility of Religion,* and *Theism*—which cannot be said to flood with light their several subjects, were given to the public after his death. These, with some volumes of *Dissertations and Discussions,* scattered papers recovered from reviews, complete the sum of Mill's contributions to our literature.

Mill's place in the history of the human mind is a tolerably definite one. It is that of an unshrinking and luminous expounder of a philosophy that subjects the mind of man to the same processes as are used in the investigation of external nature, and classes the manifestations of the human spirit with the phenomena of the material world, yet professes to educe from its principles rules of conduct that tend to the moral and social amelioration of the race. Mill is the accredited prophet of the "utilitarian school" of which his father, author of the *Analysis of the Mind*, was the founder.

LIST OF POETS LAUREATE.

Edmund Spenser	1591–1599
Samuel Daniel	1599–1619
Ben Jonson	1619–1637
(Interregnum)	
William Davenant, Knight	1660–1668
*John Dryden	1670–1689
Thomas Shadwell	1689–1692
Nahum Tate	1692–1715
Nicholas Rowe	1715–1718
†Lawrence Eusden, Clerk	1718–1730
Colley Cibber	1730–1757
William Whitehead	1757–1785
Thomas Warton, Clerk	1785–1790
‡Henry James Pye	1790–1813
Robert Southey	1813–1843
William Wordsworth	1843–1850
Alfred Tennyson (whom God preserve!)	1850–

---

* Though Dryden did not receive his letters-patent until the year 1670, he nevertheless was paid the salary for the two preceding years.

† For Eusden see 'Dunciad,' book i. line 63 ; and for Colley Cibber, see same work *passim*.

‡ "Better to err with Pope than shine with Pye," says Lord Byron, in his 'English Bards and Scotch Reviewers.' And again in the 'Vision of Judgment' the same poet represents the ghost of King George as exclaiming, on hearing Southey's recitation of *his* 'Vision'—

"What, what!
Pye come again? no more—no more of that!"

It is by these notices alone that poor Pye still hangs on the human memory.

INDEX

ADDISON.

A.

Addison, Joseph, 168-172.
Ælfric, 11.
—— another, 11.
Akenside, Mark, 201.
Alcuin, 13.
Alfred, king, 10, his trans-
 lation of Bede, 11.
Ancren Riwle, the, 16.
Angles, 8.
Anglo-Saxon, date of its
 change into English, 8.
—— language, 3, 5, 6.
—— poetry, the vernacu-
 lar, 8.
—— prose, the vernacular,
 10.
Anglo-Saxons, 3.
Anselm, 19.
Arbuthnot, Dr. John, 164.
Arden, Mary, mother of
 Shakespeare, 73.
Armstrong, John, 204.
Arnold, Dr. Thomas, 264.
Ascham, Roger, 49.
Asser, Bishop, 13.
Atterbury, Bishop, 172.
Austen, Miss, 251.

B.

Bacon, Francis, 96-102.
——, Roger, 20.
Baldwin, Richard, 52.
Bale, 63.
Ballads, 18, 212.
Barbour, 39, 50.
Barclay, Alexander, 46.
Barrow, Isaac, 148.
Battle of Finnesburh, 8.
Baxter, Richard, 113.
Beaconsfield, Earl of, 260.
Beattie, James, 199.
Beaumont, 90.
Beckford, William, 255.
Bede, 9, 11, 12.
Bell, Currer. *See* Bronte.

CAMPBELL.

Bentham, Jeremy, 273.
Bentley, Richard, 172.
Beowulf, Lay of, 8.
Berkeley, Bishop, 174.
Berners, Lord, 49.
Bible, English translation
 of, 49.
Blackstone, Sir William,
 198.
Blackwood's   Magazine,
 270.
Blair, Robert, 199.
Blind Harry, 50.
Bolingbroke, Viscount, 173.
Borron, 19.
Boswell, James, 194.
Bowles, Caroline, 234.
Boyle and Bentley Con-
 troversy, 172.
——, Robert, 152.
Britons, 1.
Bronte, Charlotte, 254.
Broome, William, 155.
Browne, Sir Thomas, 110,
 111.
——, William, 57.
Browning, Mrs., 234.
Brunanburh War Song, 9.
Brut d'Angleterre, 15, 16.
Buckingham, Duke of, 145.
Bunyan, John, 131-133.
Burke, Edmund, 195.
Burnet, Gilbert, 153.
——, Thomas, 152.
Burney, Frances, 245.
Burns, Robert, 208.
Burton, Robert, 102, 103.
Butler, Bishop, 197.
——, Samuel, 123-125.
Byron, Lord, 220-225.

C.

Cædmon, monk of Whitby,
 9.
Camden, William, 103.
Campbell, Dr. George, 198.
——, Thomas, 231.

DISRAELI.

Canute, 15.
Carew, Thomas, 106.
Carlyle, Thomas, 273.
Caxton, 45.
Celtic dialect, 2.
—— writers, 11.
Celts, 1-3.
Chapman, George, 59, 72.
Chatterton, Thomas, 206.
Chaucer, Geoffrey, 21-34.
Chesterfield, Earl of, 198.
Chillingworth, William,
 110.
Christianity, conversion of
 Anglo-Saxons to, 3.
Chronicle, the Saxon, 11.
Chronicles, Metrical, 19.
Churchill, Charles, 210.
Clarendon, Earl of, 113, 114.
Coleridge, Samuel Taylor,
 238.
Collins, William, 200.
Collier, Jeremy, 141.
Congreve, William, 140.
Cotton, Charles, 135.
Coverdale, Miles, 50.
Cowley, Abraham, 108,
 109.
Cowper, William, 203.
Crabbe, George, 207.
Crashaw, Richard, 105, 106.
Crowne, John, 141.
Cudworth, Ralph, 131.
Cymry, 2, 9.

D.

Daniel, Samuel, 56, 103.
Danish invasion, 3.
Darwin, Erasmus, 205.
Davenant, Sir W., 102.
Davies, Sir John, 57.
Deductive Method, 99.
Defoe, Daniel, 176-178.
Dekker, Thomas, 94.
Denham, Sir John, 108.
De Quincey, Thomas, 272.
Dickens, Charles, 248-50.
Disraeli. *See* Beaconsfield.

DONNE.

Donne, John, 59, 104.
Dorset, Earl of, 145.
Douglas, Gawin, 50.
Drama, English, its origin, 60.
Drayton, Michael, 57.
Dryden, John, 125–130.
Dunbar, William, 50.
Dyer, John, 210.

E.

Earle, John, 102.
Edgeworth, Maria, 252.
'Edinburgh Review,' 269.
Edwards, Richard, 64.
Egbert, Archbishop, 13.
Eliot, George, 258.
Elizabethan Age, 52, 95.
English Language, divisions of, 8.
——, origin of the name, 7; history of language, 7.
Ethelred, 13.
Ethelweard, 13.
Etherege, Sir George, 137.
Evelyn, John, 135.

F.

Fabliaux, 5, 19, 31, 37.
Fabyan, 49.
Fairfax, Edward, 59.
Falconer, William, 204
Farquhar, George, 139.
Feltham, Owen, 102.
Fenton, Elijah, 155.
Ferrers, George, 52.
Fielding, Henry, 180.
Filmer, Sir Robert, 136.
Finnesburh, Battle of (Saxon poem), 8.
Fletcher, John, 90.
——, Giles, 57.
——, Phineas, 57.
Florence of Worcester, 20.
Ford, John, 92.
Fortescue, Chief Justice, 44.
Frere, John Hookham, 231.
Froissart, Chronicle of, translated into English, 49.
Fuller, Thomas, 111.
Fust, 45.

G.

Galt, Luke, 19.
——, John, 251.

HUME.

Garth, Sir Samuel, 166.
Gascoyne, George, 58.
Gaskell, Mrs., 254.
Gay, John, 165.
Geoffrey of Monmouth, 17.
Gesta, Romanorum, 31, 39.
Gibbon, Edward, 190.
Gifford, William, 270.
Godwin, William, 245.
Goldsmith, Oliver, 185.
Gower, 32, 37–39.
Grainger, James, 204.
Grammaticus. See Ælfric.
Gray, Thomas, 202.
Green, Matthew, 199.
Greene, Robert, 71, 77.
Grimoald, Nicholas, 48.
Grote, George, 264.
Guillaume de Lorris, 24.
Gutenberg, 45.

H.

Habington, William, 107.
Hales, Alexander, 20.
——, John, 110.
Hall, 49.
——, Joseph, 58.
Hallam, Henry, 265.
Hamilton, Sir William, 268.
Hardynge, John, 49.
Harington, Sir John, 59.
Harrington, James, 136.
Harvey, Gabriel, 53.
Hathaway, Ann, wife of Shakespeare, 74.
Havelock, 4.
Hawes, Stephen, 46.
Hemans, Mrs., 234.
Henry of Huntingdon, 20.
Henryson, Robert, 50.
Heptarchy, 3.
Herbert, George, 105.
——, Lord, 103.
Hereford, translator of the Old Testament, 41.
Herrick, Robert, 106.
Heywood, John, 62.
——, Thomas, 94.
Hobbes, Thomas, 130, 131.
Hollinshed, Raphael, 95.
Home, John, 211.
Hood, Thomas, 233.
Hook, Theodore, 254.
Hooker, Richard, 96.
Hope, Thomas, 255.
Hume, David, 188.

LINDESAY.

Hunt, James Henry Leigh, 232.
Huxley, 269.
Hyde, Edward. See Clarendon.

I.

Inductive method, 99, 100, 101.
Interludes, the, 62.
Ireland, William Henry, 207.

J.

James, G. P. R., 244.
James I. of Scotland, 43
Jean de Méun, 24.
Jeffrey, Francis, 270.
John of Trevisa, 40.
—— of Salisbury, 19.
Johnson, Samuel, 191.
Jonson, Ben, 87.
Judith, 10.
Julius Cæsar, 1.
Junius, Letters of, 197.

K.

Kames, Lord, 198.
Keats, John, 230.
Knolles, Richard, 103.
Kyd, Thomas, 70.

L.

Lamb, Charles, 271.
Landon, Letitia, 234.
Landor, Walter Savage, 232.
Lanfranc, 19.
Langlande, Robert, 35.
Langue-d'Oc, the, 4.
Langue-d'Oil, the, 4.
Latin element in English language, 2, 4.
Laureate, Poets, 278.
Layamon, 15.
Lee, Nathaniel, 142.
Lewis, Matthew Gregory, 244.
——, Sir George Cornewall, 264.
Lillo, George, 144.
Lindesay, Sir David, 51.

LITERATURE.

Literature, Anglo-Saxon, in Latin, 13; influence of foreign scholars on, 11.
——, old English, 17.
Locke, John, 146–148.
Lockhart, John Gibson, 270.
Lollius, 28.
Lovelace, Sir Richard, 106.
Lydgate, John, 42.
Lyly, John, 70.
Lyttelton, Lord, 198.
Lytton, Lord, 250.

M.

Macaulay, Thomas Babington, 264.
Macpherson, James, 205.
Maculloch, 272.
Maldon, Battle of, 10.
Mallet, David, 174.
Malory, Sir Thomas, 45.
Mandeville, Bernard, 174.
——, Sir John, 40.
Mannyng, Robert, 17.
Mapes, Walter, 19.
Marlowe, Christopher, 71.
Marryat, Captain, 256.
Marston, John, 59, 94.
Marvel, Andrew, 130.
Massinger, Philip, 92.
Matthew Paris, 20.
Middleton, Thomas, 94.
Mill, James, 276.
——, John Stuart, 276.
Milman, Henry Hart, 266.
Milton, John, 114–122.
Minot, Laurence, 17.
Miracle Plays, 60.
Mitford, Miss, 255.
Montagu, Lady Mary, 174.
Moore, Thomas, 225–228.
Moralities, the, 61.
More, Henry, 131.
——, Sir Thomas, 48.
Morier, James, 255.
Mysteries or Miracles, 60, 61.

N.

Newton, Sir Isaac, 151.
Norman Conquest, effects of, 4, 5.
—— French, 5, 6.
—— influence on English language previous to the Conquest, 4.

ENG LIT.

ROBERT.

North, Christopher. *See* Wilson.
Norton, Thomas, 63.

O.

Occleve, Thomas, 23, 42
Orm or Ormin, 16.
Ormulum, the, 16.
Otway, Thomas, 142.
Overbury, Sir Thomas, 102.
Owen, 269.

P.

Paley, William, 197.
Parnell, Thomas, 166.
Pearson, John, 149.
Pecock, Bishop, 44.
Peele, George, 70.
Pepys, Samuel, 135.
Percy, Bishop, 212.
Philippa de Roet, wife of Chaucer, 22.
Philips, John, 145, 204.
Phœnicians, 1.
Picts, 2.
Plegmund, 12.
Poets Laureate, 278.
Political Songs, 18.
Pomfret, John, 145.
Pope, Alexander, 154–158.
Praed, 231.
Printing, its invention and importation into England, 45.
Prior, Matthew, 164.
Purvey, 41.

Q.

Quarles, Francis, 105.
'Quarterly Review,' 270.

R.

Radcliffe, Ann, 244.
Raleigh, Sir Walter, 95.
Ralph, Higden, 18.
Ramsay, Allan, 167.
Ray, John, 152.
Reformation, the, 21, 51.
Reviews, Edinburgh and Quarterly, 269, 270.
Ricardo, 272.
Richardson, Samuel, 178.
Robert of Brunne. *See* Mannyng.

SOUTHWELL.

Robert of Gloucester, 17
Robertson, William, 189.
Rochester, Earl of, 144.
Roger de Wendover, 20.
Rogers, Samuel, 231.
Romance languages, 4.
—— poets, 5.
Romances, 18, 19; their introduction into England from France, 5.
——, metrical, 18.
Roman invasion, 1.
Roscommon, Earl of, 144.
Rowe, Nicholas, 143.
Roy, William, 46.

S.

Sackville, Thomas, 52, 63.
Satires, 19.
Saxon element in language, 3, 4.
——, invasion, 2, 3.
Saxons, their condition under Norman rule, 4.
Scots, 2.
Scott, Michael, 257.
——, Sir Walter, 212–219.
Scottish poetry in fifteenth and sixteenth centuries, 43, 50, 51.
Scotus, Johannes Duns, 20.
Semi-Saxon, 7.
Senior, 272.
Shadwell, Thomas, 144.
Shaftesbury, Lord, 173.
Shakespeare, William, 73–86.
Sheffield. *See* Buckingham.
Shelley, Mrs., 244.
——, Percy Bysshe, 228.
Shenstone, William, 200.
Sheridan, Richard Brinsley, 211.
Sherlock, William, 150.
Shirley, James, 94.
Sidney, Philip, 53, 56.
Skelton, John, 46.
Smith, Adam, 197.
——, Horace, 231.
——, James, 231.
——, Sydney, 270.
Smollett, Tobias George, 182.
Somerville, William, 204.
South, Robert, 150.
Southerne, Thomas, 143.
Southey, Robert, 240.
——, Mrs., 234.
Southwell, Robert, 59.

SPENSER.

Spenser, Edmund, 52–56.
Sprat, Thomas, 150.
Stanley, Arthur P., 275.
Steele, Sir Richard, 169.
Sterne, Laurence, 183.
Still, John, 64.
Stillingfleet, Edward, 150.
St. John, Henry. *See* Bolingbroke.
Stow, John, 95.
Suckling, Sir John, 106.
Surrey, Earl of, 47, 48.
Swift, Jonathan, 158–164.
Sylvester, Joshua, 59.

T.

Taylor, Jeremy, 112, 113.
Temple, Sir William, 172.
Teutonic race, parentage of English nation traced to, 3.
Thackeray, William Makepeace, 246.
Thirlwall, Bishop, 264.
Thomson, James, 199.
Thrale, Mrs., 194.
Tickell, Thomas, 166.
Tillotson, Archbishop, 149.

WARTON.

Tottel's Miscellany, 48.
Traveller's Song, the, 8
Travers, Walter, 96.
Trollope, Anthony, 261.
——, Mrs., 255.
Troubadours, 5.
Trouvères, 5.
Tyndal, William, 50.

U.

Udall, Nicholas, 64.

V.

Vanburgh, Sir John, 138.
Vitalis, Ordericus, 20.

W.

Wace, 15.
Waller, Edmund, 107.
Walpole, Horace, 243.
Walton, Izaak, 134, 135.
Warner, William, 59.
Warton, Joseph, 202.
——, Thomas, 202.

YOUNG.

Webster, John, 93
Werefrith, 11.
Whately, Archbishop, 268
Whetstone, George, 64.
Whewell, 268.
White, Gilbert, 198.
——, Henry Kirke, 210.
Wicliff, 21, 24, 36, 40.
Wilfred, 13.
Wilkins, Dr. John, 151.
William of Malmesbury, 20.
—— of Occam, 20.
—— of Poitiers, 20.
Wilson, Professor John, 253, 257, 270.
Wither, George, 105.
Wordsworth, William 235-238.
Wulfstan, 11.
Wyatt, Sir Thomas, 47 48.
Wycherley, William, 139

Y.

Young, Edward, 166.

THE END.

LONDON: PRINTED BY WILLIAM CLOWES AND SONS, LIMITED.
STAMFORD STREET AND CHARING CROSS.

Telegraphic Address—
GUIDEBOOK, LONDON

MR. MURRAY'S

CATALOGUE OF

EDUCATIONAL

WORKS

LONDON
JOHN MURRAY, 50A, ALBEMARLE STREET, W.
1903

BOYLE, SON & WATCHURST,
PRINTERS,
3, 4 AND 5, WARWICK SQUARE E.C.

MR. MURRAY'S
CATALOGUE OF
EDUCATIONAL WORKS.

MR. MURRAY'S
HOME AND SCHOOL LIBRARY.

Edited by LAURIE MAGNUS, M.A.,
MAGDALEN COLLEGE, OXFORD.

This Library, which will ultimately cover, in convenient and attractive volumes, a wide field of human knowledge, is intended "A" for the general reader "B" for the special student of Literature or Technology. The line of demarcation is not absolutely rigid, for all the volumes in the Library have an educational aim, and many are adapted to definite examinations. But while the "A" Series will be found of service to the general reader, for the purpose of self-information, as well as to the special student of the subject which it treats, the "B" Series is designed more strictly for use in schools and classes.

The volumes are illustrated by maps, diagrams, &c. The following are now ready :—

"A" SERIES.

FIRST MAKERS OF ENGLAND. Julius Cæsar, King Arthur, Alfred the Great. By Lady MAGNUS, Author of "Boys of the Bible," etc. With Illustrations. F'cap 8vo. 1s. 6d.

This volume is based on the recommendations for history teaching made by Professor Withers at the invitation of the School Board for London.

"In her hands the old legends lose nothing of their beauty in force or power of inspiration. . . . Cannot fail to interest both the children for whom it is primarily intended and children of a larger growth. The moral teaching which forms the basis of the work, though not obtruded, is beyond praise."—
Educational Times.

HOME AND SCHOOL LIBRARY—*continued.*

A SHORT HISTORY OF COINS AND CURRENCY. By Lord AVEBURY, F.R.S., &c. With many Illustrations. F'cap 8vo. 2*s.*

> ". . . a treatise as fascinating as a romance."—*Outlook.*

PLATO'S 'REPUBLIC.' By Prof. LEWIS CAMPBELL, Hon. Fellow of Balliol College, Oxford. With Illustrations. F'cap 8vo. 2*s.*

> " Professor Campbell has done good service in writing this excellent book."—*Spectator.*
>
> " An excellent addition to the Home and School Library. . . . The sketch of the purpose and development of Plato's work is admirable."—*Morning Post.*

INTRODUCTION TO POETRY. (Poetic Expression, Poetic Truth, the Progress of Poetry.) By LAURIE MAGNUS, M.A. F'cap 8vo. 2*s.*

> ". . . from beginning to end it is excellent, and the delightful style, the breadth and incisiveness of view, the sidelights which it opens upon life and thought, and the frequently deep philosophy which is attractively veiled in the Author's persuasive rhetoric, make it at times fascinating."—*School World.*
>
> " He has brought to the task a critical taste and judgment almost as refined and often as illuminating as that of Ruskin."—*Yorkshire Post.*

HEROES OF THE WEST, A BIOGRAPHICAL SKETCH OF MODERN HISTORY, by the Rev. A. J. and Mrs. CARLYLE and F. S. MARVIN, M.A. 2 vols.

> Vol. I. With four Illustrations. F'cap 8vo. 2*s.*

THE FACE OF NATURE. Popular Readings in Elementary Science. By the Rev. C. T. OVENDEN, D.D., Canon of St. Patrick's, Rector of Enniskillen. With numerous Illustrations. F'cap 8vo. 2*s.*

IN ACTIVE PREPARATION.

MUSIC. By A. KALISCH, B.A.

INTRODUCTION TO PHILOSOPHY. By S. RAPPOPORT, Ph.D.

TENNYSON'S 'ŒNONE.' By LAURIE MAGNUS, M.A.

ANIMAL LIFE. By W. B. BOTTOMLEY, Professor of Botany at King's College, London University, and Professor of Biology at the Royal Veterinary College.

PLANT LIFE. By W. B. BOTTOMLEY.

ARCHITECTURE. By CECIL HEADLAM, Author of "Nuremberg" and "Chartres,' in the *Medieval Towns* Series, etc.

HOME AND SCHOOL LIBRARY—*continued.*

"B" SERIES.

ALGEBRA. Part I. By E. M. LANGLEY, M.A., Senior Mathematical Master, Modern School, Bedford, and S. R. N. BRADLY, M.A., Mathematical Master, Modern School, Bedford. F'cap 8vo. 1s. 6d.

This volume is specially adapted to the requirements of the First Stage of the Directory of the Board of Education, South Kensington.

Professor JOHN PERRY, of the Royal College of Science, South Kensington, writes:—"I never do praise a book unless I believe it to be good. Your Algebra (regarded as a book for beginners) pleases me very much indeed. I cannot imagine an Algebra prepared for schools in general, and especially for use by teachers in general, which would come nearer to my notion of what an Algebra ought to be, than yours."

A FIRST COURSE OF PRACTICAL SCIENCE, with full directions for experiments and numerous Exercises. By J. H. LEONARD. B.Sc. Lond. With a Preface by the late Dr. GLADSTONE, F.R.S. F'cap 8vo. 1s. 6d.

"This is an admirable little book. . . . The great point of Mr. Leonard's book is that he writes, as do too few instructors, for the absolutely ignorant pupil, and that unfortunate being is the one who is too often not considered. In all the experiments he gives the reason why. . . . Such books as the one before us should be scattered broadcast."—*The Lancet.*

"The author evidently understands the difficulties which assail a young boy who is starting on a course of experimental Science."—*Journal of Education.*

A FIRST COURSE OF CHEMISTRY. By J. H. LEONARD, Author of "A First Course of Practical Science." With numerous Diagrams. F'cap 8vo. 1s. 6d.

". . . An excellent little book for young students . . . expounded with admirable simplicity and good order . . . a valuable introduction to experimental knowledge of the constitution of things."—*Scotsman.*

ELECTRIC WIRING. A Primer for the use of Wiremen and Students. By W. C. CLINTON, B.Sc. (Lond.), Demonstrator in the Pender Laboratory, University College, London. With 80 Illustrations and a selection of worked examples. F'cap 8vo. 1s. 6d.

Written with particular reference to the requirements of the examinations of the City and Guilds of London Institute.

"It is written in simple and comprehensive language, free from technicalities, except such as are duly explained in the course of the text . . . the section on jointing being exceptionally good . . . this little work is replete with useful information to those engaged in electrical wiring."—*Electricity.*

GEOMETRY. An Elementary Treatise on the Theory and Practice of Euclid. Having in view the New regulations of the Oxford and Cambridge Local, the London Matriculation, The Board of Education, and other Examinations. By S. O. ANDREW, M.A., Head Master of Whitgift Grammar School, Croydon. F'cap 8vo. 2s.

IN ACTIVE PREPARATION.

TELEGRAPHS AND TELEPHONES. By Sir W. H. PREECE, K.C.B., etc., sometime President of the Institute of Civil Engineers.

THE CALCULUS FOR ARTISANS. By Prof. O. HENRICI. F.R.S., etc.

ALGEBRA. Part II. By E. M. LANGLEY and S. R. N. BRADLY

MR. MURRAY'S NEW SERIES
OF
SECONDARY EDUCATION
TEXT-BOOKS.

EDITED BY LAURIE MAGNUS, M.A.,
Magdalen College, Oxford.

COMMERCIAL FRENCH. In Two Parts. By W. MANSFIELD POOLE, M.A., Instructor in French to the Channel Squadron, formerly Assistant-Master at Merchant Taylors' School, AND MICHEL BECKER, Professor at the Ecole Alsacienne, Paris; Author of "L'Allemand Commercial," and "Lectures Pratiques d'Allemand Moderne." With a Map in each Volume. Crown 8vo. 2s. 6d. each.

"... a most careful piece of work ... an excellent book ... we warmly recommend to all who have to teach Commercial French."
—*Educational Times.*

"The good opinion formed by us on seeing Part I. is confirmed by the second instalment, really an admirable piece of work. We know of no better book to serve as an introduction to the more strictly technical study of Commercial French."—*School World.*

BRITAIN OVER THE SEA. A Reader for Schools. Compiled and edited by ELIZABETH LEE, Author of "A School History of English Literature," etc.; Editor of "Cowper's Task and Minor Poems," etc. With Four Maps of the British Empire at different periods. Crown 8vo. 2s. 6d.

MR. P. A. BARNETT (H.M. Inspector of Training Colleges).—"I congratulate you on the production of a very excellent piece of work. I hope the schools will use it; but it is almost too good for them."

COMMERCIAL KNOWLEDGE. A Manual of Business Methods and Transactions. By ALGERNON WARREN. Crown 8vo. 2s. 6d.

"The book should be used in every senior class both of our board and private schools, and as an introduction to business life it should prove of great value."—*Statist.*

INTERMEDIATE FRENCH GRAMMAR AND OUT-LINES OF SYNTAX, with Historical Notes. By G. H. CLARKE, M.A., of Hymers College, Hull, and L. R. TANQUEREY, B.ès.L. Crown 8vo. 3s. 6d.

"... In short, we like it much, for it is full without confusion, correct without pedantry, and modern without vulgarity."—*Guardian.*

ARITHMETIC MADE EASY. Lectures on method, with Illustrations for Teachers and Pupils. By MABEL A. MARSH. Crown 8vo. 2s.

This manual applies the heuristic method to arithmetic-teaching, and is especially recommended for use in Training Colleges and for all members of the teaching profession.

SECONDARY EDUCATION TEXT-BOOKS—

continued.

COMMERCIAL GERMAN. In Two Parts. By GUSTAV HEIN, University of Berlin, and Lecturer in German (Honours) to the University of Aberdeen, and MICHEL BECKER, Professor of Modern Languages in the Ecole Alsacienne, Paris.

PART I. with a Map. Crown 8vo. 3s. 6d.

This manual is uniform with the first part of *Commercial French* by Poole and Becker, and is specially adapted for the use of students in commercial classes and continuation schools.

PART II. *In the Press.*

FRENCH COMMERCIAL CORRESPONDENCE. By Professor CHARLES GLAUSER, and W. MANSFIELD POOLE, M.A. Crown 8vo. 4s. 6d.

" Both as a handbook and as a work of reference, the work seems well calculated to supply the needs of advanced students, and to be of extreme utility to persons already engaged in the practice of commercial pursuits."—*Guardian.*

CHRONIQUE DU RÈGNE DE CHARLES IX. By PROSPER MÉRIMÉE. Prepared and Edited for the use of Schools by Professor ERNEST WEEKLEY, M.A., University College, Nottingham. With Historical and brief Grammatical Notes, and a Critical Essay. Crown 8vo. 2s. 6d.

This volume which will be followed by a School edition *Le Gendre de M. Poirier*, by the same editor, and by other French and German texts, is prepared according to the most approved methods of modern language-teaching, and may confidently be recommended to the attention of masters and mistresses.

GRAMMAIRE FRANÇAISE. By W. MANSFIELD POOLE, M.A., Instructor in French to the Channel Squadron, formerly Assistant Master at Eton. Crown 8vo.

ENGLISH COMPOSITION AND ESSAY WRITING. By L. COPE CORNFORD.

THE SOIL. By A. D. HALL, M.A., Principal of the South Eastern Agricultural College. Crown 8vo. With Diagrams, etc. 3s. 6d.

This volume, by the Principal of the County Council College at Wye, is the first of a group of text-books intended for the use of students in Agriculture. Other volumes, which will be duly announced, will deal with " Plant Physiology," " Manures," etc. [*In the Press.*

ELEMENTS OF POLITICAL ECONOMY. By JAMES BONAR, M.A., LL.D., Author of " Malthus and his Work," " Philosophy and Political Economy," &c. [*In the Press.*

THEORIES OF TAXATION. By G. ARMITAGE SMITH, M.A., Principal of the Birkbeck Institute. [*In the Press.*

MERCANTILE LAW. By SIDNEY HUMPHRIES, B.A., LL.D., Principal of the City of London College. [*In the Press.*

BOTANY. By WILLIAM CROSS. [*In the Press.*

OTHER VOLUMES TO FOLLOW.

MURRAY'S
HANDY CLASSICAL MAPS.

A NEW SYSTEM.

Edited by G. B. GRUNDY, M.A.,

BRASENOSE COLLEGE, OXFORD.

These Maps have been recognised as the best and most convenient in existence for the use of scholars and students at the universities and upper classes of schools.

The old method of engraving and hatching the mountain ranges has been exchanged for that of colouring the contours with flat brown and green tints, which is now recognised as the best and most intelligible way of denoting the configuration of the land. A separate Index is included with each Map.

LIST OF MAPS IN THE SERIES:

GRAECIA	Northern Greece / South and Peloponnesus	*Two sheets in one case, 3s. cloth; 1s. 6d. net, paper.* [NOW READY.
GALLIA	- - - - -	*One sheet, 2s. cloth; 1s. net, paper.* [NOW READY.
BRITANNIA	- - - -	*One sheet, 2s. cloth; 1s. net, paper.* [NOW READY
HISPANIA	- - - - -	*One sheet, 2s. cloth; 1s. net, paper.* [NOW READY.
ITALIA	Northern Italy / South and Sicily.	*Two sheets in one case, 3s. cloth; 1s. 6d. net, paper.* [NOW READY.
GERMANIA, RHAETIA, ILLYRIA, MOESIA, etc.		*One sheet, 2s. cloth; 1s. net, paper.* [NOW READY.
PALESTINE, SYRIA, and part of MESOPOTAMIA, and a Map showing St. Paul's Voyages		*Three Maps on one sheet, 2s. cloth; 1s. net, paper.* [NOW READY.
THE ROMAN EMPIRE (at different epochs)		*Two Maps on one sheet, 2s. cloth; 1s. net, paper.* [JUST OUT.
The EASTERN EMPIRES including EGYPT		*Two Maps on one sheet, 2s. cloth; 1s. net, paper.* [JUST OUT.
* **ASIA MINOR and MARE AEGAEUM**		*Two Maps on one sheet, 2s. cloth; 1s. net, paper.* [NEARLY READY.

An Index is bound in each case.

". . . are admirable, and will prove of great assistance to students of ancient history. We have before warmly praised the colour-system of the maps and we need only say of this one (Graecia) that it will help those that use it to realize the relations and circumstances of the Ancient Greek States far better than any other map with which we are acquainted."—*Educational Times.*

* The preparation of this Map has been undertaken by Mr. J. G. C. Anderson, Christ Church, Oxford.

THE
PROGRESSIVE SCIENCE SERIES.

Large 8vo, cloth extra, 6s. per volume.

NOW READY.

THE STUDY OF MAN: An Introduction to Ethnology. By Professor A. C. HADDON, D.Sc., M.A., M.R.I.A. Illustrated.

THE GROUNDWORK OF SCIENCE. By ST. GEORGE MIVART, M.D., Ph.D., F.R.S.

EARTH SCULPTURE. By Professor GEIKIE, LL.D., F.R.S. Illustrated.

RIVER DEVELOPMENT. As Illustrated by the Rivers of North America. By Professor I. C. RUSSELL. Illustrated.

VOLCANOES. By Professor BONNEY, D.Sc., F.R.S. Illustrated.

BACTERIA. Especially as they are related to the Economy of Nature, to Industrial Processes, and to the Public Health. By GEORGE NEWMAN, M.D., F.R.S.E., D.P.H., Demonstrator of Bacteriology in King's College, London. With over 90 other Illustrations.
Corrected (2nd) Edition, and with an added Chapter on Tropical Diseases, an Account of Malarial Infection by Mosquitoes, and other Subjects.

A BOOK OF WHALES. By the Editor of the Series, F. E. BEDDARD, M.A., F.R.S. With 40 Illustrations by SIDNEY BERRIDGE.

THE COMPARATIVE PHYSIOLOGY of the BRAIN AND COMPARATIVE PSYCHOLOGY. By Professor JACQUES LOEB, M.D., Professor of Physiology in the University of Chicago.

THE STARS: A Study of the Universe. By Professor NEWCOMB. Illustrated.

EXPERIMENTS ON ANIMALS. By STEPHEN PAGET, F.R.C.S.

IN COURSE OF PRODUCTION.

HEREDITY. By J. ARTHUR THOMSON, M.A., F.R.S.E. Illustrated. Author of "The Study of Animal Life," and co-Author of "The Evolution of Sex." With numerous Diagrams and Illustrations.

PROGRESSIVE SCIENCE SERIES—*continued.*

IN COURSE OF PRODUCTION.

THE ANIMAL OVUM. By F. E. BEDDARD, M.A., F.R.S. (the Editor). Illustrated.

THE REPRODUCTION OF LIVING BEINGS: A COMPARATIVE STUDY. By MARCUS HARTOG, M.A., D.Sc., Professor of Natural History in Queen's College, Cork. Illustrated.

METEORS AND COMETS. By PROFESSOR C. A. YOUNG.

THE MEASUREMENT OF THE EARTH. By PRESIDENT MENDENHALL.

EARTHQUAKES. By MAJOR DUTTON.

PHYSIOGRAPHY; OR, THE FORMS OF LAND. By PROFESSOR DAVIS.

THE HISTORY OF SCIENCE. By C. J. PIERCE.

RECENT THEORIES OF EVOLUTION. By PROFESSOR BALDWIN.

LIFE AREAS OF NORTH AMERICA: A STUDY IN THE DISTRIBUTION OF ANIMALS AND PLANTS. By DR. C. HART MERRIAM.

PLANETARY MOTION. By G. W. HILL, Ph.D.

INFECTION AND IMMUNITY. By GEORGE S. STERNBERG, M.D., Surgeon-General of the U.S. Army.

AGE, GROWTH, SEX, AND DEATH. By PROFESSOR CHARLES S. MINOT, Harvard Medical School.

Other Volumes will shortly be announced, and the Series in its entirety will comprise volumes on every branch of Science.

MR. MURRAY'S
STUDENT'S MANUALS.

Several years have passed since the death of Sir William Smith, and the publisher of his famous dictionaries, manuals, and educational works of all kinds is now engaged in the necessary task of revision and republication. Modern scholarship has reinforced the results of previous research, and modern methods of teaching have improved the old tradition. In accordance with these new requirements, the services of competent teachers and writers have been requisitioned in order to maintain the high level of accuracy, attractiveness, and usefulness which has already raised these books to the rank of standard school classics. No pains are spared to preserve for the name of Sir William Smith the place which it has held unchallenged throughout the schools of Great Britain for more than a generation; and the publisher is confident that masters and pupils, and the general reader too, will continue to recognise the unique position which it occupies in the educational world.

The series of Student's Manuals, Ancient and Modern, issued by Mr. Murray, and most of them edited by Dr. William Smith, possess several distinctive features which render them singularly valuable as Educational Works. They incorporate, with judicious comments, the researches of the most recent historical investigators, not only into the more modern, but into the most remote periods of the history of the countries to which they refer. While each volume is thus, for ordinary purposes, a complete history of the country to which it refers, it also contains a guide to such further and more detailed information as the advanced student may desire on particular events or periods. At the end of each book, sometimes of each chapter, there are given copious lists of standard works which constitute the "Authorities" for a particular period or reign.

Before the publication of these STUDENT'S MANUALS there had been established, by the claims of middle class and competitive examiners, a large annual demand for text-books that should rise above the level of mere schoolboys' epitomes, and give to those who would master them some shadow of a scholarly knowledge of their subjects. Such books were very hard to find. Mr. Murray's Manuals, however, are the most suited for this purpose. They are most fit for use in the higher classes of good schools, where they may be deliberately studied through with the help of a teacher competent to expand their range of argument, to diversify their views by the strength of his own reading and reflection, and to elicit thought from the boys themselves upon events and the political changes to which they have led. The mature scholar also may be glad to have on his shelves these volumes, from which he can at a glance refresh his memory as to a name or date And he will not use them for reference alone : he will assuredly be tempted to read them for the clearness of statement and the just proportion with which there is traced in each of them the story of a nation.

MURRAY'S STUDENT'S MANUALS.

A Series of Class-books for Advanced Scholars.

FORMING A CHAIN OF HISTORY FROM THE EARLIEST AGES DOWN TO MODERN TIMES.

English History and Literature.

THE STUDENT'S HUME: A HISTORY OF ENGLAND, FROM THE EARLIEST TIMES TO THE REVOLUTION IN 1688. By DAVID HUME. Incorporating the Researches of recent Historians. Revised, corrected, and continued to the Treaty of Berlin in 1878, by J. S. BREWER, M.A. With Notes, Illustrations, and 7 Coloured Maps and Woodcuts. Crown 8vo. 7s. 6d.

   *** **Also in Three Parts.** 2s. 6d. each.

   I. FROM B.C. 55 TO THE DEATH OF RICHARD III., A.D. 1485
   II. HENRY VII. TO THE REVOLUTION, 1688.
   III. THE REVOLUTION TO THE TREATY OF BERLIN, 1878.

   *** *Questions on the "Student's Hume."* 12mo. 2s.

STUDENT'S CONSTITUTIONAL HISTORY OF ENGLAND. FROM THE ACCESSION OF HENRY VII. TO THE DEATH OF GEORGE II. By HENRY HALLAM, LL.D. Crown 8vo. 7s. 6d.

STUDENT'S MANUAL OF ENGLISH LITERATURE. A History of English Literature of the chief English Writers founded upon the Manual of THOMAS B. SHAW. A new Edition thoroughly revised. By A. HAMILTON THOMPSON, B.A., of St. John's Coll., Cambridge, and Univ. Extension Lecturer in English Literature. With Notes, etc. Crown 8vo. 7s. 6d.

STUDENT'S SPECIMENS OF ENGLISH LITERATURE. Selected from the BEST WRITERS, and arranged Chronologically. By T. B. SHAW, M.A. Crown 8vo. 5s.

MURRAY'S STUDENT'S MANUALS—*continued.*

Scripture and Church History.

STUDENT'S OLD TESTAMENT HISTORY. From the Creation of the World to the Return of the Jews from Captivity. With an Introduction to the Books of the Old Testament. By PHILIP SMITH, B.A. With 40 Maps and Woodcuts. Crown 8vo. *7s. 6d.*

STUDENT'S NEW TESTAMENT HISTORY. With an Introduction, containing the Connection of the Old and New Testaments. By PHILIP SMITH, B.A. With 30 Maps and Woodcuts. Crown 8vo. *7s. 6d.*

STUDENT'S MANUAL OF ECCLESIASTICAL HISTORY. A History of the Christian Church to the Reformation. By PHILIP SMITH, B.A. 2 Vols. Crown 8vo. *7s. 6d.* each.

> Part I.—A.D. 30—1003. With Woodcuts.
> Part II.—A.D. 1003—1614. With Woodcuts.

STUDENT'S MANUAL OF ENGLISH CHURCH HISTORY. By G. G. PERRY, M.A., Canon of Lincoln. 3 Vols. *7s. 6d.* each.

> 1st *Period.* From the Planting of the Church in Britain to the Accession of Henry VIII. A.D. 596—1509.
>
> 2nd *Period.* From the Accession of Henry VIII. to the Silencing of Convocation in the Eighteenth Century. A.D. 1509 —1717.
>
> 3rd *Period.* From the Accession of the House of Hanover to the Present Time. A.D. 1717—1884.

Ancient History.

STUDENT'S ANCIENT HISTORY OF THE EAST. From the Earliest Times to the Conquests of Alexander the Great, including Egypt, Assyria, Babylonia Media, Persia, Asia Minor, and Phœnicia. By PHILIP SMITH, B.A With 70 Woodcuts. Crown 8vo. *7s. 6d.*

STUDENT'S HISTORY OF GREECE. From the Earliest Times to the Roman Conquest. With Chapters on the History of Literature and Art. By Sir WM. SMITH, D.C.L. Thoroughly revised and in part rewritten by G. E. Marindin, M.A. With many new Maps and Illustrations. Crown 8vo. *7s. 6d.*

STUDENT'S HISTORY OF ROME. From the Earliest Times to the Establishment of the Empire. With Chapters on the History of Literature and Art. By Dean LIDDELL. New and Revised Edition, incorporating the results of Modern Research, by P. V. M. BENECKE, M.A., Fellow of Magdalen College, Oxford. With Coloured and other Maps and numerous Illustrations nearly all prepared specially for this Edition. Crown 8vo. *7s. 6d.*

MURRAY'S STUDENT'S MANUALS.—*continued.*

Ancient History—continued.

STUDENT'S HISTORY OF THE ROMAN EMPIRE. FROM THE ESTABLISHMENT OF THE EMPIRE TO THE ACCESSION OF COMMODUS, A.D. 180. With Coloured Maps and Numerous Illustrations. By J. B. BURY, Regius Professor of Modern History at Cambridge. Crown 8vo. 7s. 6d.

STUDENT'S GIBBON. A HISTORY OF THE DECLINE AND FALL OF THE ROMAN EMPIRE. Abridged from the Original Work by SIR WM. SMITH, D.C.L., LL.D. A New and Revised Edition in Two Parts. Crown 8vo. 5s. each.

PART I.—FROM THE ACCESSION OF COMMODUS TO THE DEATH OF JUSTINIAN. By A. H. J. GREENIDGE, M.A., Lecturer and Late Fellow of Hertford College, Lecturer in Ancient History at Brasenose College, Oxford.

PART II.—FROM A.D. 565 TO THE CAPTURE OF CONSTANTINOPLE BY THE TURKS. By J. G. C. ANDERSON, M.A., late Fellow of Lincoln College, Student and Tutor of Christ Church, Oxford. With Maps and Illustrations.

Europe,

STUDENT'S HISTORY OF MODERN EUROPE. FROM THE CAPTURE OF CONSTANTINOPLE BY THE TURKS, 1453, TO THE TREATY OF BERLIN, 1878. By RICHARD LODGE, M.A., Brasenose College, Oxford, Professor of Modern History, University of Edinburgh. 4th Edition, thoroughly revised. Crown 8vo. 7s. 6d.

STUDENT'S HISTORY OF EUROPE DURING THE MIDDLE AGES. By HENRY HALLAM, LL.D. Crown 8vo. 7s. 6d.

France.

STUDENT'S HISTORY OF FRANCE. FROM THE EARLIEST TIMES TO THE FALL OF THE SECOND EMPIRE. By W. H. JERVIS, M.A. A New Edition, thoroughly revised, and in great part rewritten, by ARTHUR HASSALL, M.A., Censor of Christ Church, Oxford. With a Chapter on Ancient Gaul by F. HAVERFIELD, M.A., Student of Christ Church, Oxford. Coloured Maps, and many new Woodcuts. Crown 8vo. 7s. 6d.

Geography.

STUDENT'S MANUAL OF ANCIENT GEOGRAPHY. By CANON BEVAN, M.A. 150 Woodcuts. Crown 8vo. 7s. 6d.

STUDENT'S GEOGRAPHY OF BRITISH INDIA. POLITICAL AND PHYSICAL. By GEORGE SMITH, LL.D. With Maps. Crown 8vo. 7s. 6d.

Sir Wm. Smith's
Smaller Manuals.

These Works have been drawn up for the Lower Forms, at the request of several teachers, who require more elementary books than the STUDENT'S HISTORICAL MANUALS.

SMALLER HISTORY OF ENGLAND. From the Earliest Times to the Year 1887. Revised and enlarged. By Prof. RICHARD LODGE, M.A. With Coloured Maps and 68 Woodcuts. Crown 8vo. 3s. 6d.

SMALLER HISTORY OF GREECE. From the Earliest Times to the Roman Conquest. With Coloured Maps, Plans, and Illustrations. Thoroughly revised by G. E. Marindin, M.A. Crown 8vo. 3s. 6d.

"Most excellently suited to its purpose; distinguished above all things by its lucidity. Altogether the book is excellent."—*Guardian.*

SMALLER HISTORY OF ROME. From the Earliest Times to the Establishment of the Empire. Thoroughly revised by A. H. J. Greenidge, M.A., Fellow of Hertford College, Oxford. With a Supplementary Chapter on the Empire to 117 A.D., by G. Middleton, M.A., under the Direction of Prof. W. M. Ramsay, M.A., D.C.L. With Coloured Map, Plans, and Illustrations. Crown 8vo. 3s. 6d.

The "Smaller History of Rome" has been written and arranged on the same plan, and with the same object, as the "Smaller History of Greece." Like that work it comprises separate chapters on the institutions and literature of the countries with which it deals.

SMALLER HISTORY OF ENGLISH LITERATURE. Giving a Sketch of the Lives of our Chief Writers. By JAMES ROWLEY. Small Crown 8vo. 3s. 6d.

SMALLER SPECIMENS OF ENGLISH LITERATURE. Selected from the Chief Authors and arranged chronologically. By JAMES ROWLEY. With Notes. Small Crown 8vo. 3s. 6d.

While the "Smaller History of English Literature" supplies a rapid but trustworthy sketch of the lives of our chief writers, and of the successive influences which imparted to their writings their peculiar character, the present work supplies choice examples of the works themselves, accompanied by all the explanations required for their perfect explanation. The two works are thus especially designed to be used together.

SMALLER CLASSICAL MYTHOLOGY. With Translations from the Ancient Poets, and Questions on the Work. With 90 Woodcuts. Small Crown 8vo. 3s. 6d.

This work has been prepared by a lady for the use of schools, and young persons of both sexes. In common with many other teachers, she has long felt the want of a consecutive account of the heathen deities, which might safely be placed in the hands of the young, and yet contain all that is generally necessary to enable them to understand the classical allusions they may meet with in prose or poetry, and to appreciate the meanings of works of art.

A carefully prepared set of QUESTIONS is appended, the answers to which will be found in the corresponding pages of the volume.

SIR WM. SMITH'S SMALLER MANUALS
—continued.

SMALLER SCRIPTURE HISTORY OF THE OLD AND THE NEW TESTAMENT. In Three Divisions:—I. Old Testament History. II. Connection of Old and New Testaments. III. New Testament History to A.D. 70. Edited by Sir WM. SMITH. With Coloured Maps and 40 Illustrations. Small Crown 8vo. 3s. 6d.
"This book is intended to be used with, and not in place of, the Bible. The result is most satisfactory,"—*The Standard.*

SMALLER ANCIENT HISTORY OF THE EAST. From the Earliest Times to the Conquest of Alexander the Great. By PHILIP SMITH, B.A. With 70 Woodcuts. Small Crown 8vo. 3s. 6d.

SMALLER MANUAL OF ANCIENT GEOGRAPHY. By Canon BEVAN, M.A. With Woodcuts. Small Crown 8vo. 3s. 6d.

MRS. MARKHAM'S HISTORIES.

HISTORY OF ENGLAND. From the First Invasion by the Romans to 1878. With Conversations at the end of each Chapter. 100 Woodcuts. 3s. 6d.

HISTORY OF FRANCE. From the Conquest of Gaul by Julius Cæsar to 1878. Conversations at the end of each Chapter. 70 Woodcuts. 3s. 6d.

HISTORY OF GERMANY. From its Invasion by Marius to 1880. 50 Woodcuts. 3s. 6d.

LITTLE ARTHUR'S HISTORIES.

HISTORY OF ENGLAND. By LADY CALLCOTT. From the Roman Invasion down to 1878. With 36 Woodcuts. 16mo. 1s. 6d.
"I never met with a history so well adapted to the capacities of children or their entertainment, so philosophical, and written with such simplicity.'—Mrs. MARCETT.

HISTORY OF FRANCE. From the Earliest Times to the Fall of the Second Empire. With Map and Illustrations. 16mo. 2s. 6d.
"The jaded schoolboy, surfeited with tales and the 'over-pressure' arising from long attention to lives and adventures, will, towards the latter part of his holiday, turn with some relief to this book, and begin feasting afresh. Those who know what 'Little Arthur's England' did to popularise the subject among little folks, will know what to expect in this 'France.' The book is capitally illustrated, and very wisely the compiler does not reject the exciting and legendary parts of the subject."—*Schoolmaster.*

HISTORY OF GREECE. By A. S. WALPOLE, M.A. With Map, Plans and Illustrations. Fcap 8vo. 2s. 6d.

SIR WM. SMITH'S
BIBLICAL DICTIONARIES.

DICTIONARY OF THE BIBLE: COMPRISING ITS ANTIQUITIES, BIOGRAPHY, GEOGRAPHY, AND NATURAL HISTORY. By Various Writers. With Illustrations. 3 vols. Enlarged and revised Edition. Medium 8vo. £4 4s.

Complete sets of the above work may be purchased through any Bookseller at reduced rates.

CONCISE DICTIONARY OF THE BIBLE. Condensed from the larger Work. For Families and Students. With Maps and 300 Illustrations. Medium 8vo. 21s.

A Dictionary of the Bible, in some form or another, is indispensable for every family. To students in the Universities, and in the Upper Forms at Schools, to private families, and to that numerous class of persons who desire to arrive at *results* simply, this CONCISE DICTIONARY will, it is believed, supply all that is necessary for the elucidation and explanation of the Bible.

SMALLER DICTIONARY OF THE BIBLE. Abridged from the larger Work. For Schools and Young Persons. With Maps and Illustrations. Crown 8vo. 7s. 6d.

"An invaluable service has been rendered to students in the condensation of Dr. Wm. Smith's Bible Dictionary. The work has been done as only a careful and intelligent scholar could do it, which preserves to us the essential scholarship and value of each article."—*British Quarterly Review.*

The two following Works are intended to furnish a complete account of the leading Personages, the Institutions, Art, Social Life, Writings, and Controversies of the Christian Church from the time of the Apostles to the Age of Charlemagne. They commence at the period at which the "Dictionary of the Bible" leaves off, and form a continuation of it.

DICTIONARY OF CHRISTIAN ANTIQUITIES. The History, Institutions, and Antiquities of the Christian Church. Edited by SIR WM. SMITH, D.C.L., and ARCHDEACON CHEETHAM, D.D. With Illustrations. 2 Vols. Medium 8vo. £3 13s. 6d.

"The work before us is unusually well done. A more acceptable present for a candidate for holy orders, or a more valuable book for any library, than the 'Dictionary of Christian Antiquities' could not easily be found."—*Saturday Review.*

DICTIONARY OF CHRISTIAN BIOGRAPHY, LITERATURE, SECTS, AND DOCTRINES. Edited by SIR WM. SMITH, D.C.L., and HENRY WACE, D.D. 4 Vols. Medium 8vo. £6 16s. 6d.

"The value of the work arises, in the first place, from the fact that the contributors to these volumes have diligently eschewed mere compilation. In these volumes we welcome the most important addition that has been made for a century to the historical library of the English theological student."—*Times.*

Sir Wm. Smith's
Classical Dictionaries.

"I am extremely glad of the opportunity of expressing to you the strong sense of obligation which I, in common with all teachers and lovers of classical literature, feel to you for your admirable Dictionaries."—Rev. Dr. HAWTREY, late Head Master of Eton College.

DICTIONARY OF GREEK AND ROMAN ANTIQUITIES. Including the Laws, Institutions, Domestic Usages, Painting, Sculpture, Music, the Drama, etc. Edited by Sir WM. SMITH, LL.D., Hon. D.C.L., Oxford, Hon. Ph.D., Leipzig; WILLIAM WAYTE, M.A., Late Fellow of King's College, Cambridge; G. E. MARINDIN, M.A., Late Fellow of King's College, Cambridge. Third Revised and Enlarged Edition. With 900 Illustrations. 2 Vols. Medium 8vo. 31s. 6d. each.

CONCISE DICTIONARY OF GREEK AND ROMAN ANTIQUITIES. Based on Sir Wm. Smith's larger Dictionary, and Incorporating the Results of Modern Research. Edited by F. WARRE CORNISH, M.A., Vice-Provost of Eton College. With over 1,100 Illustrations taken from the best examples of Ancient Art. Medium 8vo. 21s.

SMALLER DICTIONARY OF ANTIQUITIES. Abridged from Sir Wm. Smith's larger Dictionary. With 200 Woodcuts. Crown 8vo. 7s. 6d.

DICTIONARY OF GREEK AND ROMAN BIOGRAPHY AND MYTHOLOGY. By Various Writers. Edited by Sir WILLIAM SMITH, D.C.L., LL.D. Illustrated by 564 Engravings on Wood. In 3 Vols. Medium 8vo. 84s.

CLASSICAL DICTIONARY OF MYTHOLOGY, BIOGRAPHY, AND GEOGRAPHY, compiled rom Sir Wm. Smith's larger Dictionaries. In great part re-written by G. E. MARINDIN, M.A., late Fellow of King's College, Cambridge, some time Assistant Master at Eton College. With over 800 Woodcuts. Thoroughly Revised Edition. 8vo. 18s.

SMALLER CLASSICAL DICTIONARY. Abridged from the above Work. With 200 Woodcuts. In great part re-written by G. E. MARINDIN, M.A., some time Assistant Master at Eton College. Crown 8vo. 7s. 6d.

DICTIONARY OF GREEK AND ROMAN GEOGRAPHY. Illustrated by 534 Engravings on Wood. 2 Vols. Medium 8vo. 56s.

Sir Wm. Smith's Latin Dictionaries.

"I consider Dr. Wm. Smith's Dictionaries to have conferred a great and lasting service on the cause of classical learning in this country."—Dean LIDDELL.

"I have found Dr. Wm. Smith's Latin Dictionary a great convenience to me. I think that he has been very judicious in what he has omitted, as well as what he has inserted."—Dr. SCOTT.

COMPLETE LATIN-ENGLISH DICTIONARY. Based on the Works of Forcellini and Freund. With Tables of the Roman Calendar, Measures, Weights, Money, and a Dictionary of Proper Names. By Sir WM. SMITH, D.C.L., LL.D. Medium 8vo. 22nd Edition. 16s.

"This work aims at performing the same service for the Latin language as Liddell and Scott's Lexicon has done for the Greek. Great attention has beer. paid to Etymology, in which department especially this work is admitted to maintain a superiority over all existing Latin Dictionaries.

SMALLER LATIN-ENGLISH DICTIONARY. With a Separate Dictionary of Proper Names, Tables of Roman Moneys, &c. Thoroughly revised and in great part re-written. Edited by Sir WM. SMITH and T. D. HALL, M.A. The Etymological portion by JOHN K. INGRAM, LL.D. Square 12mo. 7s. 6d.

This edition of Dr. Smith's 'Smaller Latin-English Dictionary' is to a great extent a new and original Work. Every article has been carefully revised.

COPIOUS AND CRITICAL ENGLISH-LATIN DICTIONARY. Compiled from Original Sources. By Sir WM. SMITH, D.C.L., and T. D. HALL, M.A. Medium 8vo. 16s.

It has been the object of the Authors of this Work to produce a more complete and more perfect ENGLISH-LATIN DICTIONARY than yet exists, and every article has been the result of original and independent research.

Each meaning is illustrated by examples from the classical writers; and those phrases are as a general rule given in both English and Latin.

SMALLER ENGLISH-LATIN DICTIONARY. Abridged from the above Work, by Sir WM. SMITH and T. D. HALL, M.A., for the use of Junior Classes. Square 12mo. 7s. 6d.

"An English-Latin Dictionary worthy of the scholarship of our age and country. It will take absolutely the first rank, and be the standard English-Latin Dictionary as long as either tongue endures. Even a general examination of the pages will serve to reveal the minute pains taken to ensure its fulness and philological value, and the 'work is to a large extent a dictionary of the English language, as well as an English-Latin Dictionary.'"—*English Churchman*.

MR. MURRAY'S CLASS BOOKS.

Languages.

FRENCH STUMBLING BLOCKS AND ENGLISH STEPPING STONES. By FRANCIS TARVER, M.A., late Senior French Master at Eton College. Fcap. 8vo. 2s. 6d.

Mr. Francis Tarver's skill as a teacher of French to Englishmen is well known. His thorough knowledge of *both* languages, and his thirty years' experience as a master at Eton, have afforded him exceptional opportunities of judging what are the difficulties, pitfalls, and stumbling-blocks which beset the path of an Englishman in his study of French.

THE TECHNICAL SCHOOL FRENCH GRAMMAR. By DR. W. KRISCH, sometime Teacher of Latin and Greek at the Birmingham Midland Institute, Examiner in Modern Languages to the Midland Counties' Union of Educational Institutions. Crown 8vo. 2s. 6d.

A CHILD'S FIRST LATIN BOOK. COMPRISING NOUNS, PRONOUNS, AND ADJECTIVES, WITH THE VERBS. With ample and varied Practice of the easiest kind. Both old and new order of Cases given. By T. D. HALL, M.A. Enlarged Edition, including the Passive Verb. 16mo. 2s.

TRANSLATION AT SIGHT; OR, AIDS TO FACILITY IN THE TRANSLATION OF LATIN. Passages of Graduated Difficulty, carefully selected from Latin Authors, with Explanations, Notes, &c. By PROFESSOR T. D. HALL, M.A. Crown 8vo. 2s.

GREEK GRAMMAR ACCIDENCE AND SYNTAX FOR SCHOOLS AND COLLEGES. By JOHN THOMPSON, M.A., late Scholar of Christ's College, Cambridge ; Senior Classical Master, High School, Dublin. Crown 8vo. 6s.

One of the chief objects of this book is to bring within the reach of the younger generation of students and schoolboys some of the results of the linguistic discoveries of the present day. It is therefore written in accordance with the philological views of the *Grundriss der Vergleichenden Grammatik* of Professors Brugmann and Delbrück, of P. Giles' *Manual of Comparative Philology*, of G. Meyer's *Griechische Grammatik* and of other scholars. Use has also been made of the Third Edition, revised by Drs. Blass and Gerth, of Kühner's *Ausführliche Grammatik der Griechischen Sprache*, and of several school Greek Grammars in use in Germany.

The Grammar consists of two parts in one volume, Part I. containing the Accidence, and Part II. the Syntax. The forms and spelling in use in Attic Greek are given according to the latest authorities, and there are special notes on Homeric peculiarities. There are also tables of Greek verbs arranged on a new plan, including (a) a list of the chief types of verbs, (b) a list of common Attic verbs regular according to the types in (a), and (c) a list of the irregular verbs with the irregular forms printed in special type. This arrangement is intended to remove many misconceptions about Greek verbs. Brief notes on syntax, &c., are given with each verb stating the ordinary constructions and any special uses. There will also be Appendices on (1) Greek Weights, Measures, and Dates, (2) Accents, and (3) Sound Changes. Particular attention has been given to the type, so that the essential part of Greek Grammar may be made specially clear, and that the beginner may have no difficulty in distinguishing the more important sections.

MR. MURRAY'S CLASS BOOKS—*continued.*

Languages—continued.

PRINCIPIA GRÆCA. An Introduction to the Study of Greek, comprehending Grammar Delectus, and Exercise Book with Vocabularies. By H. E. HUTTON, M.A. Balliol College, Oxford. For the use of the Lower Forms in Public and Private Schools. Crown 8vo. 3s. 6d.

ELUCIDATIONS OF THE STUDENT'S GREEK GRAMMAR. By PROF. CURTIUS. From the German, with the Author's sanction. By EVELYN ABBOTT, M.A. 2nd Edition. Crown 8vo. 7s. 6d.

A SHORT PRACTICAL HEBREW GRAMMAR; WITH AN APPENDIX. Containing the Hebrew Text of Genesis I—VI, and Psalms I—VI. Grammatical Analysis Vocabulary. By the REV. STANLEY LEATHES, D.D. Crown 8vo. 7s. 6d.

PRACTICAL SPANISH. A GRAMMAR OF THE SPANISH LANGUAGE. With Exercises, Vocabularies, and Materials for Conversation.

Part I.: NOUNS, ADJECTIVES, PRONOUNS, ETC.
Part II.: VERBS, ETC., WITH COPIOUS VOCABULARIES.

By DON FERNANDO DE ARTEAGA, Taylorian Teacher of Spanish in the University of Oxford. 2 Parts. Crown 8vo. 7s. 6d.

This book has in the main been formed on the plan of Sir William Smith's well-known and deservedly popular "Principia Latina, Part I." It possesses, however, one new feature which is as novel as it is likely to prove valuable to the student who uses the book. English people, for the most part, who set themselves to learn Spanish, are not children, but either would-be travellers in the country, students of its literature, or persons engaged in commerce with Spain or Spanish-speaking countries. It has therefore been the aim of the Editor throughout to avoid the old-fashioned Ollendorfen sentences in illustration of the grammar, and instead to make use of phrases and expressions which are likely to prove of practical use to the traveller and the man of business.

Gradus.

AN ENGLISH-LATIN GRADUS, OR VERSE DICTIONARY, for Schools. By A. C. AINGER, Trinity Coll., Cambridge, Assistant-Master at Eton College, and the late H. G. WINTLE, M.A., Christ Church, Oxford. This Gradus is on a new plan, intended to simplify the Composition of Latin Verses by Classical Meanings, selected Epithets and Synonyms, etc. Crown 8vo. 9s.

MR. MURRAY'S CLASS BOOKS—*continued.*

Geography.

PREPARATORY GEOGRAPHY for IRISH SCHOOLS.
With numerous Coloured Maps, Relief Maps, Plans, and Views of
well-known Places in Illustration of Geographical Terms. By
JOHN COOKE, M.A., Lecturer in Geography, Church of Ireland
Training College; and Examiner to the Board of Intermediate
Education. Small Crown 8vo. 1s. 6d.

"Mr. Cooke's eminent services to the literature of education have seldom been
better illustrated than in this Geography for Irish Schools. . . . Mr. Cooke
claims that his Geography is suggestive rather than exhaustive. He might
reasonably have gone a step further, and claimed the high merit of charm of
attractiveness. With such a wealth of apt illustration drawn from our own
country, no child could for a moment fail to comprehend what he sees and hears."
—*The Irish Times.*

History and Literature.

THE GROWTH OF THE EMPIRE. By A. W. JOSE.
With many Coloured and other Maps and Diagrams. Cr. 8vo. 6s.
". . . . an eminently useful book . . . . as serviceable as it is readable.
It is systematic in method and accurate in statement."—*The Globe.*

**HALLAM'S CONSTITUTIONAL HISTORY OF ENG-
LAND, Chapters I. to IX.** Bound together in 1 Volume for the
special use of candidates for the London University Examinations.
Crown 8vo. 5s.

EUROPE IN THE MIDDLE AGES. By OLIVER J.
THATCHER, Ph.D., and FERDINAND SCHWILL, Ph.D.
Large Crown 8vo. 9s.

This work has been written by men who have had long experience in teaching,
to supply the want of a compendious History of Mediæval Europe, from the
middle of the Fourth to the close of the Fifteenth Century, which has been long
felt in the universities and schools. A distinguished Professor of Modern History
in one of our leading universities, to whom a copy has been sent, writes:
"The book covers ground on which it has always been hard to get a suitable
book for educational purposes, and, so far as I can judge—I have as yet only
examined the German History of the 10th Century—it is thoroughly sound and
clear

A GENERAL HISTORY OF EUROPE, 350–1900.
By OLIVER J. THATCHER and FERDINAND SCHWILL,
Authors of "Europe in the Middle Ages." Revised and adapted to
the requirements of English Colleges and Schools, by ARTHUR
HASSALL, M.A., Christ Church, Oxford. With Bibliographies at the
end of each section. With Maps, Genealogical Tables. Crown 8vo. 9s.

". . . a model of condensation, omitting no essential facts. . . . The
volume is greatly enhanced by a wealth of maps and chronological and genealogical
tables. Among general histories this will take a leading place."—
Dundee Advertiser.

MR. MURRAY'S CLASS BOOKS—*continued.*

History and Literature—continued.

A POPULAR HISTORY OF THE CHURCH OF ENGLAND. From the Earliest Times to the Present Day. By the Rt. Rev. WILLIAM BOYD CARPENTER, The Lord Bishop of Ripon. Illustrated. Crown 8vo. 6s.

> "The title is, perhaps, hardly wide enough for the contents; one would almost call the book a history of Christianity in England. . . . He has the true judicial spirit, and is passionately eager to be entirely fair to every one. His history is impartial to the last degree. . . . His book should have a very wide circulation, and can do nothing but good wherever it is read."—*Morning Post.*

THE PUBLIC SCHOOL SPEAKER. Compiled by F. WARRE CORNISH, M.A., Vice-Provost of Eton College. Large 8vo. 7s. 6d.

> This work, as its name implies, is a collection of pieces suitable for recitation at school "speeches." The Editor has made his selection in the widest manner and from various languages—Greek, Latin, English, German, French and Italian. He has included drama, general poetry, orations and other prose pieces, ancient and modern. The Editor is in hopes that no serious omissions can be found, unless it be those intentional ones from classics that are at everyone's command, which he has left out to make room for those more difficult of access.
>
> It will be noticed that he has in many cases given an extract longer than is sufficient for a single recitation—he has done this advisedly with a view to affording greater scope for individual requirements and individual taste.
>
> The publisher is of opinion that the Speaker will be found the most complete extant.
>
> "No such comprehensive work has hitherto been issued, and in our opinion 'The Public School Speaker' has leaped at a single bound into the very foremost rank, and has become the classic of its kind."—*The Bookseller.*

ELEMENTARY TEACHERS' CERTIFICATE EDITION.

STANLEY'S LIFE OF ARNOLD. With a Preface by Sir JOSHUA FITCH, LL.D., formerly H.M. Chief Inspector of Training Colleges. Large type, 800 pages, in 1 volume. With Photogravure Portrait and 16 half-tone Illustrations. Crown 8vo. 6s.

> "Stanley's Life of Arnold has been selected by the Board of Education as a subject of examination for intending teachers, so that this edition will be heartily welcomed."—*Educational Times.*

ÆSOP'S FABLES. A New Version. Chiefly from the Original Sources. By Rev. THOMAS JAMES. With 100 Woodcuts. Illustrations by John Tenniel. Crown 8vo. 2s. 6d.

> "This work is remarkable for the clearness and conciseness with which each tale is narrated; and the book has been relieved of those tedious and unprofitable appendages called 'morals,' which used to obscure and disfigure the ancient editions of the work."—*The Examiner.*

MR. MURRAY'S CLASS BOOKS—*continued*.

Classical Study.

CHAPTERS FROM ARISTOTLE'S ETHICS. By J. H. MUIRHEAD, M.A., Professor of Mental and Moral Philosophy, Mason University College, Birmingham. Author of "The Elements of Ethics." Large crown 8vo. 7s. 6d.

"We cannot commend these 'chapters' too highly, not only to teachers, but to all students of Aristotle or of moral philosophy who feel that the problems of the Old Greeks are in any way unreal in these later days, or their solutions out of date."—*Pilot*.

HERODOTUS. The Text of Canon Rawlinson's Translation. With the Notes abridged for the use of Students. By A. J. GRANT, M.A., of King's College, Cambridge; Professor of History, Yorkshire College, Leeds; Author of "Greece in the Age of Pericles." With Map and Plans. 2 Vols. Crown 8vo. 12s.

"The delightful pages of the old Greek whose flavour has been so admirably presented by Canon Rawlinson, will thus be made accessible to a far wider circle than heretofore. There is no better introduction to Greek history and literature than Herodotus, and the English reader gets him here under the best possible conditions."—*Literary World*.

THE STORY OF THE PERSIAN WARS AS TOLD BY HERODOTUS. In English. Selected, arranged and edited, so as to form a History Reading Book for Schools. By the Rev. C. C. TANCOCK, D.D., Head Master of Tonbridge School. With Illustrations, Map and Plans. Crown 8vo. 2s. 6d.

Biblical Study.

GREEK TESTAMENT READER. For Use in Schools, comprising consecutive Extracts from the Synoptic Gospel and Passages from the Epistles of St. Paul. By THEOPHILUS D. HALL, M.A. Crown 8vo. 2s. 6d.

THE SUNRISE OF REVELATION. New Testament Teachings for Secondary Schools. A Sequel to "The Dawn of Revelation." By Miss M. BRAMSTON, Author of "The Dawn of Revelation," "Judæa and her Rulers," etc. Crown 8vo. 5s. net.

"We do not think that any good judge will get far in the book without discovering that it is one of rare merit and exceptionally well suited to the class to whom it is addressed. We do not know of any book likely to be more useful to the teachers of secondary schools in the preparation of their Scripture lessons than this. It is clear, accurate, and full of instruction and suggestiveness. Miss Bramston shows a competent knowledge of the present position of criticism as to the Gospels and Acts, but she wisely keeps her learning in the background, and it only betrays itself by an occasional sentence or epithet. It is a great deal to say of any book dealing with the Scripture history that it is scholarly without being dry, and reverent without any trace of 'preaching.' Yet Miss Bramston has succeeded in all this and more. We do not often praise a book so unreservedly, but we shall be surprised if she does not attract a circle of readers far larger than that to which she has addressed herself in the first instance."—*The Guardian*.

MR. MURRAY'S CLASS BOOKS—*continued.*

Biblical Study—continued.

THE STUDENT'S COMMENTARY ON THE BIBLE.
Abridged from the " Speaker's Commentary." Edited by JOHN M.
FULLER, M.A., Vicar of Bexley, and formerly Fellow of St. John's
College, Cambridge. Crown 8vo. 7s. 6d. each.

OLD TESTAMENT.—*Vol. I.*—Genesis to Deuteronomy. *Vol. II.*—
Joshua to Esther. *Vol. III.*—Job to Song of Solomon. *Vol. IV.*—
Isaiah to Malachi.

NEW TESTAMENT.—*Vol. I.*—Gospels to Acts. *Vol. II.*—Epistles
to Revelation.

THE BIBLE IN THE HOLY LAND. Extracted from
Dean Stanley's work on Sinai and Palestine. With Woodcuts.
Crown 8vo. 3s. 6d.

Science (Elementary & General).

STUDENT'S ELEMENTS OF GEOLOGY. By SIR
CHARLES LYELL. Thoroughly revised by PROF. J. W. JUDD.
Crown 8vo. With 600 Woodcuts. 9s.

ELEMENTS OF AGRICULTURE. A Text-Book. Prepared
under the authority of the Royal Agricultural Society of England.
By W. FREAM, LL.D. New Edition (Seventh). Crown 8vo.
3s. 6d.

A HANDY BOOK OF HORTICULTURE. AN INTRODUCTION
TO THE THEORY AND PRACTICE OF GARDENING. With Illustrations
and Diagrams. By F. C. HAYES, M.A., Rector of Raheny; Lecturer
in Practical Horticulture in Alexandra College, Dublin. Crown 8vo.
2s. 6d. net.

". . . Just the book to place in the hands of young amateurs and Students,
and should find a place on the shelves of every Village and County Council
Library."—*The Field.*

THE INVISIBLE POWERS OF NATURE; SOME ELEMEN-
TARY LESSONS IN PHYSICAL SCIENCE, HEAT, LIGHT, SOUND,
GRAVITATION, SOLIDS, FLUIDS, ELECTRICITY, MAGNETISM, ETC.
By E. M. CAILLARD. Post 8vo. 6s.

"We have rarely met with a work of the kind in which so much information is
so clearly and so accurately set forth."—*Gardener's Chronicle.*

COLOUR IN NATURE: A STUDY IN BIOLOGY. By MARION
NEWBIGIN. Crown 8vo. 7s. 6d.

" All who seek for well sifted results, and not merely superficial information,
will thank her for this book, and congratulate her on a very timely contribution to
biological literature."—*Journal of Education.*

MR. MURRAY'S CLASS BOOKS—*continued.*

Science—continued.

EARLY CHAPTERS IN SCIENCE. A First Book of Knowledge of Natural History, Botany, Physiology, Physics and Chemistry for Young People. By Mrs. W. AWDRY (Wife of the Bishop of South Tokyo, Japan). Edited by W. F. Barrett, F.R.S., Professor of Experimental Physics in the Royal College of Science for Ireland. With nearly 200 Illustrations. Crown 8vo. 6s.

> "Deserves a warm welcome from all teachers of the young. . . . The illustrations are models of clear, careful, and unconventional work."—*Literature.*
> "It can be confidently recommended to the young as a sound and pleasantly written introduction to science."—*Guardian.*

ELECTRICITY. The Science of the Nineteenth Century. A Sketch for General Readers. By E. M. CAILLARD. With Illustrations. Crown 8vo. 7s. 6d.

THE FIVE WINDOWS OF THE SOUL: A Popular Account of the Human Senses. By EDWARD HAMILTON AITKEN, author of "The Tribes on my Frontier," "Behind the Bungalow," "A Naturalist on the Prowl." Crown 8vo. 6s.

> "There is probably nothing in recent literature which will so surely lead to a thirst for further and more technical knowledge than the author's treatment of these difficult subjects. . . . It is admirably written and cannot fail to give pleasure. It is so seldom that such a really good book as this is published that the hope may be expressed that it will meet with the success it deserves, and find a place in every good public and private library."—*Manchester Guardian.*

Jurisprudence.

AN ANALYSIS OF AUSTIN'S JURISPRUDENCE. By GORDON CAMPBELL. Crown 8vo. 6s.

STUDENT'S EDITION OF AUSTIN'S JURISPRUDENCE. Compiled from the larger work. By ROBERT CAMPBELL. Crown 8vo. 12s.

SIR WM. SMITH'S
EDUCATIONAL SERIES.

English Course.

PRIMARY ENGLISH GRAMMAR for Elementary Schools. With 134 Exercises and carefully graduated passing lessons. By T. D. HALL, M.A. 16mo. 1s.

SCHOOL MANUAL OF ENGLISH GRAMMAR. With Historical Introduction and copious Exercises. By SIR WM. SMITH, D.C.L., and T. D. HALL, M.A. With Appendices. Crown 8vo. 3s. 6d.

MANUAL OF ENGLISH COMPOSITION. With Copious Illustrations and Practical Exercises. Suited equally for Schools and for Private Students of English. By T. D. HALL, M.A. Crown 8vo. 3s. 6d.

French Course.

FRENCH PRINCIPIA, Part I. A FIRST FRENCH COURSE, containing Grammar, Delectus and Exercises, with Vocabularies and Materials for French Conversation. Crown 8vo. 3s. 6d.

APPENDIX TO FRENCH PRINCIPIA, Part I. Containing Additional Exercises and Examination Papers. Cr. 8vo. 2s. 6d.

FRENCH PRINCIPIA, Part II. A READING BOOK. Containing Fables, Stories, and Anecdotes, Natural History, and Scenes from the History of France. With Grammatical Questions, Notes, and copious Etymological Dictionary. Crown 8vo. 4s. 6d.

FRENCH PRINCIPIA, Part III. PROSE COMPOSITION. Containing a Systematic Course of Exercises on the Syntax, with the Principal Rules of Syntax. Crown 8vo. 4s. 6d.

THE STUDENT'S FRENCH GRAMMAR: PRACTICAL AND HISTORICAL. FOR THE HIGHER FORMS. By C. HERON-WALL with INTRODUCTION by M. LITTRÉ. Crown 8vo. 6s.

A SMALLER FRENCH GRAMMAR. FOR THE MIDDLE AND LOWER FORMS. Abridged from the above Work. Crown 8vo. 3s. 6d.

SIR WM. SMITH'S EDUCATIONAL SERIES
—continued.

German Course.

GERMAN PRINCIPIA, Part I. A First German Course. Containing Grammar, Delectus, Exercises, Vocabularies and materials for German Conversation. Cr. 8vo. 3s. 6d.

GERMAN PRINCIPIA, Part II. A Reading Book. Containing Fables, Stories, and Anecdotes, Natural History, and Scenes from the History of Germany. With Grammatical Questions, Notes and Dictionary. Cr. 8vo. 3s. 6d.

Italian Course.

ITALIAN PRINCIPIA, Part I. A First Italian Course. Containing a Grammar, Delectus, Exercise Book, with Vocabularies, &c. Thoroughly revised and in part re-written by C. F. COSCIA, Professor of Italian in the University of Oxford. Crown 8vo. 3s. 6d.

ITALIAN PRINCIPIA, Part II. A First Italian Reading-Book, containing Fables, Anecdotes, History, and Passages from the best Italian Authors, with Questions, Notes, and an Etymological Dictionary. Crown 8vo. 3s. 6d.

Spanish Course.

SPANISH PRINCIPIA. By H. J. Weintz. Crown 8vo.
[In Preparation.

Latin Course.

THE YOUNG BEGINNER'S COURSE

I. FIRST LATIN BOOK.—Grammar, Easy Questions, Exercises and Vocabularies. F'cap 8vo. 2s.

II. SECOND LATIN BOOK.—An easy Latin Reading Book with Analysis of Sentences. F'cap 8vo. 2s.

III. THIRD LATIN BOOK.—Exercises on the Syntax, with Vocabularies. F'cap 8vo. 2s.

IV. FOURTH LATIN BOOK.—A Latin Vocabulary for Beginners, arranged according to Subjects and Etymologies. F'cap 8vo. 2s.

PRINCIPIA LATINA, Part I. First Latin Course, Grammar, Delectus, Exercises, and Vocabularies. 38th Edition, Thoroughly revised so as to meet the requirements of Modern Teachers and Scholars. Crown 8vo. 3s. 6d.

APPENDIX TO PRINCIPIA LATINA, Part I. Containing Additional Exercises, with Examination Papers. Crown 8vo. 2s. 6d.

SIR WM. SMITH'S EDUCATIONAL SERIES
—*continued.*

Latin Course—continued.

PRINCIPIA LATINA, Part II. Reading Book. An Introduction to Ancient Mythology, Geography. Roman Antiquities, and History. With Notes and a Dictionary. Crown 8vo. 3s. 6d.

PRINCIPIA LATINA, Part III. Poetry. 1. Easy Hexameters, and Pentameters. 2. Eclogæ Ovidianæ. 3. Prosody and Metre. 4. First Latin Verse Book. Crown 8vo. 3s. 6d.

PRINCIPIA LATINA, Part IV. Prose Composition. Rules of Syntax, with Examples, Explanations of Synonyms, and Exercises on the Syntax. Crown 8vo. 3s. 6d.

PRINCIPIA LATINA, Part V. Short Tales and Anecdotes from Ancient History for Translation into Latin Prose. With an English-Latin Vocabulary. By Sir WM. SMITH, LL.D. Revised and considerably enlarged. By T. D. HALL, M.A. 3s. 6d

THE STUDENT'S LATIN GRAMMAR. For the Use of Colleges and the Higher Forms in Schools. By Sir WM. SMITH, LL.D., and T. D. HALL. Crown 8vo. 6s.

SMALLER LATIN GRAMMAR. For the Middle and Lower Forms. Crown 8vo. 3s. 6d.

Greek Course.

INITIA GRÆCA, Part I. A First Greek Course, containing Grammar, Delectus, Exercise Book, and Vocabularies. 26th Edition. Edited and carefully revised by FRANCIS BROOKS, M.A., Professor of Classics at University College, Bristol, and formerly Classical Scholar of Balliol College, Oxford. Crown 8vo. 3s. 6d.

APPENDIX TO INITIA GRÆCA, Part I. Containing Additional Exercises, with Examination Papers and Easy Reading Lessons with the Sentences Analysed, serving as an Introduction to Initia Græca, Part II. Crown 8vo. 2s. 6d.

INITIA GRÆCA, Part II. A Reading Book. Containing short Tales, Anecdotes, Fables, Mythology, and Grecian History. With a Lexicon. Crown 8vo. 3s. 6d.

INITIA GRÆCA, Part III. Prose Composition. Containing the Rules of Syntax, with copious Examples and Exercises. Crown 8vo. 3s. 6d.

THE STUDENT'S GREEK GRAMMAR. For the Higher Forms. By Professor CURTIUS. Edited by Sir WM. SMITH, D.C.L. Crown 8vo. 6s.

A SMALLER GREEK GRAMMAR. For the Middle and Lower Forms. Abridged from the above Work. Crown 8vo. 3s. 6d.

ETON COLLEGE BOOKS.

ETON LATIN GRAMMAR. For use in the Higher Forms. By FRANCIS HAY RAWLINS, M.A., Fellow of King's Coll., Cambridge, and Assistant Master at Eton College, and REV. W. R. INGE, M.A., Fellow of Hertford Coll., Oxford. Revised Edition. Crown 8vo. 6s.

"The Syntax has the merit of compressing a great deal of matter into a short space, and of avoiding much of the technical terminology which afflicts some of the readers of the Public School Grammar. It is also lucid in arrangement, and clear in its presentation of facts."—Prof. NETTLESHIP in the *Classical Review.*

ETON ELEMENTARY LATIN GRAMMAR. For use in the Lower Forms. Compiled with the sanction of the Head Master, by A. C. AINGER, M.A., Trinity College, Cambridge, and H. G. WINTLE, M.A., Christ Church, Oxford, Assistant Masters at Eton College. Crown 8vo. 3s. 6d.

PREPARATORY ETON LATIN GRAMMAR. Containing the Accidence and the Syntax Rules with the sanction of the Head Master. By A. C. AINGER, M.A., Trinity College, Cambridge, and H. G. WINTLE, M.A., Christ Church, Oxford, Assistant Masters at Eton College. Crown 8vo. 2s.

ETON LATIN SYNTAX AND EXERCISE BOOK. Consisting of pages 97-127 and 152-306 from the Eton Elementary Latin Grammar, together with the First Latin Exercise Book. Compiled, with sanction of the Head Master, by A. C. AINGER, M.A., Trinity College, Cambridge, and H. G. WINTLE, M.A., Christ Church, Oxford, Assistant Masters at Eton College. Crown 8vo. 5s.

A FIRST LATIN EXERCISE BOOK. Adapted to the Eton Latin Grammar. By A. C. AINGER, M.A., and H. G. WINTLE, M.A. Crown 8vo. 2s. 6d.

OVID LESSONS: being Easy Passages selected from the Elegiac Poems of OVID, with Explanatory Notes by A. C. AINGER, M.A., and H. F. W. TATHAM, M.A., of Trinity College, Cambridge, Assistant Masters at Eton College. Crown 8vo. 2s. 6d.

ETON HORACE. The Odes, Epodes, and Carmen Sæculare. With Notes. By F. W. CORNISH, M.A. In Two Parts. With Maps. Crown 8vo. 6s.

As it is considered desirable that the notes should be used only in the preparation of the lesson, and not in the class, they are bound up separate from the text.

"One good feature is that the notes are printed entirely separate from the text in a separate volume. They are just those that are suited to boys at that stage."—*Schoolmaster.*

ETON EXERCISES IN ALGEBRA. By E. P. ROUSE and A. COCKSHOTT, Assistant Masters at Eton College. Crown 8vo. 3s.

ETON EXERCISES IN ARITHMETIC. By REV. T. DALTON, M.A., Assistant Master at Eton College. Crown 8vo. 3s.

UNIVERSITY MANUALS.

Edited by PROFESSOR KNIGHT, of St. Andrew's University.

A HISTORY OF ASTRONOMY. By ARTHUR BERRY, M.A., Fellow of King's College, Cambridge With over 100 Illustrations. Crown 8vo. 6s.

Primitive Astronomy—Greek Astronomy—The Middle Ages—Copernicus—The Reception of the Copernican Theory and the Progress of Observation—Galileo—Kepler—From Galilei to Newton—Universal Gravitation—Observational Astronomy in the 18th Century—Gravitational Astronomy in the 18th Century—Herschel—The 19th Century—List of Authorities and of Books for Students—Index.

THE STUDY OF ANIMAL LIFE. By J. ARTHUR THOMSON, Regius Professor of Natural Science in the University of Aberdeen ; Joint Author of the "Evolution of Sex " ; Author of "Outlines of Zoology." With many Illustrations. Crown 8vo. 5s.

Part I.—The Everyday Life of Animals. *Part II.*—The Powers of Life. *Part III.*—The Forms of Animal Life. *Part IV.*—The Evolution of Animal Life.

THE ELEMENTS OF ETHICS. By JOHN R. MUIRHEAD, Balliol College, Oxford, Lecturer on Moral Science, Royal Holloway College, Examiner in Philosophy to the University of Glasgow. Crown 8vo. 3s.

Book I.—The Science of Ethics. *Book II.*—Moral Judgement. *Book III.*—Theories of the End. *Book IV.*—The End as Good. *Book V.*—Moral Progress.

THE REALM OF NATURE: A MANUAL OF PHYSIOGRAPHY. By DR. HUGH ROBERT MILL, Director of British Rainfall Organization. With 19 Coloured Maps and 68 Illustrations. Crown 8vo. 5s.

The Study of Nature—The Substance of Nature : Energy, the Power of Nature—The Earth a Spinning Ball—The Earth a Planet—The Solar System Universe—The Atmosphere—Atmospheric Phenomena—Climates of the World—The Hydrosphere—The Bed of the Oceans—The Crust of the Earth—Action of Water on the Land—The Record of the Rocks—The Continental Area—Life and Living Creatures—Man in Nature.

UNIVERSITY MANUALS—*continued.*

ENGLISH COLONIZATION AND EMPIRE. By A. CALDECOTT, Fellow and Dean of St. John's College, Cambridge; and Professor of Philosophy, King's College, London. Coloured Maps and Plans. Crown 8vo. 3s. 6d.

Introduction—Pioneer Period—International Struggle--Development and Separation of America—The English in India—Reconstruction and Fresh Development—Government of the Empire—Trade and Trade Policy — Supply of Labour — Native Races—Education and Religion—General Reflections—Appendix: Books of Reference.

FRENCH LITERATURE. By H. G. KEENE, Wadham College, Oxford, Fellow of the University of Calcutta. Crown 8vo. 3s.

The Age of Infancy (*a.* Birth)—The Age of Infancy (*b.* Growth)—The Age of Adolescence (XVIth Cent.)—The Age of Glory (Poetry)--The Age of Glory (Prose)—The Age of Reason—The Age of ' Nature '—Source of Modern French Literary Art: Poetry—Sources of Prose Fiction.

THE PHILOSOPHY OF THE BEAUTIFUL, Part I. By PROFESSOR KNIGHT, University of St. Andrew's. Crown 8vo. 3s. 6d.

Introductory—Prehistoric Origins—Oriental Art and Speculation —The Philosophy of Greece — The Neoplatonists — The Graeco-Roman Period — Mediaevalism — The Philosophy of Germany — The Philosophy of France—The Philosophy of Italy—The Philosophy of Holland—The Philosophy of Britain—The Philosophy of America.

THE PHILOSOPHY OF THE BEAUTIFUL, Part II. By PROFESSOR KNIGHT, University of St. Andrew's. Crown 8vo. 3s. 6d.

Prolegomena—The Nature of Beauty—The Ideal and the Real—Inadequate or Partial Theories—Suggestions towards a more complete Theory of Beauty—Art, its Nature and Functions—The Correlation of the Arts—Poetry—Music—Architecture—Sculpture—Painting—Dancing—Appendix.

UNIVERSITY MANUALS—*continued.*

THE USE AND ABUSE OF MONEY. By W. CUNNING-HAM, D.D., Fellow of Trinity College, Cambridge, Professor of Economic Science, King's College, London. Crown 8vo. 3s.

> *Part I.*—Social Problems. *Part II.*—Practical Questions. *Part III.*—Personal Duty.

THE JACOBEAN POETS. By EDMUND GOSSE. Crown 8vo. 3s. 6d.

> Preface; The Last Elizabethans; Ben Jonson—Chapman; John Dorne; Beaumont and Fletcher; Campion — Drayton—Sir John Beaumont; Heywood — Middleton — Powley; Giles and Phineas Fletcher—Browne; Tourneur—Webster—Day—Darorne; Wither—Quarles—Lord Brooke; Philip Massingen; Index.

THE RISE OF THE BRITISH DOMINION IN INDIA, FROM THE EARLY DAYS OF THE EAST INDIA COMPANY TO THE CONQUEST OF THE PANJAB. By SIR ALFRED LYALL, K.C.B. With Coloured Maps. Crown 8vo. 4s. 6d.

> "No student should be without this excellent instructor into the technicalities of the many phases through which our Empire has passed."—*Daily Telegraph.*

THE ENGLISH NOVEL, FROM ITS ORIGIN TO SIR W. SCOTT. By WALTER RALEIGH, Professor of English Literature in Glasgow University. Crown 8vo. 3s. 6d.

> The Romance and the Novel—The Elizabethan Age: Euphues Sydney and Nash —The Romances of the 17th Century — The Beginnings of the Modern Novel—Richardson and Fielding—The Novels of the 18th Century—The Revival of Romance—The Novel of Domestic Satire: Miss Burney; Miss Austen; Miss Edgeworth—Sir Walter Scott.

THE FRENCH REVOLUTION. By C. E. MALLET, Balliol College, Oxford. Crown 8vo. 3s. 6d.

> The Condition of France in the Eighteenth Century—The Last Years of the Ancien Régime—The Early Days of the Revolution—The Labours of the Constituent Assembly—Parties and Politicians under the Constituent Assembly—The Rise of the Jacobin Party—The Influence of the War upon the Revolution—The Fall of the Gironde—The Jacobins in Power—The Struggles of Parties and the Ascendancy of Robespierre—The Reaction.

UNIVERSITY MANUALS—*continued.*

AN INTRODUCTION TO MODERN GEOLOGY. By R. D. ROBERTS, sometime Fellow of Clare College, Cambridge; Fellow of University College, London; Secretary to the Cambridge and London University Extension Syndicate. With Coloured Maps and Illustrations. Crown 8vo. 5s.

> *Part I.*—PROGRESS OF GEOLOGICAL THOUGHT.
> *Part II.*—DESTRUCTION OF LAND.
> *Part III.*—CONSTRUCTION OF LAND.
> *Part IV.*—EVOLUTION OF LAND AREAS.

OUTLINES OF ENGLISH LITERATURE. By WILLIAM RENTON. With Illustrative Diagrams. Crown 8vo. 3s. 6d.

First Period.—The Old English Metric Chronicle, 600-1350 The Renascence, 1350-1500—The Reformation, 1500-1600—The Romantic Drama, 1550-1650.

Second Period.—The Serious Age, 1600-1700—The Age of Gaiety, 1650-1750—The Sententious Age, 1700-1800—The Sympathetic Age, 1800-1900—The Literature of America.

THE PHYSIOLOGY OF THE SENSES. By JOHN McKENDRICK, Professor of Physiology in the University of Glasgow, and DR. SNODGRASS, Physiological Laboratory, Glasgow. With Illustrations. Crown 8vo. 4s. 6d.

1. Touch, Taste, and Smell—2. The Sense of Sight—3. Sound and Hearing.

CHAPTERS IN MODERN BOTANY. By PATRICK GEDDES, Professor of Botany, University College, Dundee. With Illustrations. Crown 8vo. 3s. 6d.

Pitcher Plants—Other Insectivorous Plants. Difficulties and Criticisms—Movement and Nervous Action in Plants—The Web of Life—Relations between Plants and Animals—Spring and its Studies; Geographical Distribution and World-Landscapes; Seedling and Bud—Leaves—Suggestions for Further Study.

GREECE IN THE AGE OF PERICLES. By A. J. GRANT, King's College, Cambridge, and Staff Lecturer in History to the University of Cambridge. With Illustrations. Crown 8vo. 3s. 6d.

The Essentials of Greek Civilization—The Religion of the Greeks—Sparta, Argos, Corinth, Thebes—The Earlier History of Athens—The Rivalry of Athens and Sparta—Civil Wars in Greece—The Athenian Democracy—Pericles: his Policy and his Friends—Society in Greece—From the Outbreak of the Peloponnesians to the Death of Pericles—The Peloponnesian War.

UNIVERSITY MANUALS—*continued*.

LOGIC, INDUCTIVE AND DEDUCTIVE. By WILLIAM MINTO, late Professor of Logic and Literature, University of Aberdeen. With Diagrams. Crown 8vo. 4s. 6d.

Introduction—The Logic Consisting; Syllogism and Definition—The Element of Propositions—Definition—The Interpretation of Propositions — The Interdependence of Propositions — Inductive Logic or the Logic of Science.

HISTORY OF RELIGION. A SKETCH OF PRIMITIVE BELIEFS AND PRACTICES, AND OF THE ORIGIN AND CHARACTER OF THE GREAT SYSTEMS. By ALLAN MENZIES, D.D., Professor of Biblical Criticism in the University of St. Andrew's. Crown 8vo. 5s.

The Religion of the Early World—Isolated National Religions—The Semitic Group—The Aryan Group—Universal Religion.

LATIN LITERATURE. By J. W. MACKAIL, Balliol College, Oxford. Crown 8vo. 3s. 6d.

The Republic — The Augustan Age — The Empire — Index of Authors.

ELEMENTS OF PHILOSOPHY. By GEORGE CROOM ROBERTSON, late Grote Professor, University College, London. Edited from Notes of Lectures delivered at the College, 1870—1892, by (MRS.) C. A. FOLEY RHYS DAVIDS, M.A. Crown 8vo. 3s. 6d.

ELEMENTS OF PSYCHOLOGY. By GEORGE CROOM ROBERTSON, late Grote Professor, University College, London. Edited from Notes of Lectures delivered at the College, 1870—1892, by (Mrs.) C. A. FOLEY RHYS DAVIDS, M.A. Crown 8vo. 3s. 6d.

SHAKSPERE AND HIS PREDECESSORS IN THE ENGLISH DRAMA. By F. S. BOAS, Professor of English Literature, Queen's College, Belfast. Crown 8vo. 6s. Library Edition, on larger paper. 7s. 6d.

"It is impossible to part with this work without a word of cordial congratulation to the author on the vigour of his style, the originality of some of his views and theories, and the painstaking appreciation he has brought to bear on his subject —*Morning Post.*

*** *The Volumes in this Series may be obtained in the ordinary Red binding or in Library binding with uncut edges.*

WORKS FOR ADVANCED STUDENTS

Art.

THE FINE ARTS. THE ORIGIN, AIMS AND CONDITION OF ARTISTIC WORK AS APPLIED TO PAINTING, SCULPTURE AND ARCHITECTURE. By G. BALDWIN BROWN, M.A., Professor of Fine Art in the University of Edinburgh; Formerly Fellow of Brasenose College, Oxford. New Edition. With many new Illustrations. Crown 8vo. 6s. *net*.

> " It is a work that ought to be in the library of all thoughtful students of Art."
> —*Literary World*.

Banking.

THE COUNTRY BANKER. HIS CLIENTS, CARES, AND WORK. From an Experience of Forty Years. By GEORGE RAE, Author of " Bullion's Letters to a Bank Manager." With Portrait of the Author. A Cheap Edition. Crown 8vo. 2s. 6d. *net*.

Education.

NATIONAL EDUCATION. ESSAYS TOWARDS A CONSTRUCTIVE POLICY. By the Rev. BERNARD REYNOLDS, M.A.; FRANCIS STORR, B.A.; Sir JOSHUA G. FITCH, LL.D.; Prof. H. E. ARMSTRONG, LL.D., Ph.D., F.R.S.; A. D. PROVAND, formerly M.P. for Glasgow; T. A. ORGAN, B.A., L.C.C.; Prof. W. A. S. HEWINS, Director of the London School of Economics and Political Science; JOHN C. MEDD, M.A.; H. W. EVE, formerly Headmaster of University College School. Edited, with an Introductory Chapter and a Bibliography, by LAURIE MAGNUS, M.A., Magdalen College, Oxford. 8vo. 7s. 6d. *net*.

> " Professor ARMSTRONG writes vigorously on the need for 'drastic reform' in the schools in which our governing classes are educated, as the most important feature in the reorganization of a national educational programme."—*Times*.

EDUCATION AND EMPIRE. ADDRESS ON TOPICS OF THE DAY. By the Right Hon. R. B. HALDANE, K.C., M.P., LL.D. Crown 8vo. 5s. *net*.

THE SCHOOLMASTER. A COMMENTARY UPON THE AIMS AND METHODS OF AN ASSISTANT-MASTER IN A PUBLIC SCHOOL. By A. C. BENSON, Eton College. Crown 8vo. 5s. *net*.

WORKS FOR ADVANCED STUDENTS—*continued.*

Geography.

A HISTORY OF ANCIENT GEOGRAPHY AMONG THE GREEKS AND ROMANS FROM THE EARLIEST AGES TILL THE FALL OF THE ROMAN EMPIRE. By Sir E. H. BUNBURY. With Twenty Illustrative Maps. 2 Vols. 8vo. 21s.

THE DAWN OF MODERN GEOGRAPHY. By C. RAYMOND BEAZLEY, M.A., F.R.G.S., late Fellow of Merton College, Oxford. A History of Exploration and Geographical Science.

VOL. I.—From the Conversion of the Roman Empire to A.D. 900, with an account of the achievements and writings of the early Christian, Arab and Chinese Travellers and Students. With Reproductions of the Principal Maps of the Time. 8vo. 18s.

"Mr. Beazley is only at the threshold of his great subject, and the manner in which he has dealt with the obscurest part of his theme causes us to look forward with pleasant anticipations to its continuation. It is gratifying to think that the best extant account of the dawn of Geography should emanate from an Englishman."—*Athenæum.*

VOL. II.—From the Opening of the Tenth to the Middle of the Thirteenth Century (A.D. 900—1260). With Maps and Illustrations. Demy 8vo. 18s.

". . . Marked by the same admirable qualities which characterised the first volume—scholarship, immense research, and exhaustiveness . . . on the method he has adopted he has rendered an immense service to geography of the middle ages, which is accessible in no other single work."—*The Times.*

Greek.

A.—*Texts, Commentaries, etc.*

PRINCIPLES OF GREEK ETYMOLOGY. By Professor G. CURTIUS, of the University of Leipzig. Translated into English, with the Author's sanction, by A. S. WILKINS, Litt.D., LL.D., and E. B. ENGLAND, M.A., Owens College, Manchester. Fifth Edition, thoroughly revised. 2 vols. 8vo. 28s.

SOPHOCLES. The Seven Plays in English Verse. By LEWIS CAMPBELL, M.A., LL.D., Emeritus Professor of Greek in the University of St. Andrews. Demy 8vo. 10s. 6d.

THE GREEK VERB; its Structure and Development. By Professor CURTIUS. Translated by A. S. WILKINS, M.A., and E. B. ENGLAND, M.A. 8vo. 12s.

THE GREEK THINKERS. A History of Ancient Philosophy. By Professor THEODOR GOMPERZ, of Vienna University. Hon. LL.D., Dublin, Ph.D. Königsberg, &c.

VOL. I.—Translated by LAURIE MAGNUS, M.A., Magdalen College, Oxford. Demy 8vo. 14s. *net.*

"We are glad to welcome the first instalment of the authorised translation of Professor Gomperz's great history of ancient philosophy. . . . The translation is excellently done and the translator has had the benefit of untiring help from the author. Such an excellent reproduction of so important a foreign work on one of the greatest of themes is an event in its way. . . . We shall look forward with great pleasure to the appearance of the next volume."—*Spectator.*

VOL. II.—SOCRATES, THE SOCRATICS AND PLATO. Translated by G. G. BERRY, M.A., Balliol College, Oxford.   [*In the Press.*

WORKS FOR ADVANCED STUDENTS—*continued.*

Greek—continued.

A.—*Texts, Commentaries, etc.*

PLATO AND THE OTHER COMPANIONS OF SOCRATES. By GEORGE GROTE, Author of "The History of Greece." 4 vols. Crown 8vo. 5s. each.

SELECT PASSAGES FROM THE INTRODUCTIONS TO PLATO. By BENJAMIN JOWETT, M.A. Edited by LEWIS CAMPBELL, M.A., LL.D. With a Portrait. F'cap 8vo. 2s. 6d. net.

THE ILIAD OF HOMER, rendered into English Blank Verse. By the EARL OF DERBY. Portrait. 2 vols. Crown 8vo. 10s.

THE ODYSSEY OF HOMER. Books I.—VIII. Translated into English Verse by J. W. MACKAIL, Formerly Fellow of Balliol College, Oxford. Crown 8vo.

CONCISE DICTIONARY OF THE ENGLISH AND THE MODERN GREEK LANGUAGES, AS ACTUALLY WRITTEN AND SPOKEN. Being a Copious Vocabulary of all Words and Expressions Current in Ordinary Reading and in Everyday Talk, for the Guidance of Students and Travellers through Greece and the East. Compiled by Prof. A. N. JANNARIS, Ph.D., St. Andrew's University. Crown 8vo. 10s. 6d.

B.—*History.*

A HISTORY OF GREECE, from the Earliest Period to the close of Alexander the Great. By GEORGE GROTE. With Portrait, Maps, and Plans. 10 vols. 5s. each.

THE GREAT PERSIAN WAR and its Preliminaries. A STUDY OF THE EVIDENCE, LITERARY AND TOPOGRAPHICAL. By G. B. GRUNDY, M.A., Lecturer at Brasenose College, and University Lecturer in Classical Geography. With Maps and Illustrations. Demy 8vo. 21s. net.

'It is but seldom that we have the priviledge of reviewing so excellent a work in Greek history. This book on the great war which freed Greece from the attacks of Persia will long remain the standard work on the subject."—*The Athenæum.*

THE TOPOGRAPHY OF THE BATTLE OF PLATÆA THE CITY OF PLATÆA, THE FIELD OF LEUCTRA. By G. B. GRUNDY, M.A. With Maps and Plans. Demy 8vo. 7s. 6d.; sewed, 5s.

PHILIP AND ALEXANDER OF MACEDON. Two ESSAYS IN BIOGRAPHY. With Maps and Illustrations. By D. G. HOGARTH, M.A., Fellow of Magdalen College, Oxford. 14s.

WORKS FOR ADVANCED STUDENTS—*continued.*

History.

Church and Scripture.

THE HISTORY OF THE CHRISTIAN CHURCH FROM THE APOSTOLIC AGE TO THE REFORMATION, A.D. 64—1517. By JAMES C. ROBERTSON, M.A., Canon of Canterbury, Professor of Ecclesiastical History in King's College, London. 8 vols. Crown 8vo. 6s. each.

THE HISTORY OF CHRISTIANITY FROM THE BIRTH OF CHRIST TO THE ABOLITION OF PAGANISM IN THE ROMAN EMPIRE. By HENRY HART MILMAN. 3 vols. Post 8vo. 4s. each.

THE HISTORY OF LATIN CHRISTIANITY INCLUDING THAT OF THE POPES TO THE PONTIFICATE OF NICHOLAS V. By HENRY HART MILMAN. 9 vols. Post 8vo. 4s. each.

THE HISTORY OF THE JEWS FROM THE EARLIEST PERIOD DOWN TO MODERN TIMES. By HENRY HART MILMAN, D.D., late Dean of St. Paul's. 3 vols. Post 8vo. 4s. each.

LECTURES ON THE HISTORY OF THE JEWISH CHURCH FROM THE EARLIEST TIMES TO THE CHRISTIAN ERA. By the Late DEAN STANLEY. With Portrait and Maps. 3 vols. Crown 8vo. 6s. each.

THE EVOLUTION OF THE ENGLISH BIBLE. BEING AN HISTORICAL SKETCH OF THE SUCCESSIVE VERSIONS FROM 1382—1885. By H. W. HOARE, late of Balliol College, Oxford, now an Assistant Secretary to the Board of Education, Whitehall. With Portraits and Specimen-pages from Old Bibles. Second and Cheaper Edition, Revised. Crown 8vo. 7s. 6d. net.

THE REFORMATION. A RELIGIOUS AND HISTORICAL SKETCH. By the REV. J. A. BABINGTON, M.A., Assistant Master at Tonbridge School, formerly Scholar of New College, Oxford. Demy 8vo. 12s. net.

"This masterly essay . . . gives evidence on every page of wide reading and of a remarkable power of condensation. . . . It is a notable piece of work, one that deserves to be widely read."—*Daily Chronicle.*

AN INTRODUCTION TO THE STUDY OF THE NEW TESTAMENT, and an Investigation into Modern Biblical Criticism, based on the most Recent Sources of Information. By the Rev. GEO. SALMON, D.D., D.C.L., etc., Provost of Trinity College, Dublin. Crown 8vo. 9s.

WORKS FOR ADVANCED STUDENTS—*continued*.

History—continued.

Egypt.

AN ACCOUNT OF THE MANNERS AND CUSTOMS OF THE MODERN EGYPTIANS. Written in Egypt during the Years, 1833-34 and 35. Partly from Notes made during a former visit to that country in the Years 1825-26-27 and 28. By EDWARD WILLIAM LANE. Fifth Edition, with numerous additions and improvements from a copy annotated by the Author. Edited by his Nephew EDWARD STANLEY POOLE. 2 Vols. Crown 8vo. 12s.

EGYPT UNDER THE PHARAOHS. By HEINRICH BRUGSCH-BEY. Condensed and Revised by M. BRODRICK. With Maps, Plans and Illustrations. Demy 8vo. 18s.

OUTLINES OF ANCIENT EGYPTIAN HISTORY. By AUGUSTE MARIETTE. Translated and Edited with Notes by MARY BRODRICK. Second Edition. With Maps. Crown 8vo. 5s.

POPULAR ACCOUNT OF THE ANCIENT EGYPTIANS. By SIR J. GARDNER WILKINSON, F.R.S. Revised and abridged from his larger work. Illustrated with five hundred Woodcuts. 2 Vols. Post 8vo. 12s.

England.

THE CONSTITUTIONAL HISTORY OF ENGLAND FROM THE ACCESSION OF HENRY VII. TO THE DEATH OF GEORGE II. By HENRY HALLAM, LL.D. Cabinet Edition. 3 vols. Post 8vo. 12s.

HISTORY OF ENGLAND, COMPRISING THE REIGN OF QUEEN ANNE TO THE PEACE OF VERSAILLES, 1701—1783. By LORD MAHON (Earl Stanhope). Fifth Edition, Revised. Post 8vo. 9 vols. 5s. each.

Europe.

HISTORY OF EUROPE DURING THE MIDDLE AGES. By HENRY HALLAM, LL.D. Cabinet Edition. 3 vols. Post 8vo. 12s.

LITERARY HISTORY OF EUROPE DURING THE 15th, 16th and 17th CENTURIES. By HENRY HALLAM, LL.D. Cabinet Edition. 4 vols. Post 8vo. 16s.

WORKS FOR ADVANCED STUDENTS—*continued.*

History—continued.

France.

THE STATE OF SOCIETY IN FRANCE BEFORE THE REVOLUTION OF 1789 AND THE CAUSES WHICH LED TO THAT EVENT. By ALEXIS DE TOCQUEVILLE, Member of the French Academy. Translated by HENRY REEVE, D.C.L. Third Edition. Demy 8vo. 12s.

India and the East.

THE HISTORY OF INDIA. THE HINDU AND MAHOMETAN PERIODS. By the Hon. MOUNTSTUART ELPHINSTONE. Seventh Edition. With Notes and Additions by E. B. COWELL, M.A., late Principal of Sanskrit College, Calcutta. With Map Demy 8vo. 18s.

THE RISE OF THE BRITISH POWER IN THE EAST. By the late Hon. MOUNTSTUART ELPHINSTONE. Being a Continuation of his "History of India." Edited by SIR EDWARD COLEBROOKE, Bart. With Maps. Medium 8vo. 16s.

THE RISE AND EXPANSION OF THE BRITISH DOMINION IN INDIA. By SIR ALFRED LYALL, K.C.B., D.C.L. Third and Enlarged Edition. With Maps. 8vo. 12s. *net.*

CHINA: HER HISTORY, DIPLOMACY AND COMMERCE, FROM THE EARLIEST TIMES TO THE PRESENT DAY. By E. H. PARKER, Professor of Chinese at the Owens College; Acting-Consul-General in Corea, Nov., 1886—Jan., 1887; Consul in Hainan, 1891-2, 1893-4; and in 1892-3, Adviser in Chinese Affairs to the Burma Government. With 19 Maps, &c. Large Crown 8vo. 8s. net.

Netherlands.

HISTORY OF THE UNITED NETHERLANDS. FROM THE DEATH OF WILLIAM THE GREAT TO THE TWELVE YEARS TRUCE, 1609. By JOHN LOTHORP MOTLEY, D.C.L., LL.D, With Portraits. 4 Vols. Post 8vo. 6s. each.

> *Vol. I.*—1584-86. *Vol. II.*—1586-89. *Vol. III.*—1590-1600. *Vol. IV.*—1600-1609.

LIFE AND DEATH OF JOHN OF BARNEVELD (Advocate of Holland). WITH A VIEW OF THE PRIMARY CAUSES AND MOVEMENTS OF THE THIRTY YEARS' WAR. By JOHN LOTHORP MOTLEY, D.C.L., LL.D. With Illustrations. 2 Vols. Post 8vo. 6s. each.

WORKS FOR ADVANCED STUDENTS—*continued.*

History—continued.

Rome.

THE HISTORY OF THE DECLINE AND FALL OF THE ROMAN EMPIRE. By EDWARD GIBBON. With Notes by Dean MILMAN, M. GUIZOT, and Sir WILLIAM SMITH. With Portrait and Maps. Demy 8vo. 8 vols. 60s.

Complete sets of the above work may be purchased through any Bookseller at reduced rates.

Latin.

THE ANNALS OF TACITUS. FOR ENGLISH READERS. Books I.—VI. An English Translation with Introduction and Notes. By GEORGE G. RAMSAY. Litt.D., LL.D., Professor of Humanity in the University of Glasgow; Editor of Selections from Tibullus and Propertius, Latin Prose Composition, etc. With Maps. Demy 8vo.

The aim of the translator is to produce a version, which while being exact in scholarship and faithful to the original, shall be such as may be read with pleasure and profit by those who are unacquainted with Latin. The notes will be mainly historical, and designed to put the English reader in possession of all information essential to the understanding of the text, and to enable him to compare the narrative and the judgments of Tacitus with those of other authorities for the period.

VIRGIL. In English Verse. Eclogues and Æneid, Books I—VI. By the Rt. Hon Sir CHARLES BOWEN. 8vo. 12s.

Law and Politics.

LECTURES ON JURISPRUDENCE OR THE PHILOSOPHY OF POSITIVE LAW. By the late JOHN AUSTIN. Fifth Edition, Revised and Edited by ROBERT CAMPBELL, Advocate (Scotch Bar), and of Lincoln's Inn, Barrister-at-Law. 2 vols. 8vo. 32s.

FIRST PRINCIPLES IN POLITICS. By WILLIAM SAMUEL LILLY. Demy 8vo. 14s.

LAW AND POLITICS IN THE MIDDLE AGES. By EDWARD JENKS, Reader in English Law in the University of Oxford. Demy 8vo. 12s.

"By far the most important and original book relating to jurisprudence published for some years in England is Mr. Jenks's 'Law and Politics in the Middle Ages.'"—*Times.*

WORKS FOR ADVANCED STUDENTS —*continued.*

Law and Politics—continued.

Works by Sir Henry S. Maine, K.C S.I.

ANCIENT LAW; its Connection with the Early History of Society, and its Relation to Modern Ideas. Sixteenth Edition. 8vo. 9s.

LECTURES ON THE EARLY HISTORY OF INSTITU-TIONS, in continuation of the above work. 8vo. 9s.

VILLAGE - COMMUNITIES IN THE EAST AND WEST, with other Lectures, Addresses, and Essays. Seventh Edition. 8vo. 9s.

DISSERTATIONS ON EARLY LAW AND CUSTOM. 8vo. 9s.

POPULAR GOVERNMENT. Four Essays. I. Prospects of Popular Government.—II. Nature of Democracy.—III. Age of Progress.—IV. Constitution of the United States. Fifth Edition. 8vo. 7s. 6d.

INTERNATIONAL LAW. The Whewell Lectures delivered at Cambridge in 1887. 8vo. 7s. 6d.

Medical.

HANDBOOK OF PHYSIOLOGY. By W. D. HALLIBURTON, M.D., F.R.S., Professor of Physiology, King's College, London. Fourth Edition, being the Seventeenth of Kirkes' (see Note below). Again thoroughly revised, with the addition of new matter and new illustrations, and certain alteration of the arrangement in deference to the wishes and advice of numerous teachers. With upwards of Six Hundred Illustrations, including some Coloured Plates. Large Cr. 8vo. 14s.

EXTRACT FROM PUBLISHER'S NOTE TO THIS EDITION.

Three completely revised editions of KIRKES' HANDBOOK have now been published since the editorship was first undertaken by Professor W. D. Halliburton in 1896. So extensive have been the changes made in these years, that but little remains of the original work, and the manual has now obtained a higher reputation and a wider popularity than at any time before.

In these circumstances it has been suggested by several professional men and other readers of the book that it would be well to drop the time-honoured name of "Kirkes'," and to substitute for it that of the real author of the present volume—Professor Halliburton. Whatever prestige attached to the old title has now been rightly transferred to the new, and we have accordingly decided to adopt this suggestion, and to call the book in future "HALLIBURTON'S PHYSIOLOGY."

WORKS FOR ADVANCED STUDENTS—*continued*

Medical—continued.

MANUAL OF PATHOLOGY. A HANDBOOK FOR STUDENTS. By SIDNEY MARTIN, B.Sc., M.D., M.R.C.S., Professor of Pathology, University College. With numerous Woodcuts from Micro-Photographs. Medium 8vo.

A TREATISE ON MEDICAL JURISPRUDENCE. Based on Lectures delivered at University College, London. By G. VIVIAN POORE, M.D. With Illustrations. 8vo. 12s. net.

> ". . . Admirable and interesting treatise . . . the reader can almost hear Dr. Poore's genial and witty voice as he turns these instructive pages. They are marked by a kind of 'golden common-sense,' which is the most valuable lesson that any medical or legal student can lay to heart . . . an ideal handbook of the subject for the young student."—*The Spectator*

Sociology.

THE BASIS OF SOCIAL RELATIONS. A STUDY IN ETHNIC PSYCHOLOGY. By the late DANIEL G. BRINTON, A.M., M.D., LL.D., D.Sc., Author of "A History of Primitive Religions," "Races and Peoples," &c. Edited by LIVINGSTON FARRAND. 8vo. 8s. net.

> *** The above is the work upon which Professor Brinton was engaged at the time of his death.

Tides.

THE TIDES AND KINDRED PHENOMENA IN THE SOLAR SYSTEM. The substance of Lectures delivered at the Lowell Institute, Boston, Massachusetts, in 1897. By GEORGE HOWARD DARWIN, Plumian Professor and Fellow of Trinity College, in the University of Cambridge. With Illustrations. Crown 8vo. 7s. 6d.

> "Professor Darwin has succeeded in giving a very clear and lucid account of the matters of which he treats."—*Times.*

CHARLES DARWIN'S WORKS.

THE ORIGIN OF SPECIES BY MEANS OF NATURAL SELECTION. Library Edition. 2 vols. 12s.—Popular Edition. 6s.—Cheaper Edition. With a Photogravure Portrait of the Author. Large crown 8vo. 2s. 6d. net.—Also in Paper Covers. 1s. net.

> Mr. Murray desires to inform the public that the edition which has just lost copyright is the imperfect edition which was subsequently thoroughly revised by Mr. Darwin. This imperfect edition has been reprinted by other publishers without the consent or authority of Mr. Darwin's representatives.
> The only authorised and complete editions are those published by Mr. Murray, and these do not lose copyright for several years to come.

DESCENT OF MAN, AND SELECTION IN RELATION TO SEX. Woodcuts. Library Edition. 2 vols. 15s.—1 Vol. Popular Edition. 7s. 6d.—Cheaper Edition. With Illustrations. Large crown 8vo. 2s. 6d. net.

VARIATION OF ANIMALS AND PLANTS UNDER DOMESTICATION. Woodcuts. 2 vols. 15s.

EXPRESSION OF THE EMOTIONS IN MAN AND ANIMALS. With Illustrations. 12s.

VARIOUS CONTRIVANCES BY WHICH ORCHIDS ARE FERTILIZED BY INSECTS. Woodcuts. 7s. 6d.

MOVEMENTS AND HABITS OF CLIMBING PLANTS. Woodcuts. 6s.

INSECTIVOROUS PLANTS. Woodcuts. 9s.

CROSS AND SELF-FERTILIZATION IN THE VEGETABLE KINGDOM. 9s.

DIFFERENT FORMS OF FLOWERS ON PLANTS OF THE SAME SPECIES. 7s. 6d.

FORMATION OF VEGETABLE MOULD THROUGH THE ACTION OF WORMS. Illustrations. 6s.

JOURNAL OF A NATURALIST DURING A VOYAGE ROUND THE WORLD IN H.M.S. "BEAGLE." With 100 Illustrations. Medium 8vo. 21s.—Popular Edition. With Portrait. 3s. 6d.—Cheaper Edition. With 16 full-page Plates. Large crown 8vo. 2s. 6d. net.

MR. MURRAY'S MUSICAL SERIES.

Crown 8vo. 5s. net each.

—

SONGS AND SONG WRITERS. By HENRY T. FINCK, Author of "Wagner and his Works," "Chopin and other Musical Essays," etc., etc. With 8 Portraits.

THE ORCHESTRA AND ORCHESTRAL MUSIC. By W. J. HENDERSON, Author of "What is Good Music," etc., etc. With 8 Portraits and other Illustrations.

THE OPERA, PAST AND PRESENT. AN HISTORICAL SKETCH. By WILLIAM FOSTER APTHORP, Author of "Musicians and Music Lovers," etc, With Portraits.

CHOIRS AND CHORAL MUSIC. By ARTHUR MEES. With Portraits.

MUSIC: HOW IT CAME TO BE WHAT IT IS. By HANNAH SMITH. With Illustrations.

HOW MUSIC DEVELOPED. By W. J. HENDERSON, Author of "What is Good Music."

HOW TO LISTEN TO MUSIC. HINTS AND SUGGESTIONS TO UNTAUGHT LOVERS OF THE ART. By HENRY EDWARD KREHBIEL, Author of "Studies in the Wagnerian Drama," etc., etc. With 11 Portraits.

WHAT IS GOOD MUSIC? SUGGESTIONS TO PERSONS DESIRING TO CULTIVATE A TASTE IN MUSICAL ART. By W. J. HENDERSON.

A BOOK OF BRITISH SONG.
FOR HOME AND SCHOOL.

Edited by CECIL J. SHARP, Principal of the Hampstead Conservatoire. With Pianoforte Score and Words. Large 4to. 7s. 6d. net. Also a Small Crown 8vo. Edition with Words and Airs only. Cloth, 2s.; paper, 1s. 6d.

LIST OF KEYS.

These Keys are not sold to the Public, and care is taken that they do not get into the hands of boys at school.   They can only be obtained by **authenticated Teachers** *on written application to the* **Publisher,** *and their prices are* **strictly net, post free.**

ETON COLLEGE SERIES.

	s. d.		s. d.
First Latin Exercise Book	2 1	Eton Exercises in Arith-	
Eton Exercises in Algebra		metic (Answers only) ...	2 1
(Answers only)	2 1		

HALL, Professor T. D.

Translation at Sight	1 1

HOME AND SCHOOL LIBRARY.

Algebra, Part I. (Answers only)	1 1

SECONDARY EDUCATION TEXT-BOOKS.

Commercial German, Part I. ... ...

SIR WM. SMITH'S EDUCATIONAL SERIES.

ENGLISH.

	s. d.		s. d.
School Manual of English		Primary English Grammar	0 7
Grammar	2 7		

FRENCH.

	s. d.		s. d.
French Principia, Part I. ...	1 1	French Principia, Part II.	1 7
Appendix to French		French Principia, Part III.	1 7
Principia, Part I.	1 1		

GERMAN.

	s. d.		s. d.
German Principia, Part I.	1 1	German Principia, Part II.	2 7

ITALIAN.

	s. d.		s. d.
Italian Principia, Part I. ...	1 1	Italian Principia, Part II.	2 7

SPANISH.

Spanish Principia ... ...

LATIN.

	s. d.		s. d.
Principia Latina, Part I. ...	0 7	Principia Latina, Part IV.	0 7
Appendix to Principia		Principia Latina, Part V.	1 1
Latina, Part I.	0 7	Young Beginner's Latin	
Principia Latina, Part II.	2 7	Course, Part III. ...	0 7
Principia Latina, Part III.	1 7		

GREEK.

	s. d.		s. d.
Initia Græca, Part I. For		Appendix to Initia Græca,	
use with the 26th or any		Part I.	1 1
later Editions. Keys to		Initia Græca, Part II. ...	1 1
all previous Editions are		Initia Græca, Part III. ...	1 1
quite out of print ...	1 1